STAFFORD LIBRARY
COLUMBIA COLLEGE
1001 ROGERS STREET
COLUMBIA, MO 65216

THEMES IN DRAMA

Themes in Drama is a journal which brings together articles and reviews about the dramatic and theatrical activity of a wide range of cultures and periods. The articles offer original contributions to their own specialized fields, but are presented in such a way that their significance may be readily appreciated by non-specialists.

Themes in Drama

An annual publication

Edited by James Redmond

13

VIOLENCE IN DRAMA

Editorial Advisory Board

DENNIS BARTHOLOMEUSZ, Senior Lecturer in English, Monash University
EDWIN EIGNER, Professor of English, University of California, Riverside
MARTIN ESSLIN, Professor of Drama, Stanford University
INGA-STINA EWBANK, Professor of English, University of Leeds
JOHN FLETCHER, Professor of Comparative Literature, University of East Anglia
WILLIAM O. HARRIS, Professor of English, University of California, Riverside
E. W. HANDLEY, Regius Professor of Greek, Trinity College, Cambridge
PETER D. HOLLAND, Lecturer in Poetry and Drama, Trinity Hall, Cambridge
DANA SUE MCDERMOTT, Department of Dramatic Arts, University of Connecticut
MILTON MILLER, Professor of English, University of California, Riverside
P. G. O'NEILL, Professor of Japanese, School of Oriental and African Studies, University of London
H. B. NISBET, Professor of German, Sidney Sussex College, Cambridge
ANN SADDLEMYER, Professor of English, University of Toronto
S. SCHOENBAUM, Professor of English, University of Maryland
MICHAEL J. SIDNELL, Professor of English, University of Toronto
J. E. VAREY, Professor of Spanish, Westfield College, University of London
JOHN WEIGHTMAN, Emeritus Professor of French, Queen Mary and Westfield College, University of London

SUBSCRIPTIONS The subscription price to volume 13, which includes postage, is £39 (US $69.00 in USA and Canada) for institutions, £22.00 (US $42.00 in USA and Canada) for individuals ordering direct from the Press and certifying that the annual is for their personal use. Airmail (orders to Cambridge only) £6.00 extra. Copies of the annual for subscribers in the USA and Canada are sent by air to New York to arrive with minimum delay. Orders, which must be accompanied by payment, may be sent to a bookseller, subscription agent or direct to the publishers: Cambridge University Press, The Edinburgh Building, Shaftesbury Road, Cambridge CB2 2RU. Payments may be made by any of the following methods: cheque (payable to Cambridge University Press), UK postal order, bank draft, Post Office Giro (account no. 571 6055 GB Bootle – advise CUP of payment), international money order, UNESCO coupons, or any credit card bearing the Interbank symbol. Orders from the USA and Canada should be sent to Cambridge University Press, 40 West 20th Street, New York, NY 10011-4211.

BACK VOLUMES Volumes 1–12 are available from the publisher at £35.00 ($69.00 in USA and Canada).

VIOLENCE IN DRAMA

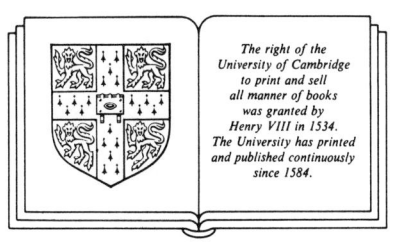

CAMBRIDGE UNIVERSITY PRESS
CAMBRIDGE
NEW YORK   PORT CHESTER   MELBOURNE   SYDNEY

Published by the Press Syndicate of the University of Cambridge
The Pitt Building, Trumpington Street, Cambridge CB2 1RP
40 West 20th Street, New York, NY 10011-4211, USA
10 Stamford Road, Oakleigh, Melbourne 3166, Australia

© Cambridge University Press 1991

First published 1991

Printed in Great Britain at The Bath Press, Avon

British Library Cataloguing in publication data
Themes in Drama, 13
1. Drama – History and criticism – Periodicals
809.2'005 PN 1601

Library of Congress catalogue card number 82-4491

ISSN 0263-676X
ISBN 0 521 403553

Contents

	page
Themes in Drama volumes and conferences	xi
List of contributors	xiii
List of illustrations	xv
Editor's preface	xvii
The uses of violence in drama by THOMAS GOULD	1
Violence in Greek tragedy by SIMON GOLDHILL	15
Violence and dramatic structure in Euripides' *Hecuba* by CHARLES SEGAL	35
Violence on the street: playing rough in Plautus by RICHARD C. BEACHAM	47
Violence and the social body in the Croxton *Play of the Sacrament* by VICTOR I. SCHERB	69
'There must be blood': mutilation and martyrdom on the medieval stage by JOHN SPALDING GATTON	79
Mixed feelings about violence in the Corpus Christi plays by RICHARD L. HOMAN	93
Shakespearean violence: a preliminary survey by JONAS BARISH	101

Cultural disintegration in *Titus Andronicus*: mutilating Titus, Vergil and Rome 123
by HEATHER JAMES

Racine's *Bajazet*: the language of violence and secrecy 141
by MAYA SLATER

Grand Guignol and the orchestration of violence 151
by VICTOR EMELJANOW

The ultimate in theatre violence 165
by JOHN M. CALLAHAN

Lesbian sexuality and violence in the plays of G. B. Shaw 177
by ELLEN GAINOR

Violence as tragic farce in Camus's *Caligula* 191
by BEN STOLTZFUS

Violence in two plays by Federico García Lorca 203
by KAY GARCÍA

Apartheid and primitive blood: violence in Afrikaans Shakespeare productions 215
by ROHAN QUINCE

A streetcar named misogyny 225
by KATHLEEN MARGARET LANT

Languages of violence: Fugard's *Boesman and Lena* 239
by MARCIA BLUMBERG

Stage violence as thaumaturgic technique 251
by MARY KAREN DAHL

Violation and implication: *One for the Road* and *Ficky Stingers* 261
by DAVID IAN RABY

The mask as sign of violence in contemporary Latin American theatre 269
by SEVERINO JOÃO ALBUQUERQUE

Contents

'night Mother and True West: mirror images of violence and
gender 277
  by RAYNETTE HALVORSEN SMITH

The role of the theatre in Czechoslovakia's 'velvet revolution' 291
  by JEREMY ADLER

Index 315

Themes in Drama volumes and conferences

Volumes already published in the series

1. *Drama and Society*
2. *Drama and Mimesis*
3. *Drama, Dance and Music*
4. *Drama and Symbolism*
5. *Drama and Religion*
6. *Drama and the Actor*
7. *Drama, Sex and Politics*
8. *Historical Drama*
9. *The Theatrical Space*
10. *Farce*
11. *Women in Theatre*
12. *Drama and Philosophy*
13. *Violence in Drama*

Forthcoming

14. *Melodrama* (pub. 1992)
15. *Madness in Drama*
16. *National Theatres*
17. *Adapted for the Stage*

Themes in Drama *conferences*

Annual conferences are held at the University of London and at the University of California, Riverside. The subject in 1992 will be 'National Theatres' and this title has been proposed and accepted for the annual journal *Themes in Drama* (volume 16). The subject for the 1993 conferences will be 'Adapted for the Stage' and this title will be proposed for publication. Details of the conference held in California may be obtained from: *Themes in Drama* Conference, University of California, Riverside, CA 92521. Details of the conference held in London may be obtained from the Editor.

Potential contributors are asked to correspond with the Editor at an early date. Papers for volume 16 should be submitted in final form to the Editor before 1 September 1992.

James Redmond, Editor, *Themes in Drama*, Queen Mary and Westfield College, University of London, Hampstead, London NW3 7ST.

Contributors

Jeremy Adler, *Department of German, Queen Mary and Westfield College, University of London*
Severino João Albuquerque, *Spanish and Portuguese, University of Wisconsin, Madison*
Jonas Barish, *Department of English, University of California, Berkeley*
Richard C. Beacham, *Theatre Studies, University of Warwick*
Marcia Blumberg, *York University, Toronto*
John M. Callahan, *Speech and Theatre, Kutztown University*
Mary Karen Dahl, *Theatre and Drama, University of Wisconsin, Madison*
Victor Emeljanow, *Department of Drama, University of Newcastle, NSW*
John Spalding Gatton, *Department of English, Bellarmine College*
J. Ellen Gainor, *Theatre Arts, Cornell University*
Kay García, *Foreign Languages, Oregon State University*
Simon Goldhill, *King's College, University of Cambridge*
Thomas Gould, *Department of Classics, Yale University*
Richard L. Homan, *Department of Fine Arts, Rider College*
Heather James, *Comparative Literature, University of California, Berkeley*
Kathleen Margaret Lant, *Department of English, California State University, San Luis Obispo*
Rohan Quince, *English and Philosophy, Georgia Southern*
David Ian Raby, *Drama Department, University College of Wales, Aberystwyth*
Victor I. Scherb, *Arizona State University, Tempe*
Charles Segal, *Department of Classics, Harvard University*
Maya Slater, *Department of French, Queen Mary and Westfield College, University of London*
Raynette Halvorsen Smith, *Theatre Department, University of California, Riverside*
Ben Stoltzfus, *Literatures and Languages, University of California, Riverside*

Illustrations

		page
1	A scene of comic violence from Hellenistic or Roman New Comedy	48
2	Replica Roman stage	52
3	Cleostrata and Chalinus	54
4	'Stabbing the Host'. The Croxton Play, The Medieval Players. Photo: Tessa Musgrave	72
5	'The Massacre of the Innocents', St Peter Mancroft, Norwich	81
6	'The Martyrdom of St Apollonia', Jean Fouquet, *The Hours of Etienne Chevalier*	85
7–12	Théâtre du Grand Guignol	152–173
13–19	November 1989: revolution in Prague	292–312

Editor's preface

This is the thirteenth volume of *Themes in Drama*, which is published annually. Each volume brings together articles on the theatrical activity of a wide range of cultures and periods. The papers offer original contributions to their own specialized fields, but they are presented in such a way that their significance may be appreciated readily by non-specialists.

Each volume indicates connections between the various national traditions of theatre by bringing together studies of a theme of central and continuing importance. The annual international conferences (see p. xi) provide an opportunity for scholars, critics and theatrical practitioners to exchange views, and many of the papers in the volumes are revised versions of papers read and discussed at the conferences. The present volume reflects the range and quality of the 1989 conferences on 'Violence in Drama'. Contributions are invited for volumes 15, 16 and 17; they should follow the style of presentation used in this volume, and be sent to

        James Redmond
        Editor *Themes in Drama*
        Queen Mary and Westfield College
        University of London
        Hampstead
        London NW3 7ST

The uses of violence in drama

THOMAS GOULD

A person who counts great drama and serious literature as indispensable sources of pleasure is likely to listen with mounting dismay to arguments against the portrayal of violence. To be deprived of the killing of Hector, the suicide of Ajax, the blinding of Gloucester, or the deaths by *plastique* in *The Battle of Algiers* – to say nothing of the brutal victimization of innocents in historical accounts and religious stories – would be intolerable. There are people (George Steiner is one) who say they are prepared to ban even *The Brothers Karamazov* if it were shown that its violence had inspired a single violent murder; but most lovers of literature hope that no cause and effect of this sort will ever be proved, and that a distinction can be made between right and wrong kinds of violence, between 'essential' and 'gratuitous' violence.

The term 'gratuitous' can mean either of two things in such a context. Violence is called 'gratuitous' if it appears to be stuck on for its own sake or if it is presented as a shocking injustice, injustice entirely uncompensated for, either by a later restitution of justice or by the splendid behavior of the victim. But alas, the elimination of violence that is gratuitous in either sense would be fatal to any attempt to exempt great tragedy from indictments against the portrayal of violence. The scene in which Gloucester is blinded is gratuitous in the first sense, a scene that need not have been shown. The pointless, almost accidental deaths of Lear and Cordelia are gratuitous in the other sense, monstrous, unredeemed miscarriages of justice. The triumphant honesty of Cordelia, the universal compassion of Lear during the storm on the heath, and the short-lived joy of the reunion and mutual forgiveness of father and daughter do not compensate for their deaths: they just make them even more bitter and pointless than they would otherwise have been. 'Why should a dog, a horse, a rat have life,' asks Lear, 'And thou no breath at all?'

Let us consider first the distinction between violence necessitated by the plot and violence that could just as well have been given much less emphasis or dropped altogether had the playwright considered only the forwarding of the action. The violent deaths of Duncan and of Macbeth himself are integral to the plot of the play. It would have been a different story without them. But Shakespeare's decision to shock us with the murder of Macduff's entire family cannot be defended in the same way. Similarly the death and dismemberment of Pentheus could not have been eliminated without destroying the plot of the *Bacchae*; but Euripides could easily have avoided, had he wanted to, the shocking scene in which Agave slowly comes to the realization that her victim's dismembered head, which she is cradling in her arms, is not that of a lion, but the head of her own son. It would be rash indeed, however, to say that these would have been better dramas had their poets avoided such scenes of unnecessary violence.

Indeed, who is to say that the playwrights were not drawn to their respective stories, in part at least, because they offered opportunities for scenes like these? The infinitely painful awakening of Agave to a non-Dionysian reality, for instance, is surely essential to Euripides' understanding of the Dionysiac, even if the scene could have been avoided without crippling the march of events. Similarly Sophocles may have been drawn to the story of Oedipus because it would allow him to move us with a scene in which the defeated king returned to the stage immediately after having put out his own eyes. In this case it seems to have been the power of the spectacle itself that attracted the poet, because he is then at pains to prevent the audience from drawing the wrong inferences from their emotional reactions. And, Nahum Tate and Dr Johnson notwithstanding, the opportunity to show the grieving Lear carrying the corpse of Cordelia may be precisely what drew Shakespeare to that particular chronicle. In fact the logic of the plot is slightly improved by Tate's happy ending; but sometimes the violence is more important than the logic.

Once we realize that in tragedy violence – or rather one kind of violence – is not something we have to apologize for, that it is the thing that makes a drama a tragedy, the distinction between violence integral to the main story and violence of the same sort introduced into the story but without that justification is seen to be of little use. And what is the kind of violence that makes a story a tragedy? It is violence that is gratuitous in the other sense, suffering or death told or staged in such a way that we feel the terrible unfairness of life. A campaign to eliminate violence that is gratuitous in this sense would be a campaign against true tragedy and a defense of one of the two obvious alternatives to tragedy in serious drama: melodrama or sentimental stories.

In sentimental stories suffering is responded to by the reader or audience with deep sympathy for the victims, just as in true tragedy. In responding to sentimental stories, however, the viewer's regret for what has happened is softened – by the suggestion that the suffering and loss in all human life are not really so terrible after all, that there are compensations, the opportunity to conduct oneself courageously, for instance, or the knowledge that at such moments we are the objects of much sympathetic attention from the world.

In antiquity reassurance of the sentimental sort is found in comedy and romance, but rarely in tragedy. For the most part the thrill of Attic drama depended on an honest facing of the cruelty or arbitrariness of divinity and the consequent injustice in human life. In post-classical drama, however, sentimental reassurances often color at least the endings of serious works thought to be in the Greek tradition. This is true of some of our best operas, for instance, such as *La Traviata*, *The Cunning Little Vixen*, and the operas of Richard Strauss that end in a sustained feeling of elevated melancholy. But examples of this sort are fairly rare. Mostly the sounding of a sentimental note at the end of a serious drama signals a retreat from tragedy, a fear of depressing the audience. Several of Dickens's best novels are spoiled in this way, as are many Broadway and West End plays, also films made in Hollywood and elsewhere. We might instance *The Breaking of the Code* and *Careful He Might Hear You*, both of which might have been tragedies had not the authors fashioned an 'upbeat' ending.

At the end of the film *On Golden Pond* we are asked to believe that dying is no worse than having to leave one's summer home at the first touch of autumn. In *My Life As a Dog* the ghastly death of the boy's mother by lung cancer is equated with the death of his beloved dog. *Love Story* invites us to picture marriage as coming to a beautiful, even enviable end while the couple is still in the flush of youthful fidelity and tenderness – suggesting that we may forget the usual expectations: declining passion, boredom, fat, ungrateful children, infidelity, old age and worse. Death in a hospital bed, our almost universal fate, is pictured as coming without any loss of looks, without great pain, or mind-distorting painkillers, without those tubes in various orifices, obscene hospital routines, dishonest role-playing by the loved ones, or terror of the unknown.

Alternatively one could give point to violence and suffering by showing that it was clearly required – to make up for a wrong, for the public safety, or for the survival of freedom and democracy. That is, one could confine oneself to melodrama. A melodrama often begins with violence of the sort that defines tragedy – grave miscarriages of justice. In this kind of drama, however, there is always a promise that the perpetrators of the preliminary violence will eventually be the victims of a new round of death and mayhem. Our appetite is whetted for a guilt-free phantasy-fulfillment of revenge for all previous set-backs, humiliations, or frustrations. The fulfillment is guilt-free for the audience because there is no reason whatever to feel sorry for the victims. They deserve what they are getting. For the good of Her Majesty's Government (or whatever) these victims must be terminated in some spectacular fashion. It is a moment eagerly looked forward to; and it is understood that the author will wait to the very end before he gives it to us.

Violence in the *Iliad*, as Plato notes, is of the tragic sort. Neither in the big set pieces, the deaths of Sarpedon, Patroclus, and Hector, nor in the countless smaller deaths on the battlefield, do we get any melodramatic satisfaction. All the deaths are regrettable. Nobody wins. The poet of the *Odyssey*,[1] however, insists that, by and large, later if not immediately, the good are rewarded and the bad punished. Zeus announces at the beginning of the *Odyssey* that the time is near for the restitution of justice for the worthy Odysseus. He may return to his homeland, reclaim his wife and kingdom, and revenge himself against his enemies, the hateful suitors. The moment we wait for finally comes: Odysseus and his noble son, with Athena at their side, perform a gratifying act of mass murder. Thud, thud go their arrows into the writhing bodies of the odious suitors. As we read – or listen to the rhapsode reciting dramatically – we experience a momentary compensation for every slight or rejection we have ever suffered, all the way back to our childhood.

In the main, the Greeks followed the Iliadic, not the Odyssean pattern in their dramas and other forms of serious literature. And even in the *Odyssey* the melodramatic pleasure is not indulged in without some embarrassment. An innocent man is included in the slaughter.[2] The killing of the maid-servants is unsettling, to say the least. When the old nurse starts to whoop with delight at the sight of the carnage, Odysseus slaps his great man-slaying hand over her mouth and tells her that such joy is not a good thing. Then Odysseus has to comfort, not only his wife, but also his grieving father, then explain it all as best he can to the angry next of kin of the suitors he has just killed. We are also reminded of the suffering that still awaits Odysseus in the future.

In Hollywood and television we rarely find this kind of hesitation and embarrassment. Melodrama is the engine that drives these billion-dollar industries. The formula is not inherently vulgar or exploitive. It would be hard to think of a more high-minded opera than Beethoven's *Fidelio*, which is pure melodrama. But it is clear that melodrama, when it is the preferred plot in playwrighting that has become big business, lends itself all too easily to the exploitation of some very unlovely instincts in the audience. First the writer proves to the audience that the victims-to-be in the climactic violence are dangerous and detestable. For the good of the perpetrators of that climactic violence – and, indeed, for the good of all of us – they must be brought to justice, vividly, before our eyes. The pleasure can be so intense that the audience at a film will shout at the most brutal moments. Even a lonely viewer before his television screen may be encouraged by thunderous music to shout as though he were in a crowd.

Sometimes the pleasure of melodrama is confined to a brief scene in an otherwise delicate scenario: Jack Nicholson getting his violent revenge on a stupid waitress or pounding his fist into the face of an odious nurse; the American captives in *The Deer Hunter* killing their Viet Cong captors in a prolonged and bloody scene; the young soldier in *Platoon* hesitating to murder the non-commissioned officer who had tormented him, then yielding to his thirst for revenge. Sometimes it is understood from the beginning of the drama that melodramatic satisfaction is the sole reason for the calculated fashioning of the sequence of events. The films of Sylvester Stallone come to mind, both the boxing series and the para-military series, also martial arts films from Hong Kong, *The Equalizer*, and several police series on television.

People who worry about regrettable social effects of the violence on the screen and in television[3] might do well to confine their concern to this kind of violence. If they made it clear right from the start that they are worried only about violence depicted in such a way that the audience identified entirely with the perpetrator, they would get a more sympathetic hearing from the lovers of tragedy. After all, violence depicted in such a way that the audience sympathizes entirely with the victim is not likely to rouse the same kinds of emotion. And it is the latter kind of violence that fuels, not only tragedy, but also serious literature of several sorts, also the holiest stories in several religions, including the biblical religions and several prominent strains of pagan religion.

Consider first the pleasures of melodrama. A 1979 film called *The Warriors* caused young viewers in Boston and other cities to go out and attack, even kill, enemies of their own. This is a story of a gang of worthy youths so bitterly wronged and in such great danger that they are entirely justified in acting with extreme violence against the gangs which are trying to injure or kill them. Scorcese's film *Taxi Driver* inspired a famous attempt to kill the President. What inspired the would-be assassin was the violent extermination by Travis Bickle (Robert DeNiro) of the man who had wronged him and who also represented an extreme danger to society.

In tragedy, by contrast, opportunities to exploit our hunger for guilt-free revenge are refused. The pitiable sacrifice of the innocent Iphigenia gave Clytemnestra, her mother, a very strong motive for killing Agamemnon; yet Aeschylus does not offer the audience the slightest reason to sympathize with her until, in the second play of the trilogy, she herself becomes the victim in the next round of violence. In *The Night of the Shooting Stars*, a film by the Taviani brothers, the most wronged of the anti-Fascists finally gets an opportunity to kill the most detested of the Fascists and his even more odious young son. He does kill them, yet the Tavianis find a way to make the audience sympathize strongly with the victims it had hated minutes before. If violence is made attractive by a drama it is in melodramas. The thrill of tragedy comes from a different kind of arousal altogether: an invitation to the pleasure of honest and realistic pity.

Aristotle thought that pity was invariably a painful emotion, since it is generated by the sight of suffering beyond the sufferer's deserts. He suggests that the pleasure of tragedy comes from the *flushing out* of this painful response. But the earlier Greeks, from Homer to Plato, knew better. A pitiable tale is the most pleasant to hear. In the Hymn to Apollo the poet tries to imagine the sweetest of all songs, the song the newborn Apollo sang when he struck his lyre for the first time and made the gods and goddesses forget everything but music. The subject of this music, he says, was 'the misery men have from the deathless gods,/ the way they must live in ignorance, unable/ to find a cure for death or help against old age' (lines 190–3). Plato explains that the part of us that delights in tragedy yearns to believe what our reason forbids us to conclude, that our happiness is not in our own power, that we need not blame ourselves for our every failure – in other words, that we are all victims. When reason is in control, this hunger is denied fulfillment; but in our dream-like state in the theatre we can suspend reason and indulge our intense yearning to pity ourselves.

Plato concludes that the joy which lovers of tragedy get from tragedy is the joy of believing, if only temporarily, that the warnings and advice of moral teachers amount to nothing. He therefore condemns tragedy as an activity that weakens moral resolve (*Republic* 10.606a–b). A case can be made, however, for this kind of holiday from a rigidly moral world-view. We know now that our internal censurer, the super-ego, can be a major source of undeserved unhappiness, something we need relief from, if only for the duration of a drama. With the return of full wakefulness after the drama has ended our moral assumptions are likely to function again – with undiminished strength, more than likely. This is because it is the unusually moral people, not the unusually weak, who are likely to have super-egos so strong that their happiness is threatened. And that, presumably, is why tragedy is an elite, not a popular taste: it brings the strongest joy to the people who have the strongest super-egos. A person who indulges himself in a phantasy of violent revenge, however, is courting lasting damage, especially if morality is not a major factor in his personality to begin with. The internal and external voices that have held him back from full expression of his indignations, frustrations, and murderous hatreds, have been momentarily tricked, as it were: they seem no longer to have a case. The resulting joy of revenge, revenge beyond his wildest dreams (as we say), continues when he spills out onto the street with his equally excited buddies. This is the kind of phantasy fulfillment that does indeed need close examination.

It is not a case of showing violence vividly as opposed to reporting it discretely. The Greeks rarely showed violence. That, however, is a consequence of the way dramas were staged in antiquity. As Horace points out in the *Ars poetica*, an attempt to convince a theatre audience that Atreus is cutting up his young nephews and cooking them for the feast he is preparing for Thyestes, their father, is bound to fall flat. At best it will be seen for what it is, sensationalism, theatrical trickery. That is why the best dramatists avoid such scenes. The poet of the *Iliad* was not hampered in the same way from presenting shocking, realistic scenes of terrible carnage; and in fact he never seems to miss an opportunity to do so. Showing us violence realistically and in impressive detail, something film is especially good at, is not dangerous in itself. It is of dubious value only if we are invited to see ourselves personally in the role, not of the victims, but of the perpetrators.

All sorts of combinations are possible: tragedies spoiled by sentimental or by melodramatic elements, for instance, or sentimental stories redeemed by tragic elements – either wholly redeemed as in Dickens and Richard Strauss, or partially redeemed, as occasionally even in Puccini. What makes a drama, or an element in a drama, tragic is its power to move us with an honest look at the terrible unfairness of life. What turns a story toward melodrama is the invitation to identify the source of suffering with certain hateful people, in order that we may feel renewed when we see these people suffer for what they have done. What turns it toward sentimentality is the suggestion that even if we suffer, as we must someday, we will be well compensated for this by the realization that we have joined a community of sufferers and will be elevated thereby to far better company than can be known by those responsible for our suffering. But these three pleasures are seldom pure in complex literature.

Sentimental pleasure is the hardest to define. Not much has been written about it. Mark Jefferson offers a general definition in an article called, 'What is Wrong with Sentimentality', which appeared in *Mind* in 1983 (NS 92, pp. 519–29). Lovers of sentimental stories, he suggests, 'misrepresent the world in order to feel unconditionally warm-hearted about bits of it' (p. 524). This would account, for instance, for the behavior of people who buy Christmas presents for their dogs. But Jefferson then blurs the lines distinguishing tragedy, sentimentality and melodrama. He says that sentimentality is objectionable because it can lead to ugly violence. He draws his main example from Forster's *Passage to India*. In this novel the English community in India commits a vile injustice as a consequence of having sentimentalized the purity and vulnerability of young English women as a class. One such young woman thinks she has been sexually assaulted by an Indian doctor and the English community wants revenge. Forster's novel avoids sentimentality because the reader rejects the sentimental judgement of the English community and is horrified by its reaction. The story is a tragedy, by and large. If it had been written in such a way as to make the reader, too, thirst for revenge against the Indian doctor, it would have been a melodrama.

Perhaps we should revise our definition of melodrama: it is the arousal of pity, *sentimental or otherwise*, done in such a way that satisfaction is possible only with the realization of vengeance. In life this kind of satisfaction motivates the victims, or the next of kin of the victims, of brutal crimes when they demand that their suffering be reckoned in when the criminal is sentenced or paroled. In politics the pleasure of melodrama fuels much misconceived passion. George Shultz, shaking with indignation, condemned the killing of innocents for political or nationalistic purposes but then dismissed the death of Qaddaffi's infant daughter in the US raid on Tripoli, saying that that was different, it was 'sending a message'. Whole movements grow strong by offering melodramatic pleasure. Anti-abortion organizations stir pity for nameless foetuses in order that satisfaction can be realized when an abortion clinic is successfully blown up. *The Phyllis Schlafly Report* advocates 'the right to life of all *innocent* persons from conception to natural death'. The 'guilty' not only can, but should be put to death, by capital punishment or just wars. 'There is a high correlation,' Gloria Steinem tells us, 'between those who are anti-abortion and those who are in favor of both capital punishment and high military spending' (*Outrageous Acts and Everyday Rebellions*, New York, 1983, p. 312).

The audiences at the most successful film and television melodramas regularly link their pity for innocent suffering to the lust for revenge in much the same way as do idealogues on the political Right. Even if it cannot be proved, therefore, that violent retribution at the climax of a popular film significantly increases violence in the streets,[4] it surely does contribute to the violence in politics and morality. Nixon saw *Patton* several times on the night before he ordered the invasion of Cambodia. Reagan imagined the bombing of Libya as an admirable Rambo plot.[5] Sentimentality, especially the dishonesty necessary for its special pleasures, deeply annoys lovers of tragedy; but the short-sighted righteousness that is appealed to in crass melodramas that have become big business is a menace of a different order. It is not what people usually have in mind when they condemn 'gratuitous' violence in popular drama, but perhaps it should be.

The term 'melodrama', drama heightened by music, is borrowed from the French who, in the eighteenth century, developed a popular dramatic form characterized by terrifying incidents, cruel acts, a build-up of tension through chance and coincidence, an exaggerated difference between the good and the bad, and, finally, a conventional happy ending, an ending in which the good utterly defeat the bad. The appeal of this kind of drama was, from the start, to the least sophisticated sections of society. At a later date the most famous Parisian theatre specializing in these plays was called the Théâtre du Grand-Guignol. Guignol is a character in Punch and Judy shows, so Grand Guignol is Punch and Judy for grown-ups.[6] To this day violent beatings are absolutely essential to puppet shows in this tradition, and so is a triumphant turning of the tables with the good finally being given a chance to whack the bad over the head with a long, heavy stick.

Of course, a taste for dramas ending in the violent triumph of the good did not begin in the eighteenth century. It did not even begin with the *Odyssey*, in all probability. We know that, at the height of Athenian sophistication, audiences even there had a 'weakness' for dramas with double endings, good for the good and bad for the bad. Aristotle says as much (*Poetics* 1453a 33). He says that this is actually only the second best of the patterns found in Attic tragedy, although a few minutes later he, too, ranks it as the best when he reserved his highest praise for plays with endings like that in *Iphigenia Among the Taurians* (1454a 4–9). As for the tragedies which end in a grim defeat for those we admire and sympathize with, Aristotle insists that they, too, must have some elements of justice in them; otherwise we would feel ourselves 'polluted' by the play (ch. 13). The poets themselves, however, have usually preferred non-melodramatic climaxes and have sometimes even taunted their audiences, not without some bitterness, for their preference for triumphant endings. Consider the surprises at the climax of Euripides' *Orestes* and Brecht's *Three-Penny Opera*.

What the Greeks in their greatest periods tended to avoid altogether was not triumphant endings, but a build-up of desire for vengeance so intense that it is almost lustful. Here is where our 'weakness' differs from that of the ancients. There is an obvious continuity from nineteenth-century melodrama, through silent films (those in which the good are sentimentalized and everyone's heightened responses are communicated by operatic acting), to 'R' rated films and the violent dramas on television. But melodrama in our own time is no longer confined to amusement for children and ways to collect pennies from the poor. A taste for violent melodrama has become so nearly universal that even the best educated of us are likely to take secret delight in its special thrill and even prefer it to Greek or Shakespearian tragedy. And evidence is mounting (see, for instance, Vladimir Konečni 'Psychological Aspects of the Expression of Anger and Violence on the Stage', forthcoming, esp. notes 68–71) that phantasies of perpetrating violent revenge may have unfortunate effects on individual and group personalities. (To be sure, it may be only a question of quantity. Violent police dramas on television may not be any worse for children than Punch and Judy shows, but the fortunate children of previous centuries did not sit before Punch and Judy shows twenty and thirty hours a week.)

And what of sentimentality? Can an unabashed indulgence in this also harm us? As Mark Jefferson showed in his example from *Passage to India*, and as we would have known anyhow from Grand Guignol and silent films, sentimental pleasure can facilitate a later pleasure in melodramatic violence. But sentimentality itself may be related to a weakness not dependent on later melodramatic victory and revenge. Nico Frijda defines sentimentality as 'the occurrence of strong emotions, mostly conducive to tearfulness, in response to relatively weak stimuli. The stimuli usually have to do with love, affection, devotion, or solitude and often have no direct personal significance for the subject: seeing brides in white wedding gowns, hearing stories about poor small boys being lost and lonely but finally finding a loving home. Tearjerkers and three-penny novels usually have such themes and readily elicit tears, secret or open, even in critical, sophisticated adults.'[7]

That this can be an embarrassing weakness is clear. Kenneth Clark, in the second volume of his autobiography (*The Other Half*, New York: 1977, pp. 54–5) tells how at a public event which he was chairing he announced the presence in the audience of a famous ballerina, an adored idol of his youth. He broke into loud, irrepressible sobs as he spoke her name. The ballerina did so as well. 'It would have been an embarrassing moment,' says Lord Clark, 'but fortunately almost everyone in the audience also wept. I am very prone to tears,' he adds, '(all that I have in common with the great soldiers of the early nineteenth century), and cannot read my favorite poems, even to myself, without weeping. For this reason I cannot quote poetry in a lecture.'

Crying at a public drama is not, of course, an invariable sign that the play must be sentimental or the audience prone to sentimentality. We today do not usually cry at tragedies, but other people have, at other times and in other nations. Different groups and individuals are brought up to feel differently about the public display of emotions even when there is no cheapness in the emotions themselves. A further distinction is needed, therefore, before we can condemn tears as sentimental. What we need is a way to distinguish between pity arising from an honest assessment of reality and pity cheaply bought because dependent on self-deception.

Milan Kundera says (*The Unbearable Lightness of Being*, New York: 1984, p. 251) that kitsch (he uses the German word instead of the French which we prefer) 'causes two tears to flow in quick succession. The first tear says: How nice to see children running in the grass! The second tear says: How nice to be moved, together with all mankind, by children running in the grass! It is the second tear that makes kitsch kitsch.' Then Kundera adds sarcastically, 'The brotherhood of man on earth will be possible only on a base of kitsch.' What is wrong with an awareness of the brotherhood of man won in this way? What is wrong is that it is achieved by reconciling us to the world as it is instead of rousing us to indignation and a demand that we struggle for true justice.[8]

There are two modern theories about the thrill of tragedy that may now be seen to be erroneous, or at least very suspect. One is Brecht's analysis of the effect of traditional tragedies like *King Lear*. The other is the equation of tragic thrills with the community-building thrills of the sacrifice. The latter idea is most frequently associated with René Girard's *La Violence et le sacré* (Paris 1972).

Brecht wanted to produce *Verfremdungseffekte*, distancing or alienation, so that the audience would be unable to identify with the hero. What he was afraid of was that such an identification would give a person in the audience the feeling that he had heroic power over his own life (whereas in fact he was the victim of vast forces he was powerless to control).[9] Plato, as we saw, feared tragedy for the opposite reason: because tragedies make us identify with victims. This, he thought, taught us to believe that we, too, are victims – not in control of our lives or responsible for our own happiness. Plato is surely the more likely to be right. Fortunately, directors of Brecht's plays, including Brecht himself,[10] have generally found it very difficult indeed to avoid stirring the audience, despite the *Verfremdungseffekte*.

The second theory, which goes back to Frazer and to Freud's *Totem and Taboo*,[11] is surely right in identifying the power of violence in tragedy with the power of the communal celebrations of violence in our past. It is wrong, however, in supposing that 'we', whether in an audience or in our community, identify with the perpetrators rather than the victims of the 'sacrifice'. What unites us in America is not our memory of what we did to the Indians, but the injustices we suffered from George III, or at Valley Forge, or the Alamo. The Japanese can be made only with great difficulty to remember that they started the Pacific war and committed many atrocities not so very long ago; but they brood with open and passionate feelings on the memory of Hiroshima and Nagasaki. Israel draws life-giving unity from thoughts about the Holocaust; brooding on their relations with Palestinians and other neighbors divides them bitterly. The Russians are currently suffering a different kind of division. Many Russians cling to the myth that Soviet history is a glorious story; a growing majority, however, fight passionately for a recognition that it has been a long nightmare. Their strength comes only from this latter vision.

If, therefore, a shared memory does sometimes have the power to draw individuals above their day-to-day affairs and unite them with the best, it is not because there is a realization that we were once, and may be again, the perpetrators of violence. Nor is our elevated feeling likely to be caused by the transference of our guilt to a surrogate. It is the cleansing memory of defeats that we cling to and find life-enhancing; and that is powerful enough. We are so prone to blame ourselves individually for our every failure to achieve complete happiness that we are deeply grateful for any authoritative voice which offers us reasons for self-forgiveness. This offer can be implicit in a dishonest sentimental or melodramatic vision; but it can also come in a truthful vision, one that makes us face the most unsatisfactory features of human existence. There is not only the violence we are all prone to but also the violence that pervades the universe. If the poet can make us understand that injustice rules, not justice, we see that, not only are we victims ourselves, which allows us to forgive ourselves, but so too are our fellow human beings, which permits us to experience universal compassion, like Lear's in the storm on the heath. 'When such as I cast out remorse', says Yeats – that is, when we are able to accept human life, not ourselves alone, as the cause of human suffering,

> So great a sweetness flows into the breast
> We must laugh and we must sing,
> We are blest by everything,
> Everything we look upon is blest.

NOTES

1 Among the Alexandrine scholars in antiquity there were at least two *chorizontes*, 'separators', interpreters who thought that the master poets of the two epics could not have been one and the same. See T. W. Allen, *Homer: the origins and the transmission* (Oxford 1924), p. 28. The idea was taken up again by Werner Jaeger in 'Solons Eunomiie', *Berliner Sitzb.* (1926), 69–85; and Reinhardt, Jacoby, and others have followed him in this. See Wolfgang Kulmann, 'Gods and Men in the *Iliad* and *Odyssey*', *Harvard Studies in Classical Philology* 89 (1985), 1–23, esp. pp. 5–6 and note 11. Richard Janko, in *Homer, Hesiod, and the Hymns* (Cambridge University Press, 1982), has produced statistics which would seem to support separate authorships, but he points out that the *Odyssey* is 'later' than the *Iliad* by no greater a margin than that which separates the *Works and Days* from the *Theogony* (p. 82).
2 On the injustices suffered, not only by some of the suitors, but also by Odysseus' men as well, see Sheila Murnaghan, *Disguise and Recognition in the Odyssey* (Princeton University Press, 1987), p. 67 and note 13.
3 'By a vote of 399 to 18, the House [of Representatives] approved a measure that would waive the Sherman Antitrust Act to permit television networks, cable channel operators and other producers of programing to meet to draw up voluntary standards to curb violence on television.' *New York Times*, 2 August 1989.
4 'A 16-year-old boy, apparently enthralled by the film character Rambo, killed his father, mother and brother and wounded his sister ... [He] wore camouflage outfits ... Police said they had found in his bedroom dozens of Rambo posters and magazines, army packs, smoke grenades ... ammunition pouches ... a revolver and four shotguns ... When the boy was booked at the

police station, he gave his nickname as "Rambo".' *New York Times* 23 March 1989.
5 Because she cooperated enthusiastically in Reagan's raid, Mrs Thatcher was dubbed 'Rambo's Daughter' by the London press.
6 See Mel Gordon, *The Grand Guignol: Theatre of Fear and Terror* (New York: Amok Press, 1988), pp. 4–43. See also Victor Emeljanow, 'Grand-Guignol and the Realization of Violence', included in the present volume.
7 *The Emotions* (Cambridge University Press, 1986), p. 352, where credit is given to J. S. Efran and T. J. Spangler, 'Why Grown-Ups Cry', *Motive Emot.* 3, pp. 63–72.
8 Cf. James Baldwin's 'revelation' at his father's funeral in Harlem: *Notes of a Native Son* (Boston, 1955), pp. 113–14. He suddenly realized that, to escape the hatred that destroyed the hater, 'we must hold in the mind forever two ideas which seemed to be in opposition. The first idea was acceptance, the acceptance, totally without rancor, of life as it is, and men as they are', which includes the comprehension that 'injustice is commonplace'. Somehow, he observes, this is not simply cancelled out by the opposite conviction, that 'one must never accept these injustices as commonplace but must fight them with all one's strength.' Cf. Plato, *Timaeus* 87b 6.
9 See K. A. Dickson, *Toward Utopia: a study of Brecht* (Oxford: Clarendon Press, 1978), p. 231.
10 See, for instance, Martin Esslin, *Brecht: a choice of evils* (London: Eyre & Spottiswoode, 1959), chapter 6.
11 See Simon Bennett, *Tragic Drama and the Family: psychoanalytic studies from Aeschylus to Beckett* (New Haven: Yale University Press, 1988), pp. 253–64. Helena Foley, *Ritual Irony: poetry and sacrifice in Euripides* (Ithaca: Cornell University Press, 1985), pp. 30–64, bibl. 24–5, notes 6–11, outlines the later developments of their ideas.

Violence in Greek tragedy*

SIMON GOLDHILL

The question of violence in Greek drama[1] has been regularly dismissed in a sentence or two.[2] The violence that makes Greek myth such a scandal for Victorian scholars,[3] tracing their place in the glory that was Greece, happens off stage in the white-sculptured world of Greek tragedy, or so generations of scholars affirm. The fratricidal, matricidal, patricidal aggression that makes Freud's turn to the ancient world seem inevitable,[4] is talked about incessantly – which also attracts Freud – but scarcely staged, at least in the sense that Shakespeare can stage a blinding, or David Storey a rape.[5] Even recent attempts to reassert the priority of action over the word for Greek theatre have failed to reinscribe violence as a term of performance studies.[6] A touch on an arm, a struggle over a bow, may become especially valorized on the Greek stage, but it is a valorization that functions in part at least by a contrast with the multifaceted violence that shakes the tragic city at the level of narration.[7] There are a few scenes which are regularly cited in mitigation of this trend – the on-stage suicide of Ajax in Sophocles' *Ajax*, the activity of the Egyptians in Aeschylus' *Suppliant Maidens* – but it is also significant that each of these scenes is in itself a crux of performance studies,[8] in the case of Aeschylus' play not least because the text has been submitted to such violence that it reads only ὀ ὀ ὀ ἀ ἀ ἀ for crucial parts of the scene in question.[9]

Yet the very qualities that may make Greek tragedy seem a strange corpus through which to discuss violence in drama, turn out to lead to the heart of the problem of representing violence and of staging violence, and indeed open in a fundamental way the question of the status of the term 'violence' itself. For the notion of 'violence' needs to be carefully situated within a cultural, rhetorical and ideological system, if it is usefully to become a subject of discussion – and the immense production of discourse about violence in Greek tragedy both provokes such an investigation, and, as we will see, makes it extremely difficult to complete.

Now it is impossible to understand Greek tragedy without Homer, the

---

* A draft of this paper was read at the *Themes in Drama* International Conference held at the University of London, Queen Mary and Westfield College, in March 1989.

texts that are constantly being *written through*[10] by the tragedians, and the *Iliad*, a poem which investigates the limits and transgressions of power, provides a privileged work for the discourse of violence throughout the ancient world. Images of the destruction of bodies in the course of war are a recurring feature of Homeric writing: the morselized, damaged body is the result of heroic military endeavour, as much as the perfected, beautiful body is a fundamental aspect of the idea and ideal of excellence projected in the *Iliad*. 'Look at me', says Achilles on the rampage, 'Do you not see how I too am fine and big', οὐχ ὁράᾳς οἷος καὶ ἐγὼ καλός τε μέγας τε (*Il.* 21. 108). The word καλός (*kalos*), with its range of senses from 'noble' to 'beautiful' indicates the inevitable overlap of social and physical excellence that Achilles – the best of the Achaeans, whose only physical flaw is his ankle – above all other evokes. The end that a hero threatens against his enemy and deprecates for himself is the mutilation of the corpse, its abandonment to be consumed by animals, rather than the proper ordering of a funeral (where the body is consumed by fire).[11] So, Achilles, in the scene from which I have just quoted, follows his self-representation by stabbing Lycaon in the neck, sinking the whole sword into his body, and then throwing his body into the river, where, he says, the fish can lick his wounds – an end set in explicit contradistinction to the care of the corpse by his mother prior to a proper funeral (*Il.* 21. 116–25):

> Ἀχιλεὺς δὲ ἐρυσσάμενος ξίφος ὀξὺ
> τύψε κατὰ κληῖδα παρ' αὐχένα, πᾶν δέ οἱ εἴσω
> δῦ ξίφος ἄμφηκες· ὁ δ' ἄρα πρηνὴς ἐπὶ γαίης
> κεῖτο ταθείς, ἐκ δ' αἷμα μέλαν ῥέε, δεῦε δὲ γαῖαν.
> τὸν δ' Ἀχιλεὺς ποταμόνδε λαβὼν ποδὸς ἧκε φέρεσθαι,
> καί οἱ ἐπευχόμενος ἔπεα πτερόεντ' ἀγόρευεν·
> 'ἐνταυθοῖ νῦν κεῖσο μετ' ἰχθύσιν, οἵ σ' ὠτειλὴν
> αἷμ' ἀπολιχμήσονται ἀκηδέες· οὐδέ σε μήτηρ
> ἐνθεμένη λεχέεσσι γοήσεται, ἀλλὰ Σκάμανδρος
> οἴσει δινήεις εἴσω ἁλὸς εὐρέα κόλπον.'

> Achilles drew his sharp sword,
> And struck him on the neck by the collar bone. He sunk
> The whole broad-sword in. Lycaon lay stretched out
> On the earth, and his black blood flowed out and drenched the soil.
> Achilles took him by the foot and carried him to the river,
> And, vaunting over him, spoke these winged words:
> 'Now lie there with the fish, who will lick off the blood
> From your wound, without a care. Nor will your mother
> Lay you on the bier and mourn, but Scamandros
> Will carry you, inside his eddies, to the broad bosom of the sea.'

The fish will not show the care of a funeral (κῆδος means 'care' also in the specific ritual sense of care for the dead corpse); the river will take the body to 'the bosom' of the sea. The mother's care is diffused through the language of the desecration that denies its possibility.

So, too, the physique of Hector and the desire to mutilate it are strongly emphasized at the moment of the Trojan leader's death, where the soldiers run up and 'they marvelled at the physique and admirable form of Hector. Nor did any one stand by him without wounding him', οἳ καὶ θηήσαντο φυὴν καὶ εἶδος ἀγητὸν Ἕκτορος· οὐδ' ἄρα οἵ τις ἀνουτητί γε παρέστη (*Il.* 22. 370– 1). It is the treatment of Hector's body after death, however, that raises a more problematic aspect of the noble body and its mutilation in this heroic military discourse. For Achilles in his wrath at the death of Patroclus grotesquely mistreats Hector's body as a part of his revenge and overwhelming grief. He ties Hector's body to a chariot and drags it round, and commits many outrages to the lifeless form. It is the only example in the Homeric poems of such behaviour. The narrator and Apollo before the gods terms it ἀεικείη, 'an outrage', and Apollo intervenes to prevent Hector's body from decomposing.[12] Even Achilles' mother, Thetis, wonders why he continues with such demonstrations of uncontrollable grief.[13] Achilles may be the best of the Achaeans, but his supremacy is not merely as an exemplary hero, or as the ideal of behaviour. Indeed, Achilles' violent reaction to Patroclus' death images the best of the Achaeans as a bestial mutilator of corpses. Achilles, as several critics have discussed, is a figure who goes beyond the limits, the norms, of social exchange in this poem.[14] And such 'going beyond' is *both* transgression *and* the achievement of outstandingness. It is in this paradigmatic expression of the double, difficult nature of heroic achievement that Achilles becomes the paradigmatic hero. The wrath that moves Achilles leads both to the heights of glory and to his (unacceptably) violent behaviour – he remains αἰναρετή, as Patroclus calls him, 'terrible in excellence'[15] – and it is the consequent difficulty of comprehending his μῆνις, 'wrath', and its place within social norms that have prompted many critical readings of the poem.

Moreover, Achilles' violent treatment of Hector and Lycaon is also part of a sequence of scenes of supplication that play a crucial role in the structuration of the epic.[16] Supplication is a ritualized pattern of behaviour, an institution, designed to limit the uncontrolled use of power by the powerful, designed to integrate the powerful and the weak in a ritualized relation of exchange.[17] It is a striking fact that in the *Iliad* the only two figures to reject supplication with a display of violence are Agamemnon and Achilles, the most kingly and the best of the Achaeans, whose clash not only motivates the epic narrative but also revolves around the ordering and transgression of the boundaries of authority and power. The conflict between the figure of greatest authority and the figure of greatest power on the battlefield is also expressed and explored through their parallel willingness to ignore the institutions and rituals for the control of power *in violence*. While the 'rules of war' exist to order the animal forces of the warrior,[18] violence in the *Iliad* is the enactment of an aggression that sets at risk the boundaries of the institutions of power. The *Iliad* in short sets the problems of extremes of power and authority (and the conflicts between these extremes of power and authority) in the frame of war and its treatment of the human body, in order to articulate the place, limits, and transgressions of social and physical violence. And the *Iliad* provides a privileged set of terms, a privileged range of questions for Greek tragedy's writing.

Indeed, the *Iliad* and the figure of Achilles in particular remain integral to Greek tragedy's depiction of violence, and in particular to Sophocles' treatment of the heroic figure's passionate commitment, excess and physical destructiveness.[19] I want to take up here, however, the institution of supplication to see first how in Aeschylus' play the *Suppliant Maidens* the drama of integration that is supplication becomes the central dramatic device for an extensive consideration of power relations and the violence which is the transgressive instantiation of such relations.

The *Suppliant Maidens* is the first play of a triology whose final two dramas have been lost:[20] it dramatizes the arrival in Argos of the Danaids – fifty black[21] virgins from Egypt – with their father, Danaus. They supplicate King Pelasgus of Argos to accept them and to defend them as Greeks from an unwanted marriage with their (fifty) Egyptian cousins, who are pursuing them. The play ends with the Danaids resisting the Egyptian herald and praying to the gods for deliverance – but since the Danaids are famous for slaughtering their husbands on their wedding night, in the remaining plays the Argives must either have been beaten in battle or to have changed their attitude towards the Danaids' pleas. The play is largely taken up with the Danaids' attempt to be accepted as suppliants within the Argos community and the difficulties that this raises for Pelasgus, the king.

As so often, the brief remarks of Jean-Pierre Vernant go closer to the heart of the issues at stake here than many a lengthier exegesis. He argues that the play is concerned with the contradictory expressions and senses of power, or, more precisely, that 'the idea of *kratos*' – that is, power, authority, strength – can be seen 'to oscillate between two contrary accepted meanings, unable to settle for one rather than the other'.[22] On the one hand, *kratos* 'refers to legitimate authority, the control rightfully exercised by the guardian over whoever is dependent upon his power'.[23] On the other, *kratos* 'is drawn into the semantic range of *bia*', that is, 'force, constraint imposed by violence'.[24] Let me gloss this division in the term *kratos* a little further. *Kratos* as legitimate authority is associated with the term *kurios*, 'master', 'figure of authority', the one who possesses *kratos*, and it refers to a series of analogous relationships each of which is dramatized in the *Suppliant Maidens*.[25] First, it refers to the authority of the male over the female, and more specifically to the authority of father over daughter and the authority of husband over wife. In Athenian culture, a female is expected at all times to have a *kurios*, and marriage is a *rite de passage*, an exchange not merely of status from παρθένος, 'unmarried female', to, finally, γυνή, 'woman/wife', but also of *kurios* from father to husband.[26] The *Suppliant Maidens* revolves around the desire of the Danaids with the connivance of Danaus, their father, to avoid – and finally violently to destroy – the transition that is marriage. Second, *kratos* refers to the authority of the city over the citizen, the stranger and the metic (resident alien). At stake in the supplication of the Danaids is the commitment of the *polis* (which necessarily implicates each citizen) to go to war to protect the strangers to whom such sanctuary has been properly offered.[27] Third, *kratos* indicates the legitimate rule of those in authority within the *polis*, and in this case the king, the father to his people. It is with the king that the Danaids deal, and then the king persuades the people in the assembly to accept the supplication. Fourth, there is the authority of god over man. In supplication, a weaker figure appeals to the stronger through the still greater authority of the gods:[28] it is at the altar that the Danaids make their supplication. Moreover, the Danaids claim their descent (and consequent obligatory ties with Argos) from Io, a mortal female, and Zeus – and this relationship is referred to again and again in the play as an expression of divine and human interaction and as an expression of the hierarchies of gender and power.[29]

The conceptualization of the enactment of each of these relations of power depends on a further commonly paired – and polarized – terms, πειθώ (*peitho*) and βία (*bia*). *Peitho* means persuasion, seduction, implying obedience, agreement – from erotics to military diplomacy.[30] *Bia* connotes force, violent constraint, rape, over a similar range of areas. The expression of *kratos* as legitimate power, dependent on *peitho* for its operation, is set in tension with the expression of *kratos* as constraint dependent on *bia* for its domination. In Athenian democratic representations, the figure of the tyrant, who exercises violent constraint over the citizens, women, and channels of power in a city, typifies the conjunction of *kratos* and *bia*,[31] and such a conjunction is dramatized with stunning boldness in the *Prometheus Bound*, where in the opening scene Prometheus is chained to the Caucasian rocks by the agents of Zeus' tyranny – the god Hephaestus, and two figures named, precisely, Kratos and Bia. (Bia is, significantly, mute.) The tyrant's transgressive rule is visibly instantiated in the violent enchainment of the civilizer of mankind by the figures of κράτος and βία, working together.[32] What is more, the tyrant's aggression – in the standard rhetoric of Athenian democratic representation – causes 'injury or annoyance whereby the sufferer is disgraced, not to obtain any advantage besides the performance of the act, but for the aggressor's own pleasure': which is exactly how

Aristotle defines *hubris*.³³ That the violence termed *hubris* involves the *disgrace* of the victim and the *pleasure* of the perpetrator demonstrates how the (evaluative) terminology of violence can never be purely or absolutely physical.

In the *Suppliant Maidens*, Pelasgus, the Argive ruler, is open to the persuasion of the Danaids, takes their proposal to the Assembly, and is prepared to back his city's decision with properly ordered military action. He questions the Danaids – and behaves himself – from an understanding of *kratos* as a legally and socially determined set of hierarchical relations. The Egyptian barbarians, however, lust for fighting and fight for their lust; they attempt to remove the Danaids from the altar; reject the Greek gods and norms of social interaction (ξενία). In short, their claims of *kratos* are established within a (transgressive) commitment to *bia*, force. It might seem at first sight, then, as if the play constructs an opposition between legitimated authority, centred on Pelasgus in Argos, and violence, as embraced by the barbarians. But such an opposition is consistently set at risk in Aeschylus' play.

First, the authority of the gods, particularly as represented in Zeus' treatment of Io, is depicted both as gentle, divine grace and as violent sexual domination: 'divine justice may frequently appear as opaque and arbitrary as violence done by a tyrant'.³⁴ The authoritative constraint of the gods offers a paradigm of an ambivalence at the heart of power relations, not an image of controlled order for the sublunary world. Second, Pelasgus is set in a specifically *tragic* position: he is forced to question his course of action and to live with the consequences of the decision made in response to the double bind in which he is trapped. The king's position is not simply one of legitimated authority, but authority placed in a problematized, even paradoxical position.³⁵ Third, and this is the area I wish to focus on, the exchanges between the Danaids and the king, which help enmesh the king in the double bind, construct a specifically questioning attitude to the legitimation of authority and the violence that is the transgression of such authority. Consider first this well-known exchange on the siting of authority in the state of Argos (*Suppliant Maidens*, 365–75):

> Βα. οὔτοι κάθησθε δωμάτων ἐφέστιοι
> ἐμῶν· τὸ κοινὸν δ' εἰ μιαίνεται πόλις,
> ξυνῇ μελέσθω λαὸς ἐκπονεῖν ἄκη.
> ἐγὼ δ' ἂν οὐ κραίνοιμ' ὑπόσχεσιν πάρος,
> ἀστοῖς δὲ πᾶσι τῶνδε κοινώσας πέρι.
> Χο. σύ τοι πόλις, σὺ δὲ τὸ δήμιον·
> πρύτανις ἄκριτος ὤν
> κρατύνεις βωμόν, ἑστίαν χθονός,
> μονοψήφοισι νεύμασιν σέθεν,
> μονοσκήπτροισι δ'ἐν θρόνοις χρέος
> πᾶν ἐπικραίνεις· ἄγος φυλάσσου.

Pe. You do not sit as claimants at my own hearth.
    If the city in common is polluted,
    it is a shared concern for the people to work for a cure.
    I could not make a prior undertaking;
    But after I have debated in common with all the citizens.
Ch. You the city! You the commonwealth!
    You are an unimpeachable president;
    You rule this altar, the hearth of the land,
    By your nod, a single vote.
    With your seat of sole authority you fulfil
    All requirements. Beware pollution!

The king asserts that the altar is not his: that the commonality of the state is set at risk with any pollution here. Indeed, he cannot make any undertaking without appraising the citzens first. The common (κοινόν) risk enjoins him to make common (κοινώσας) the decision. Whatever the supposed constitutional position of Pelasgus,[36] there is no doubt that his decision to turn to the people takes on a special force in a play for the democratic *polis*, and is expressed in the politicized language of that *polis*. The chorus's response, however, is an intense affirmation of the monarch's sole authority, sole power, as they identify Pelasgus as the city, as the sovereign people. Their terms reverse the suggestion of the collective authority that the king had used. He rules, they say, ἄκριτος, 'unimpeachable', 'unjudged', which the Scholion correctly glosses as ἀνυπεύθυνος, 'unaccountable' – without, that is, the usual procedures of accountability that define the democratic official in Athens.[37] He enjoys μονοψήφοισι νεύμασιν, 'single-voting nods'. A nod of the head is the regal sign of affirmation, and the oxymoronic adjective μονοψήφοισι, 'single-voting' points precisely to the sense of democratic majority, democratic process, that they are denying. Where he says he cannot make (κραίνοιμ') an undertaking without consulting all (πᾶσι), they say he rules (ἐπικραίνεις) all (πᾶν). It is, they conclude starkly, for him as sole ruler to guard against the religious abomination of rejecting supplicants.

This exchange articulates, then, an incommensurability in the constitution of authority, that leads into the king's recognition of the double bind in which he is placed (lines 376–80):

βα. ἄγος μὲν εἴη τοῖς ἐμοῖς παλιγκότοις
    ὑμῖν δ' ἀρήγειν οὐκ ἔχω βλάβης ἄτερ·
    οὐδ' αὖ τόδ' εὔφρον, τάσδ' ἀτιμάσαι λιτάς.
    ἀμηχανῶ δὲ καὶ φόβος μ' ἔχει φρένας
    δρᾶσαί τε μὴ δρᾶσαί τε καὶ τύχην ἑλεῖν.

Pe. May pollution be on my enemies!
    But I cannot assist you without harm.
    Nor is this well-intentioned, to dishonour these pleas.
    I am at a loss, and fear holds my mind
    Both to act and not to act and to choose chance.

To act or not to act is a source of fear: like Agamemnon in the *Agamemnon*, the *locus classicus* of tragic choice,[38] Pelasgus sees no way forward without disastrous consequences and no way of avoiding the decision.

His next attempt to control the situation is to turn to its legal status (lines 387–91):

Βα. εἴ τοι κρατοῦσι παῖδες Αἰγύπτου σέθεν
νόμῳ πόλεως, φάσκοντες ἐγγύτατα γένους
εἶναι, τίς ἂν τοῖσδ' ἀντιωθῆναι θέλοι;
δεῖ τοί σε φεύγειν κατὰ νόμους τοὺς οἴκοθεν,
ὡς οὐκ ἔχουσιν κῦρος οὐδὲν ἀμφὶ σοῦ.

Pe. If the children of Aegyptos have authority over you
By the law of the state, claiming to be nearest of kin,
Who would want to resist them?
You must defend yourselves according to your home laws,
Showing how they have no jurisdiction over you.

If the Egyptians have authority (*kratos*) by the law of the state on the basis of kinship, then no opposition would be in order; only if the claim of proper control (κῦρος) is incorrect can support be envisaged. Again, the king seeks to find an external and systematic control for authority. The Danaids' response, however, not only studiously avoids answering the legal question in the terms it has been posed, but also rejects the possibility of their coming under the authority of males *tout court*[39] (lines 392–6):

Χο. μή τί ποτ' οὖν γενοίμαν ὑποχείριος
κράτεσιν ἀρσένων· ὑπάστρῳ δέ τοι
μῆχαρ ὁρίζομαι γάμου δύσφρονος
φυγᾷ· ξύμμαχον δ' ἑλόμενος δίκαν
κρῖνε σέβας τὸ πρὸς θεῶν.

Ch. May I never in any way be in the grasp
Of the authority of males. Under the stars,
I mark out a remedy for an ill-intentioned marriage
By flight. Choose justice as an ally,
Judge by the reverence of the gods.

So in the final lines of the play they pray to Zeus to grant power (*kratos*) to the women (lines 1068–9). As so often in Aeschylus, a clash in power turns to a clash of the sexes;[40] the virgins' rejection of marriage – the role of a Greek female in Greek culture – can only be voiced as a total rejection of the hierarchies of male control, a rejection finally to be instantiated in bloody violence against men. In the Danaids' virginal rejection of marriage as violence, we see most clearly how a culturally specific discourse of violence is predicted on a culturally specific discourse of the body.[41]

Vernant sums up this 'enquiry into the true nature of *kratos*' in the *Suppliant Maidens* as follows:

What is authority, the authority of the man over the woman, of husband over wife, of the head of state over all his fellow-citizens, of the city over the foreigner and the metric, of the gods over mortal men? Does it depend on right, that is to say, mutual agreement, gentle persuasion, *peitho*? Or, on the contrary, on domination, pure force, brute violence, *bia*?[42]

Yet the very recognition and definition of *bia*, 'violence', depends always already on the recognition and definition of *kratos*, legitimate power, be it military, political, social, sexual, religious. What definition could there be beyond the interplay of such mutual implication? And what position, what critical stance is available that is not always already implicated in this discourse of power? The *Suppliant Maidens* turns on the recognition that the act of definition whereby authority is distinguished from violence is a strategy of the discourse of power that is always open to questioning and to reappropriation.

The moment in the *Suppliant Maidens* that shows the complexity of the discourse and violence most strikingly is perhaps the following exchange, crucial to the Danaids' supplication (lines 457–69):

Χο. ἔχω στρόφους ζώνας τε, συλλαβὰς πέπλων.
Βα. †τύχαν† γυναικῶν ταῦτα συμπρεπῆ πέλοι.
Χο. ἐκ τῶνδε τοίνυν, ἴσθι, μηχανὴ καλή.
Βα. λέξον· τίν' αὐδὴν τήνδε γηρυθεῖσ' ἔσῃ;
Χο. εἰ μή τι πιστὸν τῷδ' ὑποστήσεις στόλῳ
Βα. τί σοι περαίνει μηχανὴ συζωμάτων;
Χο. νέοις πίναξιν βρέτεα κοσμῆσαι τάδε.
Βα. αἰνιγματῶδες τοὖπος· ἀλλ' ἁπλῶς φράσον.
Χο. ἐκ τῶνδ' ὅπως τάχιστ' ἀπάγξασθαι θεῶν.
Βα. ἤκουσα μαστικτῆρα καρδίας λόγον.

Ch. I have belts and bands, the ties of my robes.
Pe. These would be suitable for women.
Ch. From these, you know, comes a fine device.
Pe. Speak. What is the message you will have expressed?
Ch. If you will not make a firm promise to this group . . .
Pe. What does the device of ties achieve?
Ch. To decorate these statues with new offerings.
Pe. A riddling speech. Speak simply.
Ch. To throttle ourselves as quickly as possible from these gods.
Pe. I have heard a speech to torture my heart.

The Danaids intimate gradually that they are prepared to hang themselves from the altar – a threat of pollution that prompts a horrified response from Pelasgas. If supplication consists in a weaker figure's appeal to a stronger figure according to a still stronger force – morality, the gods – what is to be made of a supplication that relies on a powerfully polluting act of self-inflicted violence? A supplication based on a powerful threat of aggressive behaviour? How are the lines of power, persuasion and violence to be drawn in this case?

There has been, then, extensive preparation in the play for the scene where the Danaids are dragged forcibly from the altar: what is perhaps the most violent scene staged in extant ancient tragedy is led up to by a complex and conflictual investigation of the constellation of terms by which a discourse of power and violence is articulated on the Athenian stage. Tragedy stages, investigates and problematizes the development of a secure discourse of power whereby violence can be (securely) comprehended.

The scene of violence in Aeschylean theatre that is most often returned to by later writers is the death of Agamemnon in the *Agamemnon*.[43] It is an archetypal scene of tragic violence in that it takes place off stage but is represented in a vast interlocking system of imagery, discussion and evaluation. The bodies of Agamemnon and Cassandra are displayed to the chorus and the audience by the triumphant Clytemnestra, whose rhetoric demonstrates a magnificently corrupt celebration of her violence. In particular, her speech perverts three key areas of what could be called culturally controlled violence:[44] hunting, sacrifice, warfare. Hunting as an act of masculine group self-definition and as an act of institutionalized force has been extensively analysed only in recent years.[45] Clytemnestra boasts her nets of destruction are too high to be leapt over (lines 1375–6): she depicts Agamemnon as a beast entrapped by deception. So she describes the cloth in which she enmeshes her husband as a net for fish (ἀμφίβληστρον, ὥσπερ ἰχθύων, line 1382). Her act of killing her husband is celebrated as a perverted form of social ritual, where the woman hunts and her prey is the male figure of authority.[46]

Athenian society, it must never be forgotten, is a warrior culture. The values of citizenship and militarism are deeply intertwined in any Athenian sense of self.[47] Warfare is a natural state of affairs for the Athenian male. Agamemnon in the carpet scene accused Clytemnestra of improperly desiring battle (line 940). If he means there the battle of words, now it is evident that Clytemnestra has enacted a further distortion of the male pursuit of military force. Like an Amazon, that paradigmatic reversal of Athenian male values,[48] she has with her man's weapon destroyed a naked man in the bath. 'I stand here' she boasts 'where I struck him, over the completed deed' (line 1379). If the Homeric hero's boast of victory is a signal of achieved status and honour, Clytemnestra stands as a violent perversion of such claims.

The role of sacrifice in Greek culture has been the subject of much analysis, as has its treatment in the *Oresteia*.[49] Clytemnestra's narrative of violence is cast not merely as a perverted sacrifice but also in her speech of triumph as a perverted act of libations at a symposium (lines 1384–7):

> παίω δέ νιν δίς, κἀν δυοῖν οἰμώγμασιν
> μεθῆκεν αὐτοῦ κῶλα, καὶ πεπτωκότι
> τρίτην ἐπενδίδωμι, τοῦ κατὰ χθονὸς
> Διὸς νεκρῶν σωτῆρος εὐκταίαν χάριν.

> I struck him twice, and with two groans
> His limbs went slack, and as he fell
> I made a third offering, a prayer of thanks
> To Zeus of the Underworld, saviour of corpses.

The three blows, the three spillings of blood are made analogous to the three libations of wine that always open the male social event of the symposium.[50] 'Zeus the Saviour', who is the third recipient of a libation, becomes 'Zeus the saviour of corpses' – a further specific manipulation of ritual language, as the queen's rhetoric of triumph violently distorts the expression of proper, controlled, masculine group performance.

In each of these areas of cultural expression, the reversal of gender role is a fundamental aspect in the representation of Clytemnestra's violence; so it is not surprising that her description of the blood spurting from the wounds of her man – giving her 'more joy than the field feels for nourishing dew' (lines 1390–2) – has been seen as an explicitly eroticized representation of the slaughter.[51] If the Danaids express hostility towards a violence of marriage, Clytemnestra revels in an eroticism of violence against her husband.

Clytemnestra's self-representation, then – which is seen immediately by the chorus as a remarkable violence of language (lines 1399–1400) – is constituted specifically as a transgression of the normative discourse of force and authority within a specific culture. (There is always a range of types of violence within a society.[52]) What's more, this act of killing continues to be discussed, defined, and delineated within the trilogy as we move towards the legal dispute and definitions of the law-court in the *Eumenides*. Developing and conflicting representations of an act of violence are integral to this triology's complex sense of human action.[53] (There is a range of types of violence within a society, but also difficulties of recognition and categorization within such a typology, difficulties which lead to *violent* dissension.) And if there is one scene in particular that problematizes the representation of Clytemnestra's violence, it is the scene which concludes the *Choephoroi*, where Orestes, Clytemnestra's son, appears over the bodies of Clytemnestra and Aegisthus. It is a scene staged to proclaim a parallel. As Clytemnestra appears over the bodies of Agamemnon and Cassandra, so Orestes appears over the bodies of Clytemnestra and Aegisthus. So Orestes displays the weapons of violence and describes his act. The scene is a constitutive factor, then, in the pattern of repeated reciprocal violence that makes up the narrative of the house of Atreus. Yet the differences between the scenes are also important. Orestes describes himself first as a tyrannicide – a figure of cult status in the democracy[54] – and portrays the horrors of reversal that the monstrous woman in charge has enacted. But he also represents himself as beginning to lose his wits; and in a mad frenzy at what he alone sees as the onset of the Furies flees the stage. This dramatic action, as Orestes turns from hunter to hunted, seems to indicate the impossibility (within the family at any rate) of any simply valorized act of revenge or punishment. It is the paradoxical double-bind of Orestes' tragic position that in order to right a transgression he must himself be involved in transgression. As he sums up the matricide in his climactic final line before leading his mother off stage (line 930): ἔκανες ὃν οὐ χρῆν, καὶ τὸ μὴ χρεὼν πάθε., 'You killed who you ought not, now suffer what you ought not.' As Orestes now stands where Clytemnestra had stood over the victims' bodies, we see a re-presentation of the scene of violence, that forcefully demonstrates the inevitable interplay of difference, ideology, commitment in the representation of violence. So it is not surprising that it is precisely with the status of Orestes' act – thus problematized in its narrative representation – that the court scene of the *Eumenides* and the discussion of the critics find such difficulties. When does violence become controlled, determined as force? By what rhetoric? By what institutionalization? When the chorus of the *Agamemnon* describe the authority of the gods and in particular of Zeus, the king of the gods, through the oxymoronic expression χάρις βίαιος (line 182), 'violent grace', 'a blessing through violence', they point to a paradox and a problem worked through at all levels of this triology's interest in authority and violence.

The *Oresteia* does not end with the law-court, but requires Athene's persuasion to realign the still-threatened violence of the Furies towards Athens. The final stanzas of praise project not a utopian vision of Athens but a more precarious sense of the conditional prosperity of the city, where humans still do not control the narratives of violent punishment, and the threats of transgression are ever present.[55] What is remarkable is that despite the representation of Athens itself on stage, despite the representation of a key political and legal institution of the city, the trilogy does not merely express a system of norms and transgressions, but also questions the very boundaries between norms and transgression, the very establishment of the system itself. The city festival in which tragedy is performed demonstrates the extraordinary process of the developing city setting its own developing system of thought at risk in the public arena, placing its language and institutions open to the violence of what Euripides calls 'the strife of warring words'.

There is, then, no notion of violence without a notion of the norms and institutions of power in society, without, indeed, a discourse of the body and its treatment in society. This has two corollaries. First, there is no representation of power, violence, the treatment of the body, that does not demonstrate these norms and institutions. Second, there is no position beyond such norms and institutions from which to speak of violence. We are all always already implicated in the system and rhetoric of power. The example of Greek tragedy not only demonstrates the cultural specificity of a notion of violence and the changing terms of power and violence within a culture, but also offers the further and more extraordinary picture of a society prepared to question in and through a public institution the terms and nature of power and violence within that society. I have discussed briefly – and I am highly conscious of the violence of interpretation in which I have indulged – only two of the works of Aeschylus, the earliest of the great Athenian tragedians. One could have mentioned Sophocles' interrogation of the limits and transgressions of commitment through his heroic figures' destructive self-esteem and passionate involvement in self-centred principle. One could have mentioned Euripides' ironic questioning of the rhetoric of war in a play like the *Troades*, or disturbing portrayal of divine violence and power in a play like the *Bacchae*, or the examination of the motivation and the force of violent revenge in the *Medea*. One could have traced these later playwrights' continuing interest in the rituals and performance of supplication. In the period of Athenian hegemony in the Greek world, the period of democracy's growth, a period of rapid social and cultural transformation, the question of power and violence is increasingly and publicly discussed and debated.

In Britain today – where the Government can at the same time ban access to the public media for certain groups in Ireland, and appeal to free speech as an international moral standard; where political rhetoric rarely goes beyond mutual accusations or claims of terrorism and national security; where 'human rights' and 'civilized values' are all too often invoked, and all too rarely analysed; it might be that Greek tragedy's sophisticated, powerful and public interrogation of the nature of violence and power in society offers us an example to be seriously considered.

NOTES

1 The following notes are not intended to be exhaustive, but to site the argument within the relevant areas of contemporary scholarship.
2 E.g. 'The fact remains that in the extant tragedies violence and murder normally occur "offstage": there are no exciting duels, no bloodthirsty spectacles.' H. C. Baldry, *The Greek Tragic Theatre* (London: Chatto, 1971), p. 50.
3 On this sense of scandal, see M. Detienne, *L'Invention de la mythologie* (Paris: Gallimard 1981), especially pp. 15–49, and *s.v.* scandale; and from a more general perspective, G. Stocking, *Victorian Anthropology* (New York: Free Press, 1987) especially pp. 78–109, 186–237.
4 On Freud and the classical world, see for bibliography and discussion P. Rudnytsky, *Freud and Oedipus*, (New York: Columbia University Press, 1987).
5 I am referring to the blinding of Gloucester (*King Lear*, II, vii) and to David Storey's *Life Class*. I have learnt in particular from the following studies of power and violence in Shakespeare: J. Dollimore, *Radical Tragedy: religion, ideology, and power in the drama of Shakespeare and his contemporaries* (Brighton: Harvester Press, 1984); F. Barker, *The Tremulous Private Body: essays in subjection* (London and New

York: Methuen, 1984); L. Tennenhouse, *Power on Display: the politics of Shakespeare's genres* (New York and London: Methuen, 1986), especially pp. 102–46. For a different sort of attempt to relate the blinding of Gloucester to the physical imagery of the play, see J. Stewart, 'The blinding of Gloster', *Review of English Studies*, 21 (1945), 264–70.

6 Except in the claim that it is not the violence but the reaction to it that is relevant: e.g. 'My claim is ... that it is the action that takes place *on* stage which *is* important ... The action off-stage is only of interest in so far as it is given attention on stage. The error comes about from a simple-minded preconception of what constitutes action; it only counts the huge violent events of narrative history – battles, riots, miracles, natural disasters and so forth. This is to miss the point that the stuff of tragedy is the individual response to such events; not the blood, but the tears.' O. Taplin, *Greek Tragedy in Action* (London: Methuen, 1978), pp. 160–1.

7 For one attempt to construct a typology of the violences that threaten the city, see F. Zeitlin, *Under the Sign of the Shield: Semiotics and Aeschylus' Seven against Thebes* (Rome: Edizioni dell Ateneo, 1982), pp. 29–36.

8 On *Ajax*, see e.g. K. Reinhardt, *Sophocles*, trans. H. Harvey and D. Harvey (Oxford University Press, 1979), pp. 28–30 (with note 17, pp. 238–9); T. Webster, *Greek Theatre Production* (London: Methuen, 2nd edition, 1970), pp. 17–18; P. Arnott, *Greek Scenic Conventions in the Fifth Century B.C.* (Oxford University Press, 1962), pp. 132–3; C. P. Gardiner, 'The staging of the death of Ajax', *Classical Journal*, 75 (1979), pp. 10–14; S. P. Mills, 'The Death of Ajax', *Classical Journal*, 76 (1980/1), 729–35; M. Heath, *The Poetics of Greek Tragedy* (London: Duckworth, 1987), pp. 192–4. On the *Suppliant Maidens*, see O. Taplin, *The Stagecraft of Aeschylus* (Oxford University Press, 1977), pp. 215–38, with bibliography of the extensive earlier discussions; also H. Friis Johansen and E. Whittle, *The Suppliants*, 3 vols (Coppenhagen: Gyldendal, 1980), pp. 171–4.

9 On which see, W. Nestle, 'Review of Walter Kranz *Stasimon*', *Gnomon*, 10 (1934), 414–15; A. Garvie, *Aeschylus' Supplices: play and trilogy* (Cambridge University Press, 1969), pp. 56–7 (with note 5); Taplin, *The Stagecraft of Aeschylus*, 213–14. E. Hall, *Inventing the Barbarian: Greek Self-definition through Tragedy* (Oxford University Press, forthcoming) sees this cry as a sign of barbarian excess.

10 I use the phrase 'written though' with the same double sense as Jane Gallop's 'thinking through' in her *Thinking Through the Body* (New York: Columbia University Press, 1988).

11 See in particular, C. P. Segal, *The Theme of the Mutilation of the Corpse in the Iliad*, *Mnemosyne* suppl. 17 (1971); J. Redfield, *Nature and Culture in the Iliad: the tragedy of Hector* (Chicago and London: University of Chicago Press, 1975), especially pp. 179–86.

12 See *Iliad* 22. 395–404; 24. 17–21; 24. 54.

13 *Iliad* 24. 128–37.

14 I have discussed this in a forthcoming book *The Poet's Voice*. See in particular, Redfield, *Nature and Culture in the Iliad*; S. Schein; *The Mortal Hero* (Berkeley: University of California Press, 1984); M. Mueller, *The Iliad* (London: Allen & Unwin, 1984); K. King, *Achilles: paradigms of the war hero from Homer to the Middle Ages* (Berkeley: University of California Press, 1987); M. Lynn-George, *Epos:*

15 *Iliad* 16.31.
16 See on this theme J. Gould,'Hiketeia', *Journal of the Hellenic Society*, 93 (1973), 74–103; J. Griffin, *Homer on Life and Death* (Oxford University Press, 1980), 24–6; C. Macleod, *Homer: Iliad xxiv* (Cambridge University Press, 1982), pp. 16–35; V. Pedrick, 'Supplication in the *Iliad* and the *Odyssey*', *Transactions and Proceedings of the American Philological Association*, 112 (1982), 125–40; A. Thornton, *Homer's Iliad: its composition and the motif of supplication* (Göttingen: Vandenhoeck und Ruprecht, 1984); Mueller, *The Iliad*, pp. 28–76; M. Lynn-George, 'Epos: word, narrative and the Iliad' (1983, unpublished dissertation, Cambridge).
17 The standard description remains Gould, 'Hiketeia', pp. 74–103. I have discussed problems with his description in *The Poet's Voice* (forthcoming).
18 On the 'animal within' the warrior, see in particular Redfield, *Nature and Culture in the Iliad* especially, pp. 160–223.
19 Achilles and the Sophoclean hero is discussed in particular by R. Winnington-Ingram, *Sophocles: an interpretation* (Cambridge University Press, 1980), pp. 11–72, in response to the seminal study of B. Knox, *The Heroic Temper: studies in Sophoclean tragedy* (Berkeley: University of California Press, 1964). I have discussed this debate in *Reading Greek Tragedy* (Cambridge University Press, reprinted 1988), pp. 154–67.
20 On the trilogy, see in particular A. Garvie, *Aeschylus' Supplices: play and trilogy* (Cambridge University Press, 1969).
21 They are described (154–5 and 279ff.) as sun-burnt and looking Egyptian. Scholars (c.f. e.g. F. Snowden, *Blacks in Antiquity: Ethiopians in the Greco-Roman experience*, Cambridge University Press, 1970, p. 157, with bibliography 311 note 10) have debated whether they are half-black or wholly black. They are clearly not white (Greek), however.
22 J-P. Vernant in J-P. Vernant and P. Vidal-Naquet, *Tragedy and Myth in Ancient Greece*, trans. J. Lloyd (Brighton: Harvester Press, 1981), p. 14. See also A. Moreau, *Eschyle: la violence et la chaos* (Paris: Les Belles Lettres, 1985), pp. 246–52.
23 Ibid. pp. 246–52.
24 Ibid. pp. 14–15.
25 In what follows, I have profitted immensely from a forthcoming study of this play by Froma Zeitlin.
26 For the legal position of women see D. Schaps, *The Economic Rights of Women in Ancient Greece* (Edinburgh University Press, 1978) and most recently V. Hunter, 'Women's Authority in Classical Athens', *Echos du Monde Classique*, 33 (1989), 39–48, who argues (against the *communis opinio*) that under very exceptional circumstances a woman could be regarded as the head of a household. I have discussed the question of the social models of gender with bibliography in *Reading Greek Tragedy* pp. 107–37, to which can be added J. Blok and P. Mason eds., *Sexual Assymetry: Studies in ancient society* (Amsterdam: Gieben, 1987); C. Sourvinou-Inwood, *Studies in Girls' Transitions: aspects of the arkteia and age representation in Attic iconography* (Athens: Kardamitsa, 1988); P. duBois, *Sowing the Body: psychoanalysis and ancient representations of women* (Chicago and London: University of Chicago Press, 1988); D. Halperin, J. Winkler, F. Zeitlin eds.,

Before Sexuality: the construction of erotic experience in the Ancient Greek world (Princeton University Press, forthcoming).

27 The categories of the 'city' (πόλις) and 'citizen' (πολίτης) are crucial to any sense of the self and authority in ancient Athens. I have discussed this with bibliography in *Reading Greek Tragedy*, pp. 57–78; and with regard to tragedy in 'The Great Dionysia and civic ideology', *Journal of the Hellenic Society*, 107 (1987), 58–76. N. Loraux's *L'Invention d'Athènes* (Paris: Mouton, 1981) is one of the best studies of these categories. For the development of Athens' special claims to receive suppliants and the role of metics, see e.g. P. Gauthier, *Symbola: les étrangers et la justice dans les cités grecques* (Nancy: Annales de l'Est, 1972).

28 For this power relation, see M. Serres, 'The Algebra of Literature: the Wolf's Game' in *Textual Strategies: perspectives in post-structuralist criticism*, ed. J.V. Harari (Ithaca: Cornell University Press, 1979).

29 On Io and Zeus in this play, see R. D. Murray, *The Motif of Io in Aeschylus' Suppliants* (Princeton University Press, 1958). And on her representation in the *P.V.*, see J-F Boittin, 'Figures du mythe et de la tragedie. Io dans le *Prométhée Enchaîné*' in *Écriture et théorie poétiques. Lectures d'Homère, Eschyle, Platon, Aristote* (Paris: Presses de l'Ecole Normale Supérieure, 1976); A. Masaracchia, 'Per l'interpretazione del Prometeo II', *QUCC*, 50 (1985), 15–26, especially 15–24.

30 On the range of sense for *peitho*, see R. Buxton, *Persuasion in Greek Tragedy: a study of Peitho* (Cambridge University Press, 1982).

31 See G. Cerri, *Il Linguaggio politico nel Prometeo di Eschilo: saggio di semantica* (Rome: Edizioni del Ateneo, 1975); D. Lanza, *Il tiranno e il suo pubblico* (Turin: Einandi, 1977); K. Waters, 'Herodotus on Tyrants and Despots', *Historia Einzelschriften*, 15 (1971); M. Taylor, *The Tyrant Slayers: the heroic image in fifth-century B.C. Athenian art* (New York: Arno Press, 1981); S. Said, *Sophiste et tyran ou le problème du Prométhée enchaîné* (Paris: Klincksiecke, 1985) especially pp. 233–340; Moreau, *Eschyle: la violence et la chaos*, pp. 209–16; H. Berve, *Die Tyrannis bei den Griechen* (Munich: Beck, 1967), pp. 190–4; G. Cerri, 'Antigone, Creonte e l'idea tirannide nell' Atene del v secolo', *QUCC*, 10 (1982), 137–55; D. Asheri, 'Tyranni et mariage forcé: essai d'histoire sociale grecque', *Annales ESC*, 32 (1977), 21–48. I have discussed the idea of rule by a single figure in the *Persae* in 'Battle narrative and politics in Aeschylus' *Persae*', *Journal of Hellenic Studies*, 108 (1988), 189–193.

32 See Said, *Sophiste et tyran*, pp. 233–340; Cerri, *Il Linguaggio politico nel Prometeo di Eschilio*; Moreau, *Eschyle: la violence et la chaos* 209–16, each with bibliography to the extensive earlier discussions of scholars. See also V. Citti, 'κράτος and βία contrapposti e congiunti nelle tragedie di Eschilio', *Vichiana* 1.3. (1964), 76–9; U. Albini, 'I tre volti del potere nel Prometeo', *Parole del Passato*, 40 1985), 414–18. V. di Benedetto's claim (*L'ideologia del potere e la tragedia greca*, Turin: Einandi, 1978, p. 56) that Zeus is described neutrally by the language of tyranny in the *Prometheus Bound* seems indefensible to me.

33 ἔστι γὰρ ὕβρις τὸ βλάπτειν καὶ λυπεῖν ἐφ' οἷς αἰσχύνη ἐστὶ τῷ πάσχοντι, μὴ ἵνα τι γένηται αὐτῷ ἄλλο ἢ ὅτι ἐγένετο, ἀλλ' ὅπως ἡσθῇ. Aristotle *Rhetoric* 1378b23ff. On this definition of *hubris* and its social and legal connotations see D. MacDowell *The Law of Classical Athens* (Ithaca: Cornell University Press, 1978), pp. 113–32; and, in particular, N. Fisher, '*Hybris* and Dishonour I', *Greece and Rome*, 23

(1976), 177–93, writing in response to D. MacDowell, '*Hybris* in Athens', *Greece and Rome*, 23 (1976), 14–31.

34 Vernant, *Tragedy and Myth in Ancient Greece*, p. 14. See also E. Whittle, 'An ambiguity in Aeschylus', *Classica & Mediaevela*, 25 (1964), 1–7; Murray, *The Motif of Io in Aeschylus' Suppliants*. H. Lloyd-Jones 'Zeus in Aeschylus', *Journal of Hellenic Studies* 76 (1956), 55–67 and G. Grube, 'Zeus in Aeschylus', *American Journal of Philology*, 91 (1970), 43–51, both underestimate the possible ambivalence of divine power and its effect on humans.

35 'It is perhaps the most purely tragic of tragic situations.' H. Kitto, *Greek Tragedy* (London: Methuen, 3rd edn, 1961). See also T. Tarkow, 'The dilemma of Pelasgus and the nautical imagery of Aeschylus' *Suppliants*', *Classica & Mediaevela*, 31 (1970=1975), 1–13.

36 A much discussed problem. See A. Garvie, *Aeschylus' Supplices. Play and trilogy* (Cambridge University Press, 1969), pp. 150–4, with good bibliography and discussion of earlier views. See also P. Burian, 'Pelasgus and politics in Aeschylus' Danaid trilogy', *Wiener Studien*, n.s.8 (1974), 5–14; A. Podlecki, *The Political Background of Aeschylean Tragedy* (Ann Arbor: University of Michigan Press, 1966), p. 46. Johansen and Whittle, *The Supplices*, ad loc. trenchantly sidestep earlier discussions.

37 On this idea, see e.g. G. de Ste.-Croix, *The Class Struggle in the Ancient World* (London: Duckworth, 1981), p. 285.

38 For a discussion of this tragic moment with bibliography, see S. Goldhill, 'Character and action: representation and reading. Greek tragedy and its critics', in C. Pelling ed., *Character and Individuality* (Oxford University Press, forthcoming).

39 This has led to an extensive discussion of motivation: see e.g. Winington-Ingram, *Studies in Aeschylus* pp. 59–61; G. Thompson, 'The Suppliants of Aeschylus', *Eirene*, (1971), 25–30; S. Ireland, 'The problem of motivation in the *Supplices* of Aeschylus', *Rheinische Museum*, 117 (1974), 14–29; F. Ferrari, 'La missandria della Danaidi', *ASNP*, 7 (1977), 1303–21; J. MacKinnon, 'The reasons for the Danaids' flight', *Classical Quarterly*, 28 (1978), 74–82; M. Detienne, *Arethusa*, (1988).

40 See e.g. F. Zeitlin, 'The dynamics of misogyny in the *Oresteia*', *Arethusa*, 11 (1978), pp. 149–84. S. Goldhill, *Language, Sexuality, Narrative: the Oresteia* (Cambridge University Press, 1984).

41 A vast bibliography on this important topic could be given. Mine would include: M. Foucault, *L'Usage des plaisirs* (Paris: Gallimard, 1984); *Le Souci de soi* (Paris: Gallimard, 1984); S. Suleiman ed., *The Female Body in Western Culture* (Cambridge University Press, 1986); E. Scarry, *The Body in Pain: the making and unmaking of the world* (Oxford University Press, 1985); H. Michie, *The Flesh Made Word: Female figures and Women's bodies* (Oxford University Press, 1987); Gallop, *Thinking Through the Body;* P. Brown, *The Body and Society* (Princeton University Press, 1988); A White and P. Stallybrass, *The Politics and Poetics of Transgression* (London: Methuen, 1986); J. Kristeva, *Polylogue* (Paris: Editions du seuil, pp. 409–35). Specifically on the question of rape and seduction, see e.g. S. Tomaselli and R. Porter, *Rape* (Oxford: Blackwell 1986) (with bibliography of earlier

studies); S. Kappeler, *The Pornography of Representation* (London: Polity Press, 1984); T. Eagleton, *The Rape of Clarissa* (Oxford: Blackwell, 1982). And from the psychoanalytic perspective, see J. Gallop, *Feminism and Psychoanalysis: the daughter's seduction* (London: Methuen, 1982); A. Jardine, *Gynesis: configurations of women and modernity* (Ithaca: Cornell University Press, 1985) especially pp. 159–223. On virginity and female bodies in ancient Greek culture, see e.g. G. Sissa, *Le Corps virginal* (Paris: Vrin, 1986); A. Rousselle, *Porneia: de la maîtrise du corps à la privation sensuelle* (Paris: Presses Universitaires de Paris, 1983); H. King, 'Bound to bleed: Artemis and Greek women', in A. Cameron and A. Kuhrt eds., *Images of Women in Antiquity* (London: Croom Helm, 1983); G. Lloyd, *Science, Folklore, Ideology* (Cambridge University Press, 1983), pp. 58–111.
42 Vernant and Vidal-Naquet, *Tragedy and Myth in Ancient Greece*, p. 15.
43 From Sophocles' *Electra* and Euripides' *Electra*, both of which return and rewrite the Aeschylean masterpiece, to T. S. Eliot and beyond.
44 I am referring here to the influential analysis of R. Girard, *Violence and the Sacred*, trans. P. Gregory (Baltimore: Johns Hopkins University Press, 1977) and W. Burkert, *Homo Necans*, trans. P. Bing (Berkeley: California University Press, 1983).
45 In particular, by P. Vidal-Naquet in *Le Chasseur noir* (Paris: Le Decouverte–Maspero, (1981).
46 On hunting in the *Oresteia* see P. Vidal-Naquet, 'Hunting and sacrifice in Aeschylus' *Oresteia*' in Vernant and P. Vidal-Naquet, *Tragedy and Myth in Ancient Greece*.
47 I have discussed this with extensive bibliography in *Reading Greek Tragedy*, chapters 3 and 6.
48 On Amazons, see W. Tyrrell, *Amazons: a study in Athenian mythmaking* (Baltimore: John Hopkins University Press, 1984); P. duBois, *Centaurs and Amazons: women and the pre-history of the great chain of being* (Ann Arbor: University of Michigan Press, 1984); M. Merck, 'The city's achievement: the patriotic Amazonomachy and ancient Athens' in S. Lipshitz ed., *Tearing the Veil: essays on feminism* (London: Routledge & Kegan Paul, 1978).
49 On sacrifice in general, see M. Detienne and J-P Vernant, *La cuisine du sacrifice en pays grec* (Paris: Gallimard, 1979); J-L Durand, *Sacrifice et labour en grèce ancienne* (Paris: La Jécouverte–Ecole française de Rome, 1986); Girard, *Violence and the Sacred*; Burkert, *Homo Necans*, trans. P. Bing; P. Vidal-Naquet, 'Valeurs religieuses et mythiques de la terre et du sacrifice dans l'Odyssée', reprinted in *Le Chasseur noir*. On the *Oresteia*, see also F. Zeitlin, 'The motif of the corrupted sacrifice in Aeschylus' *Oresteia*', *Transactions and Proceedings of the American Philological Association*, 96 (1965), 463–505; Vidal-Naquet, 'Hunting and sacrifice in Aeschylus' *Oresteia*' in Vernant and Vidal-Naquet, *Tragedy and Myth in Ancient Greece*.
50 On the significance of the third libation see D. Clay, 'Aeschylus' Trigeron Muthos', *Hermes*, 97 (1969), 1–9; P. Burian 'Zeus Σώτηρ τρίτος and some triadism in Aeschylus' *Oresteia*', *American Journal of Philology*, 107 (1986), 332–42.
51 J. Moles, 'A neglected aspect of *Agamemnon* 1389–92', *Liverpool Classical Monthly*, 4 (1979), 179–89. It is worth recalling that Aristotle defines *hubris* as being committed '*for one's own pleasure*'.

52 Here, this paper points both towards social definitions and towards legal categories, and the difficult interplay between them: see e.g. MacDowell, *The Law in Classical Athens*, pp. 113–32. If *hubris* is regarded as an assault that disgraces the sufferer and gives pleasure to the perpetrator, it is perhaps not surprising that there is little evidence of the fiercely competitive and status conscious Athenian males using this legal recourse – although *hubris* occurs frequently as a term in less formal normative contexts. See also Fisher, '*Hybris* and dishonour I', 177–93; also MacDowell, '*Hybris in Athens*', 14–31.
53 I have discussed this with bibliography in 'Character and action: representation and reading. Greek tragedy and its critics' in C. Pelling ed., *Character and Individuality* (Oxford, forthcoming).
54 See Taylor, *The Tyrant Slayers: the heroic image in fifth-century B.C. Athenian art*.
55 I have discussed this briefly with bibliography in 'Character and action: representation and reading. Greek tragedy and its critics' in Pelling ed., *Character and Individuality* and at greater length in *Language, Sexuality, Narrative: the Oresteia*, chapter 3.

Violence and dramatic structure in Euripides' *Hecuba**

CHARLES SEGAL

Since Lessing's *Laocoon* the problem of the presentation of pain and violence in art has been a major issue in European aesthetics. Greek drama, on the whole, avoids the direct visual depiction of violence on the stage. The bloody acts which dominate these plays generally occur off stage. Though we often see the results of the violence – the bodies of Agamemnon, Clytaemnestra, and Aegisthus in the *Oresteia*, the bloodied eyes of Oedipus in the *Tyrannus*, the grim corpse of the suicide in Sophocles' *Ajax*, the broken body of Pentheus in Euripides' *Bacchae* – we rarely see the violent acts themselves. Indeed, there is no place in extant Greek drama where we can be sure that a deed of bloodshed took place on stage, although the punishment of the adulterous Aegisthus in Sophocles' *Electra* and the suicide of Ajax come teasingly close. Yet violence everywhere surrounds us in these plays; and though we do not see it performed, we hear of it as something beyond sight or language, too horrible to be seen or spoken of.[1] In the *Hecuba* the protagonist calls Polymestor's murder of her son something 'unspeakable, unnamable, beyond wonder, unholy, unendurable' (lines 714f.).

The prologue of the *Hecuba* – the only extant example in Greek tragedy of a prologue spoken by a ghost – introduces us to the first victim. The shade of Polydorus, the last surviving son of Priam and Hecuba, tells how he has been murdered by his host, King Polymestor of Thrace, to whom he had been sent for safekeeping. The first half of the play, however, leaves Polydorus in the background and concentrates on the sacrifice of his sister, the young Polyxena, whom the shade of Achilles – another ghost – demands as an offering at his tomb. Despite Hecuba's pleas, the girl is killed. When a servant goes to the shore to bring water for the funeral ablutions, she finds the body of Polydorus, washed up on the beach. Thus the two murders are brought together in an overwhelming catastrophe for the aged mother.

Resolving to avenge the treacherous killing of Polydorus, Hecuba

---

* A draft of this paper was read at the *Themes in Drama* International Conference held at the University of California, Riverside, in February 1989.

enlists the help of King Agamemnon – a delicate task, as Polymestor is an ally of the Greeks. But Agamemnon has Hecuba's other daughter Cassandra, as his concubine, and Hecuba makes full use of this sexual obligation that Agamemnon has toward her. With the connivance of Agamemnon she and her women lure Polymestor and his two sons into their tent, kill the two boys – precise compensation for her own two murdered children – and blind the father. The play ends with Polymestor's demands for vengeance. In a kind of trial scene, with Agamemnon as judge, Hecuba wins her case. The enraged Polymestor prophesies Hecuba's transformation into a monster and the murder of Cassandra and Agamemnon at home. But just at this moment the long-awaited winds arrive. With the Thracian's curses ringing in his ears, Agamemnon sets sail for Greece, bringing with him, of course, the enslaved Trojan women.

The play, then, concerns the crimes of war, the terrible aftermath of revenge that they leave behind, and the justice of such revenge. But the final impression that the play leaves us with is not so much the resolution of abstract moral questions as the brutalization and barbarization that takes place on all sides. Certainly in the first half the questions of justice and morality pale beside the horror and the pathos of killing Hecuba's innocent children. Both of these murders are the direct results of war, of the betrayals that it permits on the one hand and of sheer bloodlust on the other.

The ingenious cruelty and success of Hecuba's revenge, however, render her justice problematical. We want her to succeed. With Agamemnon, we connive at the revenge. But when it bursts out on the stage, in the form of the blinded barbarian roaring like an animal (lines 1056ff.), we are horrified by it. Our *anagnorisis* (recognition) consists in part in seeing that we, like Agamemnon, have been the accomplices of something horrible and ugly. We know that this is justice, but we also perceive that it brings more degradation and brutality.

The violence done to individuals is only the specific focus for the wider reaches of violence in the background, the destruction of a once great city, now reduced to smoking ruins (cf. lines 476–8, 823, 1215). In the foreground are two of the worst offences against basic moral and religious sanctities: human sacrifice and the treacherous betrayal and murder of a guest entrusted to one's care. The first of these atrocities is, in fact, legitimated and legally enacted by the Greek army. The second leads to a further murder of the innocent: Hecuba's killing of King Polymestor's sons. And around these killings, unquestioned by anyone, are the enslavement of the women of Troy and their future forced service in the households and beds of their masters. This is something they dread, as their songs in the choral odes show repeatedly (cf. lines 444–83); but they know that they cannot change the situation. It is, as their last words say, 'hard necessity' (line 1295).

Violence and dramatic structure in Euripides' Hecuba

It is a critical commonplace to describe the *Hecuba* as one of Western literature's most powerful representations of the violence of war.[2] What has perhaps been less recognized is how Euripides has distorted what might have been a smoother, less fragmented plot in order to get the greatest dramatic impact from the outrages and degradations that war works on both sides, the victimage of the defeated, the brutalization of the victors. The relatively low valuation of the play in modern times has been due, at least in part, to the failure to appreciate fully the expressive function of the play's structure. The effect of the play depends on a calculated dissonance within a formally articulated design.

In the symmetry of the play's bipartite structure, the action moves from Polyxena to Polydorus. Each death of a child reaches some degree of closure: Hecuba pronounces a formal eulogy and lament over her daughter (lines 585–628); she punishes the killer of her son. The two children are brought together for the double funeral announced in the exodos (line 1287; cf. lines 726f., 894–7). Yet the haste with which Agamemnon orders this funeral in the closing lines (lines 1287f.) and particularly the future suffering awaiting all the protagonists – metamorphosis, murder, exile, slavery – also militate against closure. The final lines, spoken by the chorus, open upon their future life of slavery as they prepare to embark on the ships of their masters under 'hard necessity' (lines 1293–5).

The wandering shade at the beginning and the motif of metamorphosis at the end belong to a world of unstable forms, a world where physical, moral, and psychological coherence is precarious. The main figures change or lose what most firmly defines their identity. Only Polyxena is able to maintain a stable coherence of self, but at the price of her life. *Felix opportunitate mortis*, she does not have to survive and live in this nightmarish world.

In the first half of the play violence takes the form of lust for the blood of a virgin: the innocent girl will be sacrificed to Achilles' ghost by the most murderous of the Greek warriors at Troy (cf. lines 23f.). Odysseus defends this sacrifice on practical political grounds (lines 306–20). War here appears as the extension of the social order. But beneath this there lies another vision of war, war as an archaic ritual, something beyond reason, a murderous rite that demands the innocent blood of the young. Euripides has transposed into mythical terms the insights about the war that Thucydides expresses in passages like the Mytilenean debate and the Melian dialogue. He gives us the intellectual refinements of Sophistic argumentation alongside primitive levels of superstition, particularly human sacrifice.

This is a unique moment in Western society, a point of meeting between archaic, mythic ways of thought and the birth of philosophy, science, medicine, ethnography, the architecture of cities and of newly redesigned sites like the Acropolis. Only a few yards from the Parthenon, with its elegant, carefully worked out mathematics and calculated optical refinements was a sanctuary of Brauronian Artemis, with its ancient rites of passage for young girls, or the site of the Arrhephoria, where girls carry a basket with secret mystic symbols down a dark corridor hewn in the rock.

Commentators generally find what unity they allow to the play in the figure of Hecuba.[3] She is clearly the focus of the play's mood of desperate, unstable, emotions. Some critics see two Hecubas: the figure of passive suffering, crushed by grief; and the vengeful figure at the end exulting in her vengeful murder of Polymestor's sons.[4] The change in her character follows the shift from violence suffered by the women in the first half to violence done by the women in the second. The first part of the play draws on the familiar figure of the *mater dolorosa*, as we see it, for example, in Aeschylus' *Niobe*. As the play continues, it shows Hecuba's transformation into a strong woman of action, craftiness, and ruthlessness.[5]

Euripides pinpoints the exact moment of the transformation. When the herald, Talthybius, enters with the news of Polyxena's death, the chorus describes Hecuba as lying on the earth, 'closed up in her robes' (lines 485f.), a verbal and visual echo of the suffering of her daughter, who left the stage 'covering her head in her robes' (line 432).[6] Later, after the discovery of Polydorus' body, Agamemnon enters to inquire about the delay in burying Polyxena. His first word is the direct address, 'Hecuba'. She, however, says nothing. In a series of three asides, remarkable in Greek tragedy, she ponders within herself whether or not to enlist Agamemnon in her plot of revenge against Polymestor (lines 736–53). This unusual stage device shows us Hecuba in the process of undergoing radical change as she shifts her attention from helpless grief over the sacrificed daughter to active revenge for the murdered son.

This scene is one of Euripides' subtlest portrayals of violent, pathological movements in personality at the limits of human endurance. Hecuba begins the first aside with an apostrophe to the dead Polydorus, here identified only as 'unfortunate one' (line 736), and then goes on to address herself by name: 'O unfortunate one, for in speaking of you I speak of myself, Hecuba, what shall I do?' The uttering of her own name in close proximity to her 'unfortunate' son and to her nascent plot of revenge calls attention to the new Hecuba that is taking shape under the name of the old.[7] The two vocatives, 'unfortunate' and 'Hecuba', fuse her new identity with the suffering of her son.

In order to depict the full extent of the psychological disintegration that exposure to extreme violence creates, Euripides has recourse to the realm of myth. Hecuba's accomplishment of her vengeance reenacts one of the most famous episodes of Homer's *Odyssey*. Her victim, blinded by the Trojan women, returns to the stage with bestial gestures and cannibalistic cries that recall the enraged Polyphemus blinded in vengeance by the Homeric Odysseus (lines 1056ff.).[8] In the closing scene, frustrated in his attempts to get back at Hecuba, the Thracian king suddenly prophesies her transformation into a dog-like monster with fiery eyes (lines 1260ff.). This new development is startling, even in a playwright who introduces unexpected, divinely motivated turns of events at the end of his plays. In this case, however, the sudden news of 'metamorphosis' (Hecuba's word at line 1266) is of a piece with the play's irrationality and discontinuity of suffering. Even in the full enjoyment of her revenge, Hecuba remains, in a sense, still a victim. She is in a world where she no longer has control of her being. Metamorphosis is the fullest expression of that total helplessness and disorientation in the engulfing sea of loss, sorrow, and overwhelming pain.

Like the *Medea*, to which it is often compared, the *Hecuba* depicts a powerful and once loving woman's downward plunge into murderous vengeance. But the differences between the two female protagonists are revealing. Unlike Medea, Hecuba retains her claims on just action. But whereas Medea remains fully and triumphantly in control, Hecuba loses her identity. Her metamorphosis is the logical culmination of the motif of inner death that runs throughout the play. It fulfils in a horrible way her feeling of a literal or figurative death in the grief of overwhelming loss (cf. lines 168f., 284, 391–6, 431, 683). Her gradual estrangement over the course of the play from a gentler, more loving, maternal self is sealed finally in the physical change.[9] As she moves from just avenger to monster, she will become literally a stranger to herself; she becomes one with her own hatred, trickery, and murderousness.

Euripides experiments not only with the extremes of emotion but also with different kinds of dramatic plots. In this case, he combines a sacrifice-of-the-virgin play (such as his *Suppliants, Heraclidae, Erechtheus*, and *Iphigeneia at Aulis*) with a play of lamentation (like *Trojan Women*) and the revenge play (such as *Medea*).[10] There is also a typically Euripidean combination of intense emotionality and logical argumentation. We witness the army's decision to put Polyxena to death as the impersonal resolution of the assembly and the logical calculation of advantage, stemming from the necessity of honoring the great warriors and recognizing the value of those who risk their life for their country (cf. 136ff., 306ff.).

In the background is the highest image of heroic glory in Greek culture, the honor of Achilles. Yet Achilles himself is only a ghost; his successor is his bloodthirsty son, Neoptolemus (always referred to by his patronymic) who has killed Priam at an altar (lines 23f.) and is designated to wield the knife that cuts Polyxena's throat (lines 527–41, 566f.). The Greeks are the glorious victors of Troy; but the army in the foreground is a corrupt, mean-spirited mob whose leaders are governed by self-interest, greed, and lust. The strongest image of traditional heroism and innate nobility, as many critics point out, lies with the helpless young girl who dies under the knife of Achilles' son (cf. 589–603).[11]

Far from being heroic, war is seen through the eyes of its victims. All the major choral odes, from the parode to the third stasimon, express the Trojan Women's victimage in war: their grief at the destruction of their homes, the death of their husbands and sons, and the obliteration of their city. Through their eyes we witness the physical and sexual vulnerability of the women, enslaved to their new masters (especially in the third stasimon, lines 905ff.). The imagery of uprooted plants or the slaughter of young animals repeatedly presents war as the destruction of the innocent young.[12] These truncated lives mark the main stages in the action and help link the two parts of the play to one another. Polydorus, losing what remains of his ruined Trojan patrimony, is the son who will not grow up to manhood (cf. lines 14f.) or to inherit his kingdom. Polyxena, like Antigone, becomes a bride of death, 'a bride who is no bride, a maiden not-a-maiden' (line 612; cf. 416).

Various formal devices join together the deaths of the child-victims on both sides. Being led off to her sacrificial death, Polyxena bids farewell to both Cassandra and Polydorus (lines 426–8), whereupon Hecuba expresses her doubts that Polydorus is still alive (line 429). The servant then discovers his body when she goes to the shore for the water with which to perform the funerary ablutions for Polyxena (lines 658ff.; cf. 609ff.). Hecuba, overwhelmed by this additional blow, asks whether the body is that of Polyxena or Cassandra (lines 671ff.). In order to adorn Polyxena's corpse, Hecuba will make use of the jewellery that the Trojan women have managed to hide from their masters (lines 618ff.). This is the first hint of her and her women's skill as deceivers. This same wealth, and a similar deception, will serve to avenge her son's murder. But now she will use them far more ominously, luring Polymestor and his sons into her tent with the ploy of the allegedly concealed wealth (cf. lines 1012ff.). Polymestor asks if they have the valuables hidden in their garments (line 1013), but what they have in fact hidden in their robes are the daggers with which, as he says later, they kill his sons (lines 1161f.).

The second movement in the action begins with bodies. But now the cycle of violence passes from the sacrificial killing of Polyxena to the criminal murder of Polydorus. Agamemnon enters with the query, 'Why, Hecuba, do you delay to bury your child' meaning Polyxena (lines 726f.). Hecuba explains Polydorus' murder and asks Agamemnon to suspend the funeral rites for Polyxena in order to bury both children together. The two siblings are a 'double care to their mother', and she will bury them with a 'single fire' (lines 894–7). The play ends with a reference back to this scene: Agamemnon commands Hecuba to look after the two bodies of her children brought together as one by the phrase *diptychous nekrous* ('the twofold corpses', lines 1287f.; cf. 897, 1051). The play began with the murder of Polydorus, but the revenge for this crime is bracketed by the burial of Polyxena.

The motif of the two bodies serves as the signposts of increasing violence. In the prologue Polydorus stressed Hecuba's double loss of children (lines 45f.); 'The mother will see two corpses of two children' (*duoin de paidoin duo nekrô*); but the full significance of the 'two corpses of children' emerges only later in the play. This coupling of Hecuba's two children not only depicts the double suffering of the *mater dolorosa*, but also hints at a parallel with the two children of Polymestor. In lines 891–7, in fact, the doubleness of Hecuba's loss of children follows immediately upon the first allusion to Polymestor's children as part of the revenge that she is now plotting. When that revenge is complete, his children, like hers, are but 'bodies of twofold children' (*paidôn dissôn sômata*, line 1051). We are reminded of that phrase again when Polymestor, a hundred lines later, tells how the women's attack began by separating him 'from his two-fold escort' of arms (*diptychon stolisma*, line 1156).

The destruction of Hecuba's children, as we have noted, appears under images of destroying vegetal or young animal life. This vitalistic imagery is appropriate to the female, maternal perspective from which their deaths are viewed, i.e. through the eyes of Hecuba. The death of Polymestor's children, on the other hand, appears in the more abstract terms of the transmission of knowledge about hidden wealth. These are also the terms appropriate to paternity, for they concern the continuity of the male line and masculine privilege. Polymestor, who has extinguished the Trojan line by murdering its last male heir, is entrapped by an appeal to his own interest in the regular succession of the patrimony that he will hand on to his sons. He needs his sons' presence for the secret of the alleged treasure so that they can profit by it should anything happen to him (lines 1005f.). In a deeper stroke of retributive justice, Hecuba allows Polymestor to think that she is telling him about the treasure as a means of handing the secret on to her own child, Polydorus (line 1003). In this disrupted world continuity is the foremost and most obvious victim of violence.

By manipulating the tempo of the action Euripides uses physical suffering with the greatest possible effect, to make us feel the full horror of the killings on both sides. After Polyxena's death the action slows down for the scenes of lamentation and the discovery of Polydorus' body. There follows a long scene of debate and persuasion in which Hecuba resolves on her revenge and sets it into motion. Finally, the horror bursts upon us with the terrible cries of the blinded Thracian, screaming in pain and hate (lines 1056ff.). The play then modulates back to another scene of debate in the verbal and intellectual action of the trial scene between Hecuba and

Polymestor; (lines 1129–254). After this a rapid, stichomythic exchange between Hecuba and her enemy creates the mood of suspended horror and future doom in the prophecies with which the play ends (lines 1255–95).

For both Polydorus at the beginning and Hecuba at the end a fluid spatial condition or a metamorphic state points to a loss of control. The mood of instability is established from the play's opening lines. Polydorus leaves the depths of Hades and 'the gates of darkness' to visit the world above (lines 1ff.). He is a shade without a body and a body without burial. He is between Hades and the living, between sea and land, between life and death. As an incorporeal shade he is 'flitting' or 'soaring' in the air (*aiôroumenos*, line 32). His body, unburied, lying on the beach, is tossed to and fro by the random movements of the waves (lines 26ff., especially 28–9).

Hecuba, now a ruthless murderer instead of a loving mother, undergoes both inward and external transformation. Her victim, Polymestor, also experiences a kind of metamorphic disorientation in his turn. He emerges from the tent, his eyes torn, not knowing where he stands or where are the women who have blinded him and killed his sons (lines 1056ff., 1065ff.). Like his own victim, Polydorus, he is 'carried about' without apparent direction (line 1075, *pheromai*; cf. *phoroumenos* of Polydorus' sea-tossed body in line 29). He even compares himself to a ship making for land (lines 1079–82), another recall of the sea similes of Polydorus' corpse in the prologue. Like Polydorus too, he is suspended between the upper and the lower worlds, for in his pain and confusion he would leap to the heavens or plunge into Hades' dark abyss (lines 1099–106).

This sharp contrast of spatial extremes is not only appropriate to the violence of action and emotion depicted in the play; it also helps depict the erosion of the boundaries of the self in the extreme conditions of war, murder, human sacrifice, and revenge. Polymestor's closing prophecy leaves Hecuba suspended between righteous retribution and monstrosity. He himself, bloody eyes and all, is silenced by the threat of banishment to a desert island (lines 1283–6). What little moral and social authority is left is rendered problematical by the doom hanging over Agamemnon on his return to his 'bitter housekeeper' at Mycenae (lines 1277ff.).

Throughout the play the presence of the sea reinforces the effect of restlessness, unsettledness, and disorder. This extends from these opening descriptions of the sea-tossed corpse to the closing prophecy of the marine fate of Hecuba (lines 1259–73) and her attendants' voyage into slavery in the exodos (line 1289–95).[13]

The land that constitutes the spatial setting of the play has an analogous instability. The remote Thracian Chersonese vacillates between being plowland and mountain, an agrarian kingdom and a snowy wilderness of warlike peoples, a settled kingdom and a disorganized, ineffectual tribal society.[14] These spatial disorientations prepare us for the deeper disorientation of identity in Hecuba's metamorphosis at the end.

Chaos and dissolution in the individual and in the social order extend to the entire world-order. Throughout the first part of the play the winds were under the control of the shade of Achilles. Neoptolemus, as he slits the throat of Polyxena, offering the girl to the ghost, asks Achilles specifically to send the winds to the becalmed fleet (lines 538–41). Later Agamemnon, persuaded to aid Hecuba, alludes to some god (*theos*) who does not yet send the winds and thus delays his departure so that he can permit the revenge plot to go forward (lines 898–904). But at the end Agamemnon says nothing either of Achilles or of a god. He says merely, 'I see these favoring winds sending us homeward' (lines 1289f.).

The absence of any reference to gods here may, of course, reflect only Agamemnon's moral blindness, appropriately combined with a failure to take in the meaning of Polymestor's warning prophecy. But the god's absence may also be the final indication of the chaotic state of this world. Nature no longer seems to be governed by moral forces. Or, conversely, men can discern in it only the physical, external features of their world. Divine action, even if present, is invisible and thus ambiguous.[15] So too the role of the *deus ex machina* has been assumed by the greedy, homicidal barbarian, now blinded for his crime.[16] In the terms of René Girard, this society offers no hope for the sacralization of violence; and so men are condemned to see the violence feed on itself mimetically in the human world.[17]

The play began with a spatial image of a coherent cosmic order, the gulf between the human world and 'the gates of darkness where Hades dwells apart from the gods' (lines 1f.). It ends with a virtual annihilation of its large spatial frame. The distances between Troy, the Chersonese, and the Greek mainland have closed down to the small field of repetitive cycles that crime and revenge create. The Greek world will both continue and reenact the violence that we have seen here in Thrace and further back at Troy. The second stasimon, about Helen and Paris, ended with the bitter reflection that the Greek girl or mother in Sparta will be tearing hair and skin in the mourning rites just as the Trojan women have been doing in the Chersonese (lines 659–7). The expanding violence destroys and confounds the differences between Troy and Greece, Greek and barbarian, agent and victim.

Unresolved violence has the instability of the sea and the strangeness and disorientation of mythic metamorphosis. But at the same time a terrible sameness encircles Hecuba, Polymestor, and Agamemnon. This is perhaps Euripides' way of saying that evil creates its own constricted and self-destructive world. That message, if such it is, is given only implicitly, without moralizing, and almost anticlimactically. The narrowing of the inner world by hate and bitterness is all the more striking because of the large spatial frame surrounding the action: the distances between Hades and the upper world, the sea between Troy and Greece, the triangulated space of Priam's palace, the Thracian tomb of Achilles, and the palace of Agamemnon. Yet it all shrinks into the dangerous enclosures of the Trojan women's tents and its later equivalent in Mycenae. The cruel, greedy, and treacherous Thracian king will be removed to a desert island. Hecuba, victorious in her terrible revenge, will be frozen into canine shape as a landmark for sailors. And for Agamemnon an obscure doom, waiting, like Polymestor's, in a woman's chambers, adds its quiet, brooding horror to this last scene.

NOTES

1 See, e.g., Sophocles, *Oedipus Tyrannus* 465f., 996, 1289; Euripides, *Hippol.* 602, 846; also *Hecuba* 200. See Diskin Clay, 'Unspeakable Words in Greek Tragedy', *American Journal of Philology*, 103 (1982), 288–92; also my remarks in *Interpreting Greek Tragedy: Myth, Poetry, Text* (Ithaca, NY: Cornell University Press, 1986), pp. 97–9.

2 Leo Aylen, *Greek Tragedy and the Modern World* (London: Methuen, 1964), pp. 137f. Philip Vellacott, *Ironic Drama* (Cambridge University Press, 1975), p. 162; also Kenneth J. Reckford, 'Concepts of Demoralization in the *Hecuba*' in *Directions in Euripidean Criticism: A Collection of Essays*, ed. P. Burian (Durham, NC: Duke University Press, 1985), pp. 114ff., 125f. For a recent survey of changing judgements of the *Hecuba* over the centuries see Malcolm Heath, ' "Jure Principem Locum Tenet"; Euripides' *Hecuba*', *Bulletin of the Institute of Classical Studies*, 34 (1987), 40–68. To the modern critics may be added the implicit judgement of Virgil, whose second book of the *Aeneid* owes a great deal to Euripides' depiction of the suffering of war-victims in his tragedies of Troy's fall.

3 'Unity, if we seek it, exists only in the chief character, in Hecuba as a mater dolorosa', remarked Paul Decharme, *Euripides and the Spirit of his Dramas*, trans. J. Loeb (New York: Methuen, 1906), p. 224; see also Gilbert Norwood, *Euripidean Tragedy* (Berkeley and Los Angeles: University of California Press, 1954), p. 47; For further discussion and bibliography see Albin Lesky, *Die tragische Dichtung der Hellenen*, 3rd edn (Göttingen: Vandenhoeck und Ruprecht, 1972), pp. 336f.; D. J. Conacher, *Euripidean Drama: Myth, Theme and Structure* (Toronto: 1967), pp. 152ff.; Ann N. Michelini, *Euripides and the Tragic Tradition* (Madison, Wisc.: University of Wisconsin Press, 1987), pp. 133–5; Heath, 'Jure Principem', pp. 64ff.

4 G. M. Kirkwood, 'Hecuba and Nomos', *Transactions of the American Philological Association*, 78 (1947), 61ff.; G. M. A. Grube, *The Drama of Euripides* (London: Methuen, 1941), pp. 82f.

5 David Kovacs, *The Heroic Muse: Studies in the Hippolytus and Hecuba of Euripides* (Baltimore: Johns Hopkins University Press, 1987), pp. 8of. argues against any

psychological interest in this character, but offers little to put in its place. Euripides obviously does not show us the inner processes behind the emotional changes that she undergoes, but he powerfully conveys the external forces that work upon a figure in such circumstances to produce the final Hecuba from the one we see in the opening scenes. On this externalized mode of presenting inner change and development see the balanced remarks of Albin Lesky, 'Psychologie bei Euripides' in *Entretiens sur l'antiquité classique*, vol. 6, *Euripide* (Geneva: Fondation Hardt, Vandoeuvres, 1960), pp. 125–50, especially p. 148. For a useful survey of recent discussions of the characterization of Hecuba and the question of her change or development in the play see Reckford, 'Concepts of Demoralization in the *Hecuba*', p. 114, with note 1, pp. 209f.

6 This gesture of covering herself here, in turn, contrasts sharply with her uncovering herself before the army to receive, voluntarily, the blow of the sacrificial knife (line 558). The robes which mark the victimage of women here return later as instruments of the women's revenge: lines 1154, 1161.

7 Note too that in the previous scene Hecuba called herself 'unfortunate' (line 683), and the chorus repeats the epithet (line 688). Hecuba's address to Polydorus in lines 736f. also places the mother–son bond under the sign of misfortune. In the prologue he had apostrophized her (line 56), and she now addresses him in the same way. The figure of apostrophe, as a rhetoric of absence, marks the tragic emptiness of this reaching out toward one another. The chorus' commiseration for Hecuba in lines 721f., recalling Polydorus' in lines 57f., also helps us to associate the two scenes. We may add that when Hecuba, at the end of the scene, again uses the self-address, 'Hecuba', it is in the instructions that she gives to her servant, to be repeated verbatim to Polymestor as part of the trap she is laying for him (line 892).

8 For the echoes of the Homeric scene (*Odyssey* 9.395ff., 456ff.) see Wilhelm Schmid in W. Schmid and Otto Stählin, *Geschichte der griechischen Literatur* 1.3 (Munich, 1940), p. 466; also William Arrowsmith's introduction to his translation of the play in the University of Chicago Series, *The Complete Greek Tragedies: III. Euripides* (Chicago University Press, 1955). The scene of *Hecuba* 1109–19, in which Agamemnon hears Polymestor's shouts, also recalls *Odyssey* 9.399–408, where the Cyclopes hear Polyphemus' cries.

9 Kovacs, *The Heroic Muse*, pp. 108ff. argues that Hecuba's metamorphosis gives no indication of brutalization, but in fact allows an escape from the 'hard necessity' of which the chorus speaks in the last line of the play (p. 112). Such a view, however, neglects the suggestion of monstrosity in the 'blazing eyes' of line 1265 and the more general consideration that Polymestor reports this prophecy to cause Hecuba as much pain as he can.

10 For Euripides' contamination of different types of plot see Norwood, *Euripidean Tragedy*, p. 35; also Ann Burnett, *Catastrophe Survived* (Oxford University Press, 1971), chapter 1. Michelini, *Euripides and the Tragic Tradition*, p. 170 remarks, '*Hekabe* contains enough plot elements to make up several ordinary tragedies.'

11 On the degeneration of the heroic in the play see Katherine Callen King, *Achilles* (Berkeley and Los Angeles: University of California Press, 1987), pp. 88ff., especially 91–4.

12 Cf. 20, 90, 142, 205, 525. On this motif see Michelini, *Euripides and the Tragic*

Tradition, pp. 135–42; Martha C. Nussbaum, *The Fragility of Goodness* (Cambridge University Press, 1986), pp. 397f., 400.

13 The fearful sea-journey awaiting the chorus appears repeatedly, at greatest length in the first stasimon (lines 444–83) and the third (lines 937ff.). Note too their allusion to Helen and Paris's sea-journey in the second stasimon (lines 629ff.) and their curse on Helen's return over the sea in the third (lines 950–2). The image of Polydorus's sea-tossed body is kept in our minds even after the prologue: lines 698ff., 782, 797. The sea also occurs in metaphors for various forms of violence: cf. lines 116, 1025, 1081.

14 In lines 8ff. Polymestor is described as 'sowing (farming) the excellent plain of the Chersonese, ruling with his spear a horse-loving folk.' But in line 82 Thrace is 'snowy'. In lines 1088ff. Polymestor calls to his people, addressing them as warlike, fond of horses, and dedicated to Ares. Yet they do nothing to help him, and in fact he seems completely subject to Agamemnon's authority. In lines 1141ff. he speaks of the Thracian plain as if it were itself vulnerable to enemy incursions; and Hecuba repeats this view of Thrace in her rebuttal (line 1204).

15 Kovacs, *The Heroic Muse*, pp. 110f. seems to me to oversimplify the presence of divine justice (as he does also the justice of Hecuba's revenge, pp. 108f.). See my essay, 'The Problem of the Gods in Euripides' *Hecuba*', *Materiali e Discussioni per l'Analisi dei Testi Classici*, 22 (1989), pp. 9–21.

16 See Schmid, *Geschichte der griechischen Literatur*, p. 472, on Polymestor as 'ein missglückter Deus ex machina'.

17 See René Girard, *Violence and the Sacred* (1972), trans. P. Gregory (Baltimore: Johns Hopkins University Press, 1977), chapter 2.

Violence on the street: playing rough in Plautus*

RICHARD C. BEACHAM

Consider a play in which the first few lines of the opening scene have references to hanging, torture, hard labour, beatings, crippling, starvation, and to round things off, the novel punishment of being suspended in a window frame – infenestration – during which, to add a cruel refinement to the 'suspense', the victim must listen to a rival making love to his sweetheart.

The author is Plautus, and the subject is comedy: the reference is to his *Casina*.[1] Working in the late third and early second century BC, Plautus set the tone and style, together with much of the technique which would thereafter characterize farce, and in particular, the manner in which violence somehow becomes a primary source of comic pleasure just as pain and cruelty inform our response to tragedy.

In his *Poetics* Aristotle proposed the concept of Catharsis to explain the curious way in which that strange oxymoron, 'tragic pleasure' arises, using it to describe how things which in ordinary life would cause us distress to witness (much less experience), in dramatic art may become a species of pleasure and entertainment. Plautus offers an extreme example of a related phenomenon in comedy: pain, beatings, threats of torture are not only a source of peripheral fun; they are important elements of characterization and frequently motivate the plot and action. I am referring both here and subsequently to actual physical violence, whether enacted or talked about; not to Plautus' handling of what might otherwise also be termed 'violent': the misuse of power, the violation of social norms or status, transgression of matrimonial obligations and the like, all of which do indeed frequently underlie or lead to moments of real physical violence.

Of course, violence was a part of everyday existence for the Roman audience. Slaves were indeed tortured, even executed for trivial offences, without recourse to law: as mere chattel, their well-being was entirely at the will and whim of their masters. As a result of the Second Punic War and subsequent conquests, slaves became very cheap, with vast numbers

* A draft of this paper was read at the *Themes in Drama* International Conference held at the University of London, Queen Mary and Westfield College, in March 1989.

1 A scene of comic violence from Helenistic or Roman New Comedy

of war prisoners brought to Italy and set to work. Unlike the situation earlier slaves now 'were not usually part of the family unit; they had become a distinct social stratum separate from the other strata in society through their lack of rights, the harshness with which they were exploited and the contempt they suffered . . . by and large the treatment of slaves in the later Republic was worse than ever it was either earlier or later in Roman history.'[2]

As evidence for this we have the testimony of Plautus' contemporary, Cato the Elder who counted his slaves as farm equipment, alongside livestock. Enforcing the most severe discipline, he kept them working without respite, deliberately undernourished, subject to extreme punishments – if his slaves prepared a meal which displeased him he had them flogged – and when they could no longer work because of age or illness, he sold them off.[3]

In addition to the violence consequent to slavery, Plautus' audience was accustomed both to virtually continuous warfare, and from the mid-third century onwards, to the institutionalized violence of the gladiatorial displays.[4] For such spectators, violence must have almost seemed commonplace, an element of everyday life. And yet, Plautus is not otherwise greatly concerned with verisimilitude, and he rarely dwells on matters of direct social or political concern (however important they may be in providing a general context for evaluating his plays); his exuberant comic fantasy easily slips away from such moorings. Nor is violence particularly evident in his Greek comic predecessors. There are even in old comedy references to slaves being whipped, but the threat of such violence is never so pervasive as it is in Plautus nor given such prominence through detail, emphasis and repetition. By contrast, in the subsequent comedies of Terence, violence is infrequently evoked.[5] In transforming his Greek models, Plautus seems deliberately to have increased both elements of violent verbal abuse and threats of cruel physical punishment.[6] Perhaps with an eye to popular taste (clearly evident elsewhere in his treatment) he is as Chalmers suggested, 'catering for a fondness for abuse which had been formed by the Fescennine verses and the Atellane farces, and, secondly . . . pandering to the rather cruel streak in his audience which accounted for the later popularity of the bloody sports of the Amphitheatre.'[7]

General theories about the nature of the 'comic' may provide a further nudge towards understanding Plautus' love of violence, without altogether explaining it. Comedy releases tension, making us feel better as we perceive and confront incongruity while correcting and reacting to it with laughter. The spectators feel superior to the anxiety and pain of comic characters, experiencing not the pity and fear engendered by tragedy, but pleasurable relief at seeing what they might fear, being inflicted upon others.[8] It is not empathy but distance that encourages this response. Such an attitude and sense of detachment would have been particularly effective in the case of Plautus' audience, since all the plots and characters are set safely and unthreateningly in Greece; in the time-honoured tradition of ethnic and minority humour, a Plautine play is one extended 'Greek joke'.

Much laughter too is nervous; arising from such social and psychological tensions as those engendered by the relations between the sexes, class conflict, generational antagonisms, and reactions to disparities of power and authority. Because these are still felt by a modern audience, they empower the play to continue to function as a living act of comic theatre: to seem, in a word, 'funny'. If this analysis is valid, it suggests that the comic success of a Plautine play when presented before a contemporary audience depends in large part upon establishing an equivalent sense of aesthetic distance, while yet rendering the characters recognizable: tasks which must be encouraged by the translation, and nurtured by the elements of performance.

The script itself points the way. It was once fashionable for literary critics to castigate Plautus for, in effect, not writing good realist plays; lamenting (in addition to his unnatural dialogue) such 'unrealistic devices' as a stop-and-go plot, eavesdropping, audience address, and the way in which, according to them, the excellence of his Greek originals (hardly any surviving examples of which had yet come to light), was 'smothered by barbarous clownery, intolerable verbosity, and an almost complete indifference to dramatic structure'.[9] Of course, such scholars paid lip-service to the undeniable if sometimes inconvenient and irritating fact that Plautus' works were written to be performed in a theatre. Yet, for the most part, despite such recognition, the perception of all ancient drama as theatre was conditioned by received notions of what theatre was commonly understood to be: that is, by the conventions and values of realism.

All too frequently whether in critical analysis or performance, ancient texts suffered a double indignity; first by having unlikely or even alien aesthetic concepts drawn out or thrust upon them; and then forced as often as not (on the rare occasions they were performed), into the procrustean bed of the illusionistic stage. But now, with a fresh approach, scholarship is beginning to recognize Plautus not for what he never aspired to be, but for what he was: a superbly gifted comic craftsman who had mastered and employed every trick of effective theatrical technique, for the benefit and appreciation of an audience which had already acquired impressive theatrical experience and sophistication.[10]

It has been observed that one of the recurrent 'conceits' of Plautus' plays is that the characters make up the comedy as they go along: they contrive and create the very plot in which they take part. Probably this reflects the fact that his plays, although scripted, were being presented before an audience accustomed to a more tentative dramatic fare: improvised, non-literary entertainments, which, as in *commedia* later, the actors built up using stock characters and the barest outline of a scenario. Certainly Plautus' indifference to 'dramatic illusion' and his characters' frequent acknowledgement both of the audience and of the play itself lend weight to this analysis.[11]

The chief agent of this dramaturgical self-consciousness is usually the 'clever slave' who fashions the play around him to become simultaneously its author and hero. He fills this role by virtue of his wit and intelligence which triumphs over adversity and the social facts of life in a way which no actual Roman slave could ever hope to do. Indeed, according to Donatus, it was forbidden that Roman slaves be depicted in plays as cleverer than their masters; but ostensibly Greek slaves could do so while preserving the necessary distance from an audience.[12] Masters are tricked, freedom is won, and so long as the play lasts, in the words of a slave in Plautus' *Casina*, 'we victims are victors; it's our lucky day!' (line 510).[13] The audience is able to admire and derive a mildly subversive pleasure from such characters' ability to fashion something redemptive from their dramatic situation, not because, as in tragedy, they suffer in a way a spectator fears he might suffer, but because they do not suffer: they get away with it.

The clever slave does indeed enjoy impunity. In the surviving plays, nothing dire ever actually happens to him despite circumstances of ever-present peril. As Segal points out, Plautus' protagonists make a point of positively disdaining and mocking the fates which, but for their success in fashioning unlikely, anti-realist plots, would tumble down upon them. In the *Asinaria* such a slave, Libanus, speaks for them all;

> We give our great and grateful thanks to Holy Trickery,
> For by our shrewdness, wiles, deceits, and clever machinations,
> our shoulders bold displaying courage in the face of rods,
> we've just defied hot-iron tortures, crucifixion, chains,
> strappadoes, fetters, dungeons, locking, stocking, manacles,
> and harsh persuasive whippers well-acquainted with our backs![14]

In the fragile world of the play punishment is meted out to the bad guys: authority figures (who have compromised their legitimacy in some way), unscrupulous lechers, boasters, bullies, and abusers of desirable social norms, while the – by contrast merely mischievous – authors of their correction enjoy a general amnesty announced at the play's conclusion. As the prologues reiterate, today is a holiday – it is 'fun and games' but tomorrow, as the protagonists subsequently remind the audience, is another day: their little brief authority and the higher justice it sometimes

2 Replica Roman stage

brings ends with the conclusion of these lively, but unlikely revels.

Violence is potentially a crucial component of the way a theatrical event of this type functions, both dramaturgically in terms of the development and presentation of the play, and psychologically, in its impact upon an audience; in translating and producing Plautus, it must be deftly handled. This applies to the moments of actual violence directly called for by the text and represented on stage, as well as the far more frequent and sometimes extremely robust and colourful verbal violence taking the form either of threats and abuse, or as a description of violence described occurring off stage.

In addition, of course, there is a fourth type of violence associated with these plays and with the later works of farce for which they provide the earliest example, and which so often directly adapted or imitated them. Slapstick; knock-about farce: the very terms suggest the variety of on-going comic violence associated with the genre. As Plautus might have put it, punches punctuate his plays, as do the epithets by which the characters are most frequently designated, e.g. 'Mastitgia' (whipping post); 'Verbero' (flogable); and 'Furcifer' (gallowsbird). The director must intuit the moments at which such casual violence is signalled or appropriate, and arrange for the characters physically to abuse each other in a manner worthy of their names, without spoiling the fun with too much lasting damage. The pain must be acute; not chronic. Like the coyote in the popular road-runner cartoons (or Tom and Jerry), however horrible the abuse meted out, the characters must be resilient; never permanently deformed or maimed: in the next sequence, they must appear as good as new.

Examples of these four forms of Plautine violence: actual violent acts called for by the text; verbal abuse; the narration of off-stage violence; and slapstick, are found throughout the plays. In order to illustrate some ways of dealing with them, I will draw on my own experience of producing Plautus, with particular examples taken from a recent presentation of the *Casina*.[15] In this play, a markedly nasty and lascivious old man plots to have a young household servant, Casina, marry his slave, with whom he will then surreptitiously share her. The old man's wife, whom he hopes to deceive, intends instead to have the girl marry another slave, the servant of their son who is himself in love with Casina, but has been conveniently sent abroad by the father. Thus, an interesting dichotomy is set up: wife (and son) versus husband (and father); domestic discord embodied by their slave surrogates.

This essential conflict is very efficiently and graphically laid out in the opening scene of the play which is also notable for the violence of the confrontation between its protagonists, the rival slaves. These two will fight twice in the course of the play, first publicly, and then again in an

3 Cleostrata and Chalinus

obscene scene, off stage, when one of them, disguised as Casina, employs the 'bed-trick', which even when the play premiered around 185 BC might justly have been termed 'venerable'. Throughout this comedy the conflict and impetus for the violence is essentially sexual, and is here stated explicitly and then further underscored in the teasing and jealousy with which one slave torments the other. This gives their confrontation an 'edge' which the director must identify and use to good effect. However serious the underlying cause of conflict may be (or however distressing in 'real life') its theatrical expression should create not empathy but distance in the audience. Slapstick is essentially innocent, and although the director may employ it to capture the attention of the spectators, and amuse them, he must not allow them to take it seriously as violence, or lose the sense of its artifice. It must be direct, uncomplicated, and above all, playful. One model for depicting Plautine violence is that of children's play, when it is full of exaggerated threat and reaction, huffing and puffing, but little actual infliction of pain. Another might be the feigning, bluster and make-believe seen in professional wrestling. Such 'rhetorical' violence is literally incredible; a matter of style.

I found it useful to give a suggestion of clowning (deadly earnest to them, fantastic to us) to the conflict between the slaves in the opening scene, and to introduce it with appropriate music, 'The Entrance of the Gladiators', which also served to induct the audience imaginatively into the artificial world of the play. This was further facilitated by attempting to approximate in translation something of the playfulness and fanciful exuberance of Plautus' text. The two slaves (already engaged in animated conversation) came striding onto the stage, one following the other so closely that when the first suddenly halts, the other collides into him, thus immediately giving their confrontation a physically violent expression. These two, Olympio in the lead and Chalinus at his heels, as well as serving as surrogates for, respectively, the old man Lysidamus and his wife, Cleostrata, also present a contrast between rural and urban attributes. Olympio, a bumpkin fond of crude jests and prone to violence, serves as a country foreman, while Chalinus, more diffident and plaintive, is a town slave.

Olympio rebukes Chalinus for following him to which he responds 'I'm resolved to go wherever you go. Just like your shadow, I'll follow. Even if you're strung up on the cross, I'll string along' (lines 91–4). Told to mind his own business, Chalinus in turn orders the 'over-sized overseer' Olympio to get back to the farm and his 'own turf', leaving city affairs to city folks. Accusing him of planning to carry off Casina, he continues, 'Back to the farm! Get back to the outback!' (line 103) Olympio arrogantly replies that indeed he does intend to marry Casina, and once back on the farm, 'you can bet I'll bed down with my bride, on my "own turf!"' (line 110):

> *Chal.* You have her, YOU! Hang me, by Hercules, I'd sooner die than let you get her!
> *Ol.* Hang on! She's mine, my booty, baby! So your neck's for the noose.
> *Chal.* You, dug from a dungheap! She's your booty, booby? (lines 111–14)

These insulting exchanges should be underscored by a variety of escalating knock-about abuse; slaps, blows, trips and the like. Chalinus' cry in the middle of line 115, 'Vae tibi!' would serve to punctuate the moment in which Olympio grabs hold of him in some suitably cruel embrace prior to delivering an extended climactic description (interrupted only by Chalinus' two plaintive cries, 'what will you do to me?') of how he intends to torture his rival once he obtains Casina. Beginning with 'Oh, how I'll needle you at my nuptials!' (line 116), he recites a rich catalogue of first physical and then mental torment which he promises to inflict upon his opponent. Olympio chooses an appropriately countrified means of punishing the household slave, Chalinus. He will force him to carry pitchers of water to fill eight immense vats: 'and fill you will, or you'll be well full of welts!' (line 123), until Chalinus is bent like a horse's crupper – the part positioned just beneath the tail. Next he will starve him: 'when you fancy some fodder, you'll eat dirt like a worm, compliments of the compost heap ... you'll famish on the farm!' (lines 126–7; 129).

Olympio's abuse then turns sexual, as he describes how at night Chalinus will be fastened in the frame of a window and forced to listen while he makes love to Casina. This verbal violence, taken with that just preceding it, demands some physical correlation, with Olympio manhandling Chalinus throughout the sequence, while perhaps miming the sort of torments awaiting him. Thus, clasping him tightly from behind, while facing him directly towards the audience, he might now run his hand mockingly over Chalinus' immobilized body, as he describes how Casina will murmur,

> Oh, sweetie-pie, oh Olympio my darling, my little honey pot, my joy, let me kiss those cute little eyes of yours, my precious! Oh, please, please let me love you, light of my life, my little dickey-bird, my lovey-dovey, my bunny-wunny! (lines 134–8)

As well as adding variety to the miseries suffered by Chalinus, this passage, particularly if given mock-erotic physical expression, ironically foreshadows the form of Chalinus' subsequent revenge upon Olympio, and, more generally, introduces the element of gross sexuality which characterizes the play. Olympio then returns to his more normal mode of abuse, probably concluding with some final physical assault on Chalinus.

> Well then, when she's cooing these things to me, you'll flutter, gallows bird, you'll shudder like a mouse shut up in the wall. And you can shut up now. I'm going in. I'm tired of talking to you. (lines 139–43)

Olympio struts up the stairs and into Lysidamus' house, closely followed by Chalinus, 'bloodied but unbowed' and vowing to continue in hot pursuit. In this combative first scene Plautus, with deft theatrical skill, has propelled the audience into the heart of the play and its central conflict, graphically expressed in first verbally and then physically violent terms.

This sets up the next scene which opens with the entrance of the long-suffering Cleostrata, who immediately demonstrates that the strife between the servants merely parallels and pre-figures that between husband and wife.

> That monster of a man! I'll wrack that rake with hunger and thirst, curses and worse! By Pollux, I'll torture him with torment from my tongue, that dungheap dandy, the haughty debauchee, that sink of sin! (lines 151–9)

A little later the object of her wrath, Lysidamus, bustles on stage full of himself and lascivious designs. He sings to the audience an ode to love which stutters to a halt when he sees the figure of his wife glowering in the background.

> Yet I am at a loss, there's that old rugged cross
> that I bear, while she lives, called my wife.
> And she's looking quite vile – soothing words – mustn't rile!
> Ah! How goes it, sweet light of my life? (lines 227–9)

Lysidamus literally compares his married life to crucifixion, and implies a death wish (which a few lines later me makes explicit) upon his wife. In their farcical exchange, Cleostrata gruffly brushes off her husband's attempts to 'sweet-talk' her, while Lysidamus persists. As the two engage in a veritable game of verbal tag, the physical depiction of his determined (but insincere) attempts to be winsome, and her equally robust rebukes of his approaches make for a lively scene, which Plautus enhances both by the use of an unlikely simile comparing their marriage (hardly made in heaven!) to that of Jupiter and Juno, and by the device of the inadvertently overheard aside.

> *Cleo.* You shall be the death of me!
> *Lys.* (If only it were true!)
> *Cleo.* Now that I believe! (lines 233–4)[16]

The language of the scene as it builds is highly colloquial and energetic, punctuated by oaths and exclamations and coloured by suggestive imagery. After a series of quick responses and rising verbal violence it then moderates its rhythm as Lysidamus proposes a truce; 'Oh, now dear wife, please, that's enough! Get hold of yourself, and that tongue of yours! Save a bit of abuse for tomorrow's row!' (lines 248–50). They then agree to settle the question of which slave should marry Casina by drawing lots.

The subsequent scene begins with a council of war between Lysidamus and Olympio as they prepare themselves for the impending domestic battle. The master advises his servant that 'the time has come for us to draw swords and fight it out' (line 344), and when Cleostrata and Chalinus enter from the doors to his house, he suggests they 'close ranks and fight' (line 352), then gives orders a moment later to 'lift our standards and charge' (line 357). This military imagery provides the key to staging the ensuing scene. Man and wife, each with a slave ally, form opposing camps centre stage, the hostile forces glaring at one another on either side of the urn where the outcome of their struggle must be decided. In the course of the conflict there are first threats and taunts, the ritual calling upon the gods, then feigns and sorties, and finally actual physical combat, with one side fighting in the name of Jupiter, the other, Juno.

Things start off badly for Lysidamus, who by an unfortunate slip of the tongue urges that Casina be given to him (his actual wish), instead of to Olympio, which is his 'official' position. Thoroughly discomfited by this he then backtracks, attempting to avoid conflict at the last minute by a negotiated settlement.

> *Lys.* Both of us, recognizing your rights in the matter appeal to you.
> *Cleo.* For what?
> *Lys.* Why just this my sweet. To do a little favour for our foreman here in this Casina affair.
> *Cleo.* By Pollus, I won't! I wouldn't dream of it! (lines 371–3)

The lots are distributed, with mutual accusations of bad faith, followed by Olympio's insolent insults to Cleostrata. He next begins formally to invoke the gods, but each time the formula is interrupted by Chalinus.

> *Ol.* I pray the gods . . .
> *Chal.* . . . will fit you with a ball and chain . . .
> *Ol.* . . . that the lots will let me . . .
> *Chal.* . . . be hung up by your heels, by Hercules! (lines 389–90)

The prayer then descends into a series of violent verbal attacks.

> *Ol.* No! Will have you blow your brains out through your nose!
> *Chal.* What are you worried about? The noose is all ready and waiting for you!
> *Ol.* You're a dead man! . . .
> *Chal.* I beg the gods – let your lot slip out of the urn!
> *Ol.* You do do you? Since you're so slippery yourself, you want everything to imitate you?
> *Chal.* Oh, if only your lot would dissolve . . .
> *Ol.* And here's hoping you melt away yourself, soon. Warmed up with a whipping! (lines 391–3; 396–400)

These exchanges are accompanied by raised fists, and threatening postures, until, a few moments later, the formal rite which was meant to contain and resolve the conflict, breaks down altogether, and each side resorts to force. The actual physical violence (infrequent in Plautus), is in essence a punch-up between Lysidamus and Cleostrata, waged on their behalf by their slave allies. Because Cleostrata is also fighting for her son, as rival to his father, it is also a conflict between generations. Moreover, (and extending the comic to the cosmic), each side is also explicitly associated with a god. This is in effect, total war: resounding from the lowest social order of slaves, right up to heaven. Lysidamus is the aggressor, but comes off worse.

> *Lys.* Shut that man's mouth this minute! Go on, what are you waiting for?
> *Cleo.* Don't you dare raise a hand!
> *Ol.* Shall I sock him or slap him, Sir?
> *Lys.* Whichever you prefer.
> *Ol.* Take that!!
> *Cleo.* How dare you strike that man?!
> *Ol.* Why, my Jupiter here gave orders.
> *Cleop.* [to Chalinus] Well, you hit him right back!
> *Ol.* OWWWW! He's pounding me to a pulp, Jupiter!
> *Lys.* How dare you strike that man?!
> *Chal.* Why, my Juno here gave orders.

Lys. We'll just have to put up with it. My wife's already giving the orders even though I'm still alive. (lines 404–9)

Lysidamus indulges in one more bit of bluster, before the lots are drawn; Lysidamus: 'I warn you, Chalinus, keep an eye out for trouble', to which Chalinus responds, 'Oh, that's kind of you, after my eye's been blackened!' (lines 411–12). To reinforce the suggestion of a school yard brawl, Chalinus' line, and that uttered a moment earlier by Olympio, 'Why did he have to go and spoil my omen?' (line 410) can each be allowed to end in a drawn-out whimpering whine. This in turn allows Lysidamus' and Olympio's rather pompous pronouncements a few seconds later when they win the lots, to seem both incongruous as well as an indulgence of dangerous hubris in their evocation of the gods and the hallowed Roman concepts of *pietas* and of sacred custom, the *mos maiorum*.

Lys. The gods are smiling on us, Olympio, rejoice!
Ol. It's all due to the piety of me and my forefathers. (lines 417–18)[17]

In the following scene Lysidamus and Olympio plot to 'give our fallen foe, even more misery and woe' (lines 441–2), and Olympio relishes putting into effect the tortures with which he threatened Chalinus in the opening scene; 'Just wait till he comes to the farm! I'll return him to you bent double like a coalman' (lines 437–8). This prompts Chalinus (hiding in the background) to change the plan he had just confided to the audience to commit suicide, resolving instead to oppose such double-trouble. 'While one of them nails me, the other one flails me . . . That settles it. I'll postpone my passing: I won't perish till I've posted that pest off to purgatory.' (lines 445; 447–8).[18] Eavesdropping on the pair, he learns of their plot to enjoy Casina right next door, immediately after the wedding, and gleefully scurries off to inform his mistress Cleostrata of their dastardly designs.

She swiftly takes command of the play.[19] In a quick succession of scenes she deftly arranges Lysidamus's downfall. In what became the tradition of 'revolving door' farce, the characters come and go with mechanical precision and inevitability, while she tightens the plot on her husband, causing him to exclaim to the audience in consternation,

I wonder what omen I omitted when I began this love affair? Or how I incurred such Venus-envy. Why, when I'm longing to get laid, am I constantly de-layed!? (lines 616–18)

Even as he speaks fresh disasters commence with the sound of 'unholy hubbud' (line 620) in his house. Pardalisca, Cleostrata's servant, bursts out of the house, and in a frantic, mock-tragic tirade pretends to report shocking violence unfolding within. Plautus contrives for her song a piece of splendid parody, immediately evocative of high tragedy in its linguistic style, meter, and content.[20]

> I'm lost! Lost! Totally done for, and dead!
> My heart has stopped, my limbs are trembling with dread!
> Help! Safety! Shelter! Oh, where to turn for aid?
> Such things I saw inside, can scarcely be conveyed.
> Bold and brazen badness! Turmoil and alarm!
> Be careful, Cleostrata! Lest she do you harm!
> The woman's lost her senses – her mind has gone astray!
> For goodness' sake avoid her, but snatch the sword away! (lines 621–9)

In the ensuing scene, Pardalisca relates to her increasingly terrified master how Casina has run amok, 'swearing by all the gods and goddesses, that the man she sleeps with tonight . . . she'll murder!' (lines 670–1). This induces in Lysidamus another unfortunate slip of the tongue, quickly seized upon by Pardalisca to cause him even greater discomfort.

> *Lys.* Murder ME?
> *Pard.* What's it got to do with you, Sir?
> *Lys.* Damn!
> *Pard.* Why should you be concerned about that?
> *Lys.* Why I misspoke myself. I meant to say my foreman. (lines 672–4)

Pardalisca pushes her advantage relentlessly (the comedy of the scene derives from the unequal combat between master and servant), asserting that Casina does indeed intend to kill them both. After a quick gleeful aside to the audience: 'What fabulous foolery! It's all fantasy from first to finish! Mistress and her neighbour set the trap and I've been sent to spring it on him!' (lines 685–8), she raises the pressure further, claiming that Casina has *two* swords to kill them both 'this very day!' Lysidamus is in despair: 'I'm the dead-deader-deadest man alive!' (lines 693–4). Recovering slightly, he first proposes to don armour and confront Casina, but then, thinking better of it, suggests that his wife ought to be equal to the task. Told that the girl refuses to give up the swords so long as she has to marry Olympio, Lysidamus next reacts with guilty fury.

> *Lys.* Well, like it or not, the ungrateful slut
>   will be given in marriage today.
>   I won't change what's planned: she'll give me her hand . . .
>   To my FOREMAN, I meant to say!
> *Pard.* Seems you stumble a lot.
> *Lys.*   I'm so frightened, I'm not
>   giving thought to the words that I say.
>   But please beg my wife, if she values my life,
>   To get Casina out of the way!
>   And you beg her too.
> *Pard.*   Yes, I'll beg for you.
> *Lys.* Do your best, as you know how to do.
>   If you hush up these scandals, I'll buy you some sandals,
>   A gold ring, and some other treats too! (lines 700–9)

This account of violence within is immediately followed by further violence on stage in the form of slapstick. Olympio enters, returning from the market where he has purchased groceries for the wedding feast. Anxious to go into the house and assuage his hunger, he angers Lysidamus, who threatens to punish him, whereupon the slave reacts violently in turn: 'leave me alone, for the gods' sake. Do you want to make me retch, wretch?' (line 731), Lysidamus blusters, vainly attempting to remind Olympio of his subservient position, only to be threatened with a reminder of their pact, together (as the text signals) with some unspoken physical intimidation.

> *Ol.* Am I not a free man? You do remember, don't you? Don't you?
> *Lys.* Wait! Stop!
> *Ol.* Leave me alone!
> *Lys.* I'll be your slave!
> *Ol.* That's more like it. (lines 736–8)

The spectators thus have an explicit demonstration (which in performance should be reflected in some knock-about domination of master by slave), of how Lysidamus has been degraded by his unseemly and brutalizing lust: social roles have been reversed, and moreover, the master has become a suppliant. This is further underscored by Lysidamus' use of the formulaic language of submission,[21] and compounded by Olympio's contemptuous evaluation of him, even as a slave.

> *Lys.* Dear, dear Olympio, my father, my patron, I beg . . .
> *Ol.* Now you're talking sense.
> *Lys.* Yes, I'm yours, indeed I am.
> *Ol.* What do I want with such a knave of a slave?
> *Lys.* Well then. How soon can you make me over? (lines 739–42)

When the mock wedding finally occurs, at which the slave Chalinus, disguised by the women as the bride Casina, is handed over to Olympio (and Lysidamus), a scene of purest farce is again enlivened with actual physical violence. Advising the men to 'be kind to this innocent, unspoiled maiden' (line 832) as 'Casina' simpers coyly beside them, the women draw out their departure as long as possible to frustrate their avid rivals and increase the tension, then slowly depart into the house. Lysidamus and Olympio immediately advance to take possession of their spoils.

> *Lys.* . . . Almighty, mighty Aphrodite! What pleasure you gave me in giving me this treasure.
> *Ol.* Oh, your iddy, biddy, body, baby! (lines 841–4)

The mock solemnity of the wedding ceremony is now crowned by a few moments of superb slapstick as the two men attempt to paw and pet their prize before carrying her bodily off the stage and up the steps of their neighbour's house.

> *Ol.* . . . What the *hell*!?

Lys. What's wrong?
Ol. She just stamped on my foot like an elephant!
Lys. Hush up! Never a cloud was softer than this breast!
Ol. By Pollux, what an iddy, bitty, pretty, titty! *Ouch!* Goodness me!
Lys. What now?
Ol. She hit me in the chest – it wasn't an elbow; it was a battering ram!
Lys. Well, why are you handling her so roughly then? Look at me. Just treat her kind, and she doesn't mind.
Ol. Owwwww!
Lys. What's the matter now?
Ol. Damnation! What a pint-sized power-house she is!! Her elbow almost laid me low!
Lys. Maybe she'll like to be laid low – you know?[22]
Ol. Let's go!
Lys. Look lively, little, lovely, lady! (lines 844–54)

The final scene of the play begins with the triumphant entrance of the ladies (Cleostrata, Pardalisca, and the nextdoor neighbour, Myrrhina) who, having feasted within, come out to enjoy the 'wedding games' resulting from the trick played upon Lysidamus and Olympio. Myrrhina explicitly underscores the theatrical connection; 'No playwright ever conceived a plot cleverer than this masterpiece of ours!' (lines 860–1). Cleostrata, who in effect scripted the scenario, hints at the scene to come: 'Now I'd like to see the old fool come out with his face smashed!'

The doors to the house where the men have spent their brief wedding night with 'Casina' are flung open and Olympio hurdles out, howling, searching for a place to hide from the overwhelming shame as well as the violence he has just endured inside. But, this being a comedy, the character's wish to share the joke with the audience overrides verisimilitude. Despite his distress, Olympio as a conscious performer in the play acknowledges that his plight will entertain the audience, whom he asks to 'listen while I tell you all, and lend an ear./ It's worth the price; as comical to narrate as to hear/ the quite appalling mess I've made of things inside' (lines 879–80). Olympio's deliberate juxtaposing here of the world of the play and the reality of performance further encourages a pleasurable attitude of comic detachment on the part of the spectators towards the events he relates. He tells how he took Casina inside into a dark bedroom, and attempted to make love to her.

> I longed to taste in haste chaste Casina's embrace,
> and let the old man come in second place!
> And so, I closed the door to try and minimize
> the chance that in the dark he'd take ME by surprise. (lines 875–91)

The women then reveal themselves and to Olympio's intense discomfort proceed to tease and question him mercilessly, noting that 'it'll be a good lesson for our audience!' (line 902). Olympio's account and the ladies' reponse is highly ribald, as he relates how he took hold of what he thought was the hilt of Casina's sword, but then supposed it must be something else – perhaps a carrot or cucumber as the women helpfully suggest. Much of the humour of this scene in performance derives from the physical antics on stage as the women cluster around Olympio, assaulting him with questions, then reacting with shrieks and laughter to his distressed responses. Finally he relates how in desperation he tried pleading with 'Casina' to be more cooperative, whereupon she covered herself up and turning her back on him, frustrated his amorous pursuit.

> *Ol.* Since she's in that position, I ask her permission
>   to attempt the alternative route!
> *Myrr.* What a marvellous tale!
> *Ol.*   As I tried to prevail,
>   I leant over to snog with my sweet.
>   But something was weird; she'd a bristly beard!
>   Then she kicked me with both of her feet!
>   I fell flat on the ground, and she started to pound
>   and beat me just as you discern.
>   Without a word more, I ran straight out the door,
>   to let the old man have his turn. (lines 922–33)

At this point, on cue, the door is heard creaking, and all withdraw as Lysidamus, in a battered and dishevelled state, stumbles out of the house, and throws himself down before the audience in supplication. Confessing his disgrace and fear of the awful retribution 'which my wife will exact from my hide' (line 948), he pleads in vain for someone in the audience to take his place, and then, compounding and confirming his humiliation, decides to assume the most degraded of all social positions: that of a fugitive slave.

> *Lys.* Is there no one out there who'd be wanting a share
>   of the fate that awaits me inside?
>   Then I think I'll behave like a runaway slave,
>   since my back's for the rack in these parts.
>   I got beat black and blue. You may laugh, but it's true!
>   It's my folly, but by golly, it smarts! (lines 949–54)

If, as seems certain (despite the severely fragmented state of Lysidamus's account), he has indeed been beaten up by Chalinus, it marks the only occasion in Plautine drama when a master is physically punished by his slave. Lysidamus says 'I'd better make a run for it right now!', and thereby, along with the particular role which his action would suggest in its equivalent real-life situation, he also takes on the dramaturgical function and persona of *servus currens*, the 'running slave'; one of the most popular characters in new comedy, whose stereotyped behaviour Plautus parodies both here and elsewhere.[23] Lysidamus is set to flee, only to freeze at the 'starter's block' when Chalinus' cry rings out from the porch of the neighbour's house; 'Hold it right there, lover boy!' (line 955). After first asking him whether he 'yearns to return to the bedroom' (line 965), the slave (still wearing his bridal garb) threatens his master with further violence – a beating with a club – whereupon Lysidamus, reflecting that 'it's either make tracks this way, or break backs that way!' (line 968), again is poised for flight. 'Greetings! Lover boy!'. Cleostrata bellows from her place of concealment, causing Lysidamus to stop again, and cry out in despair, 'Wolves to the right of me, bitches to the left!' (line 970).[24]

The spatial arrangement on stage aptly depicts Lysidamus' predicament as he stands stock still, centre stage, 'caught in the act'. On one side his wife glowers at him from the door of their home, the honourable head of which as *pater familias* he has rendered himself unfit to fill; while, on the other, the mistaken object of his unseemly lust and agent of his disgrace – a slave – mocks and threatens him. All the characters on stage now approach and surround him, firing questions. He stands totally isolated and humiliated, surrounded by a circle of threatening accusers. Cleostrata advances grimly to deliver sentence, taking him by the ear like a naughty child and ordering him to 'just march yourself right inside' (line 998). Lysidamus capitulates. He begs her frantically to forgive him; begs Myrrhina to intercede, promises that if he should ever make love to Casina again 'or even appear to want to do so – let alone to it – if I ever again do such a thing – well then, dear wife, you can just suspend me and skin me alive!' (lines 1001–3).

Cleostrata hesitates ... Myrrhina urges clemency ... all stand waiting ... and then – she relents with a nod and a wink to the audience 'in order to keep a long play from running any longer' (line 1006). And so this rather dark and unusually violent comedy ends in reconciliation;[25] but also in the punishment of destructive excess, and the reward of domestic virtue with the triumph justly won for once by the women.

Lys. You're really not angry?
Cloe. No, I'm not really angry.
Lys. Do you promise?
Cleo. I do!
Lys. There's not a living soul with a more loving and lovely wife than mine!
(lines 1007–8)

As everyone gathers around the 'loving' couple, Chalinus, still standing behind and above them at the entrance to the neighbour's house, is told by Cleostrata to restore to Lysidamus the symbols of his manly dignity; his cloak and cane. Chalinus does so while delivering one final, and rather sophisticated joke to end the play with a laugh.

Chal. ... Just consider my plight's all I ask.
For I think it's a sin to be wed to *two* men,
neither one of whom managed the task. (lines 1010–11)

Plautus' *Casina* is a work suffused with violence. It contains more explicitly violent action taking place on stage than any other extant example, and its narration of violent episodes occurring 'behind the scenes' is also unusually detailed and extensive. Two other forms of violence: verbal abuse and moments at which it seems valid to infer some form of slapstick, while abundant, tend to repeat the pattern seen in his other works. The Roman audience evidently relished such robust comedy. As its prologue makes quite clear, *Casina*, in the version preserved to us, was already part of an admired theatrical heritage only a generation or so after Plautus composed it: our text derives from a revival. This suggests that the work, praised by the prologue for its quality, had been particularly successful.

> Now wise men – men of taste, refined,
> favour old farces, just like a vintage wine.
> They love the works and wisdom of the good old days,
> and fail to see the merit of these modern plays . . .
> . . . We've duly taken note of what the people say:
> you're longing to applaud a play by Plautus here today.
> A titillating tale, to charm, amuse and move;
> the sort of stuff the older crowd approve.
> You younger folks who don't remember Plautus,
> we'll also do our best to win your plaudits,
> with such a play! The greatest glory of its age,
> once more before you on a modern stage!
> Those dedicated, decorated, dear-departed souls, those ancient comic playwrights
> shall inspire our roles. (lines 5–9; 11–20)

As the examples of the occurrence, dramaturgical function, and suggested staging of violence discussed here demonstrate, this particular aspect of Plautus' craft (to which many other elements could be added) continues to 'inspire our roles': it has have become part of our theatrical tradition.

NOTES

1 *Casina*, lines 89–143.
2 Geza Alföldy, *The Social History of Rome*, trans. David Braund and Frank Pollock (London: Croom Helm, 1985), pp. 57–8.
3 Cato the Elder, *De Agri Cultura*, 2.1ff., 56–7. Plutarch, *Cato* 25.
4 Gladiatorial combats were first recorded at funeral games in 264 BC; (Valerius Maximus, 2.4.7; Livy, *Ep.* 16) and became ever more frequent. In 160 the public deserted the theatre during a performance of Terence's *Hecyra* (see Prologue 2, lines 31–4) in order to attend such displays.
5 For violence in Greek old comedy, see Victor Ehrenberg, *The People of Aristophanes* (Cambridge, MA: Harvard University Press, 1951), pp. 184ff. He notes that in general Greek slaves were not badly treated.
6 Eduard Frankel in his masterful analysis of the manner in which Plautus

adapted his Greek originals, notes the increased emphasis on the role of slaves, and suggests that passages which dwell on punishment are probably Plautine insertions. Rev. edn, trans. F. Munari, *Elementi Plautini in Plauto* (Florence, 1960), pp. 223ff. The same conclusion was reached by K. M. Westaway, *The Original Element in Plautus* (Cambridge University Press, 1917), pp. 49ff.

7 Walter R. Chalmers, 'Plautus and his Audience', in *Roman Drama*, ed. T. A. Dorley and Donald R. Dudley (London: Routledge & Kegan Paul, 1965), pp. 21–50; p. 28.

8 In his important essay on 'Farce' in *The Life of the Drama* (New York, 1967), pp. 219–56, Eric Bentley notes (p. 255) that comic catharsis and the release it provides is motivated not by the 'impulse to flee (or Fear), but the impulse to attack (or Hostility) . . . in farce hostility enjoys itself'. For Plautus' puritanical warrior audience, farce would have been an apt form of popular entertainment, providing release from normal repressions, and an outlet for aggression.

9 The quotation is from Gilbert Norwood, writing in 1931, who notes in the same vein, 'The construction of some among his plays is so incredibly bad that even stupidity alone, even ignorance alone, even indifference alone, seem insufficient to explain it. We can but suppose that he neither knew nor cared what drama is, and was concerned with nothing save to amuse an audience that knew and cared not indeed less, but no more. He took for this purpose amusing Greek plays and happened to produce excellent matter only when he happened to put in little of his own.' *Plautus and Terence* (Oxford: Clarendon Press, 1931), p. 19.

10 In addition to the important and innovative assessment by Erich Segal, *Roman Laughter* (Cambridge, MA: Harvard University Press, 1968), this approach has most recently been taken by Niall Slater in his superb study, *Plautus in Performance* (Princeton University Press, 1985).

11 Slater develops this analysis with great skill in his introduction, 'The Performance Dimension', pp. 3–18.

12 *Donatus ad Eunuchum* 57.

13 All quotations are from my own translation which attempts to convey the sense, imagery, playfulness and theatrical efficacy of Plautus' language; an undertaking which sometimes precludes rendering it word for word into English. Plautus is both idiomatic and inventive, and often the vitality and originality of his language, as well as the meaning it would have conveyed to his original audience, require that a translation find an equivalent rather than identical turn of phrase.

14 *Asinaria* 545–51, translated by Erich Segal; *Roman Laughter*, p. 145.

15 These productions were part of a project begun in 1984 at the University of Warwick. Following extensive research and analysis of the evidence of ancient perspective painting, I constructed a replica Roman temporary stage, and presented a series of productions of Plautus upon it. This project is the subject of a documentary video, *Pompeian Painting and Plautus: Staging Roman Comedy*, available together with extensive notes in North America from Films for the Humanities, Princeton, New Jersey, and in Britain from the Audio Visual Centre, University of Warwick.

16. Lysidamus wishes his wife dead a third time at the beginning of the lot-casting scene:

> *Cleo.* Now, Chalinus, what is it my husband wants me to do?
> *Chal.* Gee, what he'd most like is to see you going up in smoke out beyond the gates!
> *Cleo.* Goodness, I think you're right.
> *Chal.* By golly, I don't think, I know!
> *Lys.* It appears I have more servants than I thought: we seem to have a mind-reader on the staff. (lines 353–6)

17 Of course, characters in Plautus, particularly his mischievous clever slaves, are often guilty of a form of comic hubris, exalting in their ability to break the rules and come out smiling. Their triumphant capacity to 'beat the odds', lends to the comedy much of its regenerative force. But Lysidamus' case is different. Here and elsewhere he sets himself up in advance for the correction which follows, and which, as his subsequent conduct shows, he thoroughly deserves. His misbehaviour lacks the positive exuberance and life-affirming potential of Plautus' comic heroes: his lust is inhumane, degrading, selfishly destructive of other's happiness, and, worst of all, it causes him to abuse those over whom he holds power. Moreover, Lysidamus, unlike the characters whom Plautus expects his audience to admire (or at the least, condone out of respect for their wit and wiles), is not in fact strong and capable, but weak and servile: his lust is uncontrolled, and as the later scenes show, polymorphously perverse.

18 This is a case where the Latin can be translated literally into English, whose meaning is very close to it (instead of resorting to equivalent English expressions), while also echoing the alliteration of the original. 'nam illorum me alter cruciat, alter macerat . . . protollo mortem mihi; certus est, hunc Acheruntem praemittam prius.'

19 Slater's extensive analysis of this play is astute, and his discussion of the function of the matrona as playwright is particularly valuable and convincing.

20 The Latin (which I have translated into what seems the appropriate meter of the Alexandrine) rewards examination.

> Nulla sum, nulla sum; tota, tota occidi,
> cor metu mortuomst, membra miserae tremunt,
> nescio unde auxili, praeside, perfugi
> mi aut opis copiam comparem aut expetam.
> tanta factu modo mira miris modis
> intus vidi, novam atque integram audaciam.

W. T. MacCary and M. M. Willcock in their edition of the text (Cambridge University Press, 1976), p. 27, note the abundance of alliteration, assonance, repetition and (somewhat rare in Plautus) end-rhyme, which taken together give 'a jingling quality to the whole which makes it appropriate for musical rendering'. They also point out (p. 36) that her lament is reminiscent of the story, dramatized by Aeschylus, of the daughters of Danaus forced into marriage with husbands whom they then murdered on their wedding night. Leo noted in *Plautinische Forschungen* (2nd edn, Berlin, 1912; rep. Darmstadt, 1966), p. 113, that Pardalisca's report of domestic mayhem was closely similar to the account given by the Phrygian slave in Euripides' *Orestes*.

21 R. L. Hunter quotes the formula from *Captivi*, 444; 'You are now my master, you my patron, you my father', and cites other examples in Terence (*Andria*,

295; *Phormio*, 496; and *Adelphoe*, 456). *The New Comedy of Greece and Rome* (Cambridge University Press, 1985), p. 169, note 8. Segal discusses the frequent occurrences of the master-as-suppliant motif in Plautus (p. 119ff.) and devotes a chapter, 'From Slavery to Freedom', to the general topic of the reversal of status and transfer of authority which is so much a part of Plautine comic technique, and epitomized when the slave enslaves his master.

22 Plautus makes a pun upon the words for elbow and going to bed.

23 E.g. Mercury in *Amphitruo* (Lines 984–7), who runs on stage claiming the right to do so like 'paltry slaves in comedy'; or *Captivi* (lines 778–9), when the parasite Ergasilus states, 'just like slaves in comedies, I'll bundle my cloak around my neck and run ...'. R. L. Hunter notes (pp. 81–2) that 'a common feature of such scenes [is] the fact that the running slave is normally hailed by someone behind his back', and suggests that 'Roman poets, building upon a Greek foundation, elaborated the "running slave" into a cherished part of the comic apparatus'. He sees in this a self-conscious awareness by poet and public of the established conventions of the genre.

24 A reference to the proverb, 'Inter lupos et canes nullam salutem esse'; 'There's no safety twix wolves and dogs'. Lysidamus says he will 'try to change the proverb, by Hercules, and head this way; I'll hope for the best with the dog omen' (lines 971–2): in effect attempting (unsuccessfully as it turns out) to teach his old dog a new trick.

25 But not restoration. Lysidamus does not return to his position as head of the household, since henceforth, as the terms of his surrender stipulate, Cleostrata can exact punishment upon him at any time. See Slater, *Plautus in Performance*, p. 90.

Violence and the social body in the Croxton *Play of the Sacrament**

VICTOR I. SCHERB

The late medieval Croxton *Play of the Sacrament* instructs us in the many links between symbolic violence, the drama, and medieval society. In it, we see what appears to be a Holy Eucharist stolen, sold, stabbed, stretched, nailed, boiled and cooked. If a French account of a play on the same subject is any guide, the Croxton play may have been quite a gruesome spectacle. According to a stage direction in the French play, 'by a device which had been made, a large quantity of blood sprang up high from the said Host, as if it was a pissing infant and the Jew was covered and bloodied by it and it made his person very wet'.[1] At the climax of the Croxton play's violence, the bleeding, tortured Eucharist transforms itself into a bleeding child, a visceral spectacle which acts both as a final proof of the doctrine of transubstantiation and also, I contend, as a visual symbol of the social and religious divisions within the local community.

Critical attempts to deal with the symbolic violence of the late medieval stage have either found it extraneous and counterproductive or,[2] more recently, have been inclined to see it as part of the affective piety of the late Middle Ages. The York Crucifixion play's violence, drawn out in such agonizing detail, has been cogently analyzed as an example of this general trend in devotion as well as a product of the popularization of philosophical realism.[3] This critical tradition has been responsible for some excellent studies of the Croxton play. Sister Maltman, for example, has drawn our attention to how the tortures inflicted on the Host by the Jews are intended as a fairly linear re-enactment of the original Passion,[4] while such astute critics as Anne Nichols and Richard Homan have shown how many elements of the play fit in with other manifestations of late medieval devotional sensibility.[5]

Even the best of these approaches, however, seem slightly inadequate to the Croxton play, as they reduce the play's considerable violence to a simple soteriological symbol of Christ's suffering. The *Play of the Sacrament* is, after all, a highly individual drama of a fairly specific time and place:

---
* A draft of this paper was read at the *Themes in Drama* International Conference held at the University of California, Riverside, in February 1989.

late fifteenth-century Suffolk.⁶ Although no pertinent records remain to us from the town of Croxton itself, we know a good deal about the play's local environment in the later Middle Ages. In this light, we can profitably look at the violence of the *Play of the Sacrament* as a means of expressing and symbolically resolving social and religious tensions within the local community. The divisive effects of economic growth and the spread of rationalistic doubt are concretized first in the selling of the Host, and then in the brutal tortures inflicted upon it. The author in effect projects the problems of the community upon a conveniently distant scapegoat: the Jews. The playwright can thus dramatize the social and religious rifts within the contemporary community by depicting extreme and spectacular violence. At the same time, the playwright portrays the transcendental healing potential of Christ's sacrifice implicit in the Eucharist and re-enacted by the Jews on stage.

Mikhail Bakhtin has made us aware of the subversive potential of festive violence, which is often enacted in terms of the body, as well as of its potentially regenerative power.⁷ Symbolic violence has similarly been recognized by René Girard as a means of siphoning off potentially destructive tensions within a community.⁸ One possible transformation of festive release would be to have potential social violence realized on a symbolic plane around some symbol of the social body. Religious drama, which retains some elements of a ritual character while maintaining a relative freedom as to its narrative subject, would be the ideal medium for such a pattern of action. We find this pattern, I think, in the Croxton *Play of the Sacrament*.

Few symbols were so important to late medieval European man as the Blessed Sacrament. James has argued for the significance of the Corpus Christi festival in late medieval England, which he sees as a means of expressing both social wholeness and social differentiation, but I wish to focus on the significance of the Eucharist itself. According to James, the festival of Corpus Christi resolves into a Levi-Straussian binary contradiction. We find, for example, in 'the Mass of Corpus Christi Day, [that] just as social particularity involves social participation, so each fragment of the consecrated host shares in the whole of the Body of Christ'.⁹ Thus, just as the feast celebrated social wholeness in the face of the reality of social differentiation, the Host itself could become a powerful unifying symbol; at Durham, a description of the Corpus Christi day ceremonies has survived, and it is marked by a sense of unity.

> There was a goodly shrine in Sancte Nicholas church ordeyned to be caryed ye sayd daie in Prossession cauled Corpus Christi shrine all fynlye gilted a goodly thing to behould, and on ye hight of ye sayd shrine was a foure Squared Box all of christall, wherin was enclosed the holy sacrment of thaulter and was caryed ye said daie with iiij preistes vp to ye place green &

> all ye hole prossession of all ye churches in ye said towne goyng before ytt and when it was a litle space within Wyndshole yett yt dyd stand still . . . and the prior & convent with all ye whole companye of ye Quere all in there best copes dyd meet the said shrine sytting on there kneys and prayinge.[10]

After being brought into the church with all of the banners of the town gilds, the eucharistic shrine was then carried about the town, reinforcing the identity between the town and the sanctified Host. When social violence threatened to break out, as it did in London in the 1440s, a procession with the Eucharist was one means of easing tensions, the sight of the Host reminding the parties of their fraternity as members of the *corpus mysticum*.[11] The Sacrament, as one body of Christ, has an intimate symbolic relation with that other body of Christ — the community of worshipers, and an attack on the Host could be looked upon not only as sacrilege, but as an attack on the community. For example, the Bill of Riot filed by the Bungay citizens in 1514 against the men who 'brake and threw down fyve pagents of your inhabitaunts . . . the whyche we euer wont tofore to be caryed abowt the seyd Town vpon the seyd daye in the honor of the blissyd Sacrament',[12] seems to construe this as an attack on their dignity and integrity as a community.

Although those who torture the Host in the Croxton play are unequivocally described as Jews, there were few or no Jews in England in the late fifteenth and early sixteenth centuries. Instead, the dramatist seems to have superficially distanced his subject in order to more easily delineate contemporary problems at one remove. Although her view has been recently challenged by Anne Nichols,[13] Celia Cutts has to my mind persuasively argued that only in light of contemporary fears about Lollardy does the amazingly large doctrinal scope of the Croxton play make sense. According to Cutts

> Where the continental tales emphasize only the doctrine of transubstantiation, and subordinate even that to the anti-Jewish and relic aspects, the English play gives all the emphasis to pure doctrine and expands its teaching to include not only transubstantiation but also baptism, confession, penance, pilgrimage, respect for images, reverence for the Blessed Virgin, the spiritual power and authority of a priest and the reverence due him, and the superior power and authority of a Bishop, which is notably greater than that of a priest. The instruction is made more pointed by a warning that any other belief is heretical, and a passing hint at the punishment in store for the unbeliever.[14]

The playwright apparently desired to widen the doctrinal point of the play to include a large number of the sacraments and an authorization of the Church hierarchy in an effort to combat the more radical forms of belief found among the local Lollard community. Although we can't be certain of their precise number or nature, we do find occasional Lollards appear-

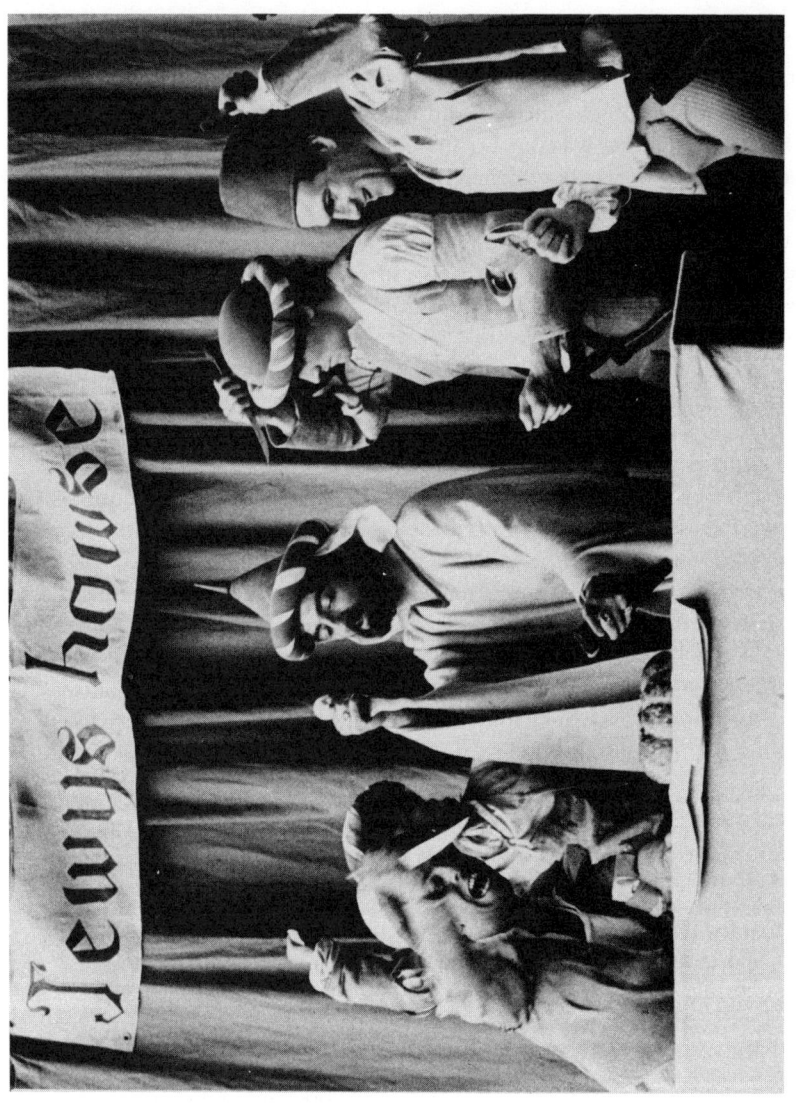

4 'Stabbing the Host'. The Croxton Play, The Medieval Players. Photo: Tessa Musgrave

ing in the region of Croxton in the 1450s and 60s,[15] while there was a more substantial resurgence at the turn of the century in Norfolk, Suffolk, Kent and, especially, Essex.[16]

The potentially violent religious divisions within the fifteenth-century East Anglian community were exacerbated by the rapidly growing and disproportionate wealth of some of its members. The collusion between Aristorius and Jonathas could easily be a satiric reflection upon the uneasy East Anglian social situation. Aristorius, for instance, would be costumed after the manner of a contemporary merchant. East Anglia was among the wealthiest areas in England, and the resultant social unrest probably played a part in both the peasants revolt of 1381 and Jack Cade's rebellion of 1450, both of which drew considerable groups of the disaffected from East Anglia.

Within the play, we find a sharp sense of the divisions and social disarray wealth can cause. Aristorius, the Christian merchant, in boasting of his wealth and power, seems to give faint praise to God and slights his priest. Although he does not seem to be a member of the nobility, he says that he lives as a 'lordys pere . . . in worthynesse' (line 119). The Jewish merchant, Jonathas, immediately follows Aristorius with another boasting speech. While Aristorius had merely asked God to 'maynteyn vs with myrth', Jonathas thanks his god who 'hayly þat hast me sent/ Gold, syluer, and presyous stonys' (lines 157–8). As theatre historian William Tydeman points out, some of these objects were almost certainly represented on stage,[17] quite possibly strewn on the same table where the Host is later to undergo the re-enactment of the Passion. The dramatist deliberately parallels their speeches in order to emphasize their identity. Two possible interpretations of this parallelism come to mind: 1) the Jew, like Aristorius, is a good merchant or 2) Aristorius, the Christian merchant, is no better than a Jew.

In the next scene, Jonathan joins Aristorius on his scaffold, the author effectually establishing the two merchants as professional and spiritual equals. Naturally enough, they discuss trade, speaking of a 'bargeyn' (line 269), 'bargeny' (line 273), and 'bartre' (line 276). Here, however, the commodity which is about to change hands is the Eucharist. The playwright draws the scene with considerable subtlety, with Aristorius at first refusing to stand bound in conscience 'for so lytell a walew' (line 290). When Jonathas increases the price to £40, the Christian merchant replies he wouldn't consider it even for £100. He is of course telling Jonathas the price he would be willing to accept, and the author makes sure the audience knows this by having Jonathas say in reply that 'hir ys [yo]wr askyng toolde pleyn' (line 313). The scene thus expresses the divisions within a community that a thriving commercial economy could create, as

Aristorius agrees to sell that community's holiest object and most perfect symbol: the Blessed Sacrament.

While appropriate to a successful, hardheaded merchant, Jonathas's actual interest in the Host is surprisingly intellectual.[18]

> þe beleve of thes Christen men ys false, as I wene;
> For þe beleue on a cake – me thynk yt ys onkynd.
> And all they seye how þe prest dothe ye bynd,
> And be þe myght of hys word make yt flessh and blode –
> And thus be a conceyte þe wolde make vs blynd – (lines 199–203)

There's no intrinsic anti-Christian feeling here, and Jonathas's reply to Aristorius later in the play further underscores his intellectual curiosity in the matter, even implying that he will become a Christian if the Cake indeed proves to be Jesus. For Jonathas, the turning of a 'cake' into flesh is impossible, and it is therefore unnatural for man to believe in such things. The supposed power of the priest to create this transformation merely compounds this lunacy. Unless proof is tangible, a belief can only be hearsay, which itself may be based upon nothing more than a foolish 'conceyte' of man. 'Machomet' has offered such proof in the form of tangible goods; God, so far, has offered only hearsay miracles. What the playwright perceives as the two sources of social discord, a rationalistic attitude toward religion and a materialistic accumulation of goods, are here seen to go hand in hand. Aristorius' later fears of condemnation 'For an heretyke' because he had sinned 'For couytyse of good, as a cursyd wyght' (lines 854–7) illustrate the potential connection between greedy materialism and heresy.

The playwright uses symbolic violence to embody these doubts and divisions within the community. It is almost as if the original Passion had lost its efficacy, and the miracle of transubstantiation in the Mass was not enough. When the Jews deny the Real Presence, they also deny that the Eucharist has a different status than any other purely material object. By extension, they also implicitly deny those social divisions between lay and cleric, as well as those between priest and bishop, that were an essential part of the structure of late medieval Christian society. Similarly, Aristorius' materialism threatens to invert both the social and spiritual hierarchies; the first, because his newly acquired wealth denies the worth of hereditary rank; the second, because his own importance devalues the relative status of the priesthood to that of a mere commodity.

Denial, either by a Jew or an unbelieving Christian, was often a prominent feature of stories of transformations of the Eucharist. The archetypal Host miracle was, of course, the Mass of Saint Gregory, which occurred when the saint prayed for a miracle to convince a doubting Christian that the sacramental blood and wine were indeed the body and blood of the Saviour. He was rewarded by the stunning transformation of the elevated

Host into the crucified Jesus. The doubt of the Jews is of course much more extreme than this, here carried to the point of a series of violent acts which take on something of the character of experimental science. As Malchus says of their actions, 'We wyll not spare to wyrke yt wrake,/ To prove in thys brede yf þer be eny lyfe' (lines 459–60). Each draws attention to the specific act of violence which he perpetrates upon the Host as they seize, strike, prick, punch, and buffet the Host with their daggers in an effort to reveal its substantial nature as bread.

Within the framework of the Mass, a priest consecrates the sacramental wine and bread, making them truly – and not just symbolically – the blood and body of Christ. Commentators such as Amalarius of Metz emphasized that, on one level at least, the events of the Mass were a careful re-enactment of the Passion.[19] The ritual structure of the Mass in effect contains and purifies the violence of the Passion, which is always potentially present in the consecrated Host.

Removed from the ritual of the Mass, the Host behaves in a frightening and even destructive way. The Host reacts to the stabbing by bleeding 'as yt were woode' (line 483), as Jonathas describes it. Jonathas' characterization of the bleeding Host as insane seems to point to what orthodox religious thought to be the fundamental limitation in the religious outlook of the Lollards. Reginald Pecock, for example, speaks in anxious tones of those lay people who 'wold be . . . redy forto resone, drive and labore in her vndirstonding vpon . . . maters touching þe sacrament of þe auter'.[20] Transubstantiation is, of course, mad to an entirely rational man, because it is not dependant on the evidence of the senses.

Outside of the ritual framework, violence is often taken for madness, and the playwright particularly identifies the Jews with madness in a series of actions that get progressively more violent. The madness of the Host is contagious, for when Jonathas picks it up he cannot remove it from his hand, saying how 'in woodnesse I gynne to wake!' (line 502). The Jews nail the Host to a post in an effort to separate Jonathas from the Host, but merely succeed in maiming their leader. The violence that the Jews had tried to perpetrate upon the Eucharist now rebounds upon Jonathas; the madness of the miraculous spray of blood escalates into the insanity of the tearing away of Jonathas' hand. As a result, Jonathas is 'nere masyd, [his] wytte ys gon' (line 655). They pluck out the nails and toss both the Hand and the Host into a cauldron, which boils up blood. Here again the blood seems to represent a kind of contagious madness,[21] for when Malcuus describes how 'owt of the cawdron yt begynnyth to rin' (line 675), he also talks about how 'I am so aferd I am nere woode' (line 676).

The violence of the play culminates in a veritable explosion of blood, as the Jews attempt to cook the Host, with Jonathas' hand still attached, and 'the owyn must ryve asunder and blede owt at þe cranys, and an image appere owt with woundys bledying' (line 712, s.d.). The Christ child's bleeding image reproaches the Jews, recalling the form if not the content of the Reproaches from the Cross, all with a very specific intent: 'To meue yow to my mercy' (line 740). The blood which just a moment before had seemed contagious and defiling, crying out to heaven for vengeance, now becomes a potentially purifying symbol of atonement. Christ's offered mercy accomplishes what the earlier bloodletting could not as first Jonathas and then all the Jews ask forgiveness and kneel. Jonathas in particular apologizes for his earlier actions, which he now sees as madness, lamenting that he had been 'In my wytt to be soo wood/ That I so ongoodly wyrk shuld soo gryll! [cruelly]' (lines 787–8). The 'madness' of the Jews' empirical denial of transubstantiation has passed; they have now accepted those doctrines that they had earlier thought to be unreasonable; miraculous violence has become rational proof, a divine sanction of Church doctrine.

Jesus directs them to go to 'his' priests, telling them to place themselves under the spiritual and sacramental authority of a priest. The violence is over and the atonement has been made, once again, by Christ. The blood of Christ, which had seemed so frightening before, now seems to prefigure the tears of contrition and the waters of baptism.

The play's action culminates in a procession which allows the spectators to objectively express their community of faith. Religious processions in general are 'for purposes of stimulating devotion, of recalling the blessings of God, of thanking Him for His graces, and of begging divine help'.[22] The play's procession heals the fractures within the community which had resulted in the steadily more violent effusions of blood. The Bishop seems to speak directly to the audience in a manner that involves them immediately in the devotional action of the play:

> Now, all ye peple that here are,
> I commande yow, euery man,
> On yowr feet for to goo bare,
> In the devoutest wyse that ye can. (lines 810–13)

Although in a different manner than the Host, the procession itself symbolizes the body of Christ, now with its divisions healed, and the transformation of the bleeding child back into the Host at the Bishop's words becomes a symbol both of that body and of the congregation's newly strengthened belief in the divinely sanctioned Church hierarchy. At the play's end the Presbytyr remarks on the unity of feeling that the events have inspired, how these new converts have their

> hartys stedfastly knett in on,
> Goddys lawys to kepe and hym to serue bydene,
> As faythfull Crystyanys euermore for to gone. (lines 985–7)

While the Priest addresses these words specifically to the Jews it is hard not to also see in them a reference to the new unity of belief among the spectators as well. Symbolically, at least, the sources of social tension have been effaced. The Jews now affirm Christian belief; Aristorius now renounces his wealth and promises to go on a penitential pilgrimage.

The symbolic violence in one sense functions as a manifestation of the principle of grotesque realism enunciated by Bakhtin, degrading all that is high, spiritual, ideal, and abstract to the gross material level.[23] The lowering is at once shockingly literal and positive; the playwright in effect attempts to destroy the ultimate symbol of Christian community in an attempt to reform it, in the process refuting rationalistic doubts about the doctrine of transubstantiation. The violence is of course a repetition of the paradigmatic Christian action of Christ's Passion, one that would have been constantly before the medieval community in the actions of the Mass, but here the violence is de-ritualized and given bloody form once again so that the action of the play can in effect both mirror and heal the divisions within the contemporary Suffolk community. In the final analysis, the violence of the play provides a symbolic sanction of the beliefs, ideals, and integrity of local society.

NOTES

1 '*Alors par une secret, qui estoit fait, sorti grand abondance de sang et sailloit en hault parmi ladite hostie, comme si ce fut ung enfant qui pissoit, et en fut le juif tout guste et dessaingé et faisoit moult bien son personnaige.*' Darryll Grantley, 'Producing Miracles' in *Aspects of Early English Drama*, ed. Paula Neuss (Cambridge: D. S. Brewer, 1983), p. 83.
2 W. A. Davenport, *Fifteenth-Century English Drama: The Early Moral Plays and their Literary Relations* (Totowa, NJ: Rowman and Littlefield, 1982), p. 75.
3 Clifford Davidson, 'The Realism of the York Realist', *Speculum*, 50 (1975), pp. 270–83.
4 Sister Nicholas Maltman, 'Meaning and Art in the Croxton *Play of the Sacrament*', *English Literary History*, 41 (1974), pp. 149–64.
5 Ann Eljenholm Nichols, 'The Croxton Play of the Sacrament: A Re-Reading', *Comparative Drama*, 22 (1988), pp. 117–37; Richard L. Homan, 'Devotional Themes in the Violence and Humour of the *Play of the Sacrament*', *Comparative Drama*, 20 (1986–7), pp. 327–40.
6 Norman Davis, introduction to *Non-Cycle Plays and Fragments*, Early English Text Society, Supplementary Series 2 (London: Oxford University Press, 1979), pp. lxxii–lxxv. All references to the play are to this edition.
7 Mikhail Bakhtin, *Rabelais and His World*, trans. Hélène Iswolsky (Bloomington: Indiana University Press, 1984), esp. pp. 18–29.
8 René Girard, *Violence and the Sacred*, trans. Patrick Gregory (Baltimore: Johns Hopkins University Press, 1972), pp. 20–1.

9 Mervyn James, 'Ritual, Drama and Social Body in the Late Medieval English Town', *Past and Present*, 98 (1983), p. 9.
10 *Rites of Durham*, ed. Canon Fowler, Surtees Society, 107 (Durham: Andres & Co., 1903), p. 107. Abbreviations have been silently expanded.
11 *Six English Town Chronicles*, ed. Ralph Flenley (Oxford University Press, 1911), p. 146.
12 Alan Nelson, *The Medieval English Stage* (Chicago and London: University of Chicago Press, 1974), p. 183.
13 Nichols, 'The Croxton Play of the Sacrament: A Re-Reading', pp. 117–20.
14 Cecilia Cutts, 'The Croxton Play: An Anti-Lollard Piece', *Modern Language Quarterly*, 5 (1944), p. 47.
15 John A. F. Thomson, *The Later Lollards, 1414-1520* (Oxford University Press, 1965), pp. 132–5.
16 Thomson, *The Later Lollards*, p. 137: 'In Essex [Lollardy] had been rife from the early years of the [sixteenth] century'; The archdiocese of Norwich instituted a commission to inquire into heresy on 28 February 1494, and the play surely reflects some of these local tensions. Thomson, *The Later Lollards*, p. 134. The results of this inquiry, if any, have been lost.
17 W. Tydeman, *English Medieval Theatre, 1400-1500* (London: Routledge & Kegan Paul, 1986), p. 63.
18 Tydeman, *English Medieval Theatre*, p. 62.
19 O. B. Hardison, Jr, *Christian Rite and Christian Drama in the Middle Ages* (Baltimore: Johns Hopkins University Press, 1965), esp. pp. 35–79.
20 Reginald Pecock, *The Reule of Crysten Religioun*, ed. William Cabell Greet, Early English Text Society, Original Series 171 (London: Oxford University Press, 1927), p. 95.
21 Girard, *Violence and the Sacred*, pp. 33–4: 'Spilt blood of any origin, unless it has been associated with a sacrificial act, is considered impure . . . wherever violence threatens, ritual impurity is present. When men are enjoying peace and security, blood is a rare sight. When violence is unloosed, however, blood appears everywhere – on the ground, underfoot, forming great pools. Its very fluidity gives form to the contagious upheavals to come. Blood stains everything it touches the color of violence and death.'
22 *New Catholic Encyclopedia*, vol. 11, p. 820.
23 Bakhtin, *Rabelais and His World*, p. 19.

'There must be blood': mutilation and martyrdom on the medieval stage*

JOHN SPALDING GATTON

According to the third-century Roman theologian Tertullian, 'The blood of the martyrs [was] the seed of the church.'[1] That inseminating fluid likewise engendered and freely flowed in medieval English miracle plays and French *mystères* based on the lives of the saints and on the wondrous deeds of Providence. In the name of sacred instruction and secular diversion, the Apostles were graphically stoned, stabbed, blinded, crucified, and flayed. Other holy men and women variously and vigorously had their teeth wrenched out, their breasts torn off, and their bodies scourged, shot with arrows, baked, grilled, and burned. Audiences were also treated to bestial scenes of infanticide and to broad comedies about divinely mutilated Jews. No torment was too extreme or too gory for representation, as medieval drama ignored the classical tenet, advanced by Horace, of not bringing upon the stage what should be performed behind the scenes.[2] An unequivocal direction in the late-fifteenth-century *Mystère du Vieil Testament* (*Mystery of the Old Testament*) provides a fitting epigraph for those plays of the Middle Ages that emphasized realistic violence: 'Il faut du sang' – 'There must be blood.'[3]

The full worth of spectacular acts of violence is scanted in scholarly discussions of miracle plays and *mystères*. Too often they are treated as exempla of Christian fortitude and faith but overlooked as the central feature – indeed, the essence – of the plays. Such highly theatrical, arresting stage business contributed significantly to the dramas' popularity, to their energy, and to their aesthetic whole, complementing plot, characterization, and message. Ironically, the depictions of these graphic, even gothic, horrors sanctioned not only virtuous behavior but sensationalism, voyeurism, sadism, and anti-Semitism, all in the name of Christian courage and love. Contemporary property lists, dialogue and directions in extant works, eyewitness accounts of plays in performance, as well as hypotheses founded on medieval theatrical conventions, permit reconstructions of the more striking mutilations and martyrdoms enjoyed

* A draft of this paper was read at the *Themes in Drama* International Conference held at the University of California, Riverside, in February 1989.

on English and French stages, to restore these essential visual effects to their central position within the genre.

The task of creating theatrical illusions in broad daylight fell to imaginative technicians, known in France as 'Les Maîtres des Secrets' or 'Les Maîtres des Feints' – 'The Masters of Hidden Places (Trapdoors)' or 'of Special Effects'. Their make-believe violence had to find favor with demanding, discriminating audiences versed in the ways of bloodshed and gruesome death past and present. Without and within medieval churches, saints holding the instruments of their torture and martyrdom – and even their severed body parts, dripping painted blood – stared down from arches, pictures, and stained glass; their ubiquitous relics gave them a physical presence among the faithful. In the secular arena, the public torture and execution of criminals served as both cautionary and entertaining spectacles for the masses, as in Mons, site of a number of dramatic productions, where, in the fifteenth century, citizens purchased a convicted brigand from a neighboring town so they could watch him be quartered. For sport, men competed to kill a cat nailed to a post by battering it to death with their heads, as the animal lashed out with its claws.[4] The sight of cruelty, suffering, and blood attracted rather than repelled men and women of the Middle Ages. Miracle plays and *mystères* were violent theatre for a violent era.

Some of the simplest but most disquieting acts of stage violence occur in plays depicting the Slaughter of the Innocents. Since the fifth century the Church had honored as martyrs the male infants two years old and younger ordered slain by King Herod in an attempt to kill the Christ Child. The episode appears in a half dozen English versions.[5] The handling of the central action is varied but consistently horrifying, given the ages of the victims and their manners of death. The babies are stabbed with a knife in the York text (lines 212–13); beheaded with a 'swappynge swerde', 'torn' at 'shanke *and* shulderyn', and impaled in the *Ludus Coventriae* script (lines 91–3, 103–10); and twice made to 'hop' upon the soldiers' 'speare ende[s]' in the Chester play (lines 321–4, 361–4, Latin stage directions after lines 344 and 376). A medieval window in the English church of St Peter Mancroft, Norwich, depicts such stage business: while Herod slices a baby in half, his soldiers spit infants on their swords.[6] In earlier, liturgical re-enactments of the Massacre of the Innocents, the 'babies' were in fact choir boys who died stylized deaths.[7] On the stage, dolls or dummies allowed the brutality to be realized with greater fidelity to Scripture and with more theatricality. As the plays in the English cycles might be repeated several times in one day, there may have been no messy blood spilled during the 'Massacre', even though one of the mothers in the Towneley/Wakefield play of *Herod the Great* cries that a soldier 'shedys [her] chyldys blood'; because his body is 'all to-rent', she

5 'The Massacre of the Innocents', St Peter Mancroft, Norwich

demands 'Veniance for thi blod thus spent!' (lines 344–5, 375, 390–1). Dolls fitted with easily pierced cloth bodies and detachable heads and limbs would have made for a moving, but neat, slaughter. This episode, as presented in the French *Passion* at Mons in 1501, used wooden figures, called *enfans fustifs* and *effans faissies*. According to the dialogue, one of these dolls had to be so constructed that it could be cut in half: 'Le velà trenchié tout d'un cop/ En deux pars' (lines G7808–9).[8] During a performance of the 'Massacre' in the *Passion* given on a fixed platform at Valenciennes in 1547, realism triumphed. The stage directions insist that when the Innocents are killed, blood must be seen 'issuing from their bodies' ('Item a l'occision des Innocents on voyait sortir le sang de leurs corps').[9] Cloth dummies could have held red liquid, such as paint, in sponges or in bags made of animal intestine or leather, all acceptable means of introducing stage blood into the action when the container was squeezed or slit.[10]

More repulsive incidents involving children are treated in the early fifteenth-century French *mystères* known collectively as *La Vengeance de Notre-Seigneur* (*The Vengeance of Our Lord*), which depict the destruction of Jerusalem by Titus in AD 70. During the siege of the city mothers are driven by famine to devour their offspring.[11] In *La Vengeance Jhesucrist* by Eustache Marcadé, three women agonize over the morality of this unthinkable atrocity, even as they defend its necessity (lines 12,694–831). Were such a scene of cannibalism actually to be shown, mimed business using one or more dolls with removable limbs and concealed receptacles for fake blood would again be a plausible staging method. But if verisimilitude were earnestly desired, a portion of the figures could be made of dough, appropriately shaped and baked. Given the degree of authenticity achieved by more intricate means in other scenes of violence, such a simple solution is not so fanciful.

Exaggerated violence, used as a source for black – and bigoted – humor, frequently befalls Jews in the medieval theatre. Long the object of Christian hatred, they were portrayed as the perpetrators of sacrilegious acts against the Eucharist and the Virgin Mary, and as the deserving recipients of fantastic punishments. The Croxton *Play of the Sacrament* (*c.* 1470) is the only complete and typical miracle play in English. *La Sainte Hostie* (*The Sacred Host*), a similarly plotted *mystère*, was seen in Metz in 1513 and in Laval in 1533. A spectator's lively account of the Metz production survives.[12] Both English and French plays make the Jews objects of divine sport. The plots also illustrate the early-thirteenth-century doctrine of transubstantiation, which holds that at the Consecration in the Mass, the whole substances of the bread (or host) and wine are changed into the body and blood of Christ, while retaining their outward forms. These plays even re-enact in miniature the central violence of Christ's Passion.

In *The Play of the Sacrament* and *La Sainte Hostie*, Jews, sceptical of the Christian belief in transubstantiation, obtain a consecrated host by theft or bribery. To see if it 'have eny blood', the English Jews stab 'woundys five' in it with their daggers (lines 377–80, 388 stage direction). 'Here the Ost must blede', specifies the text (line 400 stage direction). The French script provided that, through the use of '*secrets*' ('hidden places'), the wafer, when stuck with a knife, would spurt a quantity of blood into the air, as though it were, in the quaint imagery of the eyewitness, 'a pissing child' ('comme se ce fut ung enfant qui pissoit'). In each case, when the mutilation and subsequent miracles occur, the host is lying on a table, in deliberate mockery of the Last Supper (see particularly *The Play of the Sacrament*, lines 317–24). A stagehand hidden beneath the furniture could easily squeeze a bladder full of red liquid to create the desired stream.

The wafer in *La Sainte Hostie* is nailed to a post and jabbed with a spear, causing it to gush so much blood that, according to the spectator, the setting was drenched with crimson ('le lieu [fut] tout ensanglanté'). Bladders attached to pipes within the post would pump the 'blood' from under the stage or from behind a wall through holes concealed by the host, which would seem to spout abundantly.

In one fifteenth-century French script, the Jew is burned for his outrages, a frequent punishment in Continental dramas on this subject.[13] However, Jonathas, the leader of the Jews in *The Play of the Sacrament*, suffers temporary mutilation. After seizing the host, he is unable to release it, and, to the certain amusement of the Christian audience, he rushes madly about the stage in terror (line 423). To rescue him, Jonathas' friends nail the wafer to a post to which they have bound him then pull at his arm. His guilty right hand breaks off, remaining attached to the host; hand and host are then thrown into a cauldron of oil, which turns to blood (line 592 stage direction). Using his frenzy as a diversion, the actor could readily hide his real hand in his sleeve, proffering an artifical one that holds a host. Following this crude, anti-Semitic violence, Jonathas converts and is healed by a bleeding image of Christ when he thrusts his stump into the cauldron (lines 690–7 and stage direction).

Another apocryphal, anti-Semitic tale inspired English and French plays on the Burial of the Virgin Mary. Once again, the Jew for his villainy endures incredible physical punishment. In a lost play from York, the 'prince of the priests' tried to seize the body of the Virgin as the Apostles carried it to the grave; instead, his hand withered and remained attached to the coffin.[14] A similar piece, *The Assumption of the Virgin*, survives in the *Ludus Coventriae*. The High Priest sends three knights to attack the funeral procession; two of them succumb to madness and fear as they approach, but the First Knight (*Primus Princeps*) actually touches the coffin, only to have his body racked 'ful of peyne' and his hands 'fastened sore to this bere' (lines 382–90, 395–7). The fifteenth-century French saint play, *The Acts of the Apostles*, mined this story's violent potential, especially in the production given at Bourges in 1536. The Jews again attempt to prevent the Apostles from bearing the Virgin's coffin to the burial monument. Belzeray, Prince of the Jews, boldly lays his hands on it. Immediately, they break off and remain stuck to the litter; through the intercession of the Virgin, however, they are re-attached and he accepts Christianity. Artificial hands, made from gloves, cardboard, wood, or even animal skin, and fitted with hooks, would easily catch on the fabric of the pall, the actor's sleeves covering his own hands.[15] This episode is depicted in an early-fourteenth-century relief on the north façade of Notre-Dame de Paris. Its composition suggests a stage performance as its source. The mutilated Jew writhes on the ground between two groups of Apostles, while above him, fixed to the pall, can be seen his detached hands. His companion is held fast to the sacred cloth.

Non-discriminatory in its victims, the medieval theatre exploited with especially brutal energy, clinical accuracy, and abundant theatricality the ignoble treatment of holy women. Favorites on both sides of the English Channel include St Catherine and St Suzanna, both beheaded.[16] A vivid example of medieval staging generally and particularly of violence done to women in religious drama appears among the rich illustrations painted by the miniaturist Jean Fouquet for the fifteenth-century Book of Hours of Etienne Chevalier. The scene occurs in the *mystère* of *Sainte Apoline*, a French play now lost, but known from a bookseller's catalogue contemporary with Fouquet's painting.[17] Apollonia was an elderly deaconess in Alexandria burned alive during a third-century persecution. As part of her torture, her teeth were knocked or wrenched out, the episode Fouquet represented.

In the foreground of the acting area, Apollonia lies outstretched on a sloping, radiant board. Her brilliant white dress and pallid skin focus the eye on her and thus on her torments. Ropes already bind her to the plank in three places; two torturers are completing this task, feet braced against the board, bodies straining to draw her legs together. A third torturer yanks her golden hair; like his fellows, he leans backward to inflict greater pain. Their histrionic exertion is vastly out of proportion to the simple chores they perform, made easier by the submissiveness of the victim, who endures all with limp hands and blank expression. The principal torturer is armed with enormous pincers that, like the gestures, seem larger than necessary for the occasion and frighten by their very size; he prepares to extract a tooth at the command of the crowned Emperor. The juxtaposition of the torturers' broad efforts and Apollonia's absolute passivity intensifies her agony for the viewer, while pointing the moral of Christian courage, dignity, and acceptance in the face of the unbelievers' savagery.

6 'The Martyrdom of St Apollonia', Jean Fouquet, *The Hours of Etienne Chevalier*

But the incongruous elements also symbolize the sadism inherent in works of this type, which audiences obviously relished, given the numbers of martyrs' plays produced in the Middle Ages.

Witness St Barbara, the subject of at least a dozen dramas in France alone between 1448 and 1539.[18] As part of her martyrdom, her breasts are cut off on stage. The theatrical workings of this effect may be fairly conclusively deduced. Women's roles were often taken by men, a convention which would facilitate the 'mutilation'. In a performance of *The Life and Passion of St Barbara* given at Metz in 1485, the heroine was played by a young barber's assistant named Lyonard, whom the *Chronicles* of the city described as 'very handsome' and resembling 'a beautiful young girl'; he acted the role 'so thoughtfully and reverently that several people wept for pity'.[19] He could have attached to his bare chest breasts made of cardboard or a form of papier-mâché which, when 'amputated', would have likely revealed made-up areas of his skin simulating torn flesh, while effectively concealing his own nipples.

Theatrical violence in all its gruesome variety appears to best advantage in the fifteenth-century French episodic *Mystery of the Acts of the Apostles*, attributed to the brothers Simon and Arnoul Gréban. Extant is a richly detailed list of *feints* or special effects needed for a famous performance of the *Acts* in Bourges in 1536.[20] Following the book of the Bible from which it derives its title, this *mystère* (itself divided into nine books) dramatized the growth of the early Church from Pentecost through the journeys of the first Christian missionaries and on to their martyrdoms. An additional mystery, devoted to St Denis, a spiritual patron of France, was appended as Book x.

There are throughout the lengthy drama stonings, beatings, stabbings, and scourgings. In these scenes, live actors faced an arsenal of fake instruments of torture, collectively called *feints*, including painted-sponge rocks (*éponges peintes, pierres fainctes*), leather cudgels stuffed with hay (*bastons fraincts*), trick knives and swords, perhaps with retractable blades (*cousteaulx fraincts, poignards feincts*), and whips (*fleaulx fraincts*) fashioned from cloth or other light material that, when doctored with wet dye or paint, seemed to stripe and tear the actor's flesh.

For executions, actors were replaced by realistic, life-size dummies called *faulx corps, charnières*, and *décollations*. These would be straw-filled figures or mannequins first sculpted in stone (*en pierre*), then carefully copied in cardboard (*en carton*), and finally painted to resemble the actor cast in the martyr's role.[21] Trapdoors, trick furniture, curtains, suitable screening, diversions, and expert timing allowed the 'fake body' to be substituted for the actor – ideally, swiftly and imperceptibly.

The Acts of the Apostles depicts at least nine decapitations.[22] In all but two cases, the property list stipulates that a *décollation* lose its head. One

Mutilation and martyrdom on the medieval stage

technique for switching player for mannequin is indicated in a stage direction for the beheading of Croscus, King of the Wandres, in the *Mystery of St Didier* (French, fifteenth century): 'two soldiers force him to his knees, and then the trapdoor is used' ('deux soudards le font agenouiller par force, et là se fait le secret').[23] If the soldiers momentarily blocked the audience's view in shoving their victim down, the actor could drop through a trap as a false body was pushed up onto the stage in his stead.

On at least one occasion in *The Acts of the Apostles* a striking manner of performing an execution is called for: 'A false head is needed for the decapitation of Simon Magus, and Daru [the omnipresent executioner of most of the Apostles] must cut off the head of a sheep in his place' ('Fault une teste faincte pour une decollacion de Symon Magus, et fault que Daru descolle ung mouton au lieu de luy' (Book VII).[24] It is not clear if the sheep is alive to begin with, though likely not, or attired in a costume duplicating that of Simon Magus, but the animal certainly replaces the character before the blade falls, to the delight of an audience desirous of seeing real steel slice through real flesh, of any sort, to produce a bloody spectacle. The 'false head' would then be produced from behind the block or another hiding place and exhibited as the magician's.

In Book VI, St Matthew undergoes a gory portion of his martyrdom. To blind him, augers are bored into his eye sockets, extracting the eyeballs. The list of *feints* describes, if not all its workings, at least the basic secret of the mutilation. Two fake augers were constructed to contain artificial eyes which emerged from the tools, as if they had been extracted from the saint's face ('Fault avoir deux tarières fainctes pour crever les yeulx a St Mathieu, et fault des yeux faincts procedans dedans lesd. tarieres').[25]

A novel type of violent spectacle, appealing to the nose as well as to the eyes, distinguishes Book VI. St Barnabas, companion of St Paul, is tied to a cart wheel and burned alive. If the wheel were placed over a trapdoor, just as a stake is arranged elsewhere in the play, the requisite wood and executioners would help mask its opening as well as the switch of live and fake victims.[26] The illusion of burning a real person is heightened in this scene by stuffing the required fake body 'full of bones and entrails', as dictated by the property list: 'fauldra ung corps fainct plain d'os et de trippes'.[27] As the apparent internal organs of St Barnabas spill onto the blaze, the stench of roasting flesh complements the sight of the body being consumed by the flames.

A last clever *feint* in Book VI makes possible the martyrdom of St Bartholomew, who was flayed alive. The property list indicates that the actor of Bartholomew is laid on a table that turns ('Sera mis sainct Bartholmy sur une table tornisse'), and that hidden underneath ('dessoubz') is a mannequin, variously called 'ung nud' ('a nude') and 'une carnacion' ('a flesh-colored figure'), which appears to be a naked human body.[28] The actor is briefly covered with a sheet; at that instant, the directions state that the table must 'secretly' be flipped over ('en le couvrant dun linceul fault secretement tourner la table').[29] The man either remains concealed under the table or slips down a trap, while the fake body, now on top, is flayed, strips of cloth 'skin' (though not specified in the property list) perhaps being peeled from the dummy to enhance the effect.

With the coming of the Renaissance and the Reformation, the miracle play fell from favor on either side of the Channel. The genre did not, however, vanish. As the most widespread type of medieval religious drama, the saint play continued to appear on English and French stages, with violence still an essential element.[30] *The Virgin Martyr*, by Thomas Dekker and Philip Massinger, and dating from about 1620, is the only extant English martyrdom play treating an authentic Catholic saint.[31] Its subject is St Dorothea of Caesaria, martyred in the fourth century for refusing to marry and to worship idols. The play retains a number of violent effects popular on the medieval stage. Bound to a pillar, Dorothea is repeatedly beaten with cudgels and bats. Theophilus, 'a zealous persecutor of the Christians' ('The Actors [sic] Names'), remarks, with a nod toward earlier theatrical properties, that, although the torturing devices are 'not counterfeit', 'her skin is not scar'd' (IV.ii.62–106). In IV.iii, proclaiming with quiet dignity that 'She liu'd a virgin, and a virgin dies', Dorothea has '*Her head strucke off*' in an unspecified manner (line 179 and stage direction). Theophilus is converted to Christianity by her example. He is tortured on stage, but the rack leaves his breast 'vntorne' and 'burning pinsors' – 'their heat' perhaps red paint – cool when touched to his skin (V.ii.187–213).

In France, the saint play, as reinterpreted by Pierre Corneille, spoke with renewed power and fresh purpose, but without visible bloodshed. *Polyeucte* (c. 1642), one of Corneille's great tragedies on the conflict between love and duty, was inspired by the third-century soldier-martyr Polyeuctus.[32] The neo-classical convention of *bienséance* relegated violent actions to the wings. Polyeucte must therefore be decapitated off stage for his Christian beliefs; his wife and father-in-law, converted by his noble example in life and death, are burned alive after the play ends.

American playwright John Pielmeier offered a modern analogue to the medieval saint play in his 1982 Broadway drama *Agnes of God*. Its impetus was his uncertainty about the existence of saints and miracles today, or ever.[33] His title character is an innocent, young nun who gave birth in the convent to a baby of uncertain – but possibly supernatural – parentage, and which is later found murdered. In a scene of intense physical and emotional violence, the hypnotized Agnes relives the labor process (II.ii):

... I feel as if I've eaten glass ... I have to throw up. (*She tries*) I can't.

Mutilation and martyrdom on the medieval stage 89

(*Contraction*) It's glass! One of the sisters has fed me glass!... (*Contraction*) Oh no, please. Please. I don't want this to happen. I don't want it... (*Contraction*) Oh God. Oh my God... (*Screams and contraction*) Stay in! Please stay in! (*Several and final contractions*).

Twice in the play she experiences a partial stigmata. In I.v, she '*presents a hand wrapped in a bloody handkerchief*', explaining, 'It started this morning, and I can't get it to stop.' On the second, more graphic occasion (II.iv), she exclaims, 'my God, my God, I'm bleeding, I'M BLEEDING! (*She is bleeding from the palms of her hands*)'. Agnes stands with her hands parallel to the floor, then tilts them toward the audience, allowing the pooled blood to drip onto the stage. At the end of the scene she '*stretches out her hands like a statue of the Lady, showing her bleeding palms*'. To produce the stigmata, modern Masters of Special Effects strapped onto the actress's back a radio-controlled pneumatic device connected to plastic tubes, hidden by the sleeves of her habit, running to the center of her palms.[34] Sent to a hospital, Agnes stops eating and dies.

Pielmeier concluded that 'our determined search for *any* solution today has eliminated from our lives the mystery and wonder of the universe around us'.[35] But the quest for answers to spiritual questions undertaken by the writer and his characters in this contemporary variation on the miracle play follows the crimson path blazed and trod by its centuries-old theatrical ancestors, with its familiar and popular horrific landmarks of physical agony, infanticide, mutilation, and death. *Agnes of God*, like its predecessors, owes certain of its drama and attraction not only to its religious theme but to its spectacular violence. The medieval maxim still obtains: 'Il faut du sang' – 'There must be blood.'

NOTES

1 Tertullian, *Apologeticus*, section 50: 13. The translation is traditional.
2 Horace, *Ars Poetica*, trans. H. Rushton Fairclough (Cambridge, MA: Harvard University Press, 1926), lines 182–8.
3 *Mystère du Vieil Testament*, quoted in Gustave Cohen, *L'Histoire de la mise en scène dans le théâtre religieux français du Moyen Age* (Paris: Honoré Champion, 1951), p. 152.
4 See Andrew McCall, *The Medieval Underworld* (London: Hamish Hamilton, 1979), pp. 72–6, and Barbara Tuchman, *A Distant Mirror : The Calamitous 14th Century* (1978; New York: Ballantine Books, 1979), p. 135.
5 Lucy Toulmin Smith, ed., *York Plays* (Oxford: Clarendon Press, 1885); K. S. Block, ed., *Ludus Coventriae, or The Play Called Corpus Christi*, EETS, no. 120 (London: Oxford University Press, 1922); R. M. Lumiansky and David Mills, eds., *The Chester Mystery Cycle*, EETS, nos. 3, 9 (London: Oxford University Press, 1974); A. C. Cawley, ed., *The Wakefield Pageants in the Towneley Cycle* (Manchester University Press, 1958); F. J. Furnivall, ed., *The Digby Plays*,

EETS no. 70 (London: Oxford University Press, 1896, rpt 1930, 1967); Hardin Craig, ed., *Two Coventry Corpus Christi Plays*, EETS, no. 87 (London: Oxford University Press, 1902, 2nd edn, 1957).
6 The window is reproduced in M. D. Anderson, *Drama and Imagery in English Medieval Churches* (Cambridge University Press, 1963), plate 22b.
7 Karl Young, *The Drama of the Medieval Church* (Oxford: Clarendon Press, 1933), vol. 2, pp. 102–24.
8 In Gustave Cohen, *Le Livre de Conduite du Régisseur . . . pour le Mystère de la Passion joué à Mons en 1501* (Paris: Honoré Champion, 1925), pp. 103 and n. 13, 104; also 509 and n. 7. Cohen reprints the complete text of the Mons *Passion*.
9 In Louis Petit de Julleville, *Les Mystères*, 2 vols. (Paris: Librairie Hachette, 1880), vol. 2, p. 155.
10 For the pageant of St Thomas à Becket given at Canterbury in the sixteenth century, money was allotted for 'a new leder bag for the blode'; see E. K. Chambers, *The Mediaeval Stage*, 2 vols. (Oxford: Clarendon Press, 1903), vol. 2, p. 345. Chambers also records (vol. 1, p. 183) the use in Italy of a bladder filled with stage blood. Accounts of sponges containing red liquid to simulate wounds appear in Raymond Lebègue, *Le Mystère des Actes des Apôtres* (Paris: Honoré Champion, 1929), p. 98, n. 3; see also Lee Simonson, *The Stage Is Set* (New York: Dover, 1946; rpt of 1932 edn), pp. 194–5, 222–5.
11 Petit de Julleville, *Les Mystères*, vol. 2, pp. 451–60, esp. 459; Stephen K. Wright, *The Vengeance of Our Lord: Medieval Dramatizations of the Destruction of Jerusalem* (Toronto: Pontifical Institute of Mediaeval Studies, 1989), pp. 22, 133, 138, 155. Among other texts, Wright appends microfiche reproductions of *La Vengance Jhesucrist* by Eustache Marcadé, as edited by Andrée Marcelle Fourcade Kail (dissertation, Tulane University, 1955) and Adele Cornay (dissertation, Tulane University, 1957).
12 *The Croxton Play of the Sacrament* in *Specimens of the Pre-Shaksperean Drama*, ed. John M. Manly (1897; New York: Dover, 1967), vol. 1, pp. 239–76. *La Sainte Hostie* (extracts and eyewitness account) in Petit de Julleville, *Les Mystères*, vol. 2, pp. 103–4, 574–6.
13 Petit de Julleville, *Les Mystères*, vol. 2, p. 459.
14 Anderson, *Drama and Imagery*, p. 138.
15 Auguste-Théodore de Girardot, ed., *Mystère des Actes des Apôtres représenté à Bourges en avril 1536* (Paris: Librairie Archéologique de Victor Didron, 1854), p. 15. English examples of this story in wall-paintings and stained glass show the Jew intact and hanging by his hands from the bier; see Anderson, *Drama and Imagery*, p. 138, who unimaginatively views the effect of severed hands as 'difficult' to produce on the stage.
16 Petit de Julleville, *Les Mystères*, vol. 2, pp. 181–5; Clifford Davidson, 'The Middle English Saint Play and Its Iconography', in *The Saint Play in Medieval Europe*, ed. Clifford Davidson (Kalamazoo: Medieval Institute Publications, Western Michigan University, 1986), pp. 45–52.
17 Jean Fouquet, *The Hours of Etienne Chevalier* (New York: George Braziller, 1971), plate 45; Petit de Julleville, *Les Mystères*, vol. 2, p. 629.

In the background of the Fouquet illustration, six small elevated *mansions* or stages, crowded with actors, musicians, and properties, are arranged around

parts of the irregular oval of the *platea* or acting area. The blue-robed figure standing to the right, near the feline or ursine Hell-mouth, is identifiable as the *régisseur*, or stage manager, who carries the script from which he cues the performers or conducts the music with his staff of office.
18 Petit de Julleville, *Les Mystères*, vol. 2, p. 181, reproduces a list of performances.
19 Ibid., vol. 2, p. 48 (my translation). A year later Lyonard played St Catherine but with less success as his voice had begun to break.
20 Girardot, *Mystère des Actes des Apôtres*, pp. 9–27. See too James Hashim, 'Notes Toward a Reconstruction of the *Mystère des Actes des Apôtres* as Represented at Bourges, 1536', *Theatre Research*, 12.1 (1972), pp. 29–73.
21 See Cohen, *Mise en Scène*, pp. 148–50; Petit de Julleville, *Les Mystères*, vol. 2, p. 132; Peter Meredith and John E. Tailby, eds., *The Staging of Religious Drama in Europe in the Later Middle Ages: Texts and Comments in English Translation*, Early Drama, Art, and Music Monograph Series 4 (Kalamazoo: Medieval Institute Publications, Western Michigan University, 1983), pp. 110–13.
22 Those beheaded include St James the Greater and Josias, Book IV; St Matthew, Book VI; Simon Magus, Book VII; Sts Martinian and Processus, and St Paul, Book IX; Luby and St Rusticus, Book X.
23 Petit de Julleville, *Les Mystères*, vol. 1, p. 400.
24 Girardot, *Mystère des Actes des Apôtres*, p. 22.
25 Ibid., p. 16.
26 For the immolation of Cidrat, Titon, and Aristarcus in Book IX, the stake, surrounded by bundles of wood, is set on a trap; in place of the actors, three 'fake bodies' are attached to the post and burned ('Fault ung pilier près Paradis . . . et sera assis led. pillier sur une trappe et mis trois corps faincts en leurs lieux attachés aud. pilier qui sera environné de fagots'); Girardot, *Mystère des Actes des Apôtres*, p. 23.
27 Ibid., p. 18.
28 'Un nud' is also required for the crucifixion of St Philip in Book VI, as is *'une carnation'* for that of St Andrew in Book VII; see Girardot, *Mystère des Actes des Apôtres*, pp. 19, 21, respectively.
29 Ibid., p. 19.
30 For a discussion of plays, complete and fragmentary, on such historical English martyrs as Sir Thomas More, Thomas Lord Cromwell, and Sir John Oldcastle, see John Wasson, 'The Secular Saint Plays of the Elizabethan Era' in *The Saint Play in Medieval Europe*, ed. Davidson, pp. 241–60.
31 *The Virgin Martyr* in *The Dramatic Works of Thomas Dekker*, ed. Fredson Bowers (Cambridge University Press, 1958), vol. 3, pp. 365–480.
32 Pierre Corneille, *Polyeucte* in *Oeuvres complètes*, ed. André Stegmann (Paris: Editions du Seuil, 1963), pp. 289–313.
33 'John Pielmeier on Creating *Agnes of God*', in the unpaginated programme for the New York production, which opened at the Music Box Theatre, 30 March 1982. John Pielmeier, *Agnes of God* (Garden City, NY: Nelson Doubleday, 1982).
34 Telephone interview with John Pielmeier, 5 March 1989.
35 'John Pielmeier'.

Mixed feelings about violence in the Corpus Christi plays*

RICHARD L. HOMAN

Violent activity on stage may inspire different emotions depending on its significance. In this regard, violent activities are no different from any other class of activities. An erotic act, for instance, may inspire bliss or loathing or satirical laughter; so too, with violent acts. The climax of David Rabe's *Streamers* inspires something akin to the pity and terror supposed to attach to Greek tragedy, because the deaths with which the play ends are both unjust and inevitable. Other, equally bloody scenes affect an audience differently. In melodrama, joy comes from seeing a truly despicable villain get what is coming to him or her. We say yes to violence when it seems to re-establish a moral order; we are repelled by violence when it signals collapse into moral chaos as in horror films or Jacobean tragedies. On the other hand, as centuries of slapstick have shown, pain can be funny. The feelings of the audience during a violent scene depend as much on the context in which it occurs as on the quality of the violence itself.

Violence in English plays of the fifteenth century has long puzzled modern interpreters, perhaps because we have little understood its significance for the original audience. What, for instance, are we to make of the Crucifixion play from the York cycle, one of the four surviving collections of Corpus Christi plays? Four soldiers come onto the stage and one reminds the others how they are charged by law to put 'this fool' to death. They will be rewarded if they do it well, and punished if they do it poorly. 'Thanne to þis werke us muste take heede,/ So that oure wirking be noght wronge,' says the first soldier.[1]

As they start stretching and nailing, the first soldier calls out, 'Sir knyghtis, saie, howe wirke we nowe?' (line 97). They report that Christ seems to fit the pre-drilled holes and the nails seem to be holding pretty well. Yet, after one hand is nailed, they turn their attention to the other and find, 'It fails a foote and more!/ The senuous are so gonne inne' (lines 107–8). The first nail has pulled the sinews of Christ's hand into the nail-

---

* A draft of this paper was read at the *Themes in Drama* International Conference held at the University of California, Riverside, in February 1989.

hole so far that his other hand now will not reach the other pre-drilled hole.

This leads to an argument. Fourth soldier says somebody drilled the hole in the wrong place. Third soldier says somebody must have measured wrong. First soldier has a solution: attach a rope to the loose arm and stretch him. They do so and get the other hand nailed, but then find the same problem with the feet. So, they tie the rope to Christ's legs, and all pull together until he is long enough to reach the hole.

Once they have him securely nailed, they pause to admire their handiwork, and notice how much the stretching has increased Christ's suffering. Fourth soldier says, 'I wille goo saye to oure soveraines/ Of all this werkis howe we have wrought' (lines 151–2). Their psychology here is quite realistic: instead of admitting to themselves that they have botched the job so far, they rationalize that perhaps it was better to do it this way after all.

Next, says the first soldier, they must get him to the top of the hill. They can barely lift the cross and its victim together, and must stop to rest halfway up. It never occurs to them that it would have been easier to let Christ walk to the top of the hill, perhaps carrying the cross himself, and do the nailing up there. Now, says the first soldier, they must raise up the cross and stand it in the mortise which has been prepared. Fourth soldier suggests that they drop it into the mortise with a jolt to pay this fellow back for giving them such a heavy load to carry. They do, and notice that this causes Christ more pain than anything so far. Then, the third soldier notices the cross is wobbling. It seems the mortise is too wide – more shoddy craftsmanship. The first soldier suggests they drive wedges into the mortise around the base of the cross, and, indeed, this stabilizes it.

The first soldier then speaks to Jesus. 'Saye, sir, howe likes thou nowe/ This werke we have wrought?' (lines 249–50). Christ speaks as much to the audience as to the soldiers, asking them to 'fully feele nowe .../ If any mourning may be meete/ Or mischeve mesured unto mine' (lines 256–8). Christ goes on to pray to his Father, 'Forgiffis thes men that dois me pine. What thay wirke wotte they noght' (lines 260–1).

At first glance, it would seem that the York Realist, as scholars have named the anonymous author, has turned the Crucifixion into a slapstick farce, fit to be performed by clowns. Yet, I doubt that the original audience laughed at the difficulties with which the soldiers do their work. The key to the play is Christ's line, 'What they wirke wotte they noght.' The playwright has Crist saying 'They know not what they work' at the end of a play which has been mostly about work. The play creates dramatic irony: the soldiers do not see their work as anything more than a job of carpentry. They are tragically blind to the spiritual implications of what they do and, like all humanity, are in for a rude awakening in the final pageant, Doomsday. The violence done to Christ in this play would have inspired pity for the ignorance of the doers – especially so, considering that the soldiers are doing the kind of skilled labour performed by members of the craft guilds who in fact staged these plays.

In a chapter entitled 'The Passion and Resurrection in Play and Game' in his book, *The Play Called Corpus Christi*, V. A. Kolve describes a similar strategy of distancing the perpetrators of violence from the significance of their actions.[2] He notes the tasks as games or jokes. Thus, as in Luke 22: 63–5, Christ is blindfolded and beaten, but in the plays the action turns into 'a common children's game called "papse" in the York cycle, "whele and pylle" in the *Ludus Coventriae*, and "a new play of yoyll" (. . . [or] Hot Cockles) in Towneley' (Kolve, p. 185). Kolve demonstrates that the merry-making written into the scenes of torture was not designed to elicit joy or ridicule from the audience, but to dramatize the ignorance of the tortureres. They are not sadistic, but rather foolishly distracted by silly games. Thus the scenes of graphic violence had for the original audience a thematic significance not immediately apparent to us.

Of course, the Passion is not the only violent event dramatized in the cycles. All four extant cycles include two other explicitly violent episodes which were understood to prefigure Christ's death: Cain and Abel, and the Slaughter of the Innocents. The violence in these plays inspires varied and conflicting feelings, and does so through aesthetic strategies as ingenious as those of the Passion plays.

The Wakefield Master de-emphasizes violence in dramatizing the first murder, and concentrates instead on the character of the murderer. Like most farmers, Cain has a hard time coaxing a living from the earth. When his brother Abel invites him to offer sacrifice to God, Cain replies, 'What gifys God the[e] to rose him so?/ Me gifys him noght bot soro and wo.'[3] Cain's life is so hard, he feels he has little to be thankful for. At the altar, Abel advises Cain that God would look favourably on his offering if he would tithe. Cain blames Abel's nagging for the failure of his offering, and, in a rage, kills him. The violence is brief and unsensational. The play ends with Cain hitching up his team and starting back to work. The murder is a consequence of Cain's 'wanhope', that is, his failure to believe that the Lord will provide.

While this is a sobering theme, our emotional reaction to it is complicated by the Wakefield Master's characterization of Cain as persistently and imaginatively vulgar. When Abel enters with a greeting, Cain replies, 'Come kis mine ars!' (line 59). When Abel invites him to make an offering, Cain replies, 'Hold thy tong, yit I say,/ Even ther the good wife strokid the hay!' (lines 87–8). Some in the audience might find Cain humorous; some, offensive; still others, pitiable.

Cain's cursing may seem like realism when he is talking to Abel, but when God speaks to Cain, and Cain replies with vulgarity, it becomes blasphemy. This lack of respect for God is foreshadowed in the behavior of Cain's servant, Garcio. When Cain strikes him for doing his work badly, Garcio strikes him back. His insubordination would have shocked an audience who saw this world and the next as one, continuous hierarchy. This view of Cain was not peculiar to the Wakefield Master. In the York cycle, God sends an angel after the murder to ask 'Where hais thowe done thy broder dere?' (line 83), Cain strikes the Angel over the head, an extraordinary example of physical conflict with a supernatural character.

To further the characterization of Cain as one who subverts the order of the world, the Wakefield Master allows Cain to challenge the very conventions of the play in which he is a character. After Cain's offering fails, God rebukes him. In reply, Cain makes an apparent reference to the conditions of performance:

> Why, who is that hob over the wall?
> We! who was that that piped so small?
> Com, go we hens, for perels all.
> God is out of his wit! (lines 297–300)

Apparently, God's speeches were delivered from off stage, or from behind some 'wall', and the audience accepted the disembodied voice as the voice of God. By drawing attention to this convention, Cain threatens the very existence of the play-world in which he exists.

Such freewheeling anarchy usually provokes laughter, and the Wakefield Master may have used that laughter to trap the audience into complicity with Cain. By the end of the play, Cain's subversion of the order of things becomes more disturbing than funny when he refuses God's direct offer of mercy. In this play about the first murder, the playwright creates horror, not through explicit violence, as in the Passion plays, but through the nihilist humor of the murderer.

Some surviving dramatizations of the Slaughter of the Innocents use similar characterizations as well as explicit violence to move the audience: the plays from Chester, Wakefield and from the Digby manuscript call for explicit violence, and all surviving versions of this episode set forth a King Herod who has a lot in common with the Wakefield Master's Cain. Much has been written about the character of Herod. His ranting and raving apparently sustained his popularity, since Hamlet advises a player not to 'out-Herod Herod'. Like Cain, Herod is energetic and vulgar in his manner of speaking, and given to slapstick violence as he whacks his soldiers on the head to make them obey; and his ridiculously inflated boasts, with which each of the surviving plays begins, must have been entertaining.

Also, like Cain, Herod subverts the order of the world, although his mandate comes directly from scripture. He is the king who attempts to kill the King of Kings in order to reign unchallenged. While Herod usually appears ridiculous at the beginning of the play, after the slaughter, he becomes, in one way or another, a figure of horror. The Wakefield Master gives him a tirade in which he laughs so hard he wheezes while contemplating the flood of children's blood he has unleashed (lines 471–2). In Chester, he discovers that one of the children killed was his own son; he goes mad, dies and is dragged off to hell. As one critic has written, 'the unique force and dramatic effect of the role are rooted in the tension and interaction of the horrible and the comic'.[4]

The same might be said for the scenes of killing in some of the plays of the Slaughter of the Innocents, though not in all: in the York play, the confrontation between the soldiers and the mothers of the children is brief; the play concerns itself mostly with Herod; the N-Town follows Joseph and Mary's flight simultaneously, and switches back to find the killing already done. Yet, in the other three surviving plays the scene of killing is staged graphically and with varying claims on the emotions of the audience.

The Wakefield Master arranges the scene as a series of three murders. The first soldier approaches the first woman with mock courtesy: 'Dame, think it not ill,/ Thy knafe if I kill' (lines 330–1). The woman struggles with the soldier through a sharp exchange before he kills her child. The sequence ends with the woman's six-line lament. The second encounter intensifies the action. The second woman has a long speech of protest, indicating physical attack on the soldier, and a nine-line lament. In the third sequence, the soldier kills the child almost immediately, and the third woman, after a brief outcry proceeds to enact the vengeance which the first two have invoked in their laments. The first and second women join in, but the soldiers drive them away. Only after the women leave the stage do the knights begin boasting. The Wakefield play begins and ends with Herod's ridiculous posturing, but the central scene, with its passionate laments, evokes pure pity and terror.

By contrast, the Chester play gives this episode a different feeling through its characterization of the women and its sequence of action. Here the emphasis is less on the laments and more on the conflict between the women and the soldiers. The two soldiers greet the two women with insults and threats, and the women give as good as they get. The first woman returns an insult, calling one soldier a 'scabd bitch'.[5] The second woman returns threats by saying: 'Be thou so hardy, I thee behet,/ to handle my sonne that is so sweete,/ this distaff and thy head shall meete' (lines 301–4). The distaff, a cleft wooden pole about three feet long for spinning flax by hand, was already in the fifteenth century symbolic of women's work and women's authority (OED).

The soldiers renew their threats with grim irony. 'Dame, thy sonne, in good fay,/ he must of me learne a play:/ he must hop, or I goe away,/ upon my speare ende' (lines 321–4). The second woman makes good her threat: 'But yet wroken I wil be:/ hae here one, two, and three' (lines 333–4), apparently striking him as she says this. When the child of the first woman is killed, she has a speech of sixteen lines, only three of which lament the death of the child. The rest of the speech is combative:

> Have thou this! thow foule harlott!
> and thou knight to make a knott,
> And one buffet with this boote
> thou shalt haue to boot.
> And thou this, and thou this!
> though you both shyte and pisse,
> and if you think we do amiss,
> goe, buskes you to moote! (lines 353–60)

When the second soldier threatens the second child, the second woman replies, 'Nay! freak, thou shalt fayle,/ my child thou shalt not assayle,/ he hath II holes under the tayle,/ kyss and thou may assay!' (lines 365–8). The soldier does not believe the woman's claim that the child is female, and thus exempt from Herod's order to kill all male children under two years of age.

This central scene of the Chester play gives so little attention to the women's grief, that its emotional impact must have been very different from that of the Wakefield play. The discovery that the women are as violent and vulgar as the soldiers themselves may have had comic overtones, but would also have suggested a world gone awry, as does the behavior of Garcio, Cain's servant in the Wakefield play. The feeling of this scene may also have been meant as a contrast to the lofty tones of the play's simultaneous action in which Angelus guides Joseph and Mary with the Christ Child to safety.

In the play of the Slaughter of the Innocents from the Digby manuscript, those distaffs again figure prominently; but in this instance there is no doubt that a comic effect was intended and taken, because of the presence of Watkin.[6] This play opens with Herod's usual boasts and commands to his knights. Then, Watkin, a messenger boy approaches Herod asking to be made a knight. His request is laced with bloodcurdling threats. Herod promises him knighthood if he accompanies the knights on their present errand and proves himself. Watkin replies that he is willing to kill children, but is afraid of their mothers' distaffs. Under Herod's scorn, Watkin reasserts his merciless resolve, but says he will try to take the children when their mothers are not around.

In the encounter, the women defy the knight's threats, but not in the vulgar, scornful manner of the women in the Chester play. Here, the replies are poignant.

Prima mulier. ffye on you traitours of cruell tormentrye,
  wiche with your swerdes of mortall violens,
Secunda mulier. Our yong children, that can no socour but crie,
  wyll slee and devoure in ther Innocens. (lines 297–300)

When Watkin adds to his threats, the first woman replies, 'ffye upon the, coward, of the I will not faile/ to dubbe the knyght with my rokke rounde!' (lines 309–10). 'Rokke' is another word for distaff.

The children are killed simultaneously, and the mothers' call for vengeance is tinged with sorrow:

> And a very myscheff mut come them a-monge
> wherso-euer thei be come or goon,
> ffor thei have kylled my yong sone Iohn. (lines 319–21)

Watkin rebukes the mothers and there follows twenty lines of verbal jousting before the women beat Watkin and he is rescued by the soldiers.

There are many examples of late-medieval English plays whose apparent humor has been exposed as an illusion, seen only by the modern reader who is ignorant of the assumptions of the original audience. The Passion plays discussed here are such examples.[7] However, there is no denying that the Chester and the Digby plays focus more on ridicule of the soldiers than on the terror of the killings and the sorrow of the mothers. The vulgarity of the women in the Chester play may have brought laughter from some in the audience, and their attack on the soldiers with distaffs may have played as a comic reversal. On the other hand, their ferocity may have made anger the dominant emotion of the scene, where sorrow is the dominant emotion in the Wakefield play.

In the Digby 'Killing of the Children', there is no question that the author has attempted to mix broad comedy with profound grief. Watkin's admitted fear of the women amounts to self-ridicule. In this, he seems a forerunner of Falstaff. His mention of the distaffs before they are ever seen amounts to a comic set-up. Yet the speeches of the women have some of the nobler feeling of those in the Wakefield play. Add to this Herod's speech following the killings, in which he is overwhelmed by emotion, rends his garment, bursts his heart and dies, as well as the play's stately ending in which Joseph and Mary bring their child to Simeon, and it is clear that an extraordinary range of emotions is attempted in this play of only 566 lines.

Violence on stage may inspire various emotions, but in the English plays from the fifteenth century violence frequently inspires conflicting emotions within a single scene. This taste for mixed emotions may have grown out of devotional attitudes which became popular during the fourteenth century, partly through the influence of the Franciscan order. Meditations and devotional art focused increasingly on Christ's physical suffering. The conflicting emotions inspired by this movement are exemplified in the *Arma Christi* theme, in which the instruments used to torture Christ – the scourge, the nails, the crown of thorns, etc. – are arranged on a heraldic shield as his coat of arms.[8] The ironic message here is that the weapons which destroyed Christ physically are the weapons by which he conquered sin and death. Christians in this period seem to have become acutely aware that the violence done to their spiritual leader was their ultimate cause for rejoicing.

NOTES

1 *York Plays*, ed. Lucy Toulmin Smith (New York: Russell and Russell, 1885), p. 350, lines 25–6. Subsequent references to plays in the York Cycle are from this edition and are included parenthetically in the text.
2 (Stanford University Press, 1966). Subsequent references included parenthetically in the text.
3 *Medieval Drama*, ed. David Bevington (Boston: Houghton Mifflin, 1975), p. 278, lines 95–6. Subsequent references in the text to this play and to the Wakefield 'Slaughter of the Innocents' are to this edition.
4 Robert Weimann, *Shakespeare and the Popular Tradition in the Theater*, ed. Robert Schwartz (Baltimore and London: Johns Hopkins University Press, 1978), p. 68.
5 *The Chester Plays*, ed. Hermann Deimling, EETS, extra series no. 62 (London: Oxford University Press, 1862), I, line 297. Subsequent references in text.
6 *The Digby Plays*, ed. F. J. Furnivall, EETS, extra series no. 70 (London: Oxford University Press, 1896). References in text.
7 The *Play of the Sacrament* is another example. See Richard L. Homan, 'Devotional Themes in the Violence and Humor of the *Play of the Sacrament*', *Comparative Drama*, 20 (Winter, 1986–87), pp. 327–40.
8 Gertrude Schiller, *Iconography in Christian Art*, trans. Janet Seligman (Greenwich, CT: New York Graphic Society, 1972), vol. 2, pp. 190–1.

Shakespearean violence: a preliminary survey*

JONAS BARISH

We live, as we are often told, in a violent age, and it would seem that one of the things about the Elizabethans and Jacobeans that make us feel close to them is their own fascination with violence. As long ago as 1940 (in *Elizabethan Revenge Tragedy, 1587–1642*) Fredson Bowers cited numerous instances of violent behavior in society at large – of private duels fought in disregard of the laws forbidding them, of grudge assassinations performed by hired ruffians, of the use of lingering poison and other stealthy forms of murder for disposing of one's enemies – to demonstrate that the playwrights who brought violence onto the stage were not being merely melodramatic, not merely catering to the appetite of their audiences for bloody deeds remote from their experience, but realistic as well.[1] In both epochs we find not only the omnipresent fact of violence, but a kind of fixation on it, extending not only to violence itself but also to the representation of violence. Something about physical injuries inflicted on human bodies seems to exercise a kind of mesmerism, both over Shakespeare's generation and our own. A hasty survey, therefore, a provisional taxonomy, of Shakespearean violence may not be out of order on this occasion.

By violence I mean (following the dictionary) the inflicting of physical pain or injury by one person on another, often with the implication of excessive force, so that one might think of poisoning someone's drink as less violent than shooting or stabbing him, even if the end-result – death – were the same in both cases. Such violence, in Shakespeare as in other playwrights, may occur either before our eyes in stage action, or be reported as offstage action, or appear in the language alone. To me the most horrifying moment of violence in Shakespeare might well be Lady Macbeth's boast of what she would be capable of if bound by an oath: 'I have given suck, and know/ How tender 'tis to love the babe that milks me;/ I would, while it was smiling in my face,/ Have pluck'd my nipple from his boneless gums,/ And dash'd the brains out, had I sworn as you/

---

* A draft of this paper was read at the *Themes in Drama* International Conference held at the University of California, Riverside, in February 1989.

Have done to this' (I.vii.54–9).² Perhaps even more repellent, because we not only hear it in the language but see it performed, is the quenching of Gloucester's sight, in *Lear*. Lady Macbeth horrifies us because of the betrayal of innocence, helplessness, and trust involved, coupled with the appalling kind of *agency* whereby the smiling infant becomes the weapon of its own destruction, the wall or stony earth no more than an indifferent auxiliary. The cruelty against Gloucester makes us shrink because it puts us so intimately into the skin of the victim; Cornwall's language – 'Out, vild jelly!' (*Lear*, III.vii.83) – makes us feel our own eyes being enucleated on the point of his sword.

Compared to his predecessors, however, Shakespeare seems not much addicted to violence. He rarely goes in for bizarre or outlandish forms of it, as do a number of earlier and later playwrights. He has little to set alongside such things as the flaying of Sisamnes ('with a false skin'), the shooting of the young son of Praxaspes, followed by the cutting out of his heart and its presentation to the grieving father, in Preston's *Cambyses*; Hieronimo's biting out of his own tongue and spitting it on the ground in order not to reveal the secret he has sworn to keep – an act of madness, of course – in *The Spanish Tragedy* (here I think we should imagine the Elizabethan actor as spitting out a bit of raw calf's liver); the running against the bars of his cage so as to dash out his brains by Bajazeth the Turkish Emperor and then his wife in Marlowe's *Tamburlaine*; the writhing of the wicked Barabas in the cauldron of boiling oil in *The Jew of Malta*; the thrusting of the red-hot spit into the anus of the king in *Edward II*, if this sickening threat is indeed meant to be carried out before our eyes.

Shakespeare, as I say, on the whole avoids such perversities and bizarreries; even his most sadistic torturers rarely gloat over their own cruelty. His most frequent episodes of violence involve swordplay, often duels between mortal enemies: Richmond vs. Richard III, Mercutio vs. Tybalt, Romeo vs. Tybalt, Hal vs. Hotspur, Hamlet vs. Laertes, Edgar vs. Oswald, Edgar vs. Edmund, Macduff vs. Macbeth, Guiderius vs. Cloten, Palamon vs. Arcite, etc. In most of these cases a rough equality, of age and rank and status, obtains between the adversaries, so that the encounter takes on some of the character of a trial by combat, a feudal contest conducted according to mutually understood rules. Romeo defeats Tybalt, Macduff defeats Macbeth, Hal Hotspur, and Edgar Edmund not so much because of superior swordsmanship as because of their ethical superiority: *they* are the virtuous characters; *they* are in the right, and their malicious opponents in the wrong. In so doing they implicitly revalidate, one might say, the medieval legal concept of trial by combat, which in point of historical fact had long since lapsed.

The contest between the half-brothers in *Lear* is of course designed explicitly as a trial by combat, but so also is the earliest and in many ways the most striking of such confrontations, which takes place between commoners in a partly comic episode. In *2 Henry VI*, Peter, the Armorer's apprentice, has accused his master of treason, and been ordered to meet him in combat before the king as a test of truth. Younger than his master, and inexperienced in fighting, Peter is sure he is about to be killed by his swaggering opponent, whose neighbors are already toasting his victory. Peter, terrified at the prospect, settles his earthly affairs: he bequeaths his apron to Robin, his hammer to Will, and his money to Tom, before asking God's blessing. The two combatants then assail each other, evidently with sandbags attached to sticks – clownish weapons – and 'Peter strikes him down', whereupon the Armorer at once confesses his treason and dies. The king concludes the scene: 'Go, take hence that traitor from our sight,/ For by his death we do perceive his guilt,/ And God in justice hath reveal'd to us/ The truth and innocence of this poor fellow,/ Which he had thought to have murther'd wrongfully' (II.iii.100–5). 'For by his death we do perceive his guilt': so Richard, so Tybalt, so Hotspur, so Edmund, so Macbeth: in each case defeat signifies a moral judgement, even if no higher power is expressly invoked. So too, evidently, with Posthumus Leonatus' defeat of Iachimo, whom, however, instead of killing he simply disarms, spurred by remorse for his own attempted aggression against Imogen. And so too, no doubt, with the defeat of the French armies by the English in plays like *1 Henry VI* and *Henry V*, where the French, when they win, win only by foul means, while the English, with their victories, reconfirm and make manifest, almost magically, against impossible odds, their own moral superiority.

So too, very likely, with the death of Cornwall, following the scuffle with his servant during the blinding of Gloucester. The servant, we may recall, tries first to persuade his master to 'hold [his] hand'. Only when this attempt at restraint is met with vituperation does he challenge Cornwall physically. As they fight, Regan seizes a sword and '*runs at him behind*' (III.vii.72–80). In other words, she overcomes him by treachery. Cornwall's subsequent death, then, would seem to represent a judgement on him, along with the vindication of his socially inferior, hence presumably weaker and less able adversary, who (though fatally struck) has defeated his aristocratic master by mortally wounding him. So Albany concludes, at least, when he learns of the incident: 'This shows you are above,/ You justicers, that these our nether crimes/ So speedily can venge' (IV.ii.78–80) – a sentiment in which, I suspect, we are invited to concur.

To this we might add the fact that in such trials by combat, when the more virtuous character does go under it is usually by underhanded means, as when Tybalt thrusts at Mercutio under Romeo's arm. But at least it is Mercutio, far from blameless himself, who falls, rather than Benvolio. In Hamlet vs. Laertes, both contestants lose, Hamlet through

Laertes' perfidy, Laertes through Hamlet's energetic countermeasures and his own contrition. In all these cases one of the combatants has broken the rules. Apart from its apparent reinforcement of the moral distinction that seems to underlie such confrontations, the encounter between Cornwall and his servant and that between Tybalt and Romeo provide instances among many of the cyclical and self-perpetuating nature of violence, which even the good cannot always escape.

From time to time we also find arrested duels, such as that between Benvolio and Tybalt, interrupted by the arrival of the prince, or that between Mowbray and Bolingbroke, cut short by the histrionic and impulsive king, or that between Hector and Ajax, halted by reason of kinship and courtesy, or that between Caius Martius and Tullus Aufidius, broken off when Aufidius' men come to his rescue and retreat with him behind the city gates. In such cases the moral implications, if not already clear, remain suspended. In addition, however, to these relatively balanced duels, in which the opponents compete on a more or less equal basis, we sometimes find deliberately unbalanced encounters, killings – usually unprovoked and unexpected – of the weaker by the stronger, the defenceless by the armed, the old by the young, the innocent by the vicious, as in the sudden spitting of the nurse on Aaron's sword, in *Titus Andronicus*, or the killing of the boy Rutland by the warrior Young Clifford, the old king Henry VI by the future Richard III, the unsuspecting gull Roderigo by the perfidious Iago (in the dark), or Emilia his wife by the same Iago. From these cases we recoil as we do not from the more evenly matched contests. They represent malicious, unscrupulous, self-serving aggression.

This last category moves us toward a kind I would term 'sacrificial' killing, wherein a single defenceless individual is done to death by multiple assailants. The archetype here would be the scene in *3 Henry VI* where York, stationed on his molehill, is subjected to the taunts of the paper crown and the napkin dipped in Rutland's blood, before being cut down by Margaret and Young Clifford. I call this incident 'sacrificial' because it alludes so deliberately to the Crucifixion. York on his molehill is ridiculed like Christ on Calvary. The placing of the paper crown on his head, in savage mockery of his pretensions to be king, actually originates in the historical record, but the chronicle tells us that it took place *after* York had been killed and his head held aloft on a pole. To crown him while he is alive, cornered, and at the mercy of his enemies tightens the identification with Christ while making for a more passionate and upsetting theatrical scene. The napkin dipped in Rutland's blood, like the paper crown, intensifies the torture. Unlike St Veronica's handkerchief, of which it is surely meant to remind us, it is not designed to palliate the victim's sufferings but to aggravate them, and its effect as a talisman later on is not to stimulate faith but to spur revenge.

Of York's three tormentors, however, one is compassionate. Northumberland twice admits that the plight of their captive foe has touched him to tears: 'Had he been slaughter-man to all my kin,/ I should not for my life but weep with him,/ To see how inly sorrow gripes his soul' (1.iv.169–71). Plainly enough this spontaneous rush of fellow feeling is intended to direct our own sympathies. Despite York's past crimes, we find ourselves, like Northumberland, 'with him', and the emotional appeal gains in force when he dies invoking heavenly mercy. We cannot, at this moment, think of him as the ambitious, bullying oathbreaker he has been, brutal and dishonorable toward those to whom he has sworn faith. We see only a fellow human creature goaded beyond endurance before being put savagely to death.

If we ask to whom or to what York is being sacrificed, the only answer can be, to the heartlessness of war, of civil war especially, just as York's own child Rutland has previously been sacrificed, and as one of his least culpable enemies, Prince Edward, will later be sacrificed in the same play, pitilessly stabbed by *his* captors, the brothers Edward, George, and Richard, for refusing to play his role as prisoner meekly enough to suit them.

These cases, however, all reflect the chances of war, where the innocent are understood to be destined to suffer along with the guilty. We have every reason to think that were the positions reversed, Margaret and Young Clifford would undergo the same fate at the hands of York and his followers that they have inflicted on him, and indeed the indignities heaped on Clifford's body when he is at last killed would seem to constitute deliberate retaliation. In the case of Julius Caesar, however, also cut down by multiple assailants, the element of concerted treachery makes its appearance. He is pierced to death without warning by those he most trusts and believes loyal. His last words, '*Et tu, Brute?* – Then fall Caesar!' (III.1.77), mark the point at which our sympathies swing back to him as they have done to York. Whatever Caesar's prior arrogance and boastfulness, these are driven from our minds by the note of personal betrayal sounded in the use of the proper name and the second-person pronoun at the very moment of death.

Victim of a stealthy attack, overpowered by numbers, Caesar is explicitly likened by Mark Antony to a sacrificial animal brought low by cruel hunters, and so retrospectively ennobled: 'Here wast thou bay'd, brave hart,/ Here didst thou fall, and here thy hunters stand,/ Sign'd in thy spoil, and crimson'd in thy lethe./ O world! Thou wast the forest to this hart,/ And this indeed, O world, the heart of thee' (III.i.204–8).

Needless to say, the very killing regarded by Antony as a martyrdom of the great leader is thought by its perpetrators to be a deliverance from a prospective tyrant, a sacrificial act on behalf of republican freedom. 'Let's be sacrificers, but not butchers, Caius', Brutus has urged, and 'purgers' rather than murderers (ii.i.166–80). As events prove, of course, the violence committed in order to forestall violence only provokes worse outbreaks of new violence, the first of which turns out to be another act of mass ferocity, the lynching of the poet Cinna, torn to pieces for his name alone, as it would seem, by the inflamed mob, in whom Antony's rhetoric appears to have aroused a bloodlust that will not subside till it has wreaked itself on what in the event proves to be a simple scapegoat.

The ugliest, perhaps, of all such multiple stabbings occurs towards the end of *Troilus and Cressida*: the murder of the unarmed Hector by Achilles and his Myrmidons, in defiance of all canons of fair play, not to mention those of epic heroism. Courteous, magnanimous Hector becomes a martyr to these, a sacrifice to the outdated chivalric code which his cynical adversary exploits in order to overpower him prior to dishonoring his body in death. (A recent production of the play, at the Stratford, Ontario, Shakespeare Festival in July 1987, took literally Achilles' injunction to his followers to surround their victim and 'in fellest manner execute [their] arms' (v.vii.6). The Myrmidons turned the execution into a scene of torture, in which Hector, his *face* impaled on their swords, was made to cry out in anguish before death.) Here, as in *Julius Caesar*, the violent act engenders an overwrought mood of anarchic vengeance among Hector's survivors, with the maddened Troilus at their head.

It may be that this incident is itself outdone in ugliness by the slaughter of Lady Macduff and her child at the hands of Macbeth's hired ruffians. This comes as the bloody climax to Macbeth's other deeds of blood, which start as the honorable carving up of the merciless Macdonwald in defence of beleaguered Scotland. It is climactic not only in being morally the most abhorrent of his deeds but also in being the only one we are forced to witness for ourselves. Intensifying the horror is the fact that it is essentially so unmotivated, a kind of automatic reflex of Macbeth's increasing incapacity to feel anything at all, or to react in any situation, however inappropriate, except by ordering a bloodbath. On the other hand, reconciling us to it at least in part is the courage and dignity with which Lady Macduff and her young son confront their assassins. That their fate constitutes a sacrifice of sorts is recognized by Macduff himself: he sees that they have been struck *for him*, with the consequence that the episode marks both the low point and the turning point in the play, the moment at which the opposition to tyranny finally and irrevocably crystallizes, and so leads to its overthrow.

At the conclusion of this sequence we have the end of Coriolanus, who goes under hurling defiance at the cutthroats ringing him round and the populace clamoring for his blood, but who, rather than defend himself, welcomes their attack: 'Cut me to pieces, Volsces, men and lads,/ Stain all your edges on me' (v.vi.111–12). Aufidius' rabble-rousing turns the unruly crowd into a lynching party: 'Tear him to pieces!' they cry, 'Do it presently!' (line 120). The lords' interposition proves futile, as Coriolanus taunts his captors and dares Aufidius for the last time to personal combat – 'O that I had him,/ With six Aufidiuses, or more, his tribe,/ To use my lawful sword!' (127–9) – at which point the hired conspirators plunge their *un*lawful swords into his body. In violence of this sort, where the disparity in numbers serves to make the assault a mob attack – vengeful, irrational, and impervious to any consideration of justice – the victim dies bearing witness to the greatness of his own spirit against the meanness of his assailants.

None of these instances, however, with the partial exception of the murder of Lady Macduff and her family, is sacrificial in René Girard's sense.[3] None of them renews, restores, or regenerates. None of them turns the murder, once committed, into a sacred act. Quite the reverse: except in the case of Coriolanus, the sequel to which is left up in the air, they merely provoke further and fiercer cycles of violence, a more implacable resolve on the part of the survivor-avengers, and a thickening of the moral sensibilities of all concerned.

Something like moral restoration does seem to occur in a subcategory of the same type, wherein a pair or more of hired murderers performs an assassination ordered from above. In the Quarto version of *2 Henry VI*, for example, the following stage direction occurs: 'Then the Curtaines being drawne, Duke *Humphrey* is discouered in his bed, and two men lying on his brest and smothering him in his bed. And then enter the Duke of *Suffolke* to them' – to commend them for carrying out his wishes so efficiently, and to instruct them to 'see the cloathes laid smooth about him still,/ That when the King comes, he may perceiue/ No other, but that he dide of his owne accord.'[4] For reasons of censorship, evidently, this scene was dropped from the Folio, its outcome being simply announced to Suffolk by the hired bullies. Before they announce it, however, they engage in a significant bit of added dialogue: 'Run to my Lord of Suffolk,' says one, 'let him know/ We have dispatch'd the Duke, as he commanded', to which his companion replies, 'O, that it were to do! What have we done?/ Didst ever hear a man so penitent?' (III.ii.1–4). Clearly a new element has here entered the picture, that of the divided and guilty mind of one of the murderers.

In *Richard III* we find a more fully worked-out scene of a similar sort in which the murderers of Clarence, even before confronting Clarence himself, first struggle with their own consciences and fears of damnation, then argue justice and morality with their victim, until at length, one of them beginning to relent, the other stabs the Duke from behind and drags the body off to the malmsey-butt. His associate, remaining on stage, breaks into remorseful lament: 'A bloody deed and desperately dispatch'd!/ How fain, like Pilate, would I wash my hands/ Of this most grievous murther!' When his accomplice threatens to denounce him to Richard for his slackness, the 'slacker' retorts, 'I would he knew that I had sav'd his brother!/ Take thou the fee and tell him what I say,/ For I repent me that the Duke is slain' (I.iv.271–8). An in some ways even more highly charged moment occurs later in the soliloquy of Sir James Tyrrel, after he has successfully engineered the murder of the boy princes in the Tower. Musing in horror on the 'tyrannous and bloody act', 'The most arch deed of piteous massacre/ That ever yet this land was guilty of', he goes on to report the anguished, weeping reaction of the two crime-hardened thugs who have actually done the deed, now so speechless from 'conscience and remorse' as to be nearly incapable of telling their tale (IV.iii.1–21).

Sir Pierce Exton, in *Richard II*, performs a comparable service for the newly crowned Bolingbroke. Having killed Richard in his prison cell, he instantly recoils in dismay: 'As full of valure as of royal blood!/ Both have I spill'd; O would the deed were good!/ For now the devil that told me I did well/ Says that this deed is chronicled in hell' (v.v.113–16). All these instances thus follow a similar pattern: the instigator carefully preserves a certain distance between himself and the crime, no matter how intensely he wishes it performed. He may or may not express regret afterwards for what has happened (Bolingbroke does so, but Suffolk and Richard III do not), but in each case at least one of the paid cutthroats emerges with bitter self-reproach, either dissociating himself from the deed altogether or expressing the most passionate wish that he might undo what he has done. The direct confrontation, that is, with the flesh-and-blood victim, especially one who is patently innocent (like the young princes) or penitent (like Gloucester) or troubled in soul (like Clarence) can harrow the conscience even of the hard-shelled murderer, and arrest if it does not extinguish the thirst for reward and the ability to think of the job as nothing but a dangerous assignment for which the pay is exceptionally good. Shakespeare would seem to be implying that if violence is natural – all too natural – to our benighted species, natural too and not to be suppressed are the sometimes deeply buried instincts that pull against it, capable of emerging even in the most unlikely of representatives and under the most unpromising of circumstances.

A variant on the same theme might be the moment in *King John* when one of the 'executioners' who has helped bind Arthur and heat the iron to burn out his eyes is dismissed from the scene by Hubert. As he leaves the stage he announces with relief that he is 'best pleas'd to be from such a deed' (IV.i.85), thus intensifying the struggle already taking place within Hubert himself. What we witness in Hubert a moment later is moral renewal, brought on not *by* violence, but rather, crystallized in the decision to *refrain* from violence.

From all this it is but a step to the schizoid Macbeth, so convulsed by conscience before, during, and after the murder of Duncan, so certain of his own damnation, so hair-trigger in his remorse – 'Wake Duncan with thy knocking! I would thou couldst' (II.ii.71–2) – and then, later, following the murder of Banquo, along with the professional bravos who do his bidding, so heartless, so numb to remorse, so ready to devise new butcheries like the massacre of Macduff's family. It is as if the very hyperactivity *of* his conscience produced a corresponding hyperaggressiveness in Macbeth, an *atrophy* of conscience, exposing in almost schematic form the essential mechanism: violence fated to accomplish nothing but its own unfailing self-perpetuation.

In this case, interestingly, though Banquo's murderers are never heard to recant once they have discharged their commission, prior to receiving it they portray themselves as social rejects, so embittered as to have lost all sense of restraint. Says the first: 'I am one, my liege,/ Whom the vile blows and buffets of the world/ Hath so incens'd that I am reckless what/ I do to spite the world.' Says his comrade: 'And I another,/ So weary with disasters, tugg'd with fortune,/ That I would set my life on any chance,/ To mend it, or be rid on't' (III.i.107–13). Life, then – society – has (as they see it) by persecuting them, dehumanized these men, rendered them indifferent to the rules by which others live, sensible only of their own grievances, and left them as their sole recourse the readiness to retaliate onto others the blows and buffets they consider themselves to have suffered, if that will help them repair their own fallen fortunes. Violence in their case becomes an act of vengeance against a social order that (as they choose to think) has victimized them.

Among dramatic figures from Jacobean tragedy who come within the orbit of Shakespeare's influence, we might cite Webster's Flamineo and Bosola. Both are malcontents who regard themselves as forced by harsh economic necessity into an unsavory trade. Between them they embody both types of Shakespearean hireling. On the one hand Flamineo, the more thuggish of the two, like the assassins in *Macbeth* untroubled by conscience or any feeling for the sufferings of others, preens himself on his own criminal ingenuity and makes security of employment his sole aim in life. Bosola on the other hand, ambivalent, filled from the outset with self-loathing, resembles the more vacillating desperadoes of Shakespeare's earlier histories. Like them he feels trapped in a dirty job. Having forced himself to go through with it, he experiences a sharp revulsion, followed by a kind of revelation, which leads him to penitence and a newly awakened thirst for true justice.

To violence of such kinds we may add self-inflicted injuries. These would include mainly the suicides of characters in the Roman plays who discover that continuance in life has become impossible because (in their own view) dishonourable, and who therefore remove themselves from it, usually by the sword: Brutus and Cassius, Titinius, Enobarbus, Eros, Antony, Cleopatra. Ordinarily in such cases we are made to feel, I believe, that though reprehensible by Christian standards, which lurk always in the background, such acts of self-slaughter, springing as they do from an older code of courage and honor that survives in part into Christianity, have something noble and highminded about them. In the same category we would place the even smaller group of characters in *non*-Roman plays who follow a similar course, more or less culpably according to what they have done to bring themselves to such an extreme of desperation: Romeo and Juliet, Goneril, Timon of Athens.

To speak of the Roman plays is to recall the grisliest of Shakespeare's tragedies, *Titus Andronicus*, which outdoes even *The Spanish Tragedy* in the tempo and horrificness of its events, and introduces thus early in Shakespeare's dramatic career the motif of sexual violence, in the offstage rape of Lavinia, later to culminate in the strangling of Desdemona. Though the rape itself occurs behind the scenes, its horrendous effects are brought before us almost at once – not only in the form of the mutilated Lavinia, in the bleeding mouth and the bleeding stumps that once were hands – but in the rhetoric of her uncle Marcus, as he struggles to cope with the horror of her condition and distance us from it. Marcus compares his defiled niece to a tree whom 'stern ungentle hands/ Hath lopp'd and hew'd, and made [her] body bare/ Of her two branches, those sweet ornaments/ Whose circling shadows kings have sought to sleep in'; her mouth, he says, 'a crimson river of warm blood,/ Like to a bubbling fountain stirr'd with wind,/ Doth rise and fall between [her] rosed lips,/ Coming and going with [her] honey breath' (II.iv.16–25). With such conceits, reminiscent of Petrarchan blazonry, Marcus aims to transform and make bearable, by a certain detachment, what in anything like its immediate actuality would be too hideous to contemplate.

Later, presenting her to Titus in her mangled state, he speaks of her speechlessness in similar terms: 'O, that delightful engine of her thoughts,/ That blabb'd them with such pleasing eloquence,/ Is torn from forth that pretty hollow cage,/ Where like a sweet melodious bird it sung/ Sweet varied notes, enchanting every ear!' (III.i.82–6). Marcus seeks to lure our eyes away from what Lavinia now is and awaken our imaginations to what she once was, to summon up a vision of how graceful and

Shakespearean violence: a preliminary survey

beautiful were her hands, how melodious and birdlike her voice, and how like an aromatic fountain, even in the frightful present, seems her bleeding mouth. Shakespeare is once again drawing on the resources of figurative language to turn to favor and to prettiness that which if directly gazed at, even verbally, is – in its extremity – not to be endured.[5]

A grotesque episode of self-mutilation then follows in Titus' chopping off of his own hand, in exchange (as he thinks) for the release of his imprisoned sons – a sign, we are entitled to suspect, of his incipient madness. The wily Aaron, who has prompted the act, rapidly returns with the *heads* of the sons, and so 'wittily' fulfills his proposed bargain with Titus. The play thus presents us with images, verbal and visual, first of the human body cropped of its limbs, and then of those limbs and bodily parts themselves detached from their trunks, counterparts in the domain of the single individual to the dismemberment of Rome itself at the hands of its baleful rulers.

Heads, we may note in passing, of characters previously seen alive, appear with some frequency in Shakespeare. They are of course the products of violence, and almost always underscore the continuing inhumanity *of* the violence, which is at the same time inescapable, universal, and self-renewing: the head (for example) of the executed Suffolk, cradled in her lap by Queen Eleanor in *2 Henry VI*; the heads of Lord Say and Cromer lofted on poles by Jack Cade's followers, prompting Cade's heartless quip: 'Let them kiss one another, for they lov'd well when they were alive. Now part them again, lest they consult about the giving up of some more towns in France' (IV.vii.130–3); Cade's own head, shortly offered to the king by Iden, earning Iden his knighthood; the head of the Duke of Somerset (in *3 Henry VI*) shown proudly by Richard to testify to his achievements in battle; Yorick's skull in *Hamlet*; Macbeth's head, triumphantly flourished by the victorious Macduff; and Cloten's head, brandished by the more matter-of-fact Guiderius – all these, of course, being shown to Elizabethan playgoers quite accustomed to the displays of heads on Tower Hill and other public places following the execution of traitors.

To return to *Titus*: we see the inexorable cycle of violence renew itself and debase its victims spiritually when the abused Lavinia herself holds with her stumps the bowl into which pours the blood of her ravishers, as Titus cuts their throats before baking them in a pie to serve to their mother the Empress, in fulfillment of his revenge. *Titus*, indeed, offers the only instance in his career when Shakespeare seems to wallow in violence. The extent and terribleness of it would seem to symbolize the barbaric chaos that descends on Rome as a result of what is plainly a sacrificial act in the opening scene, the offstage ritual killing of Alarbus, the Gothic prince, by the sons of Titus, who 'for their brethren slain/ Religiously [do] ask a sacrifice' (I.i.123–4), at which the victim's mother, the Gothic queen,

Tamora, cries out, 'O cruel, irreligious piety!' (line 130). From this ill-considered immolation, stubbornly carried out by the fanatical Titus at his sons' behest, stems the fearful sequence of criminal revenges that dominate the rest of the action. Here, more crudely spelled out than in *Julius Caesar*, we see the inescapable aftermath of sacrifice: it produces an effect opposite to that intended, and worsens the situation it is designed to alleviate.

A less lethal form of violence occasionally appears, in which the weapons are stones rather than swords or knives. In *1 Henry VI*, Gloucester's men and Winchester's brawl before the Tower and are only with difficulty restrained from continuing, even in the presence of the king and their respective masters. In this case the mutual detestation of the two peers is reflected in the aggressiveness of their language. Duke Humphrey, for example, threatens his antagonist, the Cardinal of Winchester: 'Priest, beware your beard,/ I mean to tug it and to cuff you soundly./ Under my feet I stamp thy cardinal's hat;/ In spite of Pope or dignities of church,/ Here by the cheeks I'll drag thee up and down' (I.iii.47–51). To which, after further rioting among their men, and a proclamation from the Mayor forbidding weapons, the Cardinal retorts, 'Abominable Gloucester, guard thy head,/ For I intend to have it ere long' (I.iii.87–8). The weapon, in short, at least for the moment, is language. As Girard suavely phrases it, in the drama hot words often substitute for cold steel.

At the second scuffle between the factions, the terrified Mayor reports to the king that 'The Bishop and the Duke of Gloucester's men,/ Forbidden late to carry any weapon,/ Have fill'd their pockets full of pebble stones;/ And banding themselves in contrary parts,/ Do pelt so fast at one another's pate/ That many have their giddy brains knock'd out;/ Our windows are broke down in every street./ And we, for fear, compell'd to shut our shops' (III.i.76–85). Violence of this sort, which threatens innocent bystanders and verges on anarchy, seems to arouse anxiety in Shakespeare and to draw condemnatory language, as in the opening scene of *Coriolanus*, where the citizens with their bats and clubs confront Menenius with his mollifying wit. It tends also to be conveyed more powerfully in words than in stage action, since stage action, needing to be disciplined and choreographed, makes raw confusion hard to render convincingly.

In *Timon of Athens*, finally, Timon's only method of counterattack against his false friends, other than verbal denunciation, is literally to throw things – the lukewarm water he spatters in their faces at his farewell banquet, the stones he digs up in the woods with which to pelt Apemantus and drive away the Painter and Poet. Under the circumstances, such primitive implements of aggression scarcely seem comic – they seem pitiable – but their uselessness, like that of his verbal missiles, underscores the futility of Timon's life in exile, which becomes productive only when he is capable once more of bestowing gold on his visitors, on Alcibiades especially, so as to make possible the siege of Athens.

From the carnage of *Titus* and the disillusion of *Timon* we may turn to a less harrowing topic: comic violence. Like its tragic counterpart, this may occur either in the language alone, or in the language by way of narrative report, or it may be enacted on the stage. It appears most often in scenes of farce – indeed it may be said to be one of the defining characteristics of stage farce – and it also often involves beatings, with fists or broomsticks or other homely objects. It is seldom meant to do serious hurt, and it often expresses nothing worse than annoyance. It causes only temporary distress to its victims; it rarely if ever draws blood; and it has no lasting ill effects.

Like its tragic counterpart, its Shakespearean manifestations have a long history of precedent in early Tudor interludes and moralities, and in Elizabethan popular drama. Usually it is found among the Vice and the lowlife characters, sometimes augmented by the Mankind figure whom these others temporarily succeed in leading astray. It is therefore (strictly speaking) the work of the Devil, attempting to undo the efforts of guardian characters with names like Mercy or Pity, whose mission it is to keep humanity on the path of righteousness. Most commonly it consists of beatings, drubbings, fisticuffs, and other non-lethal forms of aggression, from which its victims promptly recover, or whom – like the monster Tediousness in *The Marriage of Wit and Science* – we see as so purely allegorical that it never occurs to us to feel any concern for their fates as human beings. Shakespeare, of course, is not writing allegory, and he never loses sight of the humanity of his characters. Nevertheless, the knockabout element remains prominent and vivid in the three of his comedies customarily designated as farces.

Early in *The Comedy of Errors*, Dromio of Ephesus complains to his supposed master, Antipholus of Syracuse, that the latter is late to dinner. Among other tokens of that lateness he mentions that 'The clock hath strucken twelve upon the bell:/ My mistress made it one upon my cheek' (1.ii.45–6). This simple reference sets the tone for most of the violence endured by both Dromios for most of the day. Dromio knows very well that his aching head will pay the penalty for his mistress's displeasure as well as his master's: 'I from my mistress come to you in post:/ If I return, I shall be post indeed,/ For she will score your fault upon my pate' (lines 62–5).

A moment later, having denied knowledge of the thousand marks supposedly given him, Dromio finds himself subjected to a second beating: 'What, wilt thou flout me thus unto my face,/ Being forbid?' demands his exasperated master, 'There, take you that, sir knave' – striking him.

Dromio answers, with some spirit: 'What mean you, sir? For God's sake hold your hands!/ Nay, and you will not, sir, I'll take my heels' (lines 91–4) – whereupon he runs off to complain to Adriana, this time with more wit, of his mistreatment:

> *Adr.* Say, is your tardy master now at hand?
> *E. Dro.* Nay, he's at two hands with me, and that my two ears can witness.
> *Adr.* Say, didst thou speak with him? Know'st thou his mind?
> *E. Dro.* Ay, ay, he told his mind upon mine ear. Beshrew his hand, I scarce could understand it.
> *Adr.* Spake he so doubtfully, thou couldst not feel his meaning?
> *E. Dro.* Nay, he strook so plainly, I could too well feel his blows; and withal so doubtfully, that I could scarce understand them. (II.i.44–54).

And 'in conclusion', concludes Dromio, 'he did beat me there' (line 74). Now it is Adriana's turn to threaten:

> *Adr.* Go back again, thou slave, and fetch him home.
> *E. Dro.* Go back again, and be new beaten home?
> For God's sake send some other messenger.
> *Adr.* Back, slave, or I will break thy pate across.
> *E. Dro.* And he will bless that cross with other beating:
> Between you I shall have a holy head (lines 75–80)

This sequence is quickly followed by a fresh misunderstanding between the same Antipholus and his proper Dromio, in very much the same vein, leading to another beating. Once again the beating produces an explosion of indignant punning:

> *S. Ant.* If you will jest with me, know my aspect,
> And fashion your demeanor to my looks,
> Or I will beat this method in your sconce.
> *S. Dro.* Sconce call you it? So you would leave battering, I had rather have it a head. And you use these blows long, I must get a sconce for my head, and insconce it too, or else I shall seek my wit in my shoulders. (II.ii.32–48)

One thing, it appears, that comic violence does is to unleash bouts of verbal protest from its victim, as tragic violence does not. The victims of tragic violence, like Gloucester, in *Lear*, or Lady Macduff's son, in *Macbeth*, Emilia, in *Othello*, or Coriolanus, may defy their aggressors, but they do so before, not after, they are assaulted. Once attacked, they are either dead, or else, like Lavinia or Gloucester, too brutalized to reply. In comedy, the victim strikes back in the only way permitted him, with a barrage of witty laments over his own misery. The result in the present instance is that once the interchange is over both parties return to an approximation of their former good humor.

As the tempo increases and the visiting Antipholus becomes convinced he is the sport of witches, it becomes the turn of the resident Antipholus, him of Ephesus, to lose patience with *his* Dromio – for fetching a rope instead of the money he was charged to find.

> E. Ant. To what end did I bid thee hie thee home?
> E. Dro. To a rope's end, sir, and to that end am I return'd.
> E. Ant. And to that end, sir, I will welcome you. [*Beats Dromio*].
> Officer. Good sir, be patient.
> E. Dro. Nay, 'tis for me to be patient: I am in adversity.
> Off. Good now, hold thy tongue.
> E. Dro. Nay, rather persuade him to hold his hands.
> E. Ant. Thou whoreson, senseless villain!
> E. Dro. I would I were senseless, sir, that I might not feel your blows.
> E. Ant. Thou art sensible in nothing but blows, and so is an ass.
> E. Dro. I am an ass indeed; you may prove it by my long ears. I have serv'd him from the hour of my nativity to this instant, and have nothing at his hands for my service but blows. When I am cold, he heats me with beating; when I am warm, he cools me with beating. I am wak'd with it when I sleep, rais'd with it when I sit, driven out of doors with it when I go from home, welcom'd home with it when I return; nay, I bear it on my shoulders, as a beggar wont her brat; and I think when he hath lam'd me, I shall beg with it from door to door. (IV.iv.15–39)

Here the beleaguered Dromio, even more roughly treated than his brother, appealing to the Officer and to us as witnesses, gives vent to a heartfelt outcry against his lot as underling, with its ever-present accompaniment of blows and beatings. It begins to seem as though violence in the comic world is inherent in the relations between masters and servants. Though the blows and the beatings are meant to make us laugh, and though we understand from the outset that they will cause no lasting damage, it cannot be said that they are painless. They raise welts and lumps on their victims' bodies, and they injure their fragile self-esteem still more. The victims, for their part, are far from meekly submitting; both rise to a protest of some eloquence against the life they have led since childhood, with its perpetual threat of verbal and physical mistreatment. Still, the blows are not malicious; they are not meant to humiliate or destroy but to correct, to work off a momentary impatience, and we accept them, with whatever discomfort, as belonging to farce, in which certain characters, like Bergsonian jack-in-the-boxes, are destined to be repreatedly knocked down and to rebound each time with the same manic energy.

The Taming of the Shrew is filled with similar violence, but the violence is now more varied; it has more interesting meanings and purposes. We start with a scene reminiscent of those in *The Comedy of Errors*, in which the newly arrived Petruchio, accompanied by his servant Grumio, bids him knock at Hortensio's house, and is deliberately misunderstood by the impertinent underling, who bandies words until his exasperated master '*wrings him by the ears*' (SD 1.ii.17). The difference between this scene and the exchanges between the Dromios and the Antipholuses is that in this case the cheeky groom *provokes* Petruchio, and seems neither surprised nor discountenanced by the result.

Katherina the Shrew makes her stormy entrance onto the scene dragging the rope-bound Bianca out of the house, demanding to know her opinions of her various suitors, and striking her for unsatisfactory answers, then, a moment later, taking the luckless Hortensio as her target, smashing him over the head with his lute and breaking both head and instrument in the process. Violence is evidently Katherina's specialty, one of the distinguishing marks of her identity as a shrew. The first interview between her and Petruchio leads to her rashly striking him as well. Petruchio replies without hesitation and in words of one syllable, 'I swear I'll cuff you, if you strike again' (II.i.220). From this point forward their 'chat', though charged with rage on her part and with rough good spirits on his, is conducted entirely on the verbal level. Physical roughness between them, we infer, has tacitly been declared off limits, the only possible exception being Petruchio's mock 'rescue' of his bride from her father and the wedding party, so that he may carry her off to his country estate.

We have heard, prior to this, of his antics in church, of his cuffing the priest for dropping the book, of his stamping and swearing 'as if the vicar meant to cozen him' (III.ii.168), and of his throwing the sops of the wedding wine into the sexton's face. Subsequent to this we hear from Grumio, who arrives ahead at the country house, of the turbulent journey the newlyweds have completed, a tale characteristically introduced by Grumio's boxing of Curtis's ear so as to command his attention. His narration acquaints us with more of Petruchio's antic humours *en route* ('he beat me because her horse stumbled' (IV.i.77, etc.) Arriving in person, Petruchio unloads a torrent of abuse onto his servants, cursing them as rascal knaves, loggerheaded and unpolished grooms, peasant and unmannered slaves, whoreson malt-horse drudges, as rogues, as villains, as beetle-headed, flap-ear'd knaves, as dogs, as heedless joltheads, reviling them and mauling them by turns, climaxing his tantrum by upsetting table, meat, and utensils, and swingeing any of the household foolish enough to remain within reach.

Petruchio thus enters the lists in a kind of competition of violence between himself and Katherina, except that where Katherina's violence was ill-natured, fierce, and meant to hurt, Petruchio very carefully avoids making her his target. He directs it against everyone in the neighborhood *except* her. His antics differ markedly also from the treatment of the Dromios by the Antipholuses, since it now reflects a theatrical purpose. Petruchio's anger is only mock anger. It constitutes a performance put on for Katherina's benefit, an uproar staged in order to hold the mirror to her senseless clamor, and so provide a model of unfeminine behaviour for her to contemplate, and (by inference) shun. It is intended also to wear down her resistance, to *exhaust* her into civility. And it is carried out in

Petruchio's unfailingly extravagant style, with an ever-present element of unpredictability, of *surprise*. The same applies to his plan to sustain the hubbub at night, to keep her from sleep, and to rough-handle the tailor the next day, when his vocabulary of insult waxes almost Rabelaisian in its ferocity and inventiveness: 'Thou liest, thou thread, thou thimble,/ Thou yard, three-quarters, half-yard, quarter, nail!/ Thou flea, thou nit, thou winter-cricket thou!/ Brav'd in mine own house with a skein of thread?/ Away, thou rag, thou quantity, thou remnant,/ Or I shall so bemete thee with thy yard/ As thou shalt think on prating whilst thou liv'st!' (IV.iii.107–13) – a tempest of words, that is, substituting this time for a rain of blows. This scene, however, marks the end of the violence. The tailor is stealthily promised his pay, and when next we see the wedded pair they are on the road back to Padua, where Katherina undergoes her conversion and all contention between them comes to an end.

Petruchio's violence, we may note, differs from that of the two Antipholuses not only in its being deliberately staged, but in its essential good humor, its imaginativeness, its comic high spirits, whereas that of the Antipholuses, though not malicious, sprang from furious vexation at what was perceived as the unseasonable jesting of their servants. Unlike Petruchio's, it was also relatively mechanical, monotonous, and unchanging. And it implied a somewhat unsatisfactory state of affairs between them and their Dromios. Though we hear no words of collusion between Petruchio and his domestics, and although the latter are doubtless fearful of their master's raging and storming, they nevertheless seem to take in the fact that he is play-acting, and will ultimately do neither Kate nor themselves any harm. Certainly they never respond anything like the aggrieved Dromios lamenting their aches and pains. Quite the reverse: Grumio enters into Petruchio's make-believe as zealously as the lord's servants in the Induction enter into the plot to deceive Christopher Sly; he teases Kate much in Petruchio's own vein when she is hungry; and he pinch-hits energetically for Petruchio in the dispute with the hapless tailor. Even Kate's own initial violence, we come to suspect, springs from a kind of half-conscious play-acting: having been designated all her life as the shrew, she will not bate a jot of her unprofitable role, at least not until persuaded that the role Petruchio has planned for her is a better one, that his kind of game is more amusing than her own tumultuous and fatiguing one. The happy upshot of their competition in violence, then, proves to be the total abandonment of all violence.

The most violent character in *The Merry Wives of Windsor*, Dr Caius, goes about roaring and stamping, with his rapier on the ready, but never has a chance to use it, thanks to the waggish Host of the Garter, who organizes the duel between him and Sir Hugh, sends them to wrong places, wears them out with waiting, and ends by playing the peacemaker. This leaves both of them unbloodied, but furious and thirsting for revenge. The only true violence practised on anyone in the whole mischief-ridden play has Falstaff as its butt, and Falstaff, needless to say, has it coming to him. Having survived the humiliation of his drenching in the Thames, he suffers a worse fate disguised as the old woman of Brainford, being thwacked unmercifully and at the same time strenuously berated by Ford: 'Out of my door, you witch, you rag, you baggage, you poulcat, you runnion! out, out! I'll conjure you, I'll fortune-tell you!' (IV.ii.184–6). From so much, coupled with Petruchio's verbal onslaughts, we reconfirm our impression that farce often goes in for violent language even when it refrains from violent action. Falstaff, however, has been well and truly beaten. He ponders his fate in a melancholy soliloquy:

> I would all the world might be cozen'd, for I have been cozen'd and beaten too. If it should come to the ear of the court, how I have been transform'd, and how my transformation hath been wash'd and cudgell'd, they would melt me out of my fat drop by drop, and liquor fishermen's boots with me. I warrant they would whip me with their fine wits till I were as crestfall'n as a dried pear.   (IV.v.93–100)

Not much evidence here of physical distress, nor when he tells Mistress Quickly that he was 'beaten . . . into all the colours of the rainbow' (lines 115–16), but much of wounded amour-propre and fear of disgrace. Similarly in his account to his 'confidant', Master Brook – Ford in disguise – to whom he reveals that his sweetheart's jealous husband – Ford *un*disguised – 'beat me grievously, in the shape of a woman, for in the shape of a man, Master Brook, I fear not Goliath with a weaver's beam, because I know also life is a shuttle. Since I pluck'd geese, play'd truant, and whipt top, I knew not what 'twas to be beaten till lately' (v.i.20–6).

This, unless we count the fairies' pinching in the final scene, marks the end of the violence, and of the talk of violence, in this play. The fairies' pinching, however, and the burning of Falstaff with their tapers' ends – Falstaff disguised as the ghost of Herne the Hunter, with animal horns – would seem to represent a mock sacrifice, in which a fertility spirit is done to death to allay the disruptions that have agitated the village. Prior to this moment Falstaff has been the butt of Mistress Page, Mistress Ford, and a few neighbors. He now becomes the sport of the entire populace, the irritant that must be removed if all scores are to be settled and peace is to be restored. Comic violence here, the baiting and mocking of the intruding spirit, re-establishes harmony between the Fords and advances the matrimonial designs of Fenton and Anne Page, insuring on behalf of the whole community that its wives are chaste, its husbands trusting, and its young people eager to found the next generation.

I think we may say, assuming our conventional chronology for these three farces is approximately correct, that what we see in them is a gradual progresssion *away* from violence, a growing realization on Shakespeare's part that violence in itself is not funny. And this inference would seem to be borne out by the fact that in comedies other than the farces, violence dwindles nearly to the zero point. When it threatens, however menacingly, as in Proteus' attempt to rape Sylvia, or Shylock's to exact a pound of flesh from Antonio, it fails to materialize. Swordplay is rare. Duels are more often halted or diverted than waged: Pompey vs. Armado, interrupted by the arrival of Marcade with his tidings of death; Demetrius vs. Lysander, misled into fogs and swamps and sleeps by Puck; old Leonato and old Antonio unable to provoke Claudio and Don Pedro into a quarrel to avenge the slander of Hero; Benedick vs. Claudio, their expected combat cut short by the revelation of Hero's innocence; Viola vs. Sir Andrew, swords in trembling hands, suspended by the appearance of Antonio, himself pursued by officers seeking to arrest him; Sebastian vs. Sir Toby, glaring fiercely at each other, ready to draw blood, stopped by the arrival of the outraged Olivia.

As for Orlando's match with the wrestler Charles, a formal contest staged before the court, that quickly takes on the character of a trial by combat: the self-effacing hero overthrows the boastful champion, following the champion's own defeat of three country youths whom he has left gasping on the ground with broken ribs. Charles, wrestler to the usurping Duke Frederick and an ally of Orlando's envious older brother, represents the Goliath of this contest, being rapidly dispatched – but not killed – by the David, Orlando, whose victory marks his goodness of heart and the nobility of spirit that shine through his rustical upbringing. It reassures us that we are in a comic world where virtue will eventually win out over envy and persecution.

Active violence, then, effectuated violence, violence prompted by spite or fury, plays close to no part in the comedies. Only an occasional suggestion serves to keep us mindful of the passions that can provoke it. Truly murderous violence is nowhere in evidence, or if it is, it is shunted aside before it can do serious damage. The one disturbing comic instance appears in a history play: Falstaff's stabbing of Hotspur's body on the field at Shrewsbury. Even here, however, the fact that Hotspur is after all dead and cannot be hurt by a new wound, the colossal cheek of Falstaff himself, with whose self-preserving impudence we have learned to put up, for the sake of its inventiveness, and – perhaps most of all – Hal's magnanimous allowance of the gesture as a joke rather than a desecration, tend to take the sting out of it for us.

To continue for a moment with the Lancastrian histories: at the end of *2 Henry IV*, we learn that one bit of offstage violence has had a disastrous outcome: the beadle takes Doll and the Hostess into custody, since 'the man is dead that [they] and Pistol beat amongst [them]' (v.vii.1–2).

Coming as it does at this penultimate moment in the play, the incident constitutes a sharp reminder that the world of the tavern is among other things a dark one, just as the outbreaks of violence in *Henry V* – the ferocity of Henry's speech before Harfleur, his order to his soldiers to kill their prisoners, the French butchery of 'the poys and the luggage ... expressly against the law of arms' – all throw a sordid light onto the heroic enterprise of the war and tarnish the glamor conferred on it by the Chorus, reminding us that even the most pageantlike and epically celebrated of battles has its seamy underside.

The readiness to resort to violence, in any case, even in the comic realm, remains something of a touchstone, if not of malevolence exactly, then of a rankling perversity, of an inability to conduct affairs without inflicting humiliations on others, of a preference for aggression as a way of working off irritation or bafflement. We can (I think) accept Cleopatra's furious onslaught on the luckless messenger, her striking him and haling him up and down and threatening him with horrendous torments, as an instance of comic overdoing, of the overflowing of the vessel, unlikely to have dire consequences. But the same cannot be said of Posthumus' striking of the disguised Imogen in the final moments of *Cymbeline*. That gesture really means two things: it means first of all, of course, that in spite of all that has happened in the course of the action he still does not really recognize her, really know her. It also means that he has not yet, after so long time and so much heartache, lost the habit of striking out blindly in anger. It is only when this replay, this echo of his first terrible mistake is perceived by him to be such that he can persuade us he has truly abandoned his unhealthy readiness to take to his sword or his fists. It is only when comic violence, then, is managed with good humor and a light heart, to expose swollen pride or sweeten a foul temper, as in the case of Petruchio or of the plots against Falstaff in *The Merry Wives*, that we are implicitly invited to endorse and approve it with a light heart ourselves.

I hardly need say at this point that I have dealt with this topic in an oldfashioned way. I might be taxed, by post-structuralists, with having, as they say, 'produced' the pattern I purport to discover, rather than having *found* something that was actually *there*. Furthermore, I have outlined what I take to be an implicit *morality* of violence in the Shakespearean canon, and – perhaps worst of all – the morality I claim to find is one I myself would endorse, and it is a bourgeois morality at that. But it does tally with much of what we already know about its author.

The commonest term used about Shakespeare the man in his own day was 'gentle'. I take 'gentle', here, not only in its Elizabethan senses of 'noble, generous, courteous, polite', but also in its continuing present-day sense of 'mild' – *not* rough, *not* harsh, *not* violent. To me it seems plain that the threads I have tried to follow lend support to the view of a 'gentle'

Shakespeare. They suggest a Shakespeare losing interest in violence for its own sake, gradually eliminating it from his farces, associating it increasingly with unruliness, disorder, tyranny, and whatever interferes with life. In short they suggest a civilized and a civilizing Shakespeare.

But this is not to imply a squeamish or a sentimental or a milk-sop Shakespeare. It is not to suggest that he portrays all violent acts as reprehensible in themselves – certainly not when committed in legitimate self-defense, nor when brought under some meaningful rule and order. The trial by combat, the rituals of war, have their uses, even their value. We feel no revulsion – or should feel none, I believe – when Guiderius appears with Cloten's head, or (for that matter) when Imogen awakes to find the headless body beside her, only to mistake it, significantly, for that of Posthumus. We endorse, I suspect, the intent of Fluellen's phrase – 'expressly against the law of arms' – to indicate the kind of violence Fluellen, along with Shakespeare, finds abhorrent. Shakespeare clearly believes in valor, in manly readiness, in military prowess. These qualities matter because the world we inhabit contains lawless, self-serving, aggressive human beings, ready to use others as means, ready to push them around whenever others seem to stand in the way of their own private purposes or private pleasures. And because they entail other qualities valuable in themselves, such as courage, resourcefulness, and resolution, which enable men, and women too, to assert their full humanity in the teeth of adverse fortune and dangerous enemies. The energetic captainship of Talbot against the treacherous French, the vigorous challenge of Edgar against the perfidious Edmund, conform precisely *to* the law of arms, and claim nothing short of the highest honor.

All this, no doubt, coming from our most revered culture hero, may sound too much for comfort like copybook morality. Yet I believe it to be the only lesson one can draw from the evidence I have tried to assemble.

NOTES

1 (Princeton University Press, 1940), chapter 1, passim.
2 Except where otherwise noted, all citations from Shakespeare will be to *The Riverside Shakespeare*, ed. G. Blakemore Evans, et al. (Boston: Houghton Mifflin, 1974).
3 *Violence and the Sacred*, trans. Patrick Gregory (Baltimore: Johns Hopkins University Press, 1977), passim.
4 *The First Part of the Contention*, Sig. E2, in *Shakespeare's Plays in Quarto*, ed. Michael J. Allen and Kenneth Muir (Berkeley: University of California Press, 1981), p. 60.
5 Whether this technique of combined horror and distancing works on the stage is of course another matter. See Eugene M. Waith, 'The Metamorphosis of Violence in *Titus Andronicus*', *Patterns and Perspectives in English Renaissance Drama* (Newark: University of Delaware Press, 1988), pp. 41–54, esp. p. 51.

Cultural disintegration in *Titus Andronicus*: mutilating Titus, Vergil, and Rome*

HEATHER JAMES

I

The impulse to dismember and devour pervades this revenge drama: it motivates not only the revenge plots of Titus and Tamora, but also Shakespeare's curious handling of literary authorities, particularly Vergil and Ovid. In treating the classical texts of imperial Rome, Shakespeare replicates the tragedy's patterns of competition, mutilation, and digestion – the latter a term for imitations which absorb and transform their sources. His purpose, in part, is to 'overgo' Vergil and Ovid, as well as the classicizing and violent dramas of Kyd and Marlowe. But Shakespeare's *aemulatio* and *digestio* go further to perform a critique of imperial Rome on the eve of its collapse. Re-enacting literary history, Shakespeare first invokes the *Aeneid* as the epic of empire-building, order, and *pietas*, and then allows Ovid's *Metamorphoses* to invade, interpreting the fundamental impulses of Vergil's poem as chaotic, even apocalyptic.[1] Simply put, the founding acts of Empire turn out to contain the seeds of its destruction. As we shall see, the turning point from Vergil to Ovid is the rape of Lavinia. This grisly fulcrum functions logically in the poetics of cultural disintegration, for as Shakespeare knew, Rome was founded on rape: the rape of the Sabine women, the rape of Lucrece, the rape of Ilia, Aeneas' dynastic marriage to Lavinia, which threatened to repeat the rape of Helen of Troy,[2] and, with considerable and distressing ambiguity, the seduction of Dido. (Dido's fall is overdetermined to a degree that makes it impossible to isolate agency or responsibility.) The rape of Lavinia, however, alludes to that of Ovid's Philomela, which is disturbingly spliced onto those Great Rapes which helped found Rome, and particularly – as we shall see – onto the fall of Dido. Such a conflation allows Shakespeare to perform an Ovidian critique of Rome, whose *imperium* was not, after all, *sine fine*.[3]

This is a lot to claim for a play whose overwrought rhetoric and violent

---

* A draft of this paper was read at the *Themes in Drama* International Conference held at the University of California, Riverside, in February 1989.

excesses have brought down on Shakespeare's head the famous charge that it is 'a most incorrect and indigested piece', and 'rather a heap of Rubbish than a Structure'.[4] Critics are understandably affronted by *Titus*, which of all Shakespeare's plays cites the most Latin yet hacks up the most bodies, trades on puns and body parts, and revels in a treasury of rhetorical wit, yet perversely drags on stage the physical and horribly literal signs of its 'trim invention' – such as the 'trimmed' Lavinia, who stands in ghastly contrast to the alchemical poetics her uncle Marcus produces from her maimed body. Albeit hard to stomach, such perverse links between language and action, rhetoric and violence, bear the stamp of cultural – and Ovidian – decadence. Ovidian poetics, which complicates and politicizes the referential nature of the sign, glances proleptically at the disintegration of Roman culture.[5] I shall first discuss the play's invocation of Vergil; then the Ovidian plot and critique, which unravel Vergilian values; and finally, the play's concluding attempt to re-member Vergil and to reintegrate the crumbling heritage of Roman patriarchy, a process which apparently depends on containing internal threats figured as female. For, despite Aaron's prominent role in devising plots, the play's Allecto is Tamora;[6] and while all violence performed on Titus' family devolves on Titus himself, nonetheless it is Lavinia's raped and mutilated body that stands as the most terrible sign of social disorder. The play's discourse of cultural disintegration is writ large in the two extreme signs of violation, Tamora's Pit and Lavinia's body, twin loci of violent mayhem and of literary contamination. As apocalyptic conflations of Vergil and Ovid, they are metaphors which transport Roman origins to their end.

As the *Aeneid* begins with the famous storm which comes to stand for *furor*, understood as both political and emotional upheaval, so *Titus Andronicus* begins with a political tempest whose passionate storms, thunders, and furies are heard throughout the play. Rome is beleaguered not only by the Goths, but by its own legal institutions and its worn out myths – particularly, its latter-day Romulus and Remus, who vie for the imperial seat and for Titus' daughter. The last Caesar has died, and his sons rally their factions to determine the succession. Saturninus invokes primogeniture, while Bassianus appeals to free election and to 'virtue consecrate,/ To justice, continence, and nobility' (1.i.14–15).[7] The people, however, elect as the true successor to Rome's military Caesars, Titus, who enters Rome and the stage directly from his military victory over the Goths. Titus also brings with him the cool breath of authority and order. As he formally greets Rome, then his family tomb, he has the effect of Vergil's Neptune, or more properly, of the august civic official in Vergil's simile, whose mere appearance calms the impassioned Roman mob.[8]

The Andronici, in fact, known for their 'uprightness and integrity' (1.i.48), virtually claim the *Aeneid* as family history. When Marcus announces that the people 'have by common voice,/ In election for the Roman empery,/ Chosen Andronicus, surnamed Pius' (1.i.21–3), he establishes Titus' spiritual descent from the *pius* Aeneas and embarks on an epideictic speech which refers its values to the *Aeneid*. For ten years – the duration of the Trojan war – Titus has fought 'weary wars against the barbarous Goths' and 'chastised with arms/ Our enemies' pride' (1.i.28, 32–3). His military acts against the Goths and their Queen, Tamora, satisfy Anchises' instructions to Aeneas in the Underworld, and invite an analogy of Rome's recent wars to those against Carthage, the arch-enemy civilization which in Vergil's fiction was founded by another queen, Dido: *tu regere imperio polulos, Romane, memento/ (hae tibi erunt artes), pacique imponere morem,/ parcere subiectis et debellare superbos* ('Remember, Roman, by your power to rule the people (for these will be your arts), to impose the custom of peace, spare the conquered, and battle down the proud'). He is, moreover, the 'Patron of virtue', and has for Rome's sake buried twenty-one of his twenty-five sons, 'Half the number that King Priam had' (1.i.80). He further boasts a daughter named after Aeneas' Latin bride: Lavinia, 'Rome's rich ornament', for whom Saturninus and Bassianus fight. To crown his Vergilian achievements, Titus even enters Rome with a conquered Cleopatra: Tamora, Queen of the Goths, who is 'brought to Rome/ To beautify [his] triumphs'.

Yet Vergilian *pietas* has ossified over the centuries. Titus' religious, patriotic, and familial observances conform to the letter rather than the spirit of the law. Titus' obsession with form is emblematically entwined with death, to judge by the Andronici's prominently displayed 500-year-old tomb, which Titus has 'sumptuously re-edified' (1.i.351). But Titus' actions speak loudest. Before he buries those sons who died in the wars, he interrogates his own piety:

> Titus, unkind, and careless of thine own,
> Why suffer'st thou thy sons, unburied yet,
> To hover on the dreadful shore of Styx? (1.86–8)

Yet his question is rhetorical, an occasion for an allusion to the souls of the unburied in Book VI of the *Aeneid*: *haec omnis, quam cernis, inops inhumataque turba est . . . volitantque haec litora circum* ('This crowd you see here, poor and unburied . . . flutter about the shore', VI.325–9).[9] The citation of Vergil serves less to initiate a burial rite than to authorize a dubious instance of piety, the ritual sacrifice of Tamora's eldest son, despite her plea for pity. Next, after rejecting imperial power for himself, he gives his support to Saturninus, presumably because he is elder, but gratuitously includes his daughter, who is already betrothed to Bassianus. Finally, when Bassianus, aided by Titus' sons, seizes *suum cuique*, Titus exhibits the full rigor of his *pietas*: he apparently holds no grudge against Bassianus, who seized his own 'in justice', but he kills his son Mutius for disobedience, recalling that most uncompromising Roman father, Manlius Torquatus. Tamora's memorable cry, 'O cruel, irreligious piety!' is an Ovidian oxymoron which signals the destructive rigidity of Titus and, by extension, the Roman ethos summed up in *pietas*.[10] Titus' 'by-the-book' judgements turn sympathy toward Tamora, who fluctuates between roles as a seductive Cleopatra (she marries the newly crowned Saturninus) and as a Hecuba, justified in avenging the death of her son. Her son Demetrius invokes 'The self-same gods that arm'd the Queen of Troy/ with opportunity of sharp revenge/ Upon the Thracian tyrant' (I.i.136–8).

The *Aeneid* suffers its greatest warping in the next act, whose plot turns on repeated displacements of Dido's seduction. To celebrate the supposed reconciliations of Tamora and Titus, Saturninus and Bassianus, the court arranges a royal hunt which will prove as fateful and more dire than the one which brought Dido and Aeneas to that famous cave in which they consummated their desires (Dido's, at any rate). The plot begins when Aaron finds Tamora's two sons, Demetrius and Chiron, mooning over Lavinia and ludicrously acting out Rome's fratricidal motif famously modeled by Romulus and Remus and the *Aeneid*'s contenders for the original Lavinia. When Demetrius boasts of his cuckolding techniques, 'What, hast not thou full often stroke a doe,/ And borne her cleanly by the keeper's nose?' (II.i.93–4), Aaron wrenches the figure of speech into a rally call to rape Lavinia during the next day's hunt:

> The forest walks are wide and spacious,
> And many unfrequented plots there are
> Fitted by kind for rape and villainy:
> Single you thither then this dainty doe,
> And strike her home by force . . . (II.i.113–18)

The boys jubilantly adopt Aaron's twisting of the metaphor from adultery to rape, crowing later, 'we hunt not, we, with horse nor hound,/ But hope to pluck a dainty doe to ground' (II.ii.24–5). The metaphor gains its power to chill the blood partly because it has been so violently wrenched from its original context in Vergil's famous simile of the impassioned Dido as a wounded deer:

> uritur infelix Dido totaque vagatur
> urbe furens, qualis coniecta cerva sagitta,
> quam procul incautam nemora inter Cresia fixit
> pastor agens telis liquitque volatile ferrum
> nescius: illa fuga silvas saltusque peragrat
> Dictaeos; haeret lateri letalis harundo. (IV.68–73)

Unhappy Dido burns and, frenzied, wanders through the city, even as an unwary doe, struck by an arrow, whom a shepherd hunting with darts in the Cretan woods has unwittingly pierced from far off, and left in her the flying steel. She, fleeing, wanders through the woods and dales of Dicte; the fatal shaft clings to her side.

The image, which appears in the *Aeneid* just before the fateful hunt during which Dido abandons her chastity, resurfaces again in *Titus* when Marcus presents the violated Lavinia to her father, saying he 'found her straying in the park,/ Seeking to hide herself, as doth the deer/ That hath receiv'd some unrecuring wound' (III.i.88–90). Titus takes this opportunity to pun in both Latin and English. Opening up the latent pun on *cura*, a word Vergil uses to identify a beloved or dearest 'care', Titus says, 'It was my dear, and he that hath wounded her/ Hath hurt me more than had he kill'd me dead', and, further, that of all wrongs, 'that which gives my soul the greatest spurn/ Is dear Lavinia, dearer than my soul' (III.i.91–2, 102–3). By means of puns on deer and *cura*, Titus translates the metaphor of Lavinia as a wounded deer into his own 'unrecuring wound'. The resurgence of Dido's simile is a startling reminder of the *Aeneid* and the changes it has suffered, particularly since it comes in the thick of the Ovidian plot of Philomela's rape, which should properly have nothing to do with the losses calculated into empire-building and *pietas*.

The echoes of Dido's simile are simultaneously confirmed and distorted in the plot involving Tamora. Her first appearance as a Dido figure comes when Saturninus woos her as 'lovely Tamora, Queen of Goths,/ That like the stately Phoebe 'mongst her nymphs/ Dost overshine the gallan'st dames of Rome' (I.i.315–17). The compliment alludes to the moment in Book One of the *Aeneid* when Dido first appears in a simile comparing her to Diana as she leads her chorus of nymphs and 'overshines' them all:

qualis in Eurotae ripis aut per iuga Cynthi
exercet Diana choros, quam mille secutae
hinc atque hinc glomerantur Oreades; illa pharetram
fert umero gradiensque deas supereminet omnis. (1.498–501)

As on Eurotas banks or Cynthus ridge Diana trains her dancers, and a thousand followers, mountain-nymphs, on each side gather about her; she bears her quiver on her shoulder and as she steps, overshines all the goddesses.

During the hunt in the next act, Tamora gains bow and arrow, the only circumstantial attributes of Phoebe in Vergil's simile that Saturninus does not mention (Diana's chastity and Tamora's lack of it become issues shortly). Tamora is Dido again in those woods which are, for Lavinia, 'ruthless, dreadful, deaf, and dull', but are a haven for the Queen of the Goths, who lyrically solicits Aaron the Moor to enjoy the *locus amoenus* such as 'The wandr'ing prince and Dido once enjoyed,/ When with a happy storm they were surpris'd,/ And curtain'd with a counsel-keeping cave' (II.iii.22–4). As Aaron attempts to shift Tamora's passions to revenge, pat on cue enter Lavinia and Bassianus. The pair taunts Tamora, transforming her into an obscene parody of Vergil's famous *Venus armata* – Venus, goddess of love, disguised as Diana, virgin goddess of the hunt. The Renaissance, which never tired of the figure who synthesized eroticism and chastity, may never have witnessed so violent a yoking together of Venus and Diana.[11] The queen, 'This goddess, this Semiramis, this nymph,/ This siren', is accosted by ironic comparisons to Diana, presumably in erotic drag:

> Who have we here? Rome's royal empress,
> Unfurnish'd of her well-beseeming troop?
> Or is it Dian, habited like her,
> Who hath abandoned her holy groves
> To see the general hunting in this forest? (II.iii.55–9)

Tamora, however, is no slouch at barbed classical allusions, and counters with Diana's threat to Actaeon:

> Saucy controller of my private steps!
> Had I the pow'r that some say Dian had,
> Thy temples should be planted presently
> With horns, as was Actaeon's; and the hounds
> Should drive upon thy new-transformed limbs,
> Unmannerly intruder as thou art. (II.iii.60–5)

With renewed lust for revenge, she rouses her sons to kill Bassianus and throw him in a pit, and sanctions their plan to rape Lavinia. Revenge satisfies Tamora's voracious sexual appetite: this, she says, is 'the honey we desire'.

The next scene replaces the rape of Lavinia with the fate of Titus' two sons, who are swallowed up in the pit, the 'subtle hole ... Whose mouth is covered with rude-growing briers,/ Upon whose leaves are drops of new-shed blood/ As fresh as morning dew distill'd on flowers' (II.iii.198–201). It is a 'very fatal place' (line 202), an 'unhallow'd and blood-stained hole' (line 210), a 'detested, dark, blood-drinking pit' (line 224), and 'this fell devouring receptacle,/ As hateful as Cocytus' misty mouth' (lines 236–7). The pit, into which Chiron and Demetrius have thrown Bassianus' body, sends chilling sweats through the trembling joints of Titus' sons until they grow faint and are 'pluck'd into the swallowing womb' (line 239) much as Lavinia the dainty doe is at that very moment being *plucked* to the ground in another part of the woods.[12] The 'subtile hole', by the combined powers of metaphor and synecdoche, stands for the 'subtile Queen of Goths',[13] and the scene represents a comically gruesome consummation of Tamora's lust for revenge.[14]

Ovid's tale is introduced to complete the cycle of violation when Lavinia enters, 'her hands cut off, and her tongue cut out, and ravish'd'.

When her uncle Marcus finds her, he calls upon Ovid's tale of Philomela
to make some kind of sense of the spectacle and of his own emotions.

> sure, some Tereus hath deflow'red thee,
> And, lest thou should'st detect him, cut thy tongue . . .
> Fair Philomel, why she but lost her tongue,
> And in a tedious sampler sew'd her mind:
> But, lovely niece, that mean is cut from thee;
> A craftier Tereus, cousin hast thou met,
> And he hath cut those pretty fingers off,
> That could have better sew'd than Philomel. (II.iv.26–7, 38–43)

Here is the act's final violation, one performed upon the audience. It is one thing to *read* a piece of aesthetic gore, but what is one to make of *seeing* Lavinia's mutilated body while *hearing* Marcus speak of Philomela's 'tedious sampler' and of Lavinia's body made 'bare/ Of her two branches, those sweet ornaments,/ Whose circling shadows kings have sought to sleep in' (lines 17–19) or her 'crimson river of warm blood,/ Like to a bubbling fountain stirr'd with wind' (lines 22–3) and her cheeks 'red as Titan's face/ Blushing to be encount'red with a cloud' (lines 31–2)?[15]

Marcus has inadvertently produced the play's most bizarre conflict of rhetoric and referent, and contributed the final addition to the bizarre semiotics of the pit, which is seen metamorphically to assume the shapes of Tamora, Lavinia, Philomela, and Dido, Dido's cave, the Classical Underworld, and even the Andronici's tomb, the 'sacred receptacle' retaining Titus' sons. Marcus' speech identifies both the Ovidian text that will replace Vergil's as the definitive or shaping myth of this late Roman society, and the violent poetics that separates decorative signifiers from their gruesome referents. Here, Lavinia's body is a horribly real sign of violation which Marcus attempts to contain by aestheticizing her wounds. Lavinia's body, however, is a spectacle which sucks up and annihilates his golden poetry: it is the final version of that pit. The pit and Lavinia's body condense the play's tendency to conflate and warp literary sources; as signs, moreover, they violate the norms of representation, since they both produce and consume meaning. They are semiotic black holes.

II

If Shakespeare's play and especially the pit and Lavinia's body seem compulsively to contaminate and digest literary sources and, indeed, all possible referents, they share with Ovid the practice of polemical conflations. In the tale of Tereus, Procne, and Philomela, Ovid does not single out the *Aeneid* as a rival, yet his imitations tend also to be interrogations. When Philomela is raped, she is 'like the wounded Lambe which from the Wolves hore teeth/ New shaken, thinkes hir selfe not safe', or 'as the Dove that seeth/ Hir fethers with hir own bloud stayned';[16] Dido's fall and simile as a doe wounded by the arrow of an unwitting shepherd becomes, in the retrospective view of Philomela's rape and simile, a scene of violation in which responsibility cannot be omitted. Even the most conspicuously Ovidian indulgence in the grotesque, the description of Philomela's tongue as it writhes like a snake in its dying attempt to return to its mistress throws into relief disturbing aspects of violence in the *Aeneid*, for it parodies the death paroxysms of Larides' severed hand, whose dying fingers pulsate and grope for a sword (*te decisa suum, Laride, dextera quaerit/ semianimesque micant digiti ferrumque retractant* (10.395–6). In a more seriously critical allusion, Tereus cuts out Philomela's tongue indignant and calling on her father's name (*indignantem et nomen patris usque vocantem*, 6.556), words which recall the death of Turnus: after he invoked his father's name in a vain attempt to rouse Aeneas' mercy, Turnus' spirit flew to the Underworld *indignata* – resentful of an unworthy act.

If Shakespeare had an awareness of, and sympathy for, Ovid's critical deployment of Vergil, he could not have chosen to contaminate two more startlingly relevant episodes than those treating Philomela and Dido: Dido's agentless seduction turns to Philomela's rape; Aeneas' *pietas* to Tereus' *impietas* (a word which pervades Ovid's tale); Dido nourishing the wound of love changes to Tereus and his concrete *cibus furoris* – food of passion or madness; the silencing of Dido gives way to the cutting out of Philomela's tongue; and Dido's curse to Procne and Philomela's revenge. I would not have thought to treat this particular tale as a critique of Dido's function in the *Aeneid*, yet a violent wrenching of the epic's purpose is precisely what Shakespeare accomplishes in his *contaminatio*. While I am not prepared to hold Shakespeare responsible for all the patterns set in motion, we can be reasonably certain that he designed the pit to represent this wild proliferation of meanings. Shakespeare, I suggest, found in Ovid's *Metamorphoses* a narrative and critical practice which he assimilated to the semiotics of the pit, which substitutes, inverts, confuses, appropriates, swallows up, and engenders meanings. The most significant difference between Shakespeare's and Ovid's practices of polemical literary conflations is that Shakespeare, in *Titus*, genders and metaphorizes the politics of imitation: the audience is brutally confronted with the art of contamination in the pit and Lavinia's body, both signs of social disorder. In the next section, I shall discuss Titus' brand of semiosis, and especially his practice of metaphorizing and gendering literary imitations. For through feats of literalism and displacement, Titus intends to exact poetic justice, a social destruction equal to the familial *and ideological* violence that has caused him to suffer. It will be immediately clear that Titus does not become an Ovidian author indulging in a liberating play of significations. Instead, he engages in a simpler form of subverting referentiality in order to wreak havoc on his enemies and, more importantly, on the system of values, as encoded in Augustan literature, which has disappointed him.

III

Once we have entered into the Ovidian woods of the second act, where physical and epistemological violence may and does occur at any moment, we – the audience as well as the play's characters – never return to secure Vergilian foundations.[17] In the beginning of the play, Titus exemplified the stoic belief that, in the words of one critic, 'to endure misfortune is to reveal one's true self – a pure essence of *virtus* – and, simultaneously, to discover that the universe is significantly ordered'.[18] The epic genre which had consecrated the imperial origins of Rome offered the mode of self-containment and cosmic order to Titus, the triumphant warrior but grieving father who entered Rome with an epic simile on his lips:

> Hail, Rome, victorious in thy mourning weeds!
> Lo, as the bark that hath discharg'd his fraught
> Returns with precious lading to the bay
> From whence at first she weigh'd her anchorage,
> Cometh Andronicus, bound with laurel boughs,
> To re-salute his country with his tears. (I.i.70–5)

The linguistic, cultural, and psychological integrity that Vergilian authority represents for Titus, however, fragments in those 'ruthless, dreadful, deaf, and dull woods' and even in his beloved Rome, which is 'but a wilderness of tigers' (III.i.54) for Titus once his sons are condemned to death for the murder of Bassianus. At the turning point of the play, Titus finally loosens his hold on the Andronican 'uprightness and integrity': although Aaron had persuaded Titus that sacrificing his hand would buy the lives of his sons, a messenger returns to Titus bearing the severed hand and his children's heads. Marcus drops the reins of stoicism and attempts to rouse an epic fury in his brother – 'Now is a time to storm' (III.i.263), he cries – but Titus, whose unexpected response marks his *generic* metamorphosis, is no longer an epic hero: 'Ha, ha, ha!' (III.i.264).[19] Titus comes undone in puns which strikingly contrast with the formal decorum of his former, Vergilian identity. When Marcus foolishly mentions the word 'hands', after Titus has lost his, Titus cries out that Marcus bids him, like Aeneas, to 'tell the tale twice o'er/ How Troy was burnt and he made miserable' – and then produces one of the play's worst puns, 'O, handle not the theme, to talk of hands' (III.ii.27–9). At such moments, the *Aeneid* looms as a dismembered, mutilated text of Rome's former greatness.[20]

Marcus, who fails to comprehend Titus' laughter, consistently serves to point up the shift in genre that Titus has undergone. When Marcus, Titus, and his grandson discover the identities of Lavinia's ravishers,

Marcus conjures them to kneel and swear revenge, calling young Lucius 'Roman Hector's hope' and invoking the paradigmatic rape of Lucrece to guide the Andronici's revenge: he and Titus are to swear 'as with the woeful fere/ And father of that chaste dishonoured dame,/ Lord Junius Brutus sware for Lucrece's rape/ That we will prosecute by good advice/ Mortal revenge upon these traitorous Goths' (IV.i.89–93). Titus, however, evades his brother's rite (he had, after all, already sworn revenge upon his severed hand and his sons' heads) and rejects the model of resurrection offered by the figures of Astyanax and Junius Brutus. While Titus, like Brutus, feigns imbecility, he models his actions not on those of Rome's early champion against tyranny and injustice, but on the revenge of Procne, whose domestic tragedy is antithetical to epic.[21] Marcus assumes, when Titus steers his grandson away from heroic action – young Lucius is prepared to deliver Titus' message to the empress' sons 'with my dagger in their bosoms' (IV.i.18) – that Titus has committed himself to a course of stoic patience. Yet when Titus says he will teach 'another course', he means to take up unusual weapons: the literature that encodes Rome's celebrated virtues. He seeks his revenge in exploiting the elastic nature of Roman examples and models – signs absurdly prone to hyperbolic expansion and satiric reduction.

His first lesson is inscribed in a revision of a celebrated Augustan poem: Titus sends to Chiron and Demetrius a bundle of arrows wrapped in a scroll with Horace's famous ode, *Integer vitae, scelerisque purus,/ Non eget Mauri iaculis, nec arcu* (IV.ii.20–1). He produces, quite literally, a barbed allusion. The poem has degenerated into little more than a schoolboy's verse, which Chiron 'read ... in grammar long ago' (IV.ii.23); as an allusion, however, it produces fresh meaning. Titus trusts that the ode will appear as a mere tag proclaiming a musty Roman virtue, and that the boys will fail to see the obvious referents: themselves, Aaron the Moor, and Titus, who is no longer physically whole (*integer*) and does not intend to remain free of crime. Titus' principle of inversion indicates that he is not recreating, but stripping meaning from the poem. Although he now recognizes a dead metaphor when he sees one, he apparently feels compelled to strike the final blow.

In perhaps the strangest scene of the play, Titus gathers his family to solicit the gods for justice, using an innovative method: using bow and arrow, they send petitions to the Zodiacal signs on the Capitoline Hill. Titus is actually staging an elaborate attack, not a supplication. Yet it is unclear who are the targets: Saturninus and the court or the Zodiacal signs themselves. After shooting arrows at Jove, Apollo, Pallas, and Mercury, Titus cracks the first topical joke: 'To Saturn, Caius, not to Saturnine;/ You were as good to shoot against the wind' (IV.iii.56–7). The Andronici then unite in hurling shafts of wit at the court: Lucius strikes

Virgo's lap and Publius shoots off one of Taurus' horns, providing Marcus with the occasion to complete a round of cuckolding jokes:

> This was the sport, my lord: when Publius shot,
> The Bull, being gall'd, gave Aries such a knock
> That down fell both the Ram's horns in the court;
> And who should find them but the empress' villain?
> She laugh'd, and told the Moor he should not choose
> But give them to his master for a present. (IV.iii.69–74)

Titus' arrows accomplish their mission: they not only undermine the pretensions that Saturninus and his queen might have to divine status as represented by the Zodiacal signs, but also strip the Zodiac of its power to refer to, and support, the traditional Roman sense of cosmological order the justice. Shot in the lap, the goddess of justice, Astraea, has been anatomically exposed as the whoring queen of Goths.[22]

In the most flamboyant of revenge plots based on literalism, Titus is willing to take at face value Tamora, disguised as Revenge, requesting only that she include in the allegory her sons, as Rapine and Murder. Yet it is Lavinia's body which bears most of Titus' literalisms. When Titus gathers his remaining family to swear revenge, he holds the head of one son, gives the other to Marcus, and sets in Lavinia's mouth his severed hand:

> The vow is made. Come, brother, take a head;
> And in this hand the other will I bear.
> And, Lavinia, thou shalt be employ'd in these arms:
> Bear thou my hand, sweet wench, between thy teeth. (III.i.279–82)

Titus transforms his family into a sign of mutilation, and places Lavinia at its center. As Coppelia Kahn points out, Lavinia literally represents the handmaid of revenge.[23]

Titus insistently focuses his macabre play with literalizing signs on Lavinia's body, which serves as the figurative ground for refashioning his cultural myths, his course of action, and his very identity. He calls her a 'map of woe, that thus dost talk in signs', and further says, 'Thou shalt not sigh, nor hold thy stumps to heaven,/ Nor wink, nor nod, nor kneel, nor make a sign,/ But I of these will wrest an alphabet,/ And by still practice learn to know thy meaning' (III.ii.12, 42–5). Her body, inscribed with Philomela's fate, suggests to Titus the course of his revenge and, comically, prepares for the dramatic appearance of the book itself. For, the play advertises its bookishness to the point of trotting a copy of the *Metamorphoses* on stage: Lavinia chases her nephew around the stage until she can lay hold of it and turn to Philomela's tale. Lavinia thus provides Titus with an authoritative text to replace his Vergil, and Titus concocts his revenge from Ovid's plot – a faithful act of literary digestion. 'Worse than Philomel you us'd my daughter', he says to Chiron and Demetrius,

'And worse than Progne I will be reveng'd' (v.ii.194–5). He seves up to the Queen her two sons, their flesh baked in a piecrust of their ground-up bones – a dish appropriately called 'coffin'.

As Lavinia's body serves to inspire Titus' literary revenge, so it provides his text to reveal and complete it. Titus issues his challenge to Saturninus in the form of a deadly logical proof:

> *Tit.* My lord the emperor, resolve me in this:
>   Was it well done or rash Virginius
>   To slay his daughter with his own right hand,
>   Because she was enforc'd, stain'd, and deflow'r'd?
> *Sat.* It was, Andronicus.
> *Tit.* Your reason, mighty lord?
> *Sat.* Because the girl should not survive her shame,
>   And by her presence still renew his sorrows.
> *Tit.* A reason mighty, strong, and effectual;
>   A pattern, president, and lively warrant
>   For me, most wretched, to perform the like.
>   Die, die, Lavinia, and thy shame with thee;
>   And with thy shame thy father's sorrow die! [*He kills her*] (v.iii.35–47)

It takes only fifteen more lines for Titus to clarify the exact natures of his revenge and the meal Tamora has just eaten, and a further three for Titus to kill Tamora, Saturninus to kill Titus, and Lucius to kill the emperor. These acts are riveting, but no more than the aftershocks of Titus' murder of his daughter. It seems inevitable, on reflection, that Titus should kill Lavinia; that he should use her as part of a logical proof, especially one involving a great Roman precedent which shifts responsibility to Saturninus; and that he should not place any real value in his stated textual authority. Titus regards Virginius as 'rash' and himself as 'wretched'; he had not, moreover, shared Virginius' severity when he learned of Lavinia's mutilation or its cause. Rather, he had experienced his most humanizing moment in the play: Marcus presented her, saying 'This was thy daughter', to which Titus answered simply, 'Why, Marcus, so she is' (III.i.64).

Titus' final act is perversely both to subvert and to affirm Roman paradigms of virtue. His citation of Virginius constitutes an attack on that momentous event in Roman history; for even if Titus placed value in Virginius' act, which he apparently does not, he cannot escape the fact that the heroic dimensions of the original do not pass into the repetition. One cannot monumentalize an action twice. Titus' final act has none of the wit of his earlier literary skirmishes because he has drawn his daughter into his heroic-demonic feats of emptying Roman paradigms of their virtue. Yet Titus, with equal perversity, affirms the value of his uncited *exemplum*, that of Lucrece. Titus knows that if his sorrows die with his daughter's shame, it is only because his revenge guarantees his own death.

By killing Lavinia, he can commit suicide by proxy; by appropriating her rape as an outrage committed on him (an extension which Tamora fully intended), he can assume the role of Lucrece. In slaying Lavinia, Titus commits his most alienating act. Yet if Titus gains any sympathy at the end of the play, it is paradoxically because he killed his daughter, whom he called the 'cordial of my age to glad my heart' (1.i.167). The pun on cordial and heart came early enough in the play to emphasize identity instead of disjunction, and while it testifies to paternal devotion, it also anticipates Titus' terrible inability to distinguish between himself and his children. In killing Lavinia and in casting himself as the violated Lucrece, Titus proves that his experiences in loss and injustice have failed to change him from the father who killed his son Mutius for disobedience.

In the concluding move of the play to restore order, Vergil is called upon to perform the last rites. Marcus requests Lucius to address the Senate

> as erst our ancestor,
> When with his solemn tongue he did discourse
> To love-sick Dido's sad attending ear
> The story of that baleful burning night,
> When subtile Greeks surpris'd King Priam's Troy.
> Tell us what Sinon hath bewitch'd our ears.
> Or who hath brought the fatal engine in
> That gives our Troy, our Rome, the civil wound. (v.iii.80–7)

Although the Senate places its hope in the healing powers of the *Aeneid*, master code of the Roman Empire, Vergil can do no more than bandage the civil wound. The motivations and sources of authority – literary, political, ethical – have been hopelessly confused. Titus himself, although a man more sinned against than sinning, nonetheless stands as a monument to the failings of the Roman imperial machine. No Sinon insinuated the 'fatal engine' into Rome, although that is the tale Lucius will gravely unfold. As in the first scene of the play, when Titus sacrificed Tamora's and his own sons to the rigid code of *pietas*, Roman institutions and values are dramatically emptied of all meaning. Vergil's noble rhetoric and values sound hollow; he reappears not to rejuvenate Rome, but to receive, like Titus' dead body, the last kiss of his sons. A final note: Vergil's vision of disorder and the inescapability of *furor* – madness and passion – may be sacrificed or overlooked in the Renaissance in order to gain an unambiguous champion of political order. Yet it is also possible that Shakespeare presents Rome in the late Empire as a state which made a fatally reductive icon of Vergil's poem, and ignored the double meaning of a monument – not just a tribute, but a warning.

NOTES

1 Ovid's most sustained critique of the *Aeneid* comes in the last five books of the *Metamorphoses*, which treat Aeneas' mission to found the Augustan Empire. Ovid undercuts the heroic mode primarily by evincing boredom with his task at every possible moment. The petulant Achilles, who gruesomely crushes the life out of Cygnus and who demands the sacrifice of Polyxena, the blockish Ajax, and the mean-minded, duplicitous Ulysses are enough to exhaust the epideictic powers of epic. Yet Ovid proceeds literally to overturn the *Aeneid* by elaborating on Vergil's minor characters: the left-over companion of Ulysses gains a name, Achaemenides, and a tale of his own, as do the scarcely mentioned Caenus, Picus, and Diomedes. Polyphemus reverts to his Theocritean identity, and even the Sybil gains a love life. Ovid thus dramatizes the dehumanizing aspects of heroic endeavor and the indifference of Empire to individual voice.

2 Vergil's poem opens itself to the charge of glorifying a second Trojan War based on rape when Turnus protests against the Trojans' rhetoric of divine fate:

> sat fatis Venerisque datum, tetigere quod arva
> fertilis Ausoniae Troes. sunt et mea contra
> fata mihi, ferro sceleratam exscindere gentem
> coniuge praerepta; nec solos tangit Atridas
> iste dolor, solisque licet capere arma Mycenis. (9.135–9)

> Enough has been granted to the 'fates' and to Venus, since the Trojans have touched the lands of fertile Ausonia. I have my fates to oppose theirs: since my bride was stolen, to destroy by my sword this wicked race. This sorrow does not touch the Atridae alone, and to seize arms is not allowed only to Mycenae.

All translations are mine, except where Golding's translation of the *Metamorphoses* could serve.

3 While Shakespeare's literary conflations have passed without much comment (mainly because critics elect Ovid as the master source, demoting other allusions to local color), the same cannot be said for his conflation of Roman political institutions. T. J. B. Spencer, in 'Shakespeare and the Elizabethan Romans', *Shakespeare Survey 10* (Cambridge University Press, 1969), derives a fair amount of fun in pointing out the ludicrous mixture of periods and traditions:

> In *Titus Andronicus* Rome seems to be, at times, a free commonwealth, with the usual mixture of patrician and plebeian institutions. Titus is himself elected emperor of Rome on account of his merits, because the senate and people do not recognize an hereditary principle of succession. But Titus disclaims the honour in favour of the late Emperor's elder (and worser) son. Titus is a devoted adherent ... of the hereditary monarchical principle in a commonwealth that only partly takes it into account, and he eventually acknowledges his mistake. He encourages, by his subservience, the despotic rule on which Saturninus embarks, passing to a world of Byzantine intrigue, in which the barbarians (Southern and Northern, Moors and Goths) ... exert their baneful or beneficent influence. And

finally, Lucius is elected emperor 'to order well the state' (says the second Quarto). Now, all these elements of the political situation can be found in Roman history, but not combined in this way. The play ... [is] a summary of Roman politics ... it includes all the political institutions Rome ever had. (p. 32)

Besides being genuinely funny – in a way that clocks in Rome and seacoasts in Bohemia are not, especially – there is a point to Shakespeare's summary of Roman politics. Just as the literary contamination of Vergil and Ovid carries Roman origins to their end, so does the collection of political institutions. Shakespeare is concerned with the idea of *Roma aeterna*, the eternal city with its dramatic history of upheaval. In his account of *Titus'* political shape-shifting, Spencer focuses on Titus himself, and on the ideological revisions Titus undergoes as he witnesses the terrible results of his political decisions. Spencer thus makes visible the intriguing connection between the metamorphoses of Rome and her champion, Titus.

4 Critics of *Titus* cannot resist rehearsing portions of the animated and damning criticism that the play has received over the centuries. The memorable words cited above come from Edward Ravenscroft, the seventeenth-century playwright who refurbished *Titus* for the stage. See his 'To the Reader', his preface to his own *Titus Andronicus, or the Rape of Lavinia* (London, 1686). T. S. Eliot called the play 'one of the stupidest and most uninspired plays ever written', ('Seneca in Elizabethan Translation', *Selected Essays*, new edn (New York: 1950), p. 67), and Dover Wilson recreated Ravenscroft's condemnation, saying it is 'like some broken-down cart, laden with bleeding corpses from an Elizabethan scaffold, and driven by an executioner from Bedlam dressed in cap and bells' (*Titus Andronicus*, ed. Dover Wilson (Cambridge University Press, 1948), p. xii).

5 Readers in the moralizing tradition seek to find satisfying justice in Ovid's aetiological tales, whether the metamorphoses confer an honor (Baucis and Philemon) or accomplish a revenge (e.g. Actaeon, Niobe, and Arachne). Yet Ovid dramatizes the arbitrary nature of signs in many of his metamorphoses, such as, for example, that of Daphne. When she prays to escape rape by Apollo, she is transformed into a tree. Apollo claims the laurel as his own emblem, and the boughs of the tree 'seem' to nod: but do boughs blowing in the wind signify yes or no? For Ovid, such signs can only be arbitrary in nature because passion and power assign them their meaning. See Mary Kay Gamel, 'Apollo and Daphne: The Making of a Sign', forthcoming in *Classical Antiquity*.

6 Not only does Tamora make an appearance as the spirit of Revenge, but the play's attempt to establish equilibrium at its end depends on reviling not Aaron, but Tamora. The Andronici teach the Romans 'how to knit again/ This scattered corn into one mutual sheaf,/ These broken limbs again into one body' (v.iii.70–2) by praising Titus, revealing Aaron as the architect of their woes, and saving the animus for Tamora, 'that ravenous tiger', who deserves no civilized rites of burial.

7 All references are to the third Arden edition edited by J. C. Maxwell (London: Methuen & Co., 1953).

8 While Titus calms the political storm here, he later translates himself into one. Rejecting Marcus' appeal to reason, he responds,

> If there were reason for these miseries,
> Then into limits could I bind my woes:
> When heaven doth weep, doth not the earth o'erflow?
> If the winds rage, doth not the sea wax mad,
> Threat'ning the welkin with his bid-swol'n face?
> And wilt thou have a reason for this coil?
> I am the sea. Hark how her sighs doth blow;
> She is the weeping welkin, I the earth:
> Then must my sea be moved with her sighs;
> Then must my earth with her continual tears
> Become a deluge, overflow'd and drown'd. (III.i.219–29)

9 The Arden editor points out that 'the closeness of *hover* to *volitant* suggests an actual echo' (p. 9).

10 Titus' own family points out his 'impiety' and calls him 'barbarous' (I.i.355, 378) when he kills Mutius.

11 The classic discussion of the Venus armata is found in Edgar Wind, *Pagan Mysteries in the Renaissance*, revised and enlarged edition (New York: W. W. Norton & Company, Inc., 1958).

12 A strange allusion to 'Pyramus/ When he by night lay bath'd in maiden blood' (II.iii.231–2) stresses the scene's imagery of defloration and, consequently, its capacity to substitute for the offstage scene of Lavinia's rape and mutilation. The allusion to Pyramus, especially to his 'maiden blood', fastens on the substitutive relationship of sex and death in Ovid's tale and reinforces *Titus'* obsession with substitution, the mechanism which structures much of the play's revenge plot: Tamora substitutes the rape of Lavinia and the deaths of Titus' sons for her own sexual pleasure; Titus' sons' uncanny fall into the pit substitutes for Lavinia's rape; Titus later attempts to substitute his hand for the lives of his sons and receives their heads in lieu of their whole selves; he has already substituted the textual authority on *pietas* for piety itself; and will trade that text, the *Aeneid*, for Ovid's tale of Philomela. For the insight that Aaron devises an act of synecdoche by returning the heads of Marcus and Quintus rather than the live sons, see Albert H. Tricomi, 'The Aesthetics of Mutilation in *Titus Andronicus*', *Shakespeare Survey 27* (Cambridge University Press, 1974), p. 16.

13 A. C. Hamilton notes that the pit 'becomes Hell itself, the monster who drinks Bassianus' blood and so strangely draws Titus' sons into its mouth', *Titus Andronicus*: The Form of Shakespearean Tragedy', *Shakespeare Quarterly*, 14 (1963), 212. In a footnote, Tricomi (ibid., p. 18) suggests that the connection between the Classical Underworld and female genitalia is characteristic of Shakespeare, and cites the famous lines from *Lear*:

> Down from the waist they are Centaurs,
> Though women all above:
> But to the girdle do the Gods inherit,
> Beneath is all the fiend's: there's hell, there's darkness,
> There is the sulphurous pit – burning, scalding,
> Stench, consumption; fie, fie, fie! pah, pah! (IV.vi.123–8)

David Willbern, in a provocative and careful reading of the play's association of rape and revenge, allows the internal representation of the vagina out of the footnotes in 'Rape and Revenge in *Titus Andronicus*', *English Literary Renaissance* (1977).

14 Critics have found *Titus'* gruesome humor a source of embarrassment, and have presented arguments for neutralizing the potentially uncomfortable laughter that the pit will elicit from audiences; see, for example, Alan C. Dessen, 'Two Falls and a Trap: Shakespeare and the Spectacles of Realism', *English Literary Renaissance*, 5 (1975), 291–307. Yet audiences at the brilliant production by Shakespeare Santa Cruz in 1988 had no trouble grasping either the humor or the horror of the scene, precisely because the production did not attempt to efface the specter of *vagina dentata* that looms over Marcus and Quintus' pathetic fall into the pit.

15 Orpheus, the primary narrator of Book 10 of the *Metamorphoses*, aestheticizes Hyacinthus' wounds. In Golding's translation,

> like as one
> Broosd violet stalkes of Poppie stalkes growing on
> Brown spindles, streight they withering droope with heavy heads and are
> Not able for too hold them up, but with their tops doo stare
> Uppon the ground. So *Hyacinth* in yeelding of his breath
> Chopt downe his head. His necke bereft of strength by meanes of death
> Was even a burthen too itself, and downe did loosely wrythe
> On both his shoulders, now a tone and now a toother lythe. (10.199–206)

Indulging in the aesthetics of gore is by no means exclusively Ovidian, and in fact, Ovid advertises his debt to Vergil's description of Euryalus' death in Book IX of the *Aeneid*.

Eugene Waith comments that Marcus' attempt to metamorphose Lavinia fails because 'in the presence of live actors the poetry cannot perform the necessary magic. The action frustrates, rather than reinforces, the operation of poetry', 'The Metamorphosis of Violence in *Titus Andronicus*', *Shakespeare Survey 10* (Cambridge University Press, 1969), pp. 45–6. It seems to me that far from sabotaging Ovid's aesthetics, the dramatic medium allows Shakespeare to overgo Ovid in exploiting the differences between descriptions of events, which are motivated by desire and authorized by power (in the case of Hycinthus, Apollo, god of poetry and lover of the boy, is responsible for the aesthetic representation of the boy's death) and the events themselves. The reader of Ovid is likely to juxtapose mental images of lovely bruised poppies with the boy's mangled head, and if the discontinuity is distressing, the reader can quickly resume reading the next tale; the audience of *Titus*, however, cannot escape the spectacle of Lavinia's mutilated body and the shock of Marcus' words which, if I am not stretching the metaphorizing activity of the play, perform a second 'rape' or seizure of Lavinia's body (Latin *rapere*, to seize).

16 All references to Golding's translation are to *'Shakespeare's Ovid': Arthur Golding's translation of the Metamorphoses*, ed. W. H. D. Rouse, Centaur Classics (Carbondale: Southern Illinois University Press, 1961).

17 Once Titus grasps the text of the *Metamorphoses*, he recognizes that the woods were 'ruthless, vast, and gloomy', a *locus horrendus* 'Pattern'd by that the poet here describes,/ By nature made for murthers and for rapes' (IV.i.53, 57–8).

18 Jonathan Dollimore, *Radical Tragedy* (London and Chicago: University of Chicago Press, 1984), p. 41.
19 Eugene Waith comments on Titus' 'psychic metamorphosis which provides one of the truly powerful moments in the depiction of the hero' (ibid., p. 46), although he locates the shift later, at Titus' horrifying speech to Chiron and Demetrius, when he identifies himself with Procne, only more vengeful.
20 Titus' dear-deer-cura puns also come directly after an allusion to the Troy legend: 'What fool hath added water to the sea,/ Or brought a faggot to bright-burning Troy?' (III.i.68–9).
21 Titus formalizes his anti-epic identification by overturning the genre's rhetorical conventions:
> Marcus, we are but shrubs, no cedars we;
> No big-bone'd men fram'd of the Cyclops' size;
> But metal, Marcus, steel to the very back,
> Yet wrung with wrongs more than our backs can bear. (IV.iii.45–8)

He rejects the aggranding effects of heroic similes, and adapts the iron-age discourse which is more famously recorded in the first book of the *Metamorphoses*. There, Ovid describes the degeneration of the golden to the iron age, and after the tale of Deucalion and Pyrrha, comments that men are hard as stone; Titus improves on Ovid's derivation of human durability and obduracy from stone by making explicit the connection with the iron age.
22 Frances Yates discusses *Titus'* treatment of the virgin Astraea in *Astraea: The Imperial Theme in the Sixteenth Century* (London: Routledge & Kegan Paul, 1975), pp. 74–6. She finds that although Shakespeare must surely have known about Astraea's iconographic association with Elizabeth, and that the imperial theme must be important to the play, nonetheless, his treatment of the Astraea image is 'so utterly surprising and unconventional' that it raises more questions than it answers (p. 76). Perhaps Titus' equation of Astraea with Tamora sheds light on Shakespeare's incorporation into the play of the *translatio imperii*: Rome has lost its virgin in the rape of Lavinia, and her position as 'Rome's rich ornament' is usurped by Tamora, as are her (and Elizabeth's) associations with Diana when Saturninus transfers his desires to the Gothic Queen and bestows on her the complimentary allusion to Diana. England, however, has its virgin Queen and its claim to hereditary succession of the Troy legend.
23 Coppelia Kahn, in a paper delivered at the lecture series for Shakespeare Santa Cruz' performance of the Roman plays. Lavinia is vulnerable to the Roman traffic in women, and especially to the Andronican sense of honor. In the first scene, Saturninus claims her as his bride in order, he says, to 'advance/ [Titus'] name and honorable family' (lines 238–9), to which Titus readily agrees; and Bassianus seizes her in an act Saturninus later calls 'rape' (line 404). The most telling exchange, however, occurs not between the princes but between Titus and Lucius. Titus disowns Lucius as a 'traitor', and demands that he 'restore Lavinia to the emperor', to which Lucius chillingly replies, 'Dead, if you will; but not to be his wife,/ That is another's lawful-promis'd love' (lines 296–8). Lavinia is established as an object upholding men's honor, much like Helen in *Troilus and Cressida*, who is the 'theme of honor and renown'. Worth more dead than devalued, it is no wonder that she dies in the service of Titus' symbolic play.

Racine's *Bajazet*: the language of violence and secrecy*

MAYA SLATER

In Racine's day, the staging of a tragedy in the public theatre was chaotic. Every element contributed to prevent the play from being given a fair hearing. The acting space on stage was full of rowdy members of the audience, sitting a few feet away from the actors and making rude comments; the lighting, besides being inadequate, was designed to illuminate the audience rather than the actors, and so prevent scuffles in the dark.[1] Even the actors detracted from the words of the play. Molière, mocking at the tragic actress Mlle Beauchâteau,[2] comments sarcastically: 'You should marvel at how she keeps smiling when she is most deeply afflicted.' Molière also tells us that Racine's actors opposed a naturalistic method of delivery. They wanted the rhyming couplets they used to be spoken 'avec emphase', with the last syllable of each line stressed.[3] In addition to Molière's comments, what we know of the costumes and deportment of the actors of the time reinforces the impression that the actors were not remotely concerned with rendering the text in a convincing manner.

And yet Racine's theatre is a theatre of words. There is almost no stage action, no movements, no meaningful silences. The characters exist only as a function of what they say. Racine's situation as a playwright is thus paradoxical: he was required by the conventions of classical French tragedy to write plays that relied exclusively on the spoken word for effect. But these plays were then staged in a manner that effectively distracted the audience from those same spoken words.

This paradox is important for understanding Racine. The question is, did Racine fail to address the problem of how to stage his plays, given the impossible conditions? Was he content to write as a dramatic poet, aware that even if his plays failed on stage, they would succeed with readers? Or do the texts of his plays on the contrary reveal a true playwright, concerned to find techniques for overcoming the problems that must have beset his productions? A close look at the language of violence and secrecy in *Bajazet* may provide an answer.

Bajazet (1672) was written half-way through Racine's ten-year career as

---

* A draft of this paper was read at the *Themes in Drama* International Conference held at the University of London, Queen Mary and Westfield College, in March 1989.

a successful secular playwright. It demonstrates a confident handling of language, and also an extraordinary degree of repetition of certain linguistic elements. The subjects of the reiterated material are related to two interlinking themes, *secrecy* and *violence*, which may be described as the leitmotivs of the play.

The two elements are eminently appropriate to this play, set as it is in the harem in Constantinople. The play tells of a plot within the harem to overthrow the Ottoman Sultan, engineered by his favourite concubine, the Sultana Roxane, and his brother Bajazet.[4] The traditional picture of the harem is as a taboo-ridden place and a violent one; Racine builds on this view. In his preface he implies that he is thinking in terms of violence when he explains that he feels obliged to endow the hero Bajazet, an Ottoman prince, with an unusual degree of savagery for a hero of classical tragedy: 'Bajazet retains even in love the ferocity of his race.'[5] As for secrecy, Racine in the preface stresses the importance of the harem as a setting, pointing out that it is remote and alien. And at the beginning of the play he tells us that the rooms of the harem are forbidden areas, out of bounds to all men except the Sultan.

In the action of the play Racine uses this double leitmotiv of violence and secrecy constructively, bringing the two threads together at the end with the death of Bajazet, which is both secret (a shock to characters and audience alike) and brutal (Roxane's mute slaves try to strangle him with a noose, but he fights them off, and dies surrounded by their corpses). Violence and secrecy are, indeed, incorporated into the text at all levels: the first task of this paper is to demonstrate the systematic nature of Racine's treatment by examining his use of language.

A detailed study of language is eminently appropriate to Racine's own approach to these two themes of violence and secrecy. For words have exceptional importance in *Bajazet* because of its particular setting. The brutality of the Ottoman rule, and the feeling that the characters are being spied on and are in constant danger in the harem, mean that they have to weigh every word they speak: a careless word can mean the difference between life and death. We see this immediately in 1.1 when the vizir of the harem, Acomat, claims that a single speech can change a whole empire: 'the destiny of the Ottoman empire depends on the account that you give'.[6] Later, the 'account' becomes one word: the vizir pleads with Bajazet, 'speak a word, and you will save us all'.[7] The word in question is 'yes', in answer to Roxane who is asking him to marry her. Meanwhile Bajazet's secret love, the Princess Atalide, is equally convinced of the life-saving quality of language: 'I can save him with a word'.[8] By the end of the play Bajazet is threatened with death by the violent Roxane, who has him in her power: 'If a word escapes me, your life will be forfeit'.[9] At this stage the threat is a purely symbolic expression of the fact that Roxane has power over Bajazet. But, interestingly, later, Roxane does in actual fact kill Bajazet by pronouncing one single word. She arranges a final interview with him, and tells her assassins to kill him if he leaves the room. During the interview she decides he must die, and utters the one word 'Sortez!', ('leave me!') which obliges him to go out and hence costs him his life.

Racine, then, is placing great emphasis on the importance of language in the violent action of *Bajazet*. He reinforces this by insisting on certain key words. The verb *'craindre'* (to fear, dread) occurs repeatedly in this play. Most often it is in a violent context: a character fears for his life or that of someone he loves. The most vivid of many examples is an epigrammatic description of the Sultan's relationship with his janissaries: 'Comme il les *craint* sans cesse, ils le *craignent* toujours' (line 44) ('since he fears them constantly, they fear him always'). The repetition of parts of the verb 'craindre', the symmetry of the positioning within the two hemistiches of the line, and the synonyms 'sans cesse/toujours' ('constantly/always') focus the attention on the mutual danger.

A second word that is used in a prominent manner to seem like a kind of leitmotiv is 'fatal', which in French has the useful double meaning 'disastrous/fatal' or 'fateful'. The word can seem very powerful when it sumultaneously carries both meanings. In particular, it is used of the love of Roxane for Bajazet and her plans to marry him: 'le fatal hymen que vous me proposez' 'the fateful marriage you're proposing to me' (line 492) says Bajazet, secretly meaning 'disastrous', while Roxane tells Bajazet of her intention to marry him with the portentous words: 'Prince, l'heure fatale est enfin arrivée' 'Prince, the fateful hour has finally struck' (line 421), describing a moment which will turn out to be 'fatal'. The implication of violence is combined with a subversion of the apparent meaning which reinforces the impression that there is something hidden behind the words.

These double meanings also focus attention on the vocabulary of violence. There are several cruel and frightening word-plays in *Bajazet*. The underlying brutality is reflected by numerous mentions of the word 'sang' (blood); it is used in two ways, to mean first one's life-blood, as when Bajazet says to Roxane: 'I owe all my blood to you, my life belongs to you'[10] (line 519). Secondly, it means one's race; so Bajazet is the 'reste' of the 'sang des Ottomans' ('the last remaining scion of the Ottoman blood') (line 594). Because of the frequent use of 'sang' meaning real blood, the references to race become associated with violence. At times, it is not clear which of the two meanings is the correct one, as when Atalide, terrified that Roxane is going to kill Bajazet, asks 'what blood will suffice to placate her anger?'[11] Does she mean Ottoman blood, or simply bloodshed?

Closely allied to Racine's use of 'sang' is his use of 'noeud', a 'knot'.

Again, this has an innocent and a violent meaning: an emotional bond or a noose. This double meaning gives Racine scope for some horrific word-plays. Roxane discovers that Bajazet loves Atalide, not her, so she tells her: 'Far from separating you, I intend today to tie you to him by an eternal knot'.[12] She wants Atalide to think that she is planning their marriage; in fact, she intends to strangle them both, so it is in death that she intends to unite them. Similarly, early in the play, Atalide uses both 'sang' and 'noeud' in an innocent comment that will later prove true in a completely different sense. Talking of her relationship with Bajazet, whom she has loved for years, she says 'Love tightened the knot originally tied by blood [that is, kinship]'.[13] But her words also unconsciously prefigure the violent end of the play, in which their love causes their deaths by the noose and by bloodshed.

To reinforce the feeling that violent death is imminent, Racine uses a wide variety of synonyms for death.[14] This richness is especially striking in view of the meagreness of Racine's vocabulary in general (only 2,878 different words in all his profane tragedies).[15] One should also note that *Bajazet* has a small vocabulary even for Racine,[16] which makes the huge number of death-words the more notable. We get the following synonyms for death, dying or killing: for death, 'mort', 'supplice', 'ruine', 'trépas', 'sacrifice', 'meurtre', 'chute', 'perte'. For to die: 'mourir', 'périr', 'tomber', 'expirer', 'sacrifier', 'finir'. For to kill: 'assassiner', 'trancher', 'terminer', 'achever', 'précipiter'.[17] Racine adds a further dimension by juxtaposing different forms of death-word, which avoids actual phonetic repetition. He does this repeatedly with 'mourir' and 'mort', hammering home the message, particularly with reference to Bajazet, who is in constant danger of death: 'Bajazet est *mort*, ou *meurt* en ce moment' (line 1449) ('Bajazet is dead, or dying at this moment'), or, later, the remorseless death couplet:

> Bajazet était *mort*. Nous l'avons rencontré
> De *morts* et de *mourants* noblement entouré. (lines 1700–1).

('Bajazet was dead. We found him nobly surrounded by the dead and the dying').[18]

Death is also the subject of numerous sinister idioms which add to the obsessive frequency with which this leitmotiv recurs. Within less than a hundred lines, killing is described as 'to punish a crime' (line 1692), 'to take a victim' (line 1672), 'to pierce a heart' (line 1650), 'to abandon a life to the fatal noose' (line 1697), 'to tear a life out (line 1730) and 'to ravish a life'.

More elaborately, there are violent images: 'Don't show yourself covered with my blood which you've shed with your own hands' (lines 1612–13), says Atalide to Roxane;[19] later, Atalide chides herself: 'I alone wove the ill-fated bonds whose hateful noose you have been made to endure',[20] conveying the fleeting image of her weaving the deadly noose herself. This idea of a character patiently working at death is, however, exceptional. Most of the images are much more brutal and the idea of execution haunts the characters in images like 'slice through such a beautiful life',[21] 'Don't come before me till you are carrying his head in your hands'[22] or 'Thrust aside the murderous hand'.[23] Even inanimate objects seem to exude an atmosphere of death, as in the image of the island of Rhodes, 'which has become the coffin of all who defended her'.[24]

Racine uses an interesting variation on the vocabulary of violent death to add poignancy to the plight of these vulnerable characters struggling under the threat of annihilation: he speaks of the opposite of death. This play has far more synonyms for life than any of Racine's other tragedies. But when Racine uses the word 'la vie' he is talking of a life that may well end: 'I have complete control over your life' says Roxane',[25] while Bajazet replies 'my life is in your hands'.[26] The fragility of Bajazet's existence is reflected in this use of 'la vie'. The word is used an astonishing thirty-four times in the play. In all but three cases, the context is one of death.

These examples (there are many others) should be sufficient to give an idea of the consistency of the two leitmotivs. As well as being systematic, Racine is inventive, and presents them in a variety of ways. In particular, his characters' attitude to violence colours their language, and makes for subtle differences between them.

Superficially, the characters can be divided into perpetrators and victims of violence. But matters are much more complex than this. To begin with, the Sultan is the only character who has the power to torment the others with relative impunity. But though he is constantly described using the language of violence, we never actually hear him speak because Racine never brings him on stage. The fact that he is lurking as an invisible threat makes him more frightening, although even he is not spared anxiety, and the word 'inquiet' is used to describe him several times.[27] The secrecy theme reappears in the mystery surrounding this absent character. Within the play, the nearest we get to power is in Roxane, but her ambiguous position prevents her from revelling in her cruelty. We have seen that she has power of life and death over Bajazet, but she is rightly uneasy about the Sultan, whose sinister intentions towards her remain concealed till the very end. Furthermore, despite her power over Bajazet, she is vulnerable to him because she loves him. Roxane's language reinforces this impression of constant lurking disquiet; she tells us that she is 'always uneasy' (line 295), and full of 'jealousy and suspicion' (line 751). She describes her life as 'so many sorrowful days, so many anxious nights' (line 1072). The impression is of an unhappy, uneasy character, determined to inflict her anxiety on those around her.

At the very moment when she offers her hand and heart to Bajazet, she sees fit to mention threats and violence: 'I am removing from your life a danger made manifest'.[28]

Roxane, the controlling figure and the perpetrator of cruelty, appears surprisingly insecure; Bajazet, her chief victim, also exhibits unexpected traits. I mentioned earlier that Racine pointed out that Bajazet had a ferocious side because of his Ottoman ancestry. Though Bajazet abhors the secrecy and duplicity of his tormentors, he does in fact share their aggression. He feels an immense sense of relief when he can fight and use physical violence, reflected in his language in speeches like this: 'But at last I find myself bearing arms, I am free, and I can, here and now, fight my inhuman brother for the heart of his mistress, no longer through silence helped by your cunning, but through real fighting, and noble danger.'[29] 'Silence' represents for Bajazet all the constraint that he hates, while 'fighting' and 'danger' are desirable.

The complex interplay of violence and secrecy in the characters normally reflects the contrast between their overt and their unspoken attitudes. The normal pattern of contrast is, however, curiously reversed in the case of the third major character, the Ottoman Princess Atalide, Bajazet's real love. Whereas Roxane is outwardly violent and secretly vulnerable, Atalide is outwardly touching and secretly aggressive. Though she herself is unaware of it at the time (she acknowledges it later) Atalide uses her own vulnerability as a weapon for blackmail. She uses threatened suicide as powerfully as Roxane employs the menace of assassination. At one stage she wrongly assumes that Bajazet has fallen in love with Roxane after all, and tells him she plans to die. Her 'suicide' speech is packed with synonyms for death and dying, such as 'end my life', 'sacrifice my life', 'abandon life', and even an interesting misuse of the past tense when she says 'Whilst I breathed' as though she has already ceased to do so.[30] This speech, with its overabundance of synonyms for Atalide's suicide, is a histrionic piece of polemic. This becomes clear if it is contrasted to Atalide's real suicide speech, delivered just before she kills herself on stage (lines 1721–47). This second speech is a bitter piece of self-reproach; Atalide wastes no time luxuriating in the prospect of her own death. The (rather fewer) death-words refer not to her death but to Bajazet's. She feels hateful because though responsible for his murder she is still very much alive: she is 'condemned' 'to survive him'. She despises herself because she seems able to 'endure without dying the thought' that her lover is dead. Ironically, it was the polemic of Atalide's false suicide speech that had persuaded Bajazet to adopt the course of action of defying Roxane, which leads to his death, and causes Atalide's real suicide.

The relative lack of histrionics in Atalide's final speech suggests that a character can reach a stage where death or total despair cease to appear awesome and daunting. This is in fact the case at several points in the play. Despair becomes so complete that underlying fears and anxieties disappear, and are replaced by calm language or even by the expression of a kind of pleasure – the secret uneasiness vanishes when the violence is acknowledged. Atalide accuses Bajazet of a weird enjoyment at the prospect of inflicting his own death on her.[31] Admittedly, Atalide is taunting her lover here; but her words prefigure Roxane's when her anxiety over Bajazet's feelings disappears, to be replaced by the certainty that he does not love her at all: 'I rejoice, for the traitor has betrayed himself, just once. Freed from the painful task I was setting myself, calm in my rage I need only take revenge'.[32]

The audience is not deceived, however. We know that there is no real lull in the violence, and that Roxane's fate will not be a calm one. In general, the audience is filled with a sense of constant danger which is in no way diminished by intermittent unrealistic expressions of hope or optimism expressed by various characters during the play. And when Bajazet tells Atalide 'You no longer need fear for my life, Madame',[33] we are not seduced into believing him. Rather we get a sense of hubris and dramatic irony from his words, because the atmosphere of danger has been built up so strongly.[34]

This atmosphere is greatly enhanced by the feeling that fate too is bent on destroying the characters. As in all Racine's secular tragedies, a supernatural power (which remains enigmatic and avoids any blatant indication of its presence) participates in the violence, relentlessly annihilating all the principal characters. One senses its presence through the consistent use of dramatic irony, expressed through word-play, which the audience will perceive only with hindsight: the characters' words will later be proved true in a way that destroys them. For example, when Roxane thinks she is about to marry Bajazet and achieve happiness, she tells him, in a line mentioned earlier: 'Prince, the fateful hour which heaven has reserved for your liberation has finally struck'.[35] In fact, the 'fateful hour' will bring liberation in death, not in life, for both of them; Roxane herself, of course, is unaware of this. So Fate manipulates language to confound the characters.

Not surprisingly, since words seem to provoke disaster, the characters in this play finally deny language altogether, and seek refuge from it in silence. 'Above all, keep silent', says Roxane, while the Vizir's followers are 'pledged to silence' and Bajazet 'preserves a perfidious silence' (line 997). Indeed, the entire harem 'preserves a grim silence'.[36] The harem, then, is a definitive setting to convey this sense of the danger of language. The mood can be epitomized in the implications for language of the harem killers, who lurk, unseen and menacing. They kill by strangling, that is to say they attack the voice first. More important, they are themselves mute, mutilated by being deprived of speech, condemned by violence to secrecy.

It remains to reconsider the problem posed at the outset: does Racine's use of language suggest a dramatic poet or a practical playwright? We have seen that in *Bajazet* he uses language insistently and repetitively, building up an atmosphere through this special handling of language. At any point in the play, the two leitmotivs recur with remarkable frequency. This remorseless insistence on a limited range of ideas gives an obsessive quality to the play.

It will be recalled that the audience in Racine's day was subjected to constant distractions. As a result, they might have been expected to find it difficult to follow a tragedy such as *Bajazet*, whose plot is full of complex twists and surprises. The language of the play, however, makes their task much easier: every time their wandering attention is recaptured, they will recognize the leitmotivs, and will feel less lost because they can at once recapture the mood of the play. I suggest that Racine's obsessive use of the language of violence and secrecy in this play is not simply a reflection of his personality or his concept of tragedy. Above all, it is a practical device for making the play acceptable to an audience. Could it even be that the remorseless insistence on one or two themes that is a prominent feature of all Racine's mature tragedies has a similar practical purpose in every case? It is worth noting that when *Bajazet* was first performed at the Hôtel de Bourgogne theatre in January 1672, the general public acclaimed it as 'a masterpiece *of the theatre*'.[37]

NOTES

1 Mongrédien, in his *Daily Life in the French Theatre at the Time of Molière* (London: Allen & Unwin, 1969), describes a typical performance as follows: 'The vulgar public, frothy and more interested in farces than in noble tragedies, shouted, joked or abused other spectators and sometimes organized brawls which brought in the police. Sometimes the spectators started playing cards or throwing dice. As soon as the curtain went up, the pit organized an uproar, violently applauding the actors, or cat-calling; those who were at the back could not see well and could scarcely hear the actors. Hubbub filled the hall, and from the top of the amphitheatre more specators took part in this agitation and yelling' (p. 123).
2 She performed at the Hôtel de Bourgogne, later to be Racine's accredited theatre.
3 'Admirez ce visage riant qu'elle conserve dans les plus grandes afflictions' (*L'Impromptu de Versailles*, scene i).
4 Roxane has been left in charge during the Sultan's absence, but has fallen in

love with Bajazet, who is imprisoned in the harem, under Roxane's control. Bajazet is expecting to be killed at any minute, as the Sultan regards him as a threat. Bajazet seizes the chance of freedom that Roxane offers him, though he is secretly in love with an Ottoman princess in the harem, Atalide.

5 'Bajazet . . . garde au milieu de son amour la férocité de sa nation' (p. 383). All references are to Jean Racine, *Théâtre complet*, ed J. Morel and A. Viala (Paris: Garnier, 1980). The translations are mine.

6 'du récit, Osmin, que tu vas faire/ Dépendent les destins de l'empire ottoman' (lines 14–15). E. van der Starre, in *Racine et le théâtre de l'ambiguité, étude sur 'Bajazet'* (Leiden University Press, 1966), pp. 114–15, discusses the elliptical quality of such statements.

7 'Dites un mot, et vous nous sauvez tous' (line 620). Van der Starre, *Racine*, pp. 121–2, sees Bajazet as psychologically incapable of pronouncing the word.

8 'D'un mot . . . je puis le secourir' (line 399).

9 'S'il m'échappait un mot c'est fait de votre vie' (line 542).

10 'Je vous dois tout mon sang; ma vie est votre bien' (line 519).

11 'Quel sang pourra suffir à son ressentiment?' (line 1448).

12 'Loin de vous séparer, je prétends aujourd'hui/ Par des noeuds éternels vous unir avec lui' (lines 1624–5).

13 'L'Amour serra les noeuds par le sang commencés' (line 360).

14 Raymond Picard comments 'death is present at every step' (Racine, *Oeuvres complètes*, Paris: Bibliothèque de la Pléiade, 1969, I,524). Margaret McGowan, in the Introduction to her edition of the play (University of London Press, 1968), attributes this element to the Turkish setting, since the audience would have realized that 'life was held cheaply in the Orient' (p. 15).

15 Bernet, *Le Vocabulaire des tragédies de Jean Racine* (Geneva: Slatkine, 1983), pp. 36–7.

16 Bernet demonstrates that *Bajazet* contains fewer words than all Racine's mature tragedies except *Bérénice* (p. 95).

17 See B. C. Freeman and A. Batson, *Concordance du théâtre et des poésies de Jean Racine* (Ithaca: Cornell University Press, 1968).

18 See line 1426 for another striking example, and lines 1748–9 for the same treatment of 'expirer' (to expire).

19 'Ne vous montrez point . . . couverte de mon sang par vos mains répandu' (lines 1612–13).

20 'Moi seule, j'ai tissu le lien malheureux/ Dont tu viens d'éprouver les détestables noeuds' (lines 1732–3).

21 'Trancher une si belle vie' (line 266).

22 'Ne vous présentez à moi que sa tête à la main' (line 1192).

23 'Repoussez une main meurtrière' (line 442).

24 'Rhodes . . . de tous ses défenseurs devenu le cercueil' (line 476).

25 'J'ai sur votre vie un empire suprême' (line 509).

26 line 519. See note 10.

27 For instance in line 215 and 1111.

28 'J'écarte de vos jours un péril manifeste' (line 429).

29 'Mais enfin je me vois les armes à la main;/ Je suis libre, et je puis contre un frère inhumain,/ Non plus par un silence aidé de votre adresse,/ Disputer en ces

lieux le coeur de sa maîtresse,/ Mais par de vrais combats, par de nobles dangers' (lines 947–51).
30 'Finir ma vie, sacrifier ma vie, le trépas, mourir, laisser la vie' (lines 961–74).
31 'Malgré mes pleurs, mon amant furieux/ Se fait tant de plaisir d'expirer à mes yeux' (lines 763–4) ('in spite of my tears, my lover in his madness is taking such pleasure in dying before my very eyes').
32 'ma joie est extrême/ Que le traître une fois se soit trahi lui-même./ Libre des soins cruels où j'allais m'engager/ Ma tranquille fureur n'a plus qu'à se venger' (lines 1274–7).
33 'Vous n'avez plus, Madame, à craindre pour ma vie' (line 942).
34 Or, on another occasion, the vizir says 'un calme heureux nour remet dans le port. La Sultane a laissé désarmer sa colère' (lines 844–5) (A fortunate lull brings us back to harbour. The Sultana has allowed her anger to be dispelled).
35 'Prince, l'heure fatale est enfin arrivée/ Qu'à votre liberté le ciel a réservée' (lines 421–2).
36 'Surtout garde bien le silence' (line 1330), 'engagés à se taire' (line 1387), 'garde un triste silence' (line 1339). Van de Starre, *Racine*, gives many more examples in an interesting discussion (pp. 126–31).
37 From a comment by the Ambassador of Savoy, the Comte de Saint-Maurice, in a letter of 25 February 1672. Quoted by Margaret McGowan, Introduction, p. 11. The *Mercure galant*, too, hailed the play as 'an admirable work' (6 January 1672). Quoted by Paul Mesnard in his edition *Grands écrivains de la France* (Paris: Hachette, 1911), vol. 2, p. 457.

Grand Guignol and the orchestration of violence*

VICTOR EMELJANOW

Severed heads thud on a blood soaked floor. A glistening scalpel slices open the throat of a screaming victim. Knives tear into writhing bodies. A butcher reels out a woman's intestines, two novice nuns are raped and one subsequently impaled on a blood drenched meat hook, and a crone gouges out the eye of a starving old man and feeds it to him ... And all the while the audience gasps, and cheers and bursts into nervous laughter.[1]

The state is completely dark. So is the auditorium. From the heart of deepest darkness voices are heard howling ... A shot is heard ... Sounds of furniture falling and breaking ... Screams, violent rushings to and fro ... Suddenly, through open doors ... the red light of the fire. The stage is the colour of blood ... The scene is ending amid the deafening din of a house given over to lunatics ...[2]

These two quotations might suggest the revival of an obscure Jacobean tragedy or an exhibition by a performance artist. In fact, the first is part of an article which appeared in *Newsweek* in 1974, the second, part of the stage directions which punctuate the finale of *Les Boulingrin*, a farce by George Courteline, first performed in April 1897. What links these two is the description of performances which took place in a small 230-seat theatre on the rue Chaptal in Paris, the Théâtre du Grand-Guignol, a theatre for sixty-five years devoted to the realization of both the comic and serious aspects of theatrical violence.

The extract from *Newsweek* is from a lengthy article written on the occasion of the reopening of the theatre under a new management. It had in fact closed twelve years earlier in 1962. That the reopening, however, should have attracted the attention of the magazine's European desk suggests an awareness of the theatre's importance. After all, those who had contributed to its existence included French writers as diverse as Mirbeau, Lenormand, Méténier and Courteline and the theatre had been admired by Marcel Achard, Lugné-Poë, Arrabal and even Colette.[3] Surprisingly, Antonin Artaud made no reference to it, though the descriptions

---

* A draft of this paper was read at the *Themes in Drama* International conference held at the University of California, Riverside, in February 1989.

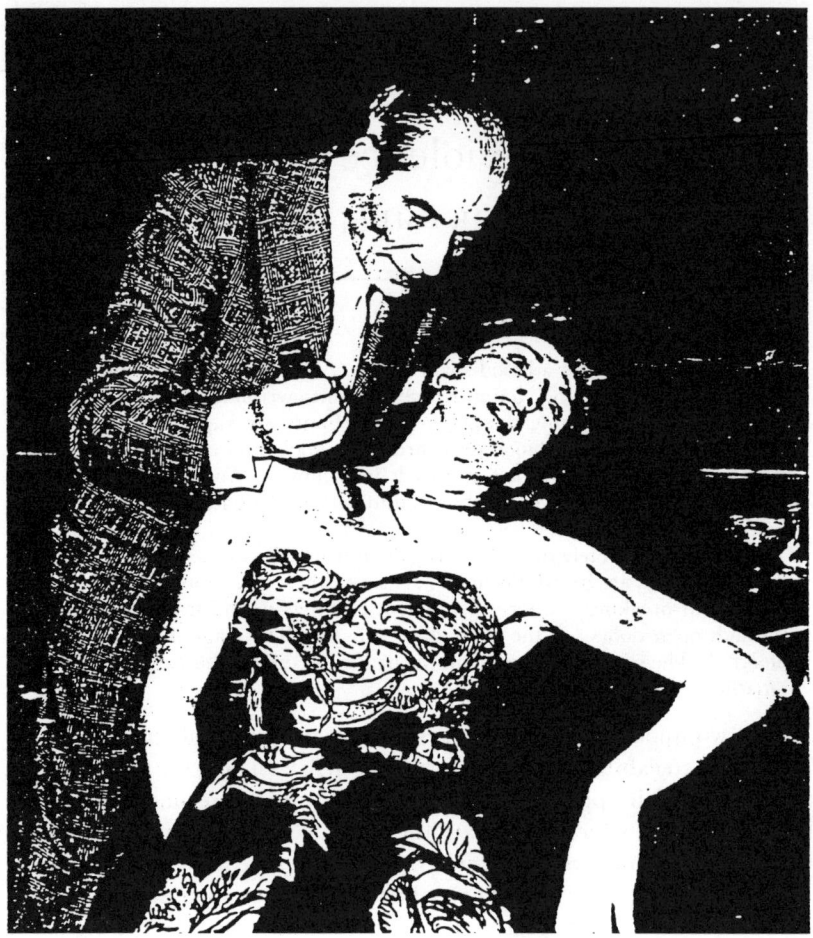

7 Théâtre du Grand-Guignol

quoted suggest the worlds of *The Revenger's Tragedy*, *Titus Andronicus*, Weiss's *Marat/Sade*, and indeed David Cronenberg's films *The Fly* and *Scanners*.

The term 'grand guignol' has itself passed into the critical vocabulary. It owes its existence to the parallel of the Petit Guignol, the child's puppet Punch and Judy show. Its origins, however, are even more ancient. The verb 'guigner' means to give someone a surreptitious glance but the implications are of possessing an evil eye, and 'guignard' refers to an unlucky person. Thus the term has embedded in it the connotations of evil, misfortune and being at the mercy of powers over which one has little control. This gives a certain credence to the French admirers of Grand Guignol who trace its origins back through Greek tragedy to the primitive exorcistic function of dramatic re-enactment.

In his books, *Théâtre d'epouvante* and *Les Maîtres de la peur*, André de Lorde, the most successful of French Grand Guignol dramatists, refers back to the paradigm of Sophocles, as well as to the Gothic antecedents of Mrs Radcliffe and Monk Lewis and those short stories of Poe and Maupassant preeminently devoted to the evocation of the terrifying and to its realization.[4] Even if his references to Oedipus or Ajax might appear rather circumstantial, the others demonstrate the enduring influence of both Romanticism and its popular counterpart, melodrama, on the French stage. Poe had after all dreamed of a theatre so frightening that spectators could tolerate only a few moments after the curtain had been raised before running out into the streets, and Maupassant's stories *The Horla* and *Fear* were intended to evoke in the reader a primitive frisson of terror which theatre ought to be able to evoke in its audience.

Since the middle of the eighteenth century, the Gothic world of clanking chains, tortured villains, dungeons and decaying castles, had been, in its theatrical manifestations, attractive both to the post-Revolution audience in France and to the new urban proletariat of England enmeshed in the Industrial Revolution. Though Gothic melodrama relied heavily on an atmosphere of mystery and the supernatural, its resolution rested on the re-establishment of an ordered world in which the values of love, selflessness and purity were sustained. Writing about the Gothic, de Lorde found its theatrical intentions admirable but its execution hampered by the constraints of convention, both theatrical and social.[5]

The Gothic remained a constant lurking thematic presence throughout the nineteenth century. As we know, the domestic form of melodrama replaced it in both England and France, though some of the same conventional constraints persisted, constraints which emanated both from the stage and the auditorium. One might recall the outrage at the representation on stage of *delirium tremens* in Reade's *Drink*, a translation of Zola's *L'Assommoir*, or at the violent behaviour in performance of Salvini's Othello to Desdemona, or at the alleged sexual impropriety of Albery's *Pink Dominoes*, or Clement Scott's angry denunciation of Ibsen's *Ghosts*.[6] It was in reaction to such constraints upon subject matter and theatre practice that we see, of course, the emergence of the Free Theatre movement in Europe, a movement associated particularly with the Parisian Théâtre Libre of André Antoine.

Thematically, the Free Theatre movement and naturalism generally addressed themselves to social issues, in particular issues of morality, sexuality, and economic repression, theatrically represented with a degree of realism which sought to authenticate and to confront. The search for authenticity and particularity extended to the use of real objects as distinct from theatre props and to the commissioning of new and authentic translations. When Antoine decided to produce the world première in 1888 of Tolstoy's *The Power of Darkness*, he asked his friend Oscar Méténier to translate it for him with the assistance of Russian emigrés. Méténier was himself a dramatic author who had contributed to the second season of plays at the Théâtre Libre with his naturalistic one-act, *In the Family*, in 1887. He was also a police reporter whose contact with the underworld and the seamy sides of society provided him with his raw material. And it was this man, with his background in journalism and the theatre, who opened the Théâtre du Grand-Guignol on 13 April 1897.

Ironically, by 1897 naturalism itself was being challenged especially in France; its ideology based on scientific investigation, observable data and scrupulous logic by one based on intuition, metaphysics and a rejection of materialism. A new Romanticism posed certain fundamental questions and none more significant than the questioning of the basis of human action and the truth of the accepted belief in the inevitability of progress. The alternative to evolution it suggested was clash, emotional violence and anarchy and these were as present in the individual as they were in society. Thus it is within this aesthetic and social context – a mixture of anarchic violence and theatrical revolution – that we should place the Grand Guignol.

From its first season, the tone of the theatre was established. Méténier presented two of his short plays – *La Brême* and *Le Loupiot*, which have been translated by Daniel Gerould as *The Meal Ticket* and *The Little Bugger* respectively – together with *Les Boulingrin* by Courteline.[7] The three plays are all characterized by a tone of subversive parody and violence which embraces attitudes to contemporary morality and dramaturgy as well. The Méténier plays, characteristic of the *comédie rosse*, cast a knowing and cynical glance at working-class domestic relationships. In *La Brême* the unmarried, middle-aged, working-class couple, just returned to the wine bar from their younger daughter's confirmation, are delighted that she will look after her parents in their old age by following her elder sister's example and become a successful prostitute. In *Le Loupiot*, the young worker is horrified to learn that his girlfriend is pregnant by her exhusband but his reaction is not morally based. It arises because the law demands that the little bugger must assume the name of his father, which will expose the worker to ridicule. Biological drives and economic considerations would appear to make the conventions of bourgeois morality irrelevant, yet ironically their trappings appear to be adhered to rigidly.

Les Boulingrin on the other hand exhibits many of the techniques of farce. Set in a middle-class drawing room, the play concerns an elderly sponger who calls on the Boulingrin family hoping to find himself a permanent lodging. He becomes, however, meat in the sandwich of a domestic confrontation. The husband and wife patently loathe one another and are quite prepared to tear the increasingly desperate lodger literally apart in a farcical confrontation which resembles a parody of a Dionysiac *sparagmos*. The play ends in the utter confusion which the stage directions quoted above suggests. Though the mechanics may be those of farce, the play's cruelty reflects psychotic behaviour and a form of madness.

Farcically deranged or abnormal behaviour would remain an enduring aspect of Grand Guignol's comic realization of violence. In *The Bronze Lady and the Crystal Gentleman* by Henri Duvernois (1921),[8] the husband has himself committed to a mental institution to get away from his overbearing wife. His wife, however, discovers the ruse, and similarly pretends to be mad. He desperately tries to disabuse the authorities but to no avail and the two are condemned to share padded cells with an interconnecting door for the remainder of their lives. The further irony lies in the fact that the trained psychiatrists are totally unable to differentiate between madness and sanity.

It was not until 1899, however, that the characteristic mix of ironic and violent comedy, complemented by dramas of violent terror (*théâtre d'épouvante*), became established. This was to be the contribution of Max Maurey, himself another fervent admirer of Antoine, who became the theatre's director.[9] Nevertheless, comedy remained a staple part of the theatre's repertoire as the most easily assimilated element of its social and emotional subversiveness. It had inherited comic subversiveness from the Free Theatre movement and it would retain this perceived role until the 1930s. Comedy furthermore provided a digestible coating to the bitter pill of aggressive amorality. Indeed, it was this aspect which allowed Grand Guignol to be accessible to audiences in England in 1908 and subsequently in the United States in 1923.[10]

Even if humour was regarded as a basic ingredient of the Grand Guignol, nevertheless the theatre's characteristic impact was achieved by a violent oscillation between it and what de Lorde called the theatre of fear. He wrote in the preface to his *Masters of Fear* anthology in 1927: 'The theatre of fear sets up a new formula which will retain its place in the history of drama next to that of the realistic theatre. This formula, furthermore, will have contributed to the introduction of some felicitous changes to theatre generally: simple unmediated action, and the precise, almost scientific, studies of social milieus so far neglected by dramatists ... the staging of physiological and medical case studies as frequently as the staging of internalized problems or examples of spiritual conflict.'[11] He thus freely acknowledges the debt to Antoine and the Free Theatre in subject matter and style. Less explicit, however, is the debt to Romanticism which would acknowledge that while Grand Guignol aimed to demonstrate its subjects with clinical exactness and show the effects of heredity with scrupulous care, in particular those of epilepsy, alcoholism and venereal disease, it also shared Romanticism's liking for the grotesque, the ugly and the exotic. More significantly, though Grand Guignol might show the processes of scientific investigation, it viewed the investigators themselves with a sceptical eye: the doctors, psychiatrists, hypnotists, lawyers and social scientists. This attitude it shared with the new Romanticism of de L'Isle-Adam and Mallarmé.

In common with Romanticism, Grand Guignol explored the condition of an individual alone and alienated. Unlike their earlier romantic counterparts, however, revelling in their isolation, the individuals in the Grand Guignol, like those of Maeterlinck, are victims rendered powerless by irreversible circumstance or the operation of forces over which they have no control. Perhaps this is best captured in de Lorde's *Au Téléphone* (1901) in which the unfortunate husband, Marex, rings his wife while on a trip away, and during the call hears her and her child being murdered.[12] (The relationship between this play and Cocteau's *The Human Voice* is an obvious one.) The problem which the play poses is totally insoluble and the dramatic situation is made more excruciating by placing the audience and the character alike in a position where neither can do anything to avert the violence which is occurring at the other end of the telephone line.

To enhance this sense of powerlessness, the individual may be trapped in the mental imprisonment of madness or obsession. Mental alienation may be further exacerbated by its existence within the closed environments of prison, colonial outpost, island, hospital, mental institution or the private world of a specific milieu: the back street wine bar or the prostitute's bedroom. In Méténier's *Him* (1897) a prostitute brings a man into her room whom she discovers to be a notorious and particularly grisly murderer. In Frederick Witney's *Say it with Flowers*, first presented in 1945[13] but itself an adaptation of a Méténier play, the young prostitute returns to the wine bar above which are situated the girls' bedrooms. She has been in hospital recovering from a breakdown brought about by her boy friend's execution for murder. Urged by the wine bar's owner to get back to work, she discovers that her most recent customer is Charcot, the public executioner. In her loathing and disgust she shoots not the public executioner but the wine bar owner who knew the identity of her customer. As he leaves, the executioner taps her on the shoulder and whispers 'I'll be seeing you.' In de Lorde's *The Last Torture* (1904), set during the Boxer Rebellion, the French consul shoots his only daughter, who has been caught and savagely tortured, in order to spare her further pain. Moments after, soldiers relieve the situation. He then goes mad, and the curtain drops. In all these, coincidence plays a pivotal role. It brings about a psychological crisis point which in turn triggers an action or a state of mind condemning the protagonist to a state of permanent alienation.

An obsessive desire for revenge or unreasoning fear usually brings about this crisis point. The energy which this obsession unleashes makes both social proprieties and theatrical conventions of characterization irrelevant. The human being is reduced to an elemental animal. In this respect Grand Guignol does indeed look back to the *Medea*, to the *Ajax* or the *Jew of Malta*. But the persecutors are not the gods nor elements of prejudiced society; as often as not they are the venal and unscrupulous agents of reform and scientific progress, the doctors, the scientists, the psychiatrists. Indeed, de Lorde posed the question in *Un Drame à la salpetrière* (1923) whether inmates were confined in institutions for their own good or to act as guinea pigs for medical investigation. Such plays, however, advance no thesis and provide no answers; a typical denouement appears in *The Laboratory of Hallucinations* (*Le Labo des hallucinations*) by de Lorde and Henri Bauche in which in a moment of lucidity the victim drives a pair of surgical scissors into the forehead of his tormenting surgeon.[14]

To illustrate how the Grand Guignol explores and orchestrates the corrosive effects of an obsession with revenge we might explore briefly Maurice Level's *Le Baiser dans la nuit* (1912), translated as *The Last Kiss* by Frederick Witney.[15] The play is written with great economy. The scene is set within a very ordinary bed sitting room decorated with the '*pictorial flotsam of a departed civilization*'. A man sits slumped at the table dimly illuminated by an outdoor street lamp. He faces away from the audience. Only after he stands and calls on the landlady to take away an uneaten meal do we see '*his face, seamed and scarred and puckered with glazed red weals where the burned flesh has healed; his nose shapeless, his mouth twisted. The hollow sockets of his eyes are hidden behind dark glasses*'. The landlady enters, breezily turns on more lights, and chats unconcernedly about his affliction:

> I always say it's better to be blind than deaf. You can't see but you can hear, you can take part in a nice conversation.

The incongruity is a deliberately grating one. In an effort to cheer him up she suggests he and his girlfriend – who, by throwing a bottle of acid in her lover's face, was responsible for his present state – should attempt a reconciliation. The girl has served her time in prison and is due for a release. With the inexorable logic of melodrama she, Minty, appears and is horrified to see that an impetuous act motivated by jealousy has resulted in such appalling damage. She is a pretty girl and he clings onto the pathetic hope that she will devote her life to his care:

> *He.* We'll begin again, Minty. We'll be lovers again, as we were in those happy days . . . before you did this to me.

But she is already shrinking away and starts to leave. She promises to write. He can do nothing except beg her for a kiss as a final consolation. Shuddering with reluctance but stricken by guilt she does so. As he pulls her down onto the bed, he reaches into his pocket for a small bottle of vitriol:

> *He.* You and I are going to be such a pair of lovers, so beautifully matched, so dependent on each other. And we shall be together for ever and ever, amen.
> *She.* Tom, not that, don't do that to me. Have mercy, Tom.
> *He.* Mercy! Look at my face and cry for mercy!
> *[He removes with his teeth the stopper from the bottle and holds the bottle over her face]*
> *He.* And the Devil said, let there be Dark – and there was Dark.
> *[Suddenly she screams and screams and screams and goes on screaming]*
> Curtain

The situation of the play is meticulously orchestrated by means of a series of violent tonal contrasts: the ordinariness of the room and the repulsiveness of the man; the matter of fact, cheerful callousness of the landlady who has seen everything before and who by extension urges us to ignore the physical manifestations; the timely appearance of the pretty girlfriend whose looks clash with those of the man; the pathetic belief in the possibility of reconciliation. We are torn between sympathy for him in his defencelessness and the realization that the scale of injury precludes any possibility of a future for these two. Furthermore, the playwright has negotiated us through an initial sensation of fear to a sensation of pity. At this point in the play, however, our sympathy begins its transformation. We realize in the discussion between the two that the action which occasions the play was a premeditated act, triggered by jealousy on her part. He in turn is revealed to have been little more than an emotional dilletante. We start to feel that perhaps these two deserve one another. As he tries to insist that she stay permanently with him we begin to realize that his physical scarring is complemented by an emotional scarring. Our initial sensation of fear returns with a premonition of impending doom. But when the curtain falls, it is not accompanied by a catharsis derived from satisfying the dictates of inescapable retribution. This is deliberately frustrated. All that is established is an amoral equilibrium accompanied by a numbing powerlessness. The play exhibits not only a stark Old Testament morality – an eye literally for an eye, but also a stern puritanism which demands that sin be punished by an ongoing life-in-death.

When reviewing Grand Guignol plays, critics, particularly English ones, tended to feel that the curtain should have come down before the final moments of violent horror. Realization, they argued, blunts the imagination.[16] Such assessment, however missed the point. Grand Guignol offered a vision of hell which left no opportunity to block off the unpleasant or to allow the comfort of the theatrical occasion to blur its implications. The primitive forces unleashed in the plays have little to do with civilized behaviour. Violence must be seen and shared, thereby stripping away the veneer of middle-class theatregoing conformity.

The contribution to the genre by Max Maurey, who directed the theatre until the middle of World War I was a technical one. Nevertheless, it was seminal. Camillo Antona-Traversi, who worked with him and also wrote for the theatre, remembered the anguish which prospective playwrights endured before their plays were granted an airing.[17] Maurey supervised every aspect of rewriting: rejecting sections over and over again, introducing special effects but above all paring the action down to a simple and inescapably logical one. Infuriating though this was, Maurey was a past master of timing. He possessed a precise ability to prolong the period of audience expectation to the moment before the anticipatory frisson turned into disbelieving laughter. This involved the engineering of suspense by means of a series of false starts and deliberate delays, thus manipulating time to intensify expectation. As well, Maurey refused to romanticize settings or to indulge in symbolic abstraction. It was essential that the world of police, doctors or domestic security be represented with meticulous detail. This extended to the dialogue, which was pared down and made deliberately ordinary less in the name of naturalism than in order to heighten incongruity and to lull the audience into a complacency soon to be shattered.

The enduring techniques of Maurey can be gauged from *Weekend Cottage*, though it is an English example of the genre written at the end of World War II when the French were becoming increasingly dominated by *romans policiers* and translations of the novels of James Hadley Chase.[18] The milieu is middle class:

> *Laura's weekend cottage in Buckinghamshire . . . a typical sitting room in a typical rural cottage which has been converted . . . to a typical pied-à-terre . . . It is typically furnished in old oak . . . A china shepherdess at one end of the mantleshelf simpers at a china shepherd at the other.*

It is a totally anonymous and unimaginative setting, a setting for a situation comedy perhaps. Its anonymity and cheap furniture, the presence of two suitcases might suggest a hotel room. A woman, Laura, enters through a doorway which obviously leads to a cellar. Carrying two bottles to a table set for two, she then waits impatiently for the arrival of a man. It is raining outside. She switches on the radio – it plays Saint Saëns' *Danse Macabre*. She switches to another station – it plays Chopin's *Funeral March*. She switches it off. Behind her two faces appear at the window. Then there is a bang at the door 'Oh, at last! Arthur!' but it isn't. Just two tramps, Butch and Nobby, hoping for a bit of food. Laura's annoyance intensifies and when she tries to shut the door in their faces, Butch keeps it open with his foot. In an effort to get rid of them, Laura agrees to give them some food and wine. They, however, ease themselves into the room and seat themselves at the table prepared for two:

> *Laura.* Listen, I'm expecting my husband any minute.
> *Butch.* Yair?
> *Laura.* He'll be frightfully annoyed if he finds you've forced your way in here.
> *Butch.* Fraightfully annoyed, will 'e? That'll be just too bad, won't it, Nobby?

Suddenly the intrusion of the two becomes a class struggle. Butch and Nobby shrewdly assess Laura: her hair, her dress, her makeup suggest that she is not waiting for husband at all:

> *Butch.* This is one of them lovenests what you read about, and it 'aint her husband she's expectin' but her fancy man.

But assures Butch:

> I'm a broadminded man . . . I like a good looking femme myself.
> *Laura.* I'm not interested.
> *Butch.* No? You would be when I got started.

Butch and Nobby then describe a man they met on the road who, they say, had been hit by a car. Laura becomes frantic at the thought it might be the absent Arthur but is stopped from leaving by Butch. An element of real danger has now been introduced as Laura notices blood on Butch's sleeve. She is isolated. Laura has no recourse but the empty threat of going to the police. Her adherence to the verities of the middle class is further shown to be inadequate when Butch suggests that going to the police would expose her to scandal particularly after she reveals that she is a public servant and Arthur is a married man. She tries to get away but is pinned down by Butch and brutally dragged to the bedroom door:

> *Butch.* I like them nice and spirited

and Laura's scream is cut off as Nobby shuts the door behind them and disappears grinning into the cellar to get more wine.

The first section of the action is complete and one of the basic western middle-class neuroses has been aired: the invasion of the barbarian working class. Butch and Nobby have exposed Laura's pretensions and paper-thin social veneer (her reliance on status, on language, on assumed norms of social behaviour). Once these have been stripped away she is completely powerless.

The action's second beat begins with the front door opening and a bloodstained Arthur staggering into the room. When he hears the sounds of Nobby's return he grabs a doublebarrelled shot gun and bails him up. Unable to identify the men who assaulted and robbed him, Arthur is convinced by Nobby that Laura has stepped out briefly. Nobby then gingerly leaves followed by Arthur and his shotgun. As this action happens, Butch sidles out of the bedroom and pretends that he too has been down in the cellar. He corroborates Nobby's account and the invaders appear to be about to get away scot free. Just then the bedroom door opens, '*Laura comes out, dishevelled, white as death, her mad eyes swollen, red rimmed*' and the third action beat begins.

Laura grabs the shotgun and forces Butch to remain. She informs Arthur that this is his assailant and that though Arthur has his stolen wallet returned, she hasn't been recompensed. Arthur is enraged when he discovers what has happened to Laura and goes to shoot Butch. Butch, however, appeals to him in terms of male solidarity and suggests that Laura's fate was her own doing:

Arthur. D'you mean she led you on?
Laura. KILL HIM!

'It's God's truth, chum' says Butch, to which Arthur replies, 'I've heard of women like that.' This is too much for Laura. She grabs the gun. There is an explosion – and Arthur's chest is perforated by the shotgun pellets.

There have been a series of rapid reversals: Arthur's unexpected but perfectly acceptable entrance, the expectation that Butch and Nobby would get away with it, the entry of Laura. Our own responses have also been made to oscillate violently. We may be appalled by Butch and Nobby as violent aggressors, but we also feel less than sympathetic to Laura's middle-class disdain. We feel relief at Arthur's safety and the fact that Arthur may be able at least to expel the intruders. When Laura, however, takes matters into her own hands, we feel with her a primitive satisfaction in the necessity for revenge. Like Laura our own veneer of comfortable distance and control has been eroded. An eye for an eye seems an appropriate though uncivilized response. Arthur's willingness to entertain Butch's monstrous accusation that Laura is a slut diminishes our support for him, so that his death at her hands, though accidental, appears a just retribution. The consequences of her action, however, make the situation even more fraught with danger.

The last action beat is a very quick one. Butch retrieves the gun and Arthur's wallet and informs Laura that she will go with him. After all, she has just murdered a man and her terror of scandal will preclude any other solution. But Laura is beyond reason. She manages to snatch up the shotgun and as Butch advances towards her, shoots him in the face and blinds him. She now sees what she can do and taunts him with his blindness: 'You're worse than dead, Butch.' As he gropes his way towards the sound of her voice, she pushes him down into the cellar, where he lands with a sickening thud. She then locks the door. What might an audience have expected her to do at this point? Collapse on the floor in relief? Investigate to see whether Arthur is indeed completely dead?

Desperately scream for help? In fact, '*She puts on her coat and hat, takes up her suitcase, and walks to the door.*' Her desire for revenge has been fulfilled and she can now resume her middle-class life. But as she reaches the door, Nobby enters:

Laura. God!
Nobby. *(grinning)* Hello, Toots.

He locks the door, puts the key in his pocket, and turns to her:

Nobby. Gonna be quite a weekend!

And the curtain comes down quickly on the world of sex, death and madness from which there is no escape, for which the norms of civilized behaviour are irrelevant. The protectors of these norms – the police, the doctors and the lawyers – are in the final analysis equally irrelevant.

When the Grand-Guignol theatre closed at the end of 1962, its director, Charles Nonon stated somewhat disingenuously, 'We could never equal Buchenwald. Before the war everyone felt that what was happening on stage was impossible. Now we know that these things, and worse, are possible in reality.'[19] As we know, the cinema was totally unaffected by the precedent of Buchenwald. The decline of the Grand Guignol coincides with the ascendancy of Hammer Films. In 1967, the director Vernon Sewell in his film, *The Blood Beast Terror*, even incorporated actors playing a scene from André de Lorde's *Horrible Experience*.[20] The real reason for the theatre's closure was that vegetable dye and strawberry syrup, the viscera made from red rubber hoses and the hand bulbs which squirted blood from spoons which gouged out the victim's eyes, had become ends in themselves. Twenty-six years later in October 1988, to explain the decline in the popularity of the 'hack and slash' movies, Richard Rubinstein, the producer of Stephen King's *Pet Semetary*, said: 'We've all become much more sophisticated in what we've grown accustomed to on the screen. If the audience cares about the characters, then they will care when they get into trouble.' In other words, we need to feel the sensation of pity first before we are subjected (in Rubinstein's words) to 'one scene that really scares people – that really makes them feel that not only is the killer beyond normal rational actions, but the film maker is too ...' Both de Lorde and Maurey would have regarded this dramaturgic principle as self-evident.

NOTES

1 'As the Stomach Turns', *Newsweek*, 18 March 1974, p. 22.
2 E. Bentley (ed.), *Les Boulingrins*, trans. as *These Cornfields*, in *Let's Get a Divorce and Other Plays* (New York: Hill and Wang, 1958), p. 193.
3 Colette, 'Pour le Grand Guignol', *Europe*, 59 (1981), p. 158.

4 See F. Rivière and F. Witkop, *Grand Guignol* (Paris: Veyrier, 1979), pp. 48–9.
5 Ibid.
6 *Daily Telegraph*, 14 March 1891.
7 D. Gerould, 'Oscar Méténier and the *Comédie Rosse*', *TDR*, 28.1 (Spring 1984), p. 15.
8 In V. and F. Vernon (eds.), *Modern One Act Plays from the French* (New York: Samuel French, 1933).
9 Rivière and Witkop, *Grand Guignol*, p. 78.
10 It was initially to the farcical elements that critics responded cf. *Illustrated London News*, 28 March 1908 and John Corbin, *New York Times*, 16 October 1923.
11 Quoted in Rivière and Witkop, *Grand Guignol*, p. 19.
12 C. Foley and A. de Lorde, *Au Téléphone* (Paris: Librairie théâtrale, 1902).
13 F. Witney, *Grand Guignol* (London: Constable, 1947).
14 This play can be found in Mel Gordon, *Theatre of the Grand Guignol* (New York: Amok Press, 1988).
15 Ibid.
16 cf. St John Ervine, *Sunday Times*, 23 January 1921.
17 C. Antona-Traversi, *L'Histoire du Grand Guignol* (Paris: Librairie théâtrale, 1933), p. 31.
18 F. Witney, *Weekend Cottage*, in *Grand Guignol*.
19 'Outdone by Reality', *Time*, 30 November 1962, p. 58.
20 Alternative theatre in the 1960s found much to admire in the Grand Guignol cf. F. Arrabal (ed), *Cahiers Le Théâtre*, 2 (1969), 193ff.

The ultimate in theatre violence

JOHN M. CALLAHAN

Le Théâtre du Grand-Guignol de Paris lasted from 1897 till late in 1962, and was devoted to horror plays designed to terrorize and amuse its audiences. The adjective *grandguignolesque* was applied in a general way to fiendish melodrama.[1] Throughout its career, the Grand-Guignol averaged four murders a night. 'Aided by trick lighting, fearsome props and make-up, the Guignolers [went] happily, if homicidally, about their business of gouging out one another's eyes, cooking villains in vats of sulphuric acid, hurling vitriol and cutting throats, all to the accompaniment of hysterical laughter and hideous shrieks.'[2]

The depiction of horror was very effective, and fainting spells were common in the audience. The Grand-Guignol was where tourists and native Parisians went to be scared to death prior to World War II. After this war the Grand-Guignol began to be regarded as tame stuff and audiences increasingly went to laugh, American tourists becoming the main clientele. The situation deteriorated until the theatre closed its doors in 1962.

The Grand-Guignol believed in the concept of *la douche écossaise*,[3] or 'the hot and cold shower', meaning the alternation of horror and humor plays. Most plays were of one act, and the Grand-Guignol usually presented four a night, two horror plays and two comedies. But while the Grand-Guignol would present farcical comedies before or after their horrifying plays, terror was always the main attraction of the evening – terror incited through the tricks of stage violence. These tricks were basically simplistic, depending upon illusionism and machinery and especially sleight-of-hand. To act at the Grand-Guignol was to be a magician. But the primary ingredient of the Grand-Guignol was the recipe for the still secret Guignol blood which changed colors as it cooled, actually coagulated and made scabs, and came in nine shades. Critics hailed this last effect as the *pièce de résistance* of the Guignol's stable of terrifying tricks.[4]

For its patrons, the Grand-Guignol offered a chance to be scared in complete safety. Audiences enjoy being frightened, as the movie box office has continued to prove. Most people are vicarious lovers of violence and

8 Théâtre du Grand-Guignol

danger, and the majority of people find the theatrical depiction of violence to be cathartic. People went to the Grand-Guignol to be scared, to be able to hug their girl friend or boy friend, to laugh, to release their own sadism and/or masochism. It was a good night out. People have enjoyed, and always will enjoy, being stimulated and shocked. The Grand-Guignol was able to last for sixty-five years simply because its violence was outrageous.

The building in which the theatre was located on the rue Chaptal in Montmartre had been built in 1786 by the Jansenists, and later made into a convent. During the purge of religion under the Revolution, the building was sacked, but the chapel survived untouched, and it was this chapel that became the physical setting for the Grand-Guignol theatre. In 1880 the chapel was closed by order of the Bishop of Paris. In 1896 when Maurice Magnier converted the chapel into an intimate theatre, he retained the chapel *motif*. Thus, some of the worst manglings, acid throwings and vile murders have been witnessed by carved cherubs and seven-foot angels, while the loges look vaguely like confessionals and the balcony seats like pews.[5]

The Guignol was begun as a part of the little theatre movement dedicated to naturalism. André Antoine's Théâtre Libre, located just off the Place Pigalle in Montmartre, not more than a ten-minute walk from the Grand-Guignol, was one of its early inspirations. The Théâtre du Grand-Guignol opened in 1897 under the leadership of Oscar Méténier, a playwright who had had several of his works produced at the Théâtre Libre. Méténier served up for his public brief, naturalistic 'slices of life-in-the-raw'. The opening bill of the Guignol, on 3 April 1897, consisted of seven short plays, including *Mademoiselle Fifi* by Méténier himself, a play which would become a Grand-Guignol classic with over 2,000 performances. *Mademoiselle Fifi* tells of a young French prostitute who knifes a German officer in the chest. Thus, from the first night of its existence, the Grand-Guignol dealt with violence, terror, and graphic representations of the seamier side of life.

In 1898, after turning over the management of the theatre to Max Maurey, Méténier (who used to arrive at the theatre between two bodyguards) simply disappeared.[6] Maurey replaced Méténier's 'slice-of-life' plays with 'slice-of-death' plays,[7] and he decreed that the staple of the Grand-Guignol was to be terror rather than naturalism. By 1900 the Grand-Guignol was a thriving enterprise.

Max Maurey advertised the Grand-Guignol as the 'House of Horror' and he reprinted newspaper cartoons showing Grand-Guignol customers having medical check-ups before purchasing their tickets. One of his best promotional schemes was to add a house physician to the staff of the theatre – a doctor who would be in attendance to administer to anyone overcome from fright. However, on the doctor's first night of duty a spectator fainted and the ushers could not locate the doctor. When the victim regained consciousness he meekly confessed that he himself was the doctor.[8]

Among the plays produced during the Maurey management were these classics of horror: *Le Système du Docteur Goudron et Professor Plume*, 1903, which features madness, eye gouging, and surgery; *La Dernière Torture*, 1904, which deals with the Boxer Rebellion in China, shows a Frenchman's hands being cut off at the wrist, and also features a father shooting his daughter in the head only to find that the approaching army is French, not Chinese, and he then goes insane; *Les Nuits du Hampton Club*, 1908, shows a self-inflicted gunshot to the head on stage (shades of *The Deer Hunter!*); *Une Leçon à la salpetrière*, 1908, presents a bottle of sulphuric acid being thrown in a character's face; and finally, *L'Horrible Expérience*, 1909, shows a doctor using electric shock to restore his dead daughter to life, however, the doctor only succeeds in causing his daughter's arms to grab him at the neck and choke him to death.

When World War I began, Maurey chose as his successor Camille Choisy, and it was under the Choisy management that the theatre attained its greatest successes and world-wide fame. Some of the more popular plays during this management were *Le Laboratoire des hallucinations*, 1916, which depicts insanity, open brain surgery with the back of the victim's head visible to the audience, an extramarital love affair, and finally a chisel through a man's forehead – this play, not surprisingly, became a Grand-Guignol classic. In *Au Petit Jour*, 1921, the guillotine beheads a man on stage, and in *Les Jardin des supplices*, 1922, the playwright shows the flesh being cut off of a young girl, and a red-hot needle piercing a woman's eye; in *La Maison des hommes vivants*, 1923, murderers drink the blood of their victims; and in another Grand-Guignol classic, *Un Crime dans une maison de fous*, 1925, one can see an eye gouging with long surgical scissors and a woman's face sizzling on a hot plate; and in *Le Baiser de sang*, 1929, a man amputates his own finger on stage (for an idea of just how grisly a finger amputation can be, see the Clint Eastwood movie, *Escape from Alcatraz*).

Between the world wars the undisputed Queen of the Grand-Guignol was 'a generously proportioned actress called Maxa. No character in the Comte de Sade's novels ever suffered so many wrongs. Not an inch of her body was spared. She died more than 10,000 times in some sixty different ways, and was raped more than 3,000 times. Only one other performer ever came close to her, Maryse Leroy, who, as a result of her thousands of deaths, came to be called "The Lady of the Père-Lachaise" (Paris's largest cemetery). This did not prevent her from fainting on stage one evening when her partner was seized with a genuine nosebleed.'[9]

In 1930 Choisy left the Grand-Guignol and Jack Jouvin took control,

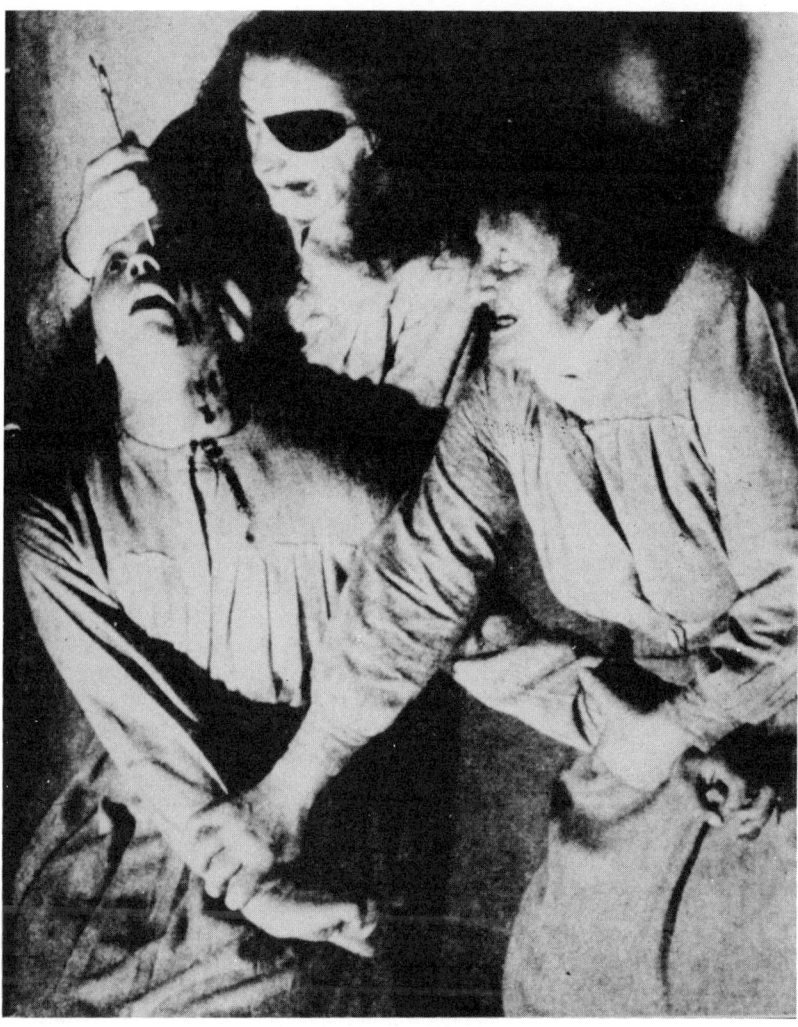

9 Eye-gouging with surgical scissors is a high point of *Crime in a Madhouse*

and Jouvin gave up his reins in 1937 to an Englishwoman, Eva Bergson. Miss Bergson fled to England after the fall of France but the Grand-Guignol continued to operate during the Occupation and was very popular with the Germans. Miss Bergson returned in 1945, only to find that Parisians now laughed at what had previously terrified them. The theatre became an important tourist attraction, but was hopelessly out-of-touch with post-war Parisians. Among the famous people who attended the Grand-Guignol during this period were Hermann Goering, Robert

Anderson and Ho Chi Minh (although not on the same night). General George S. Patton, old 'Blood and Guts' himself, watched a performance prompting Paris newspapers to write ' "Blood and Guts at the Grand Guignol", whereupon the box office received large numbers of orders for tickets to the new spectacle – "Blood and Guts." '[10] The theatre's decline was further documented by *Time* magazine in 1947: 'It was not like the old days; there were only three gruesome murders, and there was no torture more horrendous than a barehanded strangulation. Nobody in the audience even fainted. The spectators ... lounged around on rough wooden benches and had a modest emotional binge. A few couples in screened *baignoires* had another kind of binge on the indifferent house champagne.'[11]

The Grand-Guignol continued to flounder after World War II, and in 1951 Miss Bergson retired. The theatre went through a series of temporary managements, then settled upon Madame Raymonde Machard from 1954 to 1958. Fred Pascale succeeded her, and after him came Charles Nonon, the last director of the Grand-Guignol. The theatre closed in late 1962 and *Time* magazine reported on the demise of what had long been a venerable institution:

> The last clotted eyeball has plopped onto the stage. The last entrail has been pulled like an earthworm from a conscious victim. ... Only recently audiences watched a nude and lissome actress nailed to a cross and carved to pieces by a group of gypsy magicians chanting something that sounded like a Protestant hymn sung backwards. Still another victim – popular with modern fans – was bound, gagged and whipped; then the tips of her breasts were clipped off with hedge shears and her eyes were scooped out with a soupspoon and a jackknife. 'We are very proud of that sequence,' said Charles Nonon ... 'We consider it original, at least onstage.'
>
> World War II began the end of the Grand Guignol. 'We could never equal Buchenwald,' moaned Nonon. Where audiences once cowered in fear, they started to whinny.
>
> Technically, the postwar Grand Guignol was as good as ever. First-rate viscera were made from red rubber hose and sponges soaked in blood. Hand bulbs squirted blood through a hollow in the spoons that gouged out victims' eyes. The blood really curdled. It came in nine shades, and was mixed daily by Director Nonon.
>
> In a sense, Charles Nonon was the Escoffier of the Grand Guignol. For eye-gouging scenes, he bought eyeballs from taxidermists, coated them with aspic, and stuffed them with three anchovies marinated in blood. In Paris last week, there was a rumor that Nonon will soon open a quiet little restaurant on the Rue Morgue.[12]

Along with eyeballs stuffed with anchovies, the Grand-Guignolers excelled in make-up tricks, with one speciality being a 'boiled, partly skinned head (the actor is wrapped in a silk stocking and covered with putty, sponge, cloth and "blood").'[13]

10 Poster for *Les Crucifiés*

The extraordinarily effective Grand-Guignol violence was created by essentially simple tricks of lighting, mirrors, make-up and sleight-of-hand on the imagination of the audience. For example, in an Italian documentary movie titled *Ecco* (1965), a Grand-Guignol actor cuts off a woman's

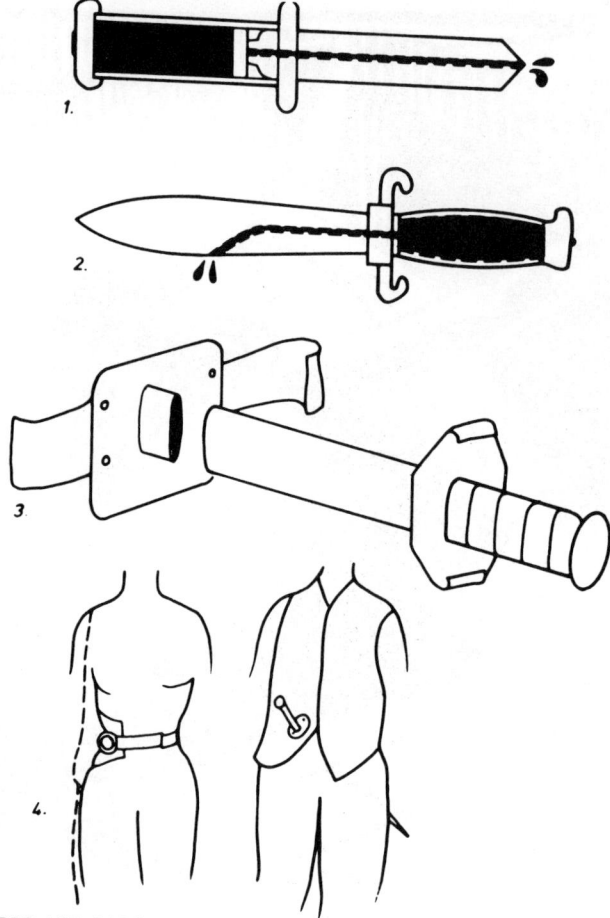

SWORDS AND DAGGERS

1. Stabbing knife
The blade is retractable and the piston handle squirts 'blood' from the point of the blade.

2. Cutting knife
When the rubber handle is squeezed, 'blood' flows from the knife edge.

3. Dagger socket
Worn under the clothing, such a socket holds a sawn-off dagger.

11 Swords and daggers in catalogue

arm at the shoulder while she is strapped to a table. This trick was accomplished by the woman pushing her arm down hard on a slat of the table made to roll over when pushed, the reverse side having been prepared with a fake arm dressed to match the actress's arm at the

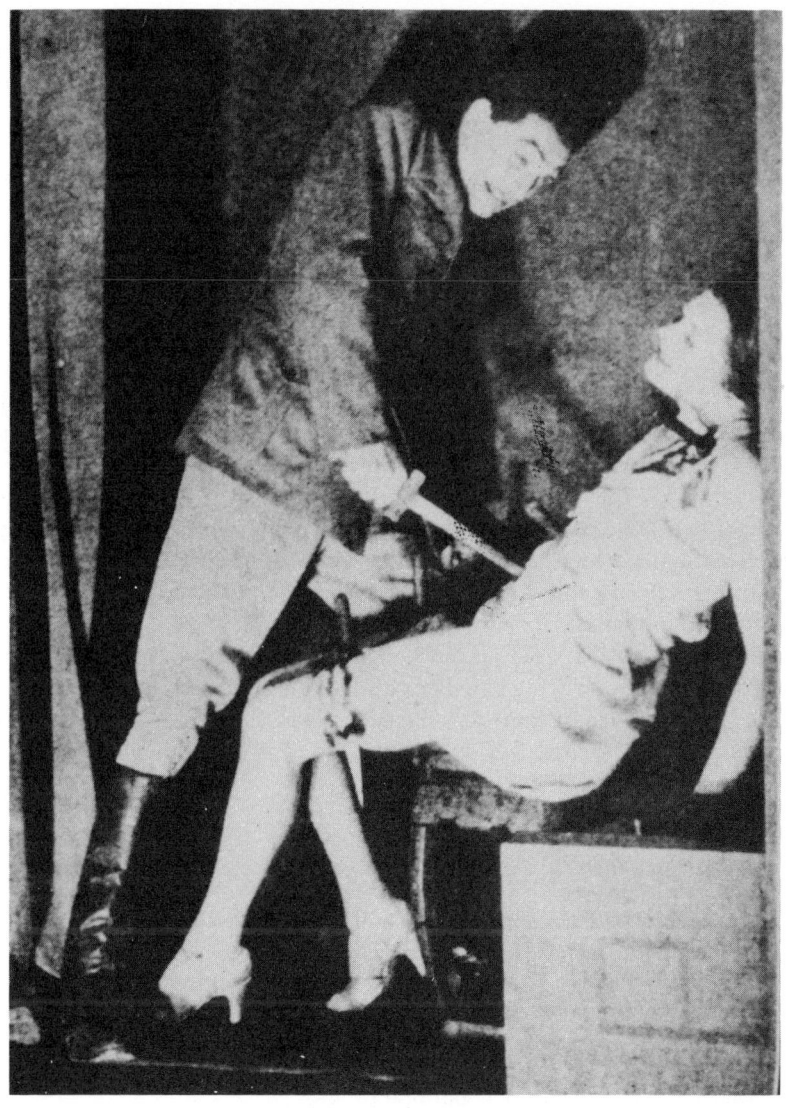

12 Swords and daggers in performance

shoulder. At the moment the slat rolls over, the actor crosses in front of her to keep the audience from seeing the manoeuvre. He then proceeds to dissect the fake arm, with much blood coming from the handle of the cutting instrument, being squeezed out through the blade. A device similar to this has been used for centuries to represent decapitation.

The girl whose nipples were cut off with hedge shears could have been wearing a bra with a realistic breast and foam rubber nipple placed on the outside of the cup; or an even simpler method of doing this trick, one favored many times in the movies for amputation, is to hire a woman with a mastectomy, place a prosthetic breast over her scar tissue, and then slice away the fake nipple.

In a trick that goes back to the Middle Ages, chewing on a bar of soap imitates the foaming at the mouth of a madman, or a victim of rabies. Knives have dull blades which retreat into the handle upon contact. The trick of having a bend or half-circle loop in the blade of a knife or the shaft of an arrow is well known, and even used for comedy effect by Steve Martin, but as is the case with many well-known tricks, it is still effective when used by actors who play the scene with the appropriate skills.

In 1956 in *L'Orgie dans le phase* the Grand-Guignol hung a girl on a hook, but hanging tricks have been done for centuries. In this same play, fire effects were achieved with a lycopodium torch, a device which Paris first saw in 1765;[14] this device produces brilliantly bright red flames with little danger because it burns its vegetable powder-fuel almost instantaneously. Lycopodium powder was commonly used in the nineteenth century for lightning effects and for when performers needed to appear to be enveloped in flames.[15]

For sixty-five years the Grand-Guignol entertained audiences through terror and laughter, stage trickery and skilful acting. Like many of the people it portrayed, it came to a sad end, but le théâtre du Grand-Guignol de Paris left the theatre world with many fond, if gruesome, memories.

NOTES

1 'Speaking of Pictures', *Life*, 22 (28 April 1947), p. 15.
2 Ibid.
3 Mary Elizabeth Homrighous, 'The Grand Guignol' (unpublished Ph.D. diss., Northwestern University, 1963), preface, p. i.
4 'Murders in the Rue Chaptal', *Time* (10 March 1947), p. 45.
5 Ibid., p. 44. See also P. E. Schneider, 'Fading Horrors of the Grand Guignol', *New York Times Magazine* (17 March 1957), p. 13.
6 Homrighous, 'The Grand Guignol', p. 7.
7 Schneider, 'Fading Horrors', pp. 13–14.
8 Ibid., p. 58.
9 Ibid., p. 56.
10 Ibid., p. 60.
11 'Murders in the Rue Chaptal', pp. 44–5. See also 'Paris Writhes Again', *Time* (16 January 1950), p. 46.
12 'Outdone by Reality', *Time* (30 November 1962), pp. 78, 80.
13 'Murders in the Rue Chaptal', p. 45.
14 M. J. Moynet, *L'Envers du Théâtre* (1873), translated as *French Theatrical Production in the Nineteenth Century*, trans. Allan S. Jackson with M. Glen Wilson, ed.

Marvin A. Carlson (no city: published by the Max Reinhardt Foundation with the Center for Modern Theatre Research, 1976), p. 16.
15 For information about this play I am indebted to Barry Alan Richmond of New York City. Mr Richmond controls the production rights to all Grand-Guignol plays staged in the United States.

Lesbian sexuality and violence in the plays of G. B. Shaw*

J. ELLEN GAINOR

We do not usually think of George Bernard Shaw's plays as violent – impassioned, perhaps, in their rhetorical and intellectual fervor, but a far cry from the Artaudian Theatre of Cruelty or the Shepardesque dramas of psychological violence on the contemporary stage. Yet a strain of sexually related aggression lurks in Shaw's plays, a motif of domination and violation masked by the larger social context in which these scenes appear. Shaw's comedies and problem plays, often conforming to conventionally romantic plots, feature sprightly young lovers engaged in the 'duel of sex', but these battles are fought with words alone, as the men try to withstand the magnetic pull of the Life Force, embodied by women. Perhaps Shaw's quintessential example of this contest comes at the climax of *Man and Superman*:

> Tanner. I will not marry you. I will not marry you.
> Ann. Oh, you will, you will.
> Tanner. I tell you, no, no, no.
> Ann. I tell you, yes, yes, yes.
> Tanner. No.
> Ann. [*coaxing – imploring – almost exhausted*] Yes. Before it is too late for repentance. Yes.
> Tanner. [*struck by the echo from the past*]. When did all this happen to me before? Are we two dreaming?
> Ann. [*suddenly losing her courage, with an anguish that she does not conceal*]. No. We are awake; and you have said no: that is all.
> Tanner [*brutally*]. Well?
> Ann. Well, I made a mistake: you do not love me.
> Tanner [*seizing her in his arms*]. It is false. I love you. The Life Force enchants me. I have the whole world in my arms when I clasp you. But I am fighting for my freedom, for my honor, for my self, one and indivisible.[1]

Obscured behind these dominant and pervasive matrimonial and amatory struggles, however, lie ones of a decidedly different kind – contests between women. These encounters feature distinctively physical – as

---

* A draft of this paper was read at the *Themes in Drama* International Conference held at the University of California, Riverside, in February 1989. It will be reprinted as a chapter in the author's forthcoming book, *Shaw's Daughters: Dramatic and Narrative Constructions of Gender* (University of Michigan Press).

opposed to verbal – methods of achieving dominance, revealing a theme of lesbian brutality in Shaw masked by the heterosexual, affectional context of the women's dialogue. Yet these scenes between women always revolve around, or take their motivation from, men. Engaged in seemingly innocuous activity, such as conversing about a male suitor or helping prepare a package for mailing, these women actually play out deeper intentions of physical violence against each other, cloaked by, and interspersed with, their superficial conversation or action. The subtextual content of these scenes discloses this very different agenda, revealing Shaw's sense of female brutality, blatancy, and cruelty that he does not allow to surface in these same women's interactions with other, male characters.

Readers and audiences familiar with Shavian dramaturgy may recall one notable scene of overt physical, heterosexual violence in *Major Barbara*, but the moments when Bill Walker punches Rummy Mitchens and slaps Jenny Hill in Act II are unique to the canon in their overt expression of rage and frustration stemming from social injustice. And although these are instances of male hostility directed physically towards women, neither Rummy nor Jenny is sexually or emotionally tied to Bill. Shaw thereby keeps their interaction solely in a social realm, saving the sexually related, but thwarted, hostility of Bill toward 'his woman', Mog Habbijam, off stage.[2]

In a more exclusively literary vein, Shaw also manipulates and pacifies a classic myth of heterosexual rape in *Candida*. By calling Reverend Morell's lovesick assistant Proserpine, he invokes the myth of Pluto and Proserpine, with its central incident of abduction and ravishment. But Shaw inverts the classical story by making Prossy the driving force and Morell a charismatic Christian Socialist who has unwittingly attracted her, and by turning the mythic rape into Prossy's voluntary self-victimization – not overtly sexual, but with desire clearly evident in her speech and action. Shaw removes the onus of rape from the male character and replaces it with female emotional masochism, thereby rendering the male guiltless in his revision. In two other plays, he similarly associates a taste for masochism with a female character, or with conventional femininity. In the historical drama *The Man of Destiny*, Shaw's Napoleon asks his antagonist, the Strange Lady, who has stolen his despatches:

> *Napoleon.* . . . Have you any sense of personal danger? Or are you one of those women who like to be beaten black and blue?
> *Lady.* Thank you, General: I have no doubt the sensation is very voluptuous; but I had rather not.[3]

And in *The Music Cure*, where Shaw explores gender conventions by characterizing a masculine woman as the lover of a feminized man,

Reginald admits, 'Don't laugh at this ridiculous confession; but ever since I was a child I have had only one secret longing, and that was to be mercilessly beaten by a splendid, strong, beautiful woman.'[4] Although the Strange Lady rejects Napoleon's overture, and the audience is meant to understand the parody and exaggeration behind Reginald's admission, these scenes nevertheless point toward a complex, and perhaps contradictory attitude toward the depths of female sexuality for Shaw. Distinct from the scenes of social violence in *Major Barbara* and literary violence in *Candida*, these last two moments of what Shaw intends as comic violence belie the darker vision of women's nature inherent in the scenes I wish to examine here in greater detail – ones which contain much more intimate, personal aggression distinctive for both its separation from the dialogic context of the action – unlike their integral relation in *Major Barbara* – and the subtlety of its textual incorporation – dialogue interwoven with seemingly innocent individual stage directions which, examined in progressive isolation, have more troubling implications.

Shaw's first play, *Widowers' Houses* (1898), exposes slum landlordism and the hypocrisy surrounding this practice in the upper middle class. Sartorius, the prosperous tenement manager (whose name suggests the duplicity of his nature – a sartorial persona masking the real one beneath) tries to keep his daughter Blanche (whose name suggests innocent purity) ignorant of the source of his income. But when she falls in love with Harry Trench (whose name points toward the depth of his own involvement in their sordid financial dealings), an eligible young gentleman whose family, unbeknownst to him, derives its fortune from the ownership of these same properties, a conflict develops between the lovers over who will support them financially. When Trench learns the origin of Blanche's wealth, he rejects this income, and insists that Blanche and he live off his small but adequate salary as a doctor. Blanche, still uninformed about the problem concerning the property and used to a more comfortable lifestyle, prefers that Trench accept additional money from her father if they are to marry. He refuses, and she breaks their engagement, leaving them both depressed, angry, and frustrated.

Immediately afterward, with the audience's mind occupied with these obstacles to the love plot, Shaw inserts a scene between Blanche and her maid, the main action of which concerns Blanche's preparations to return Trench's letters and love tokens. We see Blanche at her worst here, demonstrating her violent temper and inconsiderateness toward those who care for her. The maid enters first, inexplicably sniffling and trying to suppress sobs. Shaw's stage directions then read:

> [*Blanche's*] *expression is that of a strong and determined woman in an intense passion. The maid looks at her with abject* wounded affection *and* bodily terror. (my emphasis)[5]

The dialogue and action which follow more closely resemble those of a conventional love scene between a violently passionate gentleman and a lower-class girl than that between a lady and her maid.

> *Blanche.* . . . What are you crying for?
> *The Parlormaid [plaintively].* You speak so brutal to me, Miss Blanche; and I do love you so. I'm sure no one else would stay and put up with what I have to put up with.
> *Blanche.* Then go. I dont want you. Do you hear? Go.
> *The Parlormaid [piteously, falling on her knees].* Oh no, Miss Blanche. Dont send me away from you: dont –
> *Blanche [with fierce disgust].* Agh! I hate the sight of you. . . .
> *The Parlormaid [weeping].* Oh, how could you say such a thing to me, Miss Blanche: me that –
> *Blanche [seizing her by the hair and throat].* Stop that noise, I tell you, unless you want me to kill you.
> *The Parlormaid [protesting and imploring, but in a carefully subdued voice].* Let me go, Miss Blanche: you know youll be sorry: you always are. Remember how dreadfully my head was cut last time.
> *Blanche [raging].* Answer me, will you. Have they gone?
> *The Parlormaid.* Lickcheese has gone, looking dreadf– *[she breaks off with a stifled cry as Blanche's fingers tighten furiously on her].* . . . *[in a gasp]* Theyre staying to lunch.
> *Blanche [looking intently into her face].* He?
> *The Parlormaid [whispering with a sympathetic nod].* Yes, miss. *[Blanche lets her drop, and stands forlorn . . . The parlormaid, recognizing the passing of the crisis of passion, and fearing no further violence, sits discomfitedly on her heels, and tries to arrange her hair and cap, whimpering a little with exhaustion and soreness].* Now youve set my hands all trembling; and I shall jingle the things on the tray at lunch so that everybody will notice me. Its too bad of you, Miss Bl– *[Sartorius coughs outside].*
> *Blanche [quickly].* Sh! Get up.[6]

Arthur Ganz describes this scene as a 'sado-masochistic relationship with overtones of barely repressed lesbianism'.[7] The scene, of course, also bears striking resemblance to the interaction of Claire and Solange, the title characters in Jean Genet's 1947 play, *The Maids*. The homoerotic content of this play, with its central scenes of sexual violence between 'mistress' and 'maid', may have prompted Ganz's reading of Shaw, despite the gay, as opposed to lesbian, implications of the Genet text. Regardless of the source of Ganz's interpretation, the mixture of brutality and emotion in this section of *Widowers' Houses* is unmatched in any later Shaw play, perhaps in part because his audience responded so unfavorably to the harshness of the characters in this first dramatic effort.[8]

The scene between Blanche and her maid is striking for its subtext of spurned love. The parlormaid enters, already in a state of emotional distress, and soon throws herself on her knees before the object of her devotion, begging to continue their relationship. We see and hear that it is a dynamic fraught with violence. In a fit of passion Blanche has earlier wounded the maid's head; the mistress now pulls her hair and attempts to strangle her. As the parlormaid tries to express her caring and devotion, to remind her mistress of her acts of loyalty and love, she is repeatedly silenced. Blanche cuts off the vocalization of 'the love that dare not speak its name', and ultimately the two distractedly and hurriedly separate from their encounter at the sound of Sartorius's cough, much like two guilty lovers pretending there has been no questionable contact between them while they have been alone together.

The Alfred Douglas allusion is particularly relevant here, for Shaw wrote *Widowers' Houses* at the *fin de siècle*, at the same time that scientific and public attention focused with increasing interest on issues of human sexuality, especially the broad phenomenon known as sexual inversion, which incorporated studies of the practice of homosexuality. Recently, critics have begun to examine early theories of male and female homosexuality, and one of the striking observations they have made concerns the theorists' assumption of a heterosexual model for homosexual interaction. In other words, these early investigators posited a single-sex relation as they understood the male–female relation to be: they assumed the homosexual dynamic conformed to Victorian conventions of feminine passivity and masculine dominance. Thus in a homosexual relationship, they believed one partner took on the 'male' role, while the other behaved as the 'female'. This paradigm of male as initiator, female as passive participant reflected Victorian belief in the absence of feminine desire. Some theorists also proposed a further model of homosexual 'male' aggression and 'female' reluctance – a seduction scenario that removed the stigma of inversion from the participant who was the object of the other's advances.[9]

Shaw certainly knew the work of two of the better known of these theorists, Havelock Ellis and Edward Carpenter. He had professional contact with each of them, and he came to know Carpenter personally through their mutual friendship with Kate Salt, a lesbian and the wife of Shaw's fellow Fabian, Henry Salt. Shaw's writing in the late Victorian and Edwardian periods reflects an awareness of the terminology and characteristics of sexual inversion, and his closeness with Kate Salt may well have made him sensitive to the concept of lesbian sexuality, if not to its practice.

As a progressive writer and thinker, Shaw publicly supported sexual and artistic freedom, championing the cause of such writers as Radclyffe Hall, whose novel *The Well of Loneliness* came under the attack of the censor for its sexual content. In a 1928 note to the Very Reverend Albert Victor Baillie, Shaw comments on the letter recently published in the major London papers which Shaw, Baillie, and other prominent literary figures had signed in support of the book's publication:

> The letter we sent to the papers was drafted by me very carefully so as to keep us completely off the ground of any sympathy with the propaganda of homosexualism (I write *ism* advisedly) which goes on, and not to commit us even on the point of the book's appeal for the humane consideration of inversion as a natural misfortune. It might have been signed by persons who had not read the book, and did not know nor care what it was about.
>
> We had better leave it at that. It would be impossible to go further without involving ourselves and one another in the discussion we have evaded. We are in the difficulty that the least expression of emotional abhorrence contributes to the morbid atmosphere in which all sexual aberrations flourish and make their practitioners feel heroic, whilst anything less than that – unless at volume length on the Havelock Ellis scale – is interpreted as sympathetic.[10]

As the tone and diction of this letter suggest, Shaw, like many other forward-thinking individuals of his era, made a number of contradictory statements about homosexuality, essentially avowing a person's right to freedom of sexual choice, yet privately loathing any deviation from 'normalcy'. This is certainly the case in Shaw's attitude toward Oscar Wilde, whom he supported professionally while condemning personally. In an essay in *Pen Portraits and Reviews*, Shaw expressed his 'disgust at "the man Wilde" ', noting that his behavior 'represented a real degeneracy produced by his debaucheries'.[11] It is not surprising that at this time Shaw would, perhaps unconsciously, incorporate a concern with this form of sexuality into his drama, or that he would maintain the theorists' heterosexual paradigm while avoiding the extremely problematic and sensitive issue of male homosexuality by projecting his interest onto women, whose sexual orientation did not, in general, receive as much attention as men's.[12] Yet, given the increased public awareness and disapproval of homosexuality, it is also understandable that he would not even depict a scene between women with homoerotic content again for some time, until well after the furor connected with the Wilde case had died down.

Many critics believed Wilde to have been the victim of Alfred Douglas's seductive advances,[13] and Shaw duplicates the theorists' model of heterosexual seduction for the image of homosexuality in his subsequent scenes of lesbian contact. But he also retains the superstructure of a legitimate heterosexual context for these scenes of lesbian sexuality, as he did in *Widowers' Houses*. This surface context effectively masks the homoerotic thrust of the stage directions, which are the locus of the lesbian content – the silent dynamic which underscores the problematic heterosexual love relations of the young heroines in these plays. As with the interaction of Blanche and her maid, the structure of the relationships depicted through language and action both follow heterosexual models. This ironically contrasts with the essential sexual difference in the rapports we simultaneously hear about and see. Shaw's heterosexual dramatic conflicts, which motivate the conversations between women and provide a rationale for their scenes' action, may also accurately reflect his grasp of his society – a milieu where overt homosexuality was proscribed, and conversation and physical action were forced to contain a subtextual code to obscure homoerotic intention.

Heartbreak House, published in 1919, depicts the last days of 'cultured, leisured Europe before the war'.[14] The Shotover household and its inhabitants display elements of the decadence we associate with that historical moment. Amongst other theatrical devices, Shaw uses the ship setting (metaphorically on the rocks), Hector's Arab costume, and the fascinating polymorphous sexuality of the characters Hesione and Ariadne to demonstrate this theme tangibly for his audience. The retrospective vision of England immediately before the outbreak of war also imbues the play with a sense of tension about to erupt into violence – a pre-apocalyptic moment in which dialogue and action all seem to foreshadow the destruction to come.

The unconventional sexual attitudes and behavior of Hesione dominate the action and coincide with the sense of abandonment of the temporal setting. Hesione is a seductress, the demon daughter of Captain Shotover who enraptures men and makes all the other characters conform to her will. She has similarly charmed the young woman Ellie Dunn and, during the course of the play, tries to dissuade her from marrying Boss Mangan, an old capitalist whom Ellie does not love but regards as a good match financially. As Hesione and Ellie discuss the pros and cons of this marital arrangement, as well as Ellie's attraction for the mysterious and romantic 'Marcus Darnley' (who turns out to be Hesione's husband Hector Hushabye), Shaw gives Hesione a series of stage directions that appear startlingly like those of a seduction scene, suggesting a lesbian attraction of the older woman for the younger. '*She snatches at Ellie's waist, and makes her sit down on the sofa beside her*',[15] '*catching her dress*',[16] '*caressing her*',[17] '*laying Ellie down at the end of the sofa*',[18] and finally '*fondling her*',[19] a gesture from which Ellie '*disengages herself with an expression of distaste*'.[20] The dialogue throughout this scene, which covers ten pages in the printed text, works against the subtextual grain, however, revolving solely around Ellie's various heterosexual involvements with Mangan and Hector. The exchange that ostensibly prompts Ellie's final 'disengagement' is a reference to the 'distasteful' Mangan.

> Ellie [*staring at her thoughtfully*]. Theres something odd about this house, Hesione, and even about you. I dont know why I'm talking to you so calmly. I have a horrible fear that my heart is broken, but that heartbreak is not like what I thought it must be.
> Mrs Hushabye [*fondling her*]. Its only life educating you, pettikins. How do you feel about Boss Mangan now?

Ellie [disengaging herself with an expression of distaste]. Oh, how can you remind me of him, Hesione?
Mrs Hushabye. Sorry, dear. I think I hear Hector coming back. You dont mind now, do you, dear?[21]

Thus the speeches of Ellie and Hesione contain no overt mention of the physical activity occurring simultaneously, although Ellie's 'distaste' could have textual and/or subtextual significance. And, given contemporary directors' penchant for eliminating all the playwright's stage directions at the first rehearsal, these gestures could easily be omitted from production altogether. But examined collectively, the dialogue and action here present a fascinating network of images. At the same time that Hesione appears removed from Ellie's personal life, probing the relations with Mangan and Marcus Darnley, she physically represents a third suitor, clearly the most sexually aggressive of the group. Shaw's depiction of her homoerotic attraction parallels the model of heterosexual behavior proposed by the theorists, but he makes the lesbian dynamic appear more intense when he juxtaposes it to heterosexual activity. Hesione, as the aggressor, takes the traditionally 'male' role, but is more overt than either of Ellie's male lovers have been. But Hesione's sexual forwardness is also perfectly in keeping with Shaw's distinctive concept of Life Force women, much like Blanche with her advances on Harry Trench in *Widowers' Houses*.[22] This reverse of traditional sex roles in Shaw resonates with the Victorian/Edwardian concept of sexual inversion, where a key signifier for lesbianic tendencies could be a woman's display of strong sexual desire. Paradoxically, Shaw's heterosexual Life Force women are the *real* women in his plays, yet when he places these same women in a lesbian relation, displaying the same behavior as they do in heterosexual contexts, they theoretically become 'male'. Ellie, as the 'victim' of Hesione's aggressive advances, must evade her both linguistically and physically, and Shaw leaves the interpretation of the young woman's reactions tantalizingly ambiguous. Does the interaction of Hesione and Ellie have any impact, ultimately, on Ellie's gravitation toward the patriarchal figure Shotover, who shares with his daughters their intense fascination, but who poses no sexual threat to the young woman? In other words, does Ellie's disillusionment with her sexually active male suitors, Mangan and Marcus Darnley, coupled with her distaste – or perhaps Shaw's distaste and anxiety – over the decadent advances of Hesione propel her toward a relationship with Shotover, the ancient mariner with no interest in the wedding 'feast'?

The erotic complications of another surrogate father/daughter relation underlie the action of *Pygmalion* (1913), a play which, like *Heartbreak House*, Shaw infuses with the dark tones of impending violence – this time, pointedly sexual violence toward the heroine Eliza. Martin Meisel centers this action in 'the seduction scene of the second act', where 'everyone suspects Higgins' designs'.²³ But the theme is introduced much earlier, in the opening scene of the play, with Eliza's first 'terrified' and 'hysterical' insistence on her respectability and her fear of losing her 'character'.²⁴ Eliza's concerns operate on two levels here: she not only fears a loss of reputation (meaning actually the acquisition of one as a loose woman), but the speech also foreshadows the larger issue of Eliza's loss of self – the transformation into a new identity and 'character' created by Higgins. From her Act I protestation that 'I'm a good girl, I am'²⁵ through her Act v taunt to Henry, 'Wring away. What do I care? I knew youd strike me some day',²⁶ Eliza consistently expresses concern for her physical and moral well-being at the hands of her teacher and surrogate father.

Higgins, of course, takes advantage of Eliza's innocence and naiveté when she comes to his home requesting elocution lessons. He plays upon her concerns for her safety, as well as her sensitivity to the class differences between them, to bully her into behaving as he desires. The diction that he uses towards her, calling her 'cheap' and a 'dirty slut',²⁷ resonates with the motifs of socio-sexual disparagement that encapsulate his initial attitude toward his pupil.

Mrs Pearce, the housekeeper, echoes Higgins's defamation of Eliza, and she becomes his minion in the fairytale-like transformation of Eliza from flower seller to social triumph. Higgins informs Eliza in Act II, 'If youre naughty and idle you will sleep in the back kitchen among the black beetles, and be walloped by Mrs Pearce with a broomstick.'²⁸ Yet despite Higgins's numerous threats of physical violence, he never actually hurts Eliza, mental and emotional cruelty notwithstanding. Instead, Shaw projects onto Mrs Pearce the physical, sexual violation of Eliza that Henry suppresses throughout, in a lesbian 'rape' scene added to the original script at the time it was filmed (1938).²⁹ Eliza's loss of her profession as a flower seller – her 'defloration' – with the aid of Henry's servant, the aptly named Mrs Pearce ('pierce'), are such blatantly Freudian elements of the text that they cannot have been accidental.

Shortly after Eliza's arrival at Wimpole Street, Higgins insists that Mrs Pearce '[b]undle her off to the bath-room'³⁰ to clean her as a first step toward respectability. Mrs Pearce conducts Eliza to 'a spare bedroom' on 'the third floor'. Eliza had 'expected to be taken down to the scullery',³¹ but she begins her transformation by a physical elevation that metaphorically parallels her expected rise in social stature. She is told 'to make [herself] as clean as the room: then [she] wont be afraid of it'³² – a simile that reinforces the theme of the girl's dehumanization that runs throughout the play.³³ Eliza associates cleanliness with death, however – the metaphoric, sexual sense of death being perhaps subtextual:

> *Eliza.* You expect me to get into that and wet myself all over! Not me. I should catch my death. I knew a woman did it every Saturday night; and she died

of it.... [*weeping*] ... its not natural: it would kill me. Ive never had a bath in my life.³⁴

Mrs Pearce counters with inducements and slurs: 'Well, dont you want to be clean and sweet and decent, like a lady? You know you cant be a nice girl inside if youre a dirty slut outside.'³⁵ The reasoning is the twisted logic of upper-class male seducers of lower-class women in eighteenth- and nineteenth-century romance: submit and receive the outer embellishments of higher social status, and pay no attention to what you actually become as a result (i.e. a 'slut'). The ambiguity of the term 'slut', which can mean either a physically dirty or morally questionable woman, stands out strongly; Eliza's claims of being a 'good girl' are thrown into question by the alternative, sexual connotation of the label. This indeterminacy resonates with the link between physical cleanliness and sexual purity that is inverted by the scene's subtext into physical cleanliness and sexual defloration.

Despite Eliza's cries of protest, she is ordered to 'take off all [her] clothes'.³⁶ Shaw's stage directions then read:

> *Mrs Pearce puts on a pair of white rubber sleeves ... then takes a formidable looking long handled scrubbing brush and soaps it profusely with a ball of scented soap. Eliza comes back with nothing on but the bath gown ... a piteous spectacle of abject terror ... [D]eftly snatching the gown away and throwing Eliza down on her back ... [s]he sets to work with the scrubbing brush. Eliza's screams are heartrending.*³⁷

The blatancy of these stage directions suggests Shaw's cognizance of their sexual implications. The phallic brush and cleansing ball are applied with the clinical coldness of the bath/laboratory's rubber gloves. That Eliza should be thrown on her back to be 'cleaned', which in a bathtub would literally lead to drowning, cements the rape imagery, foregrounding for the reader the symbolic interpretation over the literal. Using a female surrogate for the male rapist, Shaw again conceives of this lesbian encounter in a heterosexual context, in keeping with the late Victorian/Edwardian medical paradigm for a lesbian relation. But perhaps more importantly, he transfers the onus of sexual violence onto a woman, thereby safeguarding the gruff geniality of Higgins and insuring his respectability at the same time that he fulfills the dark threat to Eliza that the play's opening dialogue foreshadows.

The film version, which facilitated the inclusion of this scene, quite graphically follows the outline of Shaw's directions, and creates a profoundly disturbing atmosphere on screen. At the start of the bath scene, Mrs Pearce wraps herself in a sheet/apron (instead of the printed 'sleeves') and promptly corners Eliza in the bathroom, trying to talk her into removing her clothes. She finally pushes Eliza out into the adjacent bedroom to change into a robe, leaving Mrs Pearce alone. At this point, ominous music begins quietly, and almost like the witch whose broom stick has been alluded to earlier, she begins to mix bath salts in a tub that quickly foams with the appearance of a bubbling cauldron. Mrs Pearce looks toward the bedroom door with a determined glint in her eye, as if to say, 'this will do the trick', and picks up the scrubbing brush and soap. After another brief tangle getting Eliza to remove the robe – the camera having cut to Mrs Pearce draping the bathroom mirror with a towel – Eliza is seen in the tub, screaming and struggling with Mrs Pearce, who, like Blanche before her, has Eliza by the hair, grabbing hold of it to keep Eliza submerged in the bathwater. Interspersed with her genuinely 'heartrending' screams, Eliza cries: 'I've never done this kind of thing before, really I haven't ... No, Mrs Pearce, no, don't ... stop it ... this has never happened to me before ... oh help, help ... I've never been ... stop it ... help.'[38] Amidst her screams, the camera cuts to a shot of Higgins and Pickering at the foot of the stairs below. They are staring up at the sound of the cries, and they exchange a bemused look. Higgins shrugs and turns back into his study, while Pickering remains, with an expression on his face which can only be described as a smirk. The camera cuts back to Eliza, still screaming, eyes shut (to keep out soap), hand groping along the tile wall of the tub. Her hand grasps hold of a handle, and suddenly the shower head above explodes with a cascade of shooting water. This ejaculatory conclusion to the scene clearly literalizes the subtextually heterosexual paradigm controlling the attack on Eliza.

Although the actors, screenwriters, and directors[39] must be credited for the overall production, Shaw's close involvement with the film implicates him in its creation and impact as well.[40] The thrust of this scene in particular is patently clear; the 'innocuous' bath barely masks the reality of female violation conveyed by the dialogue and action. That the male characters should find this an amusing and easily dismissed event – one in fact that they ordained and by which they are briefly entertained – establishes this film as just one of the overwhelming number that condone violence toward women and present it as light entertainment. The revised ending for the film, in which Eliza decides to return to 27A Wimpole Street, only cements the acceptability of this action. After all, she voluntarily chooses to stay with the man who initiated this action, and who treats her callously throughout, suggesting her acceptance of, and willingness to continue being treated in like fashion, all of which perpetuates the sense that such male behavior is 'what women really want'.

The motif of violent lesbian activity, which runs throughout Shaw's work, suggests a disturbingly dark and problematic view of female sexuality and the potential for positive female interaction. There are no close female friendships in Shaw's plays, indicating his reluctance, or inability, to grasp the complete range of female experience in his society. Some critics feel his portrayal of woman as the sexual aggressor in such plays as *Man and Superman* helped to break down the restrictive, conventional views of women at the end of the Victorian era. Yet the extrapolation of this forwardness to the potential of such women as Blanche and Hesione for sexual violence calls into question the ultimate impact of this aspect of his dramaturgy. Shaw never depicts male sexual violence, either hetero- or homosexual, furthering the skewed angle from which he handles the grim reality of sexual aggression in society. The comic conclusions of these dramas, with their generically heterosexual focus, cannot efface the undercurrents of female sexual violence that recurrently trouble his theatrical waters.

NOTES

1 Bernard Shaw, *Man and Superman: A Comedy and a Philosophy* (Harmondsworth: Penguin Books Ltd, 1983), p. 205.
2 I also wish to distinguish this kind of brutal violence from the more farcical pratfalls and stunts inherent to the physical business of *The Millionairess*. Epifania Ognisanti di Parerga's superior strength, which she uses to hurtle scorned male lovers down flights of stairs, is again off-stage action, and is treated only comically, in virtual cartoon-like fashion.
3 Bernard Shaw, *The Man of Destiny: A Fictitious Paragraph of History* in *Plays Pleasant* (London: Penguin, 1988), p. 192.
4 Bernard Shaw, *The Music Cure* in *Ten Short Plays* (New York: Dodd, Mead, 1960), p. 167.
5 George Bernard Shaw, *Widowers' Houses: A Play* in *Play Unpleasant* (Harmondsworth: Penguin, 1983), pp. 74–5.
6 Ibid., pp. 75–6.
7 Arthur Ganz, *George Bernard Shaw* (New York: Grove, 1983), p. 86.
8 By contrast, in *Caesar and Cleopatra* (1900), Shaw's heroine, in an early exercise of her newly discovered queenly power in Egypt, wants to beat her female servant Ftatateeta, with whom she shares a particularly close relationship, but is prevented from doing so by Caesar. Instead, she whips a young serving boy, an action which is treated as indicative of childishness, and carries no other subtextual weight.
9 An excellent summary of these scientific and theoretical studies can be found in George Chauncey, Jr, 'From Sexual Inversion to Homosexuality: Medicine and the Changing Conceptualization of Female Deviance', *Salmagundi*, 58–9 (Fall 1982–Winter 1983), 114–46.
10 Bernard Shaw, *Collected Letters*, ed. Dan H. Laurence, vol. 4 (London: Max Reinhardt, 1988), pp. 117–18.
11 Bernard Shaw, *Pen Portraits and Reviews* in *The Collected Works of Bernard Shaw: Ayot St Laurence Edition*, vol. 29 (New York: William H. Wise, 1932), pp. 302–3.
12 Shaw also felt the need to assure his biographer Frank Harris of his own sexuality: 'If you have any doubts as to my normal virility, dismiss them from your mind. I was not impotent; I was not sterile; I was not homosexual.' *Sixteen Self Sketches* (New York: Dodd, Mead, 1949), p. 175.

13 For Shaw's view of the situation, and for a detailed account of the Wilde and Douglas trials, see *Bernard Shaw and Alfred Douglas: A Correspondence*, ed. Mary Hyde (New Haven: Ticknor & Fields, 1982).
14 Bernard Shaw, *Heartbreak House: A Fantasia in the Russian Manner on English Themes* (New York: Penguin, 1977), p. 7.
15 Ibid., p. 63.
16 Ibid., p. 70.
17 Ibid., p. 70.
18 Ibid., p. 71.
19 Ibid., p. 72.
20 Ibid., p. 72.
21 Ibid., p. 72.
22 Blanche has both initiated their relationship, by engaging him in conversation aboard ship, and resolved it, ending their quarrel by overtly flirting with him to arouse his passions in the play's final scene.
23 Martin Meisel, *Shaw and the Nineteenth Century Theater* (New York: Limelight Editions, 1984), pp. 175–6.
24 Bernard Shaw, *Pygmalion: A Romance in Five Acts* (New York: Penguin, 1982), p. 15.
25 Ibid., p. 17.
26 Ibid., p. 108.
27 Ibid., p. 38.
28 Ibid., p. 36.
29 Arnold Silver has read this sequence as a rape scene, but he makes no mention of the lesbian content. *Bernard Shaw: The Darker Side* (Stanford University Press, 1982), pp. 270–2. Shaw incorporated his own versions of some of the added film scenes in his revised edition of the play, published by Penguin in 1941. Donald P. Costello, *The Serpent's Eye: Shaw and the Cinema* (Notre Dame University Press, 1965), p. 54.
30 Bernard Shaw, *Pygmalion*, p. 38.
31 Ibid., p. 38.
32 Ibid., p. 38.
33 Eliza is repeatedly associated with inanimate objects such as 'a lost umbrella' (p. 89) and 'the squashed cabbage leaves of Covent Garden' (p. 97).
34 Bernard Shaw, *Pygmalion*, p. 38.
35 Ibid., p. 38.
36 Ibid., p. 39.
37 Ibid., pp. 39–40.
38 All dialogue taken from the soundtrack to the film version, readily available on videocassette. *Pygmalion*, prod. Gabriel Pascal (Loew's Inc., 1938).
39 The film was directed by Anthony Asquith and Leslie Howard, who also played Henry Higgins.
40 For a detailed discussion of Shaw's involvement in the making of the film, see Costello, *The Serpent's Eye*, pp. 50–82. The film was a tremendous box office success, and Shaw claimed major responsibility for this.

Violence as tragic farce in Camus's *Caligula**

BEN STOLTZFUS

Violence is a leitmotif that runs through most of Albert Camus's novels, essays, and plays: there is murder in *The Stranger* and *The Misunderstanding*, suicide in *The Myth of Sisyphus*, organized terror in *The Just Assassins* and *The Rebel*, and the deadly ravages of disease in *The Plague*. In none of Camus's works, however, is violence dramatized as systematically as it is in *Caligula*.

There are two levels of violence in the play: an overt one based on the Emperor's intentional acts of rape and murder, and a covert one that foregrounds transgressive behavior. There is also a didactic element in Caligla's violence designed to alter the behavior of his fellow Romans. Although he fails in his intent, it is not because he is assassinated, but because his assailants, in miming his violence, miss the message. There are also two narrative levels: Caligula may have his Roman audience, but Camus has his implied twentieth-century audience, even as Caligula's acting is directed at both.

In Caligula's eyes, the death of his sister Drusilla is a grave miscarriage of justice that underscores the terrible unfairness of life. Because her death is the symptom of the world's random violence, Caligula will transform this gratuitous force into essential violence. He impersonates the world in order to dramatize his vision of its terrible unfairness. His acts are not motivated by revenge, since his victims are chosen at random; they are based instead on a personal pedagogical urgency.

Although the play is ostensibly a tragedy, it is difficult to identify with Caligula's victims or with him. For the patricians, who will eventually assassinate the Emperor, his playacting is tragic because he kills their wives and fathers; but the play is also melodramatic because the patricians' vengeance leads to their satisfaction. For us, it is neither tragedy nor melodrama but tragic farce, as we shall see.

What then is Caligula's intended message? It is Camus's own neo-existentialist notion of freedom and the absurd. A brief overview of critical

---
* A draft of this paper was read at the *Themes in Drama* International Conference held at the University of California, Riverside, in February 1989.

readings of the play will perhaps put Camus's philosophy in perspective. John Cruickshank, in *Albert Camus and the Literature of Revolt*, defines the play as metaphysical tragedy, and Caligula's dilemma as a quintessential drama of the absurd.[1] Raymond Gay-Crosier, in 'Camus et le Donjuanisme', states that *Caligula* offers an extension of Camus's philosophy of the absurd as developed in *The Myth of Sisyphus*,[2] where it is put forward as the origin of his freedom, his passion, and his rebellion.[3] Thus, Edward Freeman, in *The Theater of Albert Camus: A Critical Study*, asserts that Caligula's revolt against the world as death is as important as the context of the absurd.[4] Gay-Crosier, in pursuing this lead, in 'Le Jeu dans le jeu ou la tragi-comédie des *Justes*', gives revolt high status, but he acknowledges that although rebellion challenges the absurd, it does not circumvent it.[5] Robert de Luppé, in *Albert Camus*, also states that for Caligula the essential absurdity of the world unleashes powers of destruction that devalue the emotional bonds between people.[6] R. W. B. Lewis, in '*Caligula*: Or the Realm of the Impossible', affirms that Caligula's error is in dehumanizing the universe,[7] whereas for Kenneth Harrow, in '*Caligula*, A Study in Aesthetic Despair', Caligula's dehumanization is an escape from the self by retreating into the impossible, a realm in which he avoids 'the absurd confrontation with death by playing its role'. Caligula dreams of enjoying an absolute freedom, but every crime succeeds only in returning him to the prison of his finitude. 'He was more than a pedagogue', says Harrow, 'he was an actor lost in a play of his own creation.'[8] The function of the play within the play is developed by Jeanette Laillou-Savona in 'La Pièce à l'intérieur de la pièce et la notion d'art dans *Caligula*'.[9] However, before we link specular modes with freedom, violence, and play, let us look at the notion of the absurd as a generator of freedom.

As Camus's *persona*, Caligula strives to communicate the fact that 'men die and they are not happy' (p. 16, line 19).[10] This is the world's terrible unfairness. He turns Rome upside down, he opposes convention, he disrupts the accepted ways of doing business, he asserts an imperial disregard for the rights, feelings, and beliefs of other people, he mimes the randomness of chance, he violates ideology: in short, he imposes disorder onto an order that Rome's patricians had taken for granted. The consequences of his attempts to dramatize the absurd are that he is pronounced mad and killed because his brand of freedom is perceived as too disruptive to social stability and the people's peace of mind. Caligula's violence – the lesson in logic that he wished to transmit – fails to enlighten his constituents. Except for Scipio and Cherea, none understands the meaning of his mad behavior. No one appreciates the way he foregrounds radical ideas, and no one likes the dictatorial artifice that is being acted out for their benefit, every day, on the stage of life.

Caligula is assassinated allegedly because he raped wives and daughters and murdered husbands and fathers, because he disrupted public order, and because of his whimsical, unpredictable behavior. However, lurking behind the assassins' decision to restore law and order is their refusal to accede to Caligula's belief that all men are free and that the world is absurd. What is this freedom and how does absurdity manifest itself?

Blaise Pascal, referring to death, once said that the last act was bloody.[11] This metaphorical allusion led him to make a leap of faith into the unknown, and, in his now famous 'bet', to wager on the existence of God. He reasoned that life after death, if it exists, will make instant winners of us all because in betting on God we have nothing to lose and everything to gain. Camus, however, refused to make the leap because faith, he said, gains nothing. To believe in an afterlife is to lose this life, which is the only one we have. For Camus, to leap or not to leap is the question and, in choosing one way or the other, men define their essence. Those who refuse to leap are free to define an essence, whereas those who leap abdicate their freedom by choosing to subordinate their will to God's. Camus believed that men who opt for an afterlife are necessarily complacent about this one. Their attention, he says, is focused on a nebulous future, whereas in fact the present requires every ounce of energy we have. The conclusion that all men are mortal beyond redemption precipitates an urgency that, in Caligula's case, leads him to act violently and behave madly.

For Camus, however, although the urgency is there, violence is not inevitable, and he wrote much of his work, including *Caligula*, in order to demonstrate that although everything is possible, not everything is desirable. At the end of the play, shattering the mirror in which he sees his reflected image, Caligula says that his freedom was not the good kind (p. 108, line 2). 'The absurd', says Camus in his *Notebooks*, 'is tragic man in front of a mirror (Caligula). He is therefore *not alone*.'[12] Tragic man is man confronting his own mortality, and what he sees reflected in the mirror is not only his future death, but the image of total freedom. This freedom, this glimpse of the possible, exists always in the present. Moreover, the absurd posits the equivalence and permissibility of all acts. In his essay *Existentialism is a Humanism*, Jean-Paul Sartre, paraphrasing Dostoevsky, asserts that if God does not exist, everything is allowed.[13] Indeed, within a framework of total permissibility Sartre advocates revolutionary violence (his book *On Cuba* is one example) as a necessary antidote to the inequities of the class struggle.[14] Camus, in opposition to Sartre, wrote *The Rebel* in order to demonstrate that the bloodletting that is endemic to revolutions fails to solve socio-political problems because the new regime, using violent means to consolidate its power, inevitably, becomes as unjust as the regime it has supplanted.[15]

Caligula may have been cruel and even mad, but it is clear, in assassinating him, that the conspirators are perpetuating the status quo that Caligula wished so desperately to eradicate. Caligula scorns the insincerity, dishonesty, and duplicity of his countrymen. 'Everything around me', he says, 'is lies, and I want everyone to bask in the truth' (p. 16, lines 25–6). He respects only Cherea and Scipio who are not afraid to speak honestly, directly and even bluntly. The grovelling, cowardly, and insincere patricians are abused, humiliated, and executed. Caligula would impose new priorities on an old order that values falsehood and deceit. If money is more important than life, then the public treasury will be enriched at men's expense. If sex is all-important, then licentiousness will be compulsory. He refuses to wage war because, he says, he 'respects human life' (p. 68, line 20).

Caligula plays a privileged role. He is the Emperor and therefore the highest link in the chain of command. In principle he speaks the truth, since all truth, by decree, emanates from him. But since he is labeled 'mad', his dramatization of total freedom is suspect. Like other mad kings, Shakespeare's King Lear, Strindberg's Eric xiv, Pushkin's Boris Godunov, Pirandello's Henry iv, Caligula imposes disorder and devalues conventional reality in favor of a system stressing the man-made, the arbitrary, and the profane. Established customs, sacred values, and 'natural' ideals are parodied and desacralized. It is as though Caligula had taken ideology and inverted it like a gove. This inversion – the freedom of the absurd – allows him to play with ideology. He imposes whimsical taxes rather than the always 'justifiable' ones. He decrees that there will be famine instead of surfeit. He makes brothel attendance compulsory, he impersonates Venus, he pardons the guilty, he strangles the innocent, he tolerates the clandestine meetings of conspirators, and he does nothing to prevent his own assassination which he knows is imminent. All this is a form of calculated madness designed to reveal the structures of sanity. 'I wish to confound the sky and the sea, blend ugliness and beauty, infuse suffering with laughter' (p. 27, lines 22–3).

Caligula devalues ideology by playing with, dramatizing, and exaggerating its different components. He strikes at the heart of encratic language. The violence is in the collision between Caligula's creative will and Rome's conventions – the very space and stage where freedom manifests itself. Caligula's purpose is to foreground this freedom, and the best way to do that is to act as though life were a game for which he alone invents the rules. This power to invent and break the rules has its own internal and relentless logic whose sole aim is to instruct. Caligula impersonates Venus, imposing a ritual of obeisance, adoration, prostration, and donation: 'Instruct us in the truth of this world which is that it has none' (p. 63, lines 20–1). His game and his art evolve as he improvises a variety of performances. In one of them, while executing ridiculous shadowy gestures behind the transparency of a Chinese screen, Caligula appears wearing flowers on his head and the short dress of a female dancer. When the dance is over, a guard says: 'The spectacle has ended' (p. 88, lines 11–12). Cherea says that, in a sense, this has been great art (p. 88, line 34), but surely his intent is ironic even as Camus foregrounds the play within the play.

On another occasion Caligula feigns death, and one patrician offers two hundred thousand sisterces to the state treasury for Caligula's resurrection. Another offers to give up his life to Jupiter, if only Caligula will get well. The cat-and-mouse game that Caligula plays with the patricians' insincerity, since he promptly recovers, will force one of them to pay the amount he offered, and the other one to die. It is Caesonia who draws our attention to this dire game with the verb *jouer*, which in French means 'to act', 'to play', and 'to gamble'. She says: 'My friend, had you loved life more, you would not have gambled it away with such imprudence' (p. 93, lines 26–7). Scipio also opposes Caligula's games by saying: 'It is a game without boundaries. It is the amusement of a madman' (p. 23, lines 32–3). Fearful that Caligula will uncover their conspiracy, one of the plotters says: 'We are gambling with our lives' (p. 86, line 23). Perhaps the most emphatic use of the verb occurs in the exchange between Caligula and Scipio. Scipio, convinced that the bond between them, as they both evoke the beauties of the earth, the night, and the sky, is but another one of Caligula's tricks, says:

> *Scipio.* You monster, you lousy monster. You tricked me again. You are play-acting, aren't you? Are you happy with what you have done? (p. 58, lines 34–5)
>
> *Caligula.* There is some truth in what you say. I was acting. (p. 59, line 2)

Caligula exercises the inordinate freedom of a man and actor whose behavior is not prescribed and cannot be proscribed. As Emperor, he has the power to oppose and change the laws of Rome, and his play-acting is a daring, if tragic, demonstration of total freedom. It is the freedom of a man-god who plays with reality and who spontaneously invents roles for himself with which to test the limits of his power. 'I have now, at last, understood the usefulness of power. It gives the impossible a chance. Today, and for all time to come, my freedom no longer has any boundaries' (p. 24, line 7).

Caligula hopes that his dramatization of total freedom will provide distance and insight, but the personal tragedies of the people who have lost their wives and fathers are too close and too recent for any distancing effect to occur. For his audience, Caligula's message is deflected, but not for us. If the notion of play enables us to distance ourselves from both the victims and the executioner, then we are ready to receive Caligula's urgent communication. We, the other audience, are not touched by the corpses on stage because, for us, Camus is dramatizing an idea.

The *Caligula* manuscript has as its subtitle *Le joueur*,[16] meaning the 'player', and the 'gambler'. Edward Freeman in *The Theater of Albert Camus* and Germaine Brée, in 'Camus' *Caligula*: Evolution of a Play', interpret the word *joueur* as 'gambler', arguing that Caligula is an emperor who 'gambles on the side of an intellectual absolute'.[17] Is there a contradiction between staging one's own 'superior suicide', as Camus calls it in his preface to the American edition of *Caligula*,[18] and gambling on an 'intellectual absolute?' Perhaps not. Even if we admit that Caligula is a gambler, the French word *joueur* also applies to someone who *plays* with reality while simultaneously *acting* out roles on the improvised stage of life. Although, in 'Le Jeu dans le jeu ou la tragi-comédie des *Justes*', Gay-Crosier alludes to Camus's ludic point of view,[19] neither he nor Camus's other commentators develop the theme of play beyond the context of acting or gambling. Violence, as free play – Caligula's manifestation of gratuitous freedom – is thus a theme original to this essay.

Throughout the play, Caligula has been projecting an image of cruelty which he hopes will transform the ways of Rome. However, as *The Myth of Sisyphus* so poignantly affirms, 'we always end up wearing the image of our truths'.[20] Caligula may not rejoice in the fact that existence precedes essence, but nonetheless he vigorously proclaims that he is free to choose whatever essence he desires: 'Every man is allowed to act out the celestial tragedies and to become god' (p. 69, lines 19–20). This freedom to choose anything from the *tabula rasa* of existence is the 'truth' Caligula is staging and the lesson he would impose.

Nietzsche, who also proclaimed the death of God, once said that he knew of no other way than play for coping with great tasks.[21] Caligula's task seems forbidding enough, and he certainly does play. Meanwhile, Camus's use of ludic structures has given us a play of conflicting ideologies. Caligula's desire to assert his freedom, and Camus's desire to assert it for him, are thus at the heart of a discourse where, in the Saussurian sense, *langue* and *parole* clash, where the determinism of manners and of society's ready-made values vie with the gratuitous and the spontaneous acts of a man who would create new forms of consciousness. Caligula may rape and murder at random, but his assault on *doxa*, adumbrating Roland Barthes' and Michel Foucault's ideas on the violence of power, is a calculated gesture designed to expose the lies and the deceit that form the basis of social intercourse.[22]

However, by attacking encratic language Caligula breaks the bonds of human solidarity. By miming the randomness of death, the arbitrariness of nature, and the vagaries of fate, he threatens social organization at its core: 'We will make all these people die according to an arbitrarily established list' (p. 22, lines 10–11). Caligula is the incarnation of a plague which decimates and whose blind and dispassionate cruelty must, he feels, transform, alter, and inform: 'I am replacing the plague' (p. 94, line 3). His theatre of cruelty reminds us of Antonin Artaud's attack on all forms of rational discourse which, he says, had been the stock-in-trade of western playwrights from the Renaissance until Alfred Jarry's *King Ubu* (1896).[23] However, Camus's play, even though its modernity draws attention to its own internal dramatic devices, does not parody conventional theater the way Jarry's does.[24] Jarry's play, if formally more violent, is also more playful, whereas the essential violence in Camus's play stems from Caligula's parody of ideology. Formally, *Caligula* is conventional, insofar as it has four acts, plausible flesh-and-blood characters, and realistic settings, as opposed to Jarry's fantasy props and cardboard characters. With the play's ludic leitmotif in mind, Pol Gaillard urges future directors to stage *Caligula* as a 'tragic farce', and 'tragic farce' is what Eugène Ionesco calls *The Chairs*.[25]

When Artaud compared his 'theatre of cruelty' to the plague – a disease that leaves the body intact externally but ravaged internally – he was trying to imbue the theater with a new, radical, generative power. Not a lethal power, but one which, nonetheless, would transform the mind of its audience as violently as the plague alters the chemistry and the blood of the circulatory system. Camus's play, in its overt and covert violence, bears all the signs of 'cruelty'. It is surely not gratuitous that Caligula compares himself to the plague. As a demigod he is a theatrical scourge, a man who breaks the body while hoping to transform the mind.

Caligula's 'cruel' dramatizations of freedom are based on a deification of man. The reasoning is that if he is free, then other men must also be free. If, as Nietzsche, Sartre, and Foucault affirm, God and man are dead, then man, who should be free, but is not, struts and frets compulsions, repressions, and outmoded ideologies on the stage of life, unaware of the implications of freedom, unconscious of the *doxas* that imprison him. However, as Alain Robbe-Grillet says, paraphrasing Martin Heidegger, man like things, before being anything, is *there*, on stage, contingent, yet free to create an essence out of his existential and phenomenal self.[26] This awareness of unlimited choice confers on Caligula a sense of freedom that manifests itself as a flouting of codes, conventions, and rules. Caligula wants the impossible and, in order to 'capture the moon', he stages outrageous acts by dramatizing his freedom of choice. As an artist miming the gods, he plays with ideology, thereby foregrounding its man-made origins.

Every culture, in one way or another, as structuralists and post-structuralists affirm, communicates its values. They are encoded in language and in patterns of behavior. To parody these values and to play with them is a form of communication with an implied message. The distinguishing characteristic of reality, as Caligula so brutally demonstrates, is that it is played. The play's message, like any theory of information, implies a theory of play as well as a game theory. In poetics, the narrator, like the narrative, is simultaneously the subject and object of play. Camus's and Caligula's verb 'to play', connoting gambling, play-acting, and deception resonates throughout the play. Indeed, play articulates the text, Caligula's theatricality, and reality, opening and closing them through language.

Since the 1960s, game theory has elicited a renewed and heightened critical interest. Eugen Fink, in *Le jeu comme symbole du monde*, believes that the essence of the world is play, that Being, in its totality, functions like play, and that man can find his true essence only in relation to forces that transcend him. Fink asserts that in playing man experiences the meaning of the Universe.[27] Caligula says that 'all men are free to play the celestial tragedies and to become god' (p. 69, lines 19–20). Heraclitus believed that the course of the world was a child at play moving figures on a board. Hegel once said that play, in its indifference and frivolity, was 'at the same time the most sublime seriousness and the uniquely true'. Schiller observed that 'man plays only when he is man in the full sense of the word and *he is totally man only when he plays*'.[28] Camus himself suggests that we invert the classical formula which once made idleness the fruit of work, whereas, in fact, he wanted work to be the fruit of idleness.[29] Recent studies on the theory of play by Roger Caillois, Fink, Jacques Hizinga, Kostas Axelos, Jacques Ehrmann, Michel Beaujour, and others, emphasize the importance of play in man's ontological makeup.[30] Françoise Baqué, in *Le nouveau roman*, believes that society might be changed if exposed to forms of ludic art. 'After the bankruptcy of the divine order (of bourgeois society) and, in its wake, of rationalist order (of bureaucratic socialism), we must understand that henceforth the only viable forms of organization are ludic ones.'[31]

Since the 1950s, the French New Novel, like the Theatre of the Absurd, and works such as Ionesco's *The Bald Soprano*,[32] have been playing with language and the generative power of language. Philippe Sollers observes on the covernote of his novel *Drame* that 'we are now in the present, on the stage of language' (*parole*).[33] Robbe-Grillet, in an essay in *Le Nouvel Observateur*, says that 'love is a game, poetry is a game, life must become a game'.[34] Caligula's experimental violence thus adumbrates the recent, proliferating interest in the ontology of play.

Having decreed that Rome's greatness is no different than its residents' arthritic crises, and having decided to be 'logical' to the end, Caligula announces that he will exterminate contradictors and contradictions:

'You should thank me, since I am playing your game and playing with your cards' (p. 23, lines 11–13). An absurd world in which arthritis and greatness are equivalent, like a deck of cards, is a world without depth. Robbe-Grillet asserts that this is a world reduced to the play of its appearances. For a soothsayer, the implied meaning of the queen of spades may be death, but for a player of blackjack, the card is no more than a flat surface whose value is determined by the arbitrary rules of the game. Caligula's game is significant because he plays with human lives, not with cards. Also at stake are the values and the order of the old regime. Rome is under siege even as the overt violence of Caligula's behavior masks the covert assault that he is scripting, staging, and directing. Caligula's play and game strategy is directed not only at duplicity and lying, but at the myth of the state and its priorities, such as, for example, the importance of the treasury over human life, or the priority of war, or the myth of greatness.

If man is free, then play, directed at the repressive forces of society, exposes their man-made origin. Caligula's error, however, was in subscribing to violence. Instead of undermining the repressive forces of society he exacerbates them. Before strangling his mistress, he says: 'Caesonia, you have followed this singular and curious tragedy to its very end. It is time to lower the curtain on you' (p. 106, lines 10–11). Caesonia's death anticipates Caligula's, even as he and Camus blend life and art into the tragic spectacle of an emperor who would be god.

Caligula is simultaneously actor, director, choreographer, and script writer for a tragedy whose subject is death – the bloody final act that Pascal refers to. Caligula's life, since the death of his sister Drusilla, has been a theatrical performance whose purpose has been to elicit the consciousness of death.

> The only possible freedom [says Camus] is a freedom face to face with death. A truly free man is a man who, in accepting the reality of death, also accepts the consequences, namely, to overthrow all the traditional values of life. Ivan Karamasov's 'Everything is allowed', is the only possible expression of a coherent freedom.[35]

Caligula's last words before the curtain falls – 'I am still alive' – focuses the consciousness of the audience on the spectacle, on death, and on life – the life Caligula has been living and for which he is now dying. Death is the only force over which he has no dominion, and, in order to dramatize its force, Caligula, all along, has been impersonating the cruelty and violence of nature and of the gods whose freedom he believes is the corollary of play. However, in his alienated state of mind he has been staging the opposite of Camus's neo-Cartesian *cogito*. Although the world is absurd and everything is possible, the 'good kind' of freedom, as opposed to Caligula's 'bad kind', will stress life over death, solidarity over violence, and love over cruelty. And so, by the circuitous process of art calling attention to itself as a creative force, Camus returns to the idea that there are perhaps *a priori* values without which life has no meaning. 'The analysis of rebellion', says Camus in *The Rebel*, 'leads us at least to suspect, as the Greeks thought, that there is a human nature, contrary to the postulates of contemporary thought.'[36] Unless there were something for which to rebel – human dignity – rebellion would have no meaning. Caligula's error, says Camus in his 'preface' to the American edition of his plays, 'lies in negating what binds him to mankind. . . . one cannot be free at the expense of others.'[37]

Caligula expresses his freedom at the expense of others. His actions degrade the dignity of his subordinates and they rebel because things have gone too far. However, unlike Scipio and Cherea who refuse to participate in the conspiracy against Caligula, because they understand the Emperor's thinking and distress, the others do not grasp the meaning of what has transpired. Since Caligula's cruelty backfires, are we to conclude that non-violence would have succeeded where violence has failed? Perhaps. In any case I tend to think so. Indeed, the bulk of Camus's work points toward non-violence whenever he dramatizes ideas that are inherent in the philosophy of the absurd.

NOTES

1 (New York: Oxford University Press, 1960), pp. 192–207.
2 *French Review*, 41 (1968), 818–30.
3 In *Essais* (Paris: Gallimard–Pléiade, 1965), p. 145.
4 (London: Methuen, 1971), p. 43.
5 *Albert Camus* (Paris: Minard, 1975), pp. 47, 66.
6 (Paris: Le temps présent, 1951), pp. 80–2.
7 *Yale French Studies*, 25 (1960), p. 54.
8 *Contemporary Literature*, 14 (1973), pp. 31–48.
9 *Albert Camus* (Paris: Minard, 1975), pp. 87, 93.
10 'Caligula', in *Théâtre, Récits, Nouvelles* (Paris: Gallimard–Pléiade, 1962), p. 16. Subsequent references to this edition will appear within the text. All of the translations are mine.
11 *Les Pensées* (Paris: Les éditions du cerf, 1982), p. 107, line 20.
12 *Carnets II* (Paris: Gallimard, 1964), p. 94.
13 (Paris: Nagel, 1952), p. 36.
14 (New York: Ballantine, 1961).
15 'L'homme révolté', in *Essais* (Paris: Gallimard–Pléiade, 1965), pp. 421–712.
16 *Carnets I* (Paris: Gallimard, 1962), p. 58.
17 (London: Methuen, 1971), p. 44; *Symposium*, 12 (1958), p. 45.
18 *Caligula and Three Other Plays*, trans. Stuart Gilbert (New York: Random House, 1958), p. vi.
19 In *Albert Camus*, p. 66.

20 In *Essais*, p. 174.
21 'Ecce Homo' in *Nietzsche's Werke* (Leipzig, 1911), part 2, vol. 15, p. 47.
22 *Roland Barthes* (Paris: Seuil, 1975); pp. 51, 75, and *Mythologies* (Paris: Seuil, 1957); Foucault, *Histoire de la sexualité, 1: La volonté de savoir* (Paris: Gallimard, 1976).
23 *Le théâtre et son double* (Paris: Gallimard, 1964).
24 'Ubu roi' in *Théâtre* (Paris: Gallimard, 1954).
25 'Les chaises' in *Théâtre* (Paris: Gallimard, 1954).
26 *Pour un nouveau roman* (Paris: Minuit, 1959), p. 95.
27 Trans. Hans Hildenberg and Alex Lindberg (Paris: Minuit, 1966).
28 As quoted by Kostas Axelos in 'Planetary Interlude', *Yale French Studies*, 41 (1968), 7.
29 *Carnets I*, p. 115.
39 'Game, Play, Literature', *Yale French Studies*, 41 (1968).
31 (Paris: Bordas, 1972), p. 132.
32 'La cantatrice chauve' in *Théâtre* (Paris: Gallimard, 1954).
33 (Paris: Seuil, 1965).
34 'Après *L'éden et après*', no. 294 (26 June–5 July 1970), p. 35.
35 *Carnets I*, p. 118.
36 'L'homme révolté' in *Essais*, p. 425.
37 *Caligula and Three Other Plays*, p. vi.

Violence in two plays by Federico García Lorca*

KAY GARCÍA

Lorca was a creative and controversial poet and dramatist, whose life ended tragically in violence. When he was gunned down, he lived out a scene that he had already written, predicting the grisly details. Violence was a common theme in his work, although it was rarely presented physically on stage. For example, in Lorca's well-known play *La casa de Bernarda Alba* (*The House of Bernarda Alba*), four repressed sisters are all yearning for the same man. Bernarda, who is trying to keep the lid on this boiling cauldron of emotions, hits one of her daughters. That's the only violent act on stage, but off stage a shot is heard, and the youngest daughter hangs herself, believing that her lover is dead. The real violence on stage is spiritual: the oppressive captivity of the sisters, shut off from the world and from life, with tragic consequences.

Another of Lorca's plays, *Bodas se sangre* (*Blood Wedding*), tells the story of forbidden love between a young woman and a married man. At her wedding, he 'kidnaps' her, and they ride off together on his horse. The bridegroom goes after them and both men die in the ensuing knife fight. The fight occurs off stage, but violence permeates the dialogue throughout the play. It begins as a low hum (a lullaby about a wounded horse, with a silver dagger in its eye); the volume increases as blood is mentioned over and over again; the tone becomes strident as the groom's mother tells how her husband and first son were murdered; and the verbal violence finally reaches a crescendo as the knife fight is described repeatedly by different people, and the mother laments the death of her second son.

As these examples indicate, violence is an important element in many of Lorca's plays. However, there are two works that are notable for the richness and variety of their violent techniques, and for the contrast between them: *The Shoemaker's Prodigious Wife* and *The Public* (*La zapatera prodigiosa* and *El público*). In this study, a distinction is made between physical violence and aesthetic violence. The former includes on-stage violence, off-stage violence, and the threat of physical violence. The latter

---

* A draft of this paper was read at the *Themes in Drama* International conference held at the University of California, Riverside, in February 1989.

refers to the use of violent colors and sounds, violent emotions, shocking vocabulary and concepts, and breaking with the traditional conventions of the theatre. Violence in *The Shoemaker's Prodigious Wife* will be analyzed first, then violence in *The Public*, and finally a contrast will be made between the two plays.

The first play is about a pretty, young woman who has married an old shoemaker. Driven mad by her constant flirting, the old man leaves town, and returns some time later, disguised as a puppeteer. He discovers that she has set up a bar in their home, and although she continues to flirt, she has remained loyal to him. There is a fight between two of her suitors, and the enraged townspeople want to drive her out of the village. The shoemaker and his wife make a united stand to defend themselves and their home.

The first indication of the importance of violence in this play is the subtitle: 'Farsa violenta en dos actos y un prólogo' ('A Violent Farce in Two Acts and a Prologue').[1] The prologue offers another warning: 'No se extrañe el público si [la zapatera] aparece violenta o toma actitudes agrias' ('Don't be surprised if the shoemaker's wife appears violent or has a bitter attitude').[2]

In this quote, Lorca is not using the term 'violent' in the traditional sense. His work is a farce, and one of its goals is to make the audience laugh. Violence in this work is an example of Andalusian[3] exaggeration, the effect of which is comical, not threatening. Lorca himself mentioned the amusing aspect of the work: 'el grito cómico y el humor se levantan, claros y sin trampas, en los primeros términos' ('the comic outburst and humour appear in the foreground, clearly and without tricks').[4]

As the play begins, the first thing that assaults the eye is a violent color. The shoemaker's wife enters, wearing a raging green dress ('*un traje rabioso*', which could also be translated as '*a rabid green dress*'), which reflects her interior fury. The neighbor ladies enter at the end of the act, dressed with other violent colors that reflect the anger, hatred and envy that they feel.

Nevertheless, at the end of Act I, when the ladies are dancing around the shoemaker's wife, mocking her because her husband has left, the stage direction indicates: '*Todos adoptan una actitud cómica de pena*' ('*They all adopt a comic, mortified attitude*', p. 193). This comic attitude softens the ladies' characters, giving them a touch of humor.

Violent emotions provide the driving force of the play: love/hate; courage/fear; despising the husband when he's present; missing the absent spouse; the neighbors' horrible envy; and the shoemaker's jealousy, which is so powerful that it drives him to abandon his wife.

The wife is a very emotive character: she enters furiously, she protests, scolds, flirts outrageously, laments, cries out loud, and at the end she gives the reader the impression that her love is so strong that it will conquer all. This optimistic interpretation of the end is based in part on the stage direction in the first act: '*Toda la escena tendrá un aire de optimismo y alegría, exaltada en los más pequeños detalles. Una suave luz naranja de media tarde invade la escena*' ('*The whole scene has an air of optimism and joy, accentuated by every detail. A soft, orange, mid-afternoon light invades the scene*', p. 173).

The secondary characters, like planets around the sun, also exhibit extreme emotions. Besides envy and jealousy, the suitors express a burning love for the shoemaker's wife. The character called a 'young man with a hat', enraged by her rejection of him, exclaims with typical Andalusian exaggeration:

> Tengo tanto coraje que agarraría a un toro de los cuernos, le haría hincar la cerviz en las arenas y después me comería sus sesos crudos con estos dientes míos, en la seguridad de no hartarme de morder. (pp. 197–8)

> (I am so angry that I could grab a bull by the horns, force him to thrust his snout into the sand, and then I would eat his raw brains with these teeth of mine, knowing that I would never get tired of biting.)

It is insinuated that this vehement love is the cause of the knife fight in the second act, in which two men are wounded.

This fight, the only radically violent action in the play, occurs off stage. When the characters speak of the fight, the stage direction indicates, '*Tiemblan todos cómicamente*' ('*Everybody trembles comically*', p. 211). This ludicrous trembling implies that nothing is seriously wrong, and the audience need not worry.

The play is full of humorous threats. In the first act the wife's stomping scares her neighbor boy, and he hides. In the next act, she threatens to stuff a hot pepper in his mouth, but it is obvious that the threat will not be carried out. The second act's stage direction includes the author's suggestion that the director threaten his actor physically: '*Al actor que exagere lo más mínimo en este tipo, debe el director de escena darle un bastonazo en la cabeza*' ('*If the actor exaggerates even just a little on this character, the director should hit him over the head with his cane*', p. 195). Obviously, this is a joke, especially in light of the good relationship Lorca had with his actors, which is revealed in the book *La Barraca*.[5]

The most serious threat occurs at the end, when the townspeople gather together to throw the wife out of town. The play ends with this threat still pending, but the shoemaker and his wife, now united, are prepared to defend themselves.

Why is there so much violence in this work? One explanation is that it reflects the wife's internal struggle. The author says in the prologue that the wife is struggling with reality and with fantasy. It seems that the reality she fights is her boring, limited, daily life, and her lamentable situation as a young woman married to an old man. The fantasy she combats has been created by her neighbors, who want to condemn her for what they imagine she is doing. She must also resist her own fantasy, so that she doesn't get so carried away that she commits adultery.

The wife's struggle has been analyzed by Mario Hernández, who confirms the optimistic interpretation of the play:

> El anunciado implica que no se trata de una lucha de planos abstractos, en un planteamiento estático y sin solución, sino, más bien, de un proceso en el que las fantasías se resuelven en realidades, para ser de nuevo rechazadas y sustituidas. Este proceso dinámico, o, en otros términos, dramático, determina el ímpetu vital del personaje y su íntima alegría en el fracaso. Pieza, en último término, afirmativa y optimista, mientras el personaje tenga fracasos para proyectarlos sobre nuevas ilusiones; capacidad humana en la que tal vex resida, para decirlo con gravedad que no me gusta, el secreto de la vida. (p. 307).

(This implies that it is not a question of a struggle on abstract planes, in a static setting with no solution, but rather, it is a process in which fantasies are resolved in realities, to then be rejected and substituted. This dynamic or dramatic process determines the vital impetus of the character, and her intimate joy in failure. It is a play, after all, that is both affirmative and optimistic, as long as the character has failures to project on new illusions; a human capability in which perhaps resides – to say it with a seriousness that I don't like – the secret of life.)

Lorca explained the struggle in this way:

> La zapatera lucha constantemente con ideas y objetos reales porque vive en su mundo propio, donde cada idea y cada objeto tienen un sentido misterioso que ella misma ignora. No ha vivido nunca ni ha tenido novios nunca más que en la otra orilla, donde no puede ni podrá nunca llegar.

(The shoemaker's wife struggles constantly with ideas and real objects because she lives in her own world, where each idea and each object has a mysterious meaning which she herself does not know. She hasn't ever lived nor has she ever had boyfriends except on the other bank, where she can't go, nor will she ever be able to arrive.)[6]

Lorca himself was struggling; he fought against the theatre 'of and for pigs' that he described so disparagingly in an interview published in *La Barraca* (chapter 2), and against the boring theatre of poor taste, written to appease petulant actors and an audience whose main interest was to excape from problems. Violence provides a shock to this audience, to shake them up a bit. It is a rebellion against accepted formulae. Edwin Honig confirms this interpretation: 'it may be noted that . . . he mocks the devices of the conventional drama'.[7] According to Honig, Lorca wanted to be a dramatic inventor: 'Lorca, as the poet turned dramatic inventor and impresario, was seeking to re-educate as well as to astound a twentieth-century audience grown sluggish on the prosaic face of a "realistic" theatre' (p. 203).

Violence in *The Shoemaker's Prodigious Wife*, then, has various purposes: to make the audience laugh, to create a shock, and to reflect the struggle of the wife and of the author. It is principally aesthetic violence; the limited physical violence that occurs on stage has a comic purpose.

Both physical and aesthetic violence reach a much greater degree in *The Public*, a posthumous, incomplete work that the critic Martínez Nadal called 'la obra más avanzada y atrevida del poeta' ('the most advanced and daring work of the poet').[8]

In this work a theatrical group is trying to put on the play *Romeo and Juliet*, not in the open air, but rather underground. The purpose of the play is to reveal human beings' true nature, supposedly hidden in the traditional above-ground theatre that in Lorca's time had become quite complacent. The characters change identity frequently, and there is not a conventional plot, only a series of scenes that represent variations on the two main themes: the need for a new kind of theatre, and the nature of homosexual love/hate relationships.

In one draft of the play, Lorca included the subtitle, 'Drama en veinte cuadros y un asesinato' ('Drama in Twenty Scenes and One Assassination'), an ambiguous reference to the murder of Juliet, the death of the First Man, or the abstract assassination of traditional conventions and ideas.

There are only a few examples of physical violence on stage. In the first *cuadro* (hereafter translated as 'act'),[9] the Third Man lashes the Director with a whip, threatening to finish him off without mercy. Later the Third Man squeezes Elena's wrists, but she remains indifferent to the torture.

In the third act, the Director and the First Man struggle, disappearing from the stage. Later the Second Man and the Third Man fight, pushing each other from the stage. According to the stage directions, neither struggle appears very spectacular or violent. In the same act, the First Man exits violently, according to the stage directions, and later the Egg-faced Figure hits himself in the face incessantly.

These violent actions do not seem very important by themselves, but rather they reflect the characters' struggle with themselves and with each other, as they attempt to remove their masks and find their true identity. This struggle is developed further by the characters' speaking of violence, and referring to violent actions that occur off stage. In the second act, the Figure of Vine Leaves says to the Figure of Bells, 'Si yo no tuviera esta flauta te escaparías a la luna, a la luna cubierta de pañolitos de encaje y gotas de sangre de mujer' ('If I didn't have this flute, you would escape to the moon, to the moon covered with lace handkerchiefs and drops of women's blood', p. 57). A verbal battle ensues, between the desire to dominate and the desire to be dominated, and the Figure of Bells exclaims, 'Llévame al baño y ahógame. Será la única manera de que puedas verme desnudo. ¿ Te figuras que tengo miedo a la sangre?' ('Take me to the bathroom and drown me. It will be the only way in which you can see me nude. Do you imagine that I am afraid of blood?' p. 59). And the Figure of Vines replies, 'Toma un hacha y córtame las piernas. Quisiera que tú calaras hasta lo más hondo' ('Take an ax and cut my legs. I wish that you would cut down deep', p. 59). In the same act the Emperor brags of having cut the throats of more than forty boys who refused to say that 'one is one' ('one' is the ideal love). In this scene, sex is intimately associated with violence. The Figure of Vines insists that he is one, and declares, 'Si me besas yo abriré la boca para clavarme después tu espada en el cuello' ('If you kiss me I will open my mouth to plunge your sword into my neck', p. 71).

The Fourth Student informs us in the fifth act that the first bomb of the revolution knocked off the head of the rhetoric professor. The surprising reaction is: 'Con gran alegría para su mujer, que ahora trabajará tanto que tendrá que ponerse dos grifos en las tetas' ('With great joy for his wife, who now will work so much that she will have to put two faucets on her tits', p. 125). In this same act, the Ladies give reports of other off-stage action. Lady Four announces that the scene of the tomb is being performed again, but a raging fire has broken out, and it will soon burn down the doors (p. 135).

At the end of this act the students enthusiastically discuss the violent destruction of traditional love. They make plans to destroy families, and ransack homes wherever love is mentioned. They intend to burn holy books, and create havoc by hooking four hundred bulls to the rocks (pp. 141–3).

Besides speaking of violent actions and revealing their destructive desires, the characters also threaten each other, or feel threatened themselves. For example, the Director feels threatened by the Mask of Morals; he believes the mask is going to devour him, or hang him from a tree. He also feels threatened by the audience: he is afraid that the audience will not accept him as a homosexual, and that they will not accept a play whose theme is homosexuality. The First Man acknowledges him as his lover, and reminds him of when he put two roses behind his ears. The Director becomes more frightened, and protests that the First Man is deviating from the plot. Then he calls for Elena, the symbol of heterosexual love, in order to hide his true identity. After the presentation of *Romeo and Juliet*, in which Juliet is replaced by a young man, there is a great tumult and Boy One explains that the audience wants the poet to be dragged by the horses (p. 127). That is what Lorca feared from his own audience. The Director perceives the threatening atmosphere and laments, ' ¿ Qué cortina se puede usar en un sitio donde el aire es tan violento que desnuda a las gentes y hasta los niños llevan navajitas para rasgar los telones?' ('What curtain can be used in a place where the air is so violent that it strips people and even the children carry little knives to slash the curtains?' p. 151).

Besides the menacing atmosphere that surrounds the theatre, the characters threaten each other with whips and knives, which are obvious phallic symbols. In the first act, when the Director wants to get rid of the horses, he asks for a whip. In the second act (Roman Ruin), a game of imaginary metamorphoses between the Figure of Vines and the Figure of Bells ends when the former says that he would change into a knife. The Figure of Bells stops dancing, disturbed by the threat. The Emperor also uses the threat of a knife. In the same act, the centurion affirms that the Emperor will guess which of the figures is 'one', by using a knife or by spitting. When they start to change Juliet into a man, she wakes up just as the knives are shining, and the horses are speaking of yearning for blood.

In the fifth act, the Red Nude (previously called the First Man) has been emptied of fifty cups of blood, and at eight o'clock they plan to wound him with the scalpel. 'They' are the audience, or the public in general. The Red Nude says, 'Padre mío, perdónalos, que no saben lo que se hacen' ('Forgive them, Father, they know not what they do to themselves', p. 133). This reference to the crucifixion indicates that the Nude will soon die. The use of the expression 'do to themselves' suggests that the people are not only crucifying the Nude (the Director's lover), but also themselves, or the homosexual impulse that may exist in all of them.

In the same act the poets want to assassinate Elena for having sounded the alarm for what was happening in the Theatre. According to Student Four: 'Y aunque los poetas pusieron una escalera para asesinarla, ella siguió dando voces y acudió la multitud' ('Even though the poets put up a ladder to assassinate her, she kept screaming and the crowd came running', p. 125).

As the examples show, on-stage, physical aggression contributes only a little to the violent ambience of the play. The atmosphere is charged with an overwhelming and shocking violence, principally because of the reference to off-stage occurrences and the constant threat of physical assault.

There is another kind of violence that occurs in the play: the transformation of the characters. Sometimes the change is openly aggressive. Masks and costumes are torn off. They threaten to put a little clay phallus and a mustache on Juliet, by force. At other times the transformation occurs as if by magic, as a character passes behind a screen, although some characters are pushed behind the screen. These transformations radically change the identity of the characters: they are equivalent to castration or its opposite, putting a phallus on a woman against her will. By means of these transformations, the true identity of the characters may be exposed.

In spite of the above-mentioned examples of physical violence, it seems that aesthetic violence is of even greater importance in Lorca's work, since it may provide a clue to the real message behind his literary mask. The author breaks with various traditional conventions in this play. He uses vulgar and scatological language, he presents revolutionary ideas, he exposes theatrical devices to ridicule, and finally he tries to destroy the theatre itself as it was known in his time. The women in the play are humiliated, mistreated, raped, and immolated because of the homosexual love of the men. In the third act the First Man affirms that the head of the Emperor (symbol of homosexual power) burns the bodies of all women.

Homosexual love was a very controversial topic in Lorca's time, and the author does not treat this central theme with reticence, nor does he soften it or try to make it acceptable (or even comprehensible) to the public. In the play the homosexuals hate, betray, and kill each other, hiding from themselves and lamenting their fate. The First Man proclaims:

> El ano es el fracaso del hombre, es su vergüenza y su muerte. Los dos tenían ano y ninguno de los dos podía luchar con la belleza pura de los mármoles que brillaban conservando deseos íntimos defendidos por una superficie intachable. (p. 75)

> (The anus is man's failure, his shame and his death. Both of them [the Figure of Vines and the Figure of Bells] had an anus and neither could fight with the pure beauty of marble that shone, maintaining intimate desires defended by a faultless surface.)

Besides presenting shocking ideas, Lorca has unconventionally exposed some theatrical components for the audience's examination, thereby creating a multi-dimensional, metatheatrical mimesis, the infinite return of the mirror within the mirror. Some common occurrences that would normally be avoided or concealed are part of the manuscript in this work. The prompter is late because a fake beard was lost. Characters arrive at the wrong time and are reprimanded on stage, and then they are warned not to lose their wigs in the artificial wind. The scenery is criticized by the characters, and the Magician denigrates the theme of Romeo and Juliet, asking the Director why he chose a worn-out tragedy instead of doing an original drama. The Director explains his choice in a revealing speech:

> [Escogí *Romeo y Julieta*] Para expresar lo que pasa todos días en todas las grandes ciudades y en los campos, por medio de un ejemplo que, admitido por todos a pesar de su originalidad, ocurrió sólo una vez. Pude haber elegido el Edipo o el Otelo. En cambio, si hubiera levantado el telón con la verdad original, se habrían manchado de sangre las butacas desde las primeras escenas. (p. 153).

(I chose *Romeo and Juliet* in order to express what happens every day in all the big cities and in the country, by means of an example that was accepted by all in spite of its originality, and it happened only once. I could have chosen Oedipus or Othello. On the other hand, if I had raised the curtain with the original truth, the theatre seats would have been stained with blood from the first scenes.)

Lorca is using metatheatre as a critical device. *Romeo and Juliet*, the play within the play, is a worn-out cliché, but it is accepted by the public. The outer play, *The Public*, appears to be an attempt at presenting 'the original truth', with the risk of bloodshed. In other words, the public is so averse to the truth, that it would kill to avoid having to face it.

The public is also chastised for its participation in the play, even though the Director has repeatedly invited the audience to enter into the action. When the audience reacts negatively to Juliet as a man, the students comment that the public's attitude is detestable, since a spectator should never take part in a drama. Student One explains:

Cuando la gente va al acuario no asesina a las serpientes de mar ni a las ratas de agua, ni a los peces cubiertos de lepra, sino que resbala sobre los cristales sus ojos y aprende. (pp. 137–9)

(When people go to the aquarium, they don't assassinate the sea snakes and the water rats, and the fish covered with leprosy, but rather they slide their eyes over the glass, and they learn.)

It seems that the purpose of this criticism and of the shocking violence in the work is to break with the traditional theatre, to destroy the old in order to form a new theatre. Edwin Honig has said, 'There is further proof that it [*The Public*] was intended as a violent blast against the commercialized theatre, which Lorca was always combatting' (p. 204).

In the text of the play, the Director exclaims, '¡ Hay que destruir el teatro o vivir en el teatro! No vale silbar desde las ventanas' ('One must destroy the theatre or live in the theatre! It's no good whistling from the windows', p. 155). Later he explains, 'Hemos roto las puertas, hemos levantado el techo y nos hemos quedado con las cuatro paredes del drama' ('We have broken the doors, we have raised the roof and we have been left with the four walls of the drama', p. 163). The Director expounds on the need to progress and to make changes in the theatre, in order to avoid the death (or stagnation) of the theatre. Afterwards he adds, 'Es rompiendo todas las puertas el único modo que tiene el drama de justificarse, viendo, por sus propios ojos, que la ley es un muro que se disuelve en la más pequeña gota de sangre' ('Breaking all the doors is the only way that the drama has to justify itself, seeing with its own eyes that law is a wall that dissolves in the smallest drop of blood', p. 159).

The Public appears to be a precursor of the 'Theatre of Cruelty', whose manifestos were published a few years after Lorca began to write this play. In the first manifesto, Antonin Artaud proclaims, 'Without an element of cruelty at the root of every spectacle, the theatre is not possible. In our present state of degeneration it is through the skin that metaphysics must be made to re-enter our minds.'[10] In the second manifesto he says:

> The Theatre of Cruelty intends to reassert all the time-tested magical means of capturing the sensibility.
> These means, which consist of intensities of colours, lights, or sounds, which utilize vibration, tremors, repetition, whether of a musical rhythm or a spoken phrase, special tones or a general diffusion of light, can obtain their full effect only by the use of dissonances.[11]

The similarities between *The Public* and the 'Theatre of Cruelty' include: the use of dissonances, the technique of shocking the senses with intense colors, lights, and sounds, the portrayal of violence and eroticism, and the creation of a total spectacle. Lorca was working toward a new theatre, and his ideas, or similar ideas, were carried out by the 'Theatre of Cruelty'.

The Public is a much more serious work than *The Shoemaker's Prodigious Wife*. Both the physical and the aesthetic violence in the latter play reflect the Spanish tradition and the Andalusian exaggeration. It is a comic violence appropriate to farce that animates the play and gives it vigor. The brilliant colors provide visual recreation, and the actors' outbursts allow the audience to share their powerful passions, in an emotional purge, or catharsis. The optimisitc tone is an affirmation of love between man and woman, while facing an outside threat.

Andalusian exaggeration becomes extreme in *The Public*, as it loses its jovial character. Both the physical and aesthetic violence become destructive, and it appears that the author might wish to raze the old theatre in order to make room for something new, something which he did not manage to create, but which is found, in part, in the manifestos and works of the 'Theatre of Cruelty'.

In Lorca's prophetic poem, 'Canción de jinete' ('The Horseman's Song')[12] the poet describes himself as a horseman riding towards Cordoba, even though he knows he will be killed before he reaches that Andalusian city. In reality, Lorca was shot before he reached 'Cordoba', which could symbolize his professional and artistic maturity. This is the real tragedy of his life and work. We can only speculate about what Lorca would have created if he had been allowed to mature.

NOTES

1 All translations are by the author of this article.
2 Federico García Lorca, *Teatro selecto* (*La zapatera prodigiosa*) (Madrid: Escelicer, 1969), p. 172.

3 Andalusia is the region in southern Spain where Lorca was born.
4 'Declaraciones de Lorca sobre *La zapatera prodigiosa*' ('Declarations by Lorca about *The Shoemaker's Prodigious Wife*'), (Buenos Aires, 1933).
5 Luis Sáenz de la Calzada, *La Barraca* (Madrid: Biblioteca de la Revista de Occidente, 1976).
6 'Declaraciones de Lorca sobre *La zapatera prodigiosa*' ('Declarations by Lorca about *The Shoemaker's Prodigious Wife*'), (Buenos Aires, 1933).
7 Edwin Honig, *García Lorca* (New York: New Directions, 1944 and 1963), p. 130.
8 R. Martínez Nadal and M. Laffranque, *El público y Comedia sin título* (Barcelona–Caracas–Mexico: Biblioteca Breve, 1978), p. 169. All page numbers referring to *The Public* are from this critical edition.
9 The most complete manuscript of *The Public* includes only five *cuadros* (one, two, three, five and six), which are long enough to be considered acts. It appears that Lorca changed his mind about the number of *cuadros*, and he probably intended the sixth *cuadro* to be the last.
10 Antonin Artaud, 'The Theatre of Cruelty' in *The Theory of the Modern Stage*, ed. Eric Bentley (Harmondsworth: Penguin, 1968), p. 64.
11 Ibid., p. 69.
12 This poem can be found in Carmelo Virgillo et al., *Aproximaciones al estudio de la literatura hispánica* (New York: Random House, 1983).

Apartheid and primitive blood: violence in Afrikaans Shakespeare productions*

ROHAN QUINCE

It is now a commonplace that Shakespeare's plays, open to a variety of interpretations on the stage, are used by every age and society not only as cultural showcases, but also as a public arena for trying out current myths, ideologies and systems of belief. The first Shakespeare production in Afrikaans took place in 1947 at His Majesty's Theatre in Johannesburg, a production of *Hamlet* which saw the play in terms of the rightful inheritance of land. In other words, Hamlet has a moral imperative to fight the usurper Claudius for possession of the country which rightfully belongs to him. Performed one year before the Afrikaner National Party came to power in 1948, this production accurately reflected the mood of Afrikaner nationalism, the attitude of Afrikaners towards the other language and racial groups in South Africa.

During the 1950s and 60s, the Afrikaners consolidated their grip on power. Laws enforcing racial segregation were passed. Police met peaceful black opposition with violence, culminating in the shooting of sixty-nine blacks at Sharpeville in 1960. The African National Congress was banned; Nelson Mandela was arrested and sentenced to life imprisonment. Forced removal of blacks to tribal homelands was speeded up in order to achieve the design of Grand Apartheid – based on the belief that blacks and whites are fundamentally different and must be kept separate, by force, if necessary.

Throughout the period of Afrikaner political hegemony in South Africa, Afrikaans Shakespeare productions have continued to reflect Afrikaner ideological and cultural values. In most cases, the primary aim, consciously or unconsciously, is to validate Afrikaner culture by demonstrating three things: first, that Afrikaners are capable of staging productions as impressive as those of the English-speaking white community; second, that Afrikaans as a language is capable of expressing the genius of Shakespeare's poetry; and third, that the fundamental beliefs of the apartheid ideology are implicitly validated in the world's greatest drama.

* A draft of this paper was read at the *Themes in Drama* International conference held at the University of California, Riverside, in February 1989.

In those plays which depict violence, the aim is to show, wherever possible, that the violence is the result of primitive blood, a fundamental lack of civilized values on the part of the Other. A significant counter-culture does exist in Afrikaans theatre, offering productions which interrogate the prevailing apartheid ideology. Even here, however, when the production aims to confront white South Africans with the violence in their own society, resulting from the apartheid system, their response is to deflect attention away from home, to perceive, instead, the relevance of the play to the brutality in Eastern Europe, the Soviet Union, or the rest of Black Africa. Three controversial productions from the early 1970s – *Titus Andronicus*, *King Lear*, and *Othello* – offer intriguing insights into the relationship between theatre, ideology, and the political power structure in South Africa.

In 1970, CAPAB, the state-sponsored Performing Arts Council of the Cape, invited Dieter Reible, the young German director, to come out to South Africa to direct a Shakespeare play at the Hofmeyr Theatre in Cape Town. After some discussion, Reible suggested *Titus Andronicus* because, as he explained to me in a 1985 interview:

> I thought it would be interesting for South African audiences: a black man gets involved in a love story with a white princess and they have a coloured kid. Of course, her brothers get terribly upset and try to kill the little 'bastard'. I thought this would be a good story for South Africans. (Personal interview, 18 July 1985).

At this time, of course, the Immorality Act, which forbade sex across the colour line, was strictly enforced in South Africa. (The Act was finally repealed in 1985.) Reible suggested that the real significance of *Titus Andronicus* for South African audiences, however, lay in the violence of the play and the society. He said:

> South Africa is a very violent society, but the violence is removed from the people in their nice houses. If there was a message, it was to confront white audiences, who are part of the very violent society, with a production which exposes the violence. (ibid.)

Breyten Breytenbach, a leading Afrikaner poet, was commissioned to translate the play into Afrikaans. Living in Paris because his Vietnamese wife was considered 'non-white' in South Africa, Breytenbach produced an earthy, muscular translation which was hailed as a worthy contribution to Afrikaans literature. Nevertheless, his anti-apartheid activities made him a controversial figure among Afrikaners, and there was an outcry against CAPAB's choice of translator. (Three years later he was jailed for trying to organize an underground resistance movement in South Africa.) Numerous letters appeared in the Afrikaans press, asking why the commission had been given to 'an open supporter of the anti-apartheid movement, which doesn't let a chance escape to paint South Africa black . . .' (*Sunday Times*, 13 September 1970). Until the outcry, Breytenbach's name had been boldly featured in press advertisements for the play, but following the publication of the letters, his name was suddenly omitted. It was restored to the advertisements in the final week before the production.

Breyten Breytenbach was not the only controversy to discomfit the Nationalist establishment. *Titus Andronicus*, as one newspaper pointed out, contains 'a sex scene between a non-white and a white woman from which a black child is later born'. This being a time of absolute apartheid, with no racially 'mixed' casts or audiences allowed, Aron the Moor was played by a white Afrikaans actor. Nevertheless, rumours started circulating that the Board of Censors was insisting on certain cuts in the production. A member of the board attended a rehearsal, and suggested 'a slight change concerning less than four seconds' (*Cape Times*, 10 September 1970) of a scene between Aron the Moor and Tamora, the white Gothic queen.

Dieter Reible told me that other rumours circulating suggested that the Cabinet had discussed banning the production altogether, but were warned of an adverse reaction if Shakespeare were banned.

In a programme note, Pieter Fourie, the artistic director of CAPAB, wrote:

> Our *Titus Andronicus* is not an experiment to join the latest theatre fashion . . . No, it will serve the essence of theatre: to confront mankind, society or civilization with itself. And it will, because the monster of cruelty and revenge is always everywhere under the thin skin of civilization. A South African production is of special interest. Since the turn of the century we have become more and more aware that we are part of this troubled continent. Since the decolonization of Africa, our position on the continent has changed and the rest of Africa has become a new Africa. The bloodshed, rape, cruelty and political revenge in Africa today make this play look like a conventional report in a daily newspaper.

Mr Fourie's note suggests the usual white South African tendency to perceive clearly the link between violence in Shakespeare's plays and violence in other parts of Africa, thereby deflecting the focus from the applicability to South Africa itself.

The set consisted of one white oblong room. The white blocks suggested both ancient Rome and the clean atmosphere of a slaughterhouse. To one critic, they were 'symbolic of many things; a prison; a Roman palace; a home; Wall Street; the White House' (*Cape Times*, 21 September 1970). Few props were used, among them an antique bathtub in which Chiron and Demetrius had their throats cut by Titus.

The play opened with Titus's triumphal procession into Rome. At its head were carried 'realistic crucified male nudes with barbed wire around their genitals' (Williams, *Star*, 1 October 1970). Brecht-like headlines were projected during the blackouts between scenes. They were 'a mixture of poetic and double meanings', said Reible, like *Blood Harvest* near the end. Heavy rock music reinforced the parallels between then and now.

The first performance was a special preview for the black stagehands and their families, their presence being forbidden at an official performance. The house was packed and expectant, Dieter Reible told me. When Aron the Moor reached the part where he held up his black child and proclaimed that he would take him to the woods and turn him into a warrior, the black audience rose screaming to their feet. Women ran down towards the stage holding up their babies. 'It was hair-raising', said Reible. 'The officials didn't know what to do!'

White audiences were equally shocked, though perhaps for different reasons. One critic reported that 'Aron's "Black Power" speech had many of the audience tittering nervously and squirming uneasily in their seats' (*Pretoria News*, 23 October 1970). In keeping with the theatre-of-cruelty style, the violence was gory, explicit, and shocking. Stanley Uys wrote:

> In one scene the twice ravished Lavinia staggers on to the stage with her hands severed and her tongue cut out. Pointing her bleeding stumps at the audience she tries to speak, but blood froths from her mouth. Behind me a young man groaned, and clutching his stomach, rushed out of the theatre. He returned later and dosed himself with what I assume were tranquillisers.
> (Uys, *Star*, 20 October 1970)

Members of the audience fainting, rushing out to the toilets and vomiting, and then returning to their seats, became a fairly common occurrence.

Others stayed away from the production altogether. Fifteen invited white VIPs, including one Cabinet Minster, declined invitations to attend the premiere. Critics speculated that this was because Breyten Breytenbach had translated the play, but CAPAB denied that this was the case. Apparently they all 'had other commitments for the night' (*Daily Dispatch*, 22 September 1970). Two members of the Board of Censors did attend the opening night.

The critics were effusive in their praise. Owen Williams called it 'a metaphor of slavering beasts, of images of blood and mangled flesh, of life in a universal human abattoir' (*Star*, 1 October 1970).

Cobus Rossouw told me:

> The production was very gory, with blood spurting all over the stage, but at the same time very clinical, very analytic, very neat and precise, like a scalpel.
> (Personal interview, 17 June 1985).

The play ended with Aron the Moor centre stage, buried up to his neck. 'On the enormous white stage you could see only this black head', Dieter Reible told me. Then the audience heard the ominous sound of thousands of seagulls crying as the lights faded. This controversial production resonated powerfully in the South African context, interrogating racist ideology and confronting white audiences with the institutionalized violence which underpins the apartheid system.

In 1971, CAPAB invited Dieter Reible to direct Uys Krige's Afrikaans translation of *King Lear* for the opening of the lavish Nico Malan Theatre in Cape Town as part of the Tenth Anniversary Republic Festival.

A storm of controversy arose over the decision to restrict the Nico Malan Theatre for use by whites only, the majority of people in Cape Town being classified as Coloured. The so-called 'Coloured problem' has always been a thorny issue for the Nationalist government, partly because the Coloureds can claim among their ancestors the same Dutch forebears who gave rise to the Afrikaners, also because the majority speak Afrikaans as their home language, and are sometimes referred to a 'brown Afrikaners'. The translator wrote to the *Cape Times* to protest the ban. Referring to Prime Minister B. J. Vorster's infamous remark that the government had no long-term policy on the Coloureds whose future would therefore have to be decided by 'our children', Uys Krige wrote:

> Let us not give our children yet another reason for feeling ashamed of us when in due course they come to assess the full extent and scope of our inhumanity to our fellow men. (*Cape Times*, 15 March 1971).

Nevertheless, the ban remained in force, and though it was lifted some years later, the Nico Malan Theatre is still boycotted by many Coloureds.

Against this background of bitterness and acrimony, Dieter Reible's production took place. It was, no doubt, hoped that this Republic Festival production, attended by the State President, would serve to validate the glories of Afrikaner culture after ten years out of the British Commonwealth. Reible, however, had other ideas. His production emphasized the themes of violence and power in a primitive society.

He told me that he was struck by the idea of a primitive society, a small kingdom in which Lear could ride from Goneril's to Gloucester's castle in a day. The set consisted of a large hill with three flights of steep steps leading to three primitive huts covered with reeds, branches, and animal hides – all on a central revolve. A fence of sharpened stakes was built on an outer revolve.

The costumes also emphasized the primitive look. Much use was made of feathers, bones, hides, and beads. When Edgar transformed himself into mad Tom, he draped two dead puff-adders about his body. The actors wore heavy white mask-like make-up, highlighted with red, similar to Xhosa tribal dress. As Reible confessed to me with a chuckle, the costumes and set ended up looking like a tribal society – Zulu or Xhosa.

The opening scene was by all accounts magnificent. As the members of the court flung themselves to the ground in obeisance, Lear made his grand entrance from the central hut, 'looking like an African king', said Reible. He wore foot-high clogs to increase his stature, supported himself with two huge staffs, and dragged behind him a forty-foot cloak made of peacock feathers. As he gave his kingdom away, he slowly removed the cloak, the sticks, and the clogs, getting smaller and smaller as the scene progressed. His entrance alone took four minutes. The first scene lasted for thirty minutes. The entire play took longer than four hours.

As in *Titus Andronicus*, Reible emphasized the violence in the play. The blinding of Gloucester was graphically portrayed. One character was killed with a knobkerrie (a traditional African club with a rounded head), literally 'bashed to death', Reible told me. David Haynes, who played Edgar, remembers the duel with Edmund fought with twelve-foot-long swords. When he finally stabbed Edmund, a blood bag released a copious amount of blood onto the stage. By the end, the stage was literally strewn with bodies.

To say that the critics condemned the production would be an understatement. Michael Venables wrote:

> Imagine, if you will, palaces represented by three crude cane huts with the hides of African buck, King Lear looking for all the world like an African witchdoctor, Goneril dressed as a Japanese nobleman, Cordelia looking vaguely Chinese and the King of France resembling an Egyptian ... (*Rand Daily Mail*, 1 June 1971)

W. E. G. Louw's review ran the headline, 'Shakespeare's King Lear becomes a circus'. He said he left the theatre overwhelmed with anger which by the next morning had changed to shame and humiliation (*Burger*, 31 May 1971). He attributed some of his anger to the fact that the production was part of the Republic Festival performed before 'the highest in the land'.

If the critics were scathing, CAPAB officials were horrified at the ruin of their official opening which was supposed to be the climax of the Republic Festival. Mr F. D. Conradie, vice-chairman of CAPAB, wrote to an Afrikaans newspaper:

> An insult to the State President and his wife – that was my overwhelming feeling while I had to endure the four-hour trial of Dieter Reible's production of Koning Lear. Only the rules of etiquette and decency because of the presence of the State President and Mrs Fouche prevented my wife and me from leaving the theatre early. I think CAPAB should appologise to the State President and other guests of honour present ... (*Burger*, 2 June 1971).

Phillippa Breytenbach called on the Minister of Cultural Affairs to do something about the importing of foreign directors, adding 'to think that even the President and Mrs Fouche gave up an evening!' (*Transvaler*, 3 June 1971).

Reible noted that a four-hour production, while acceptable in the European theatrical tradition, was still out of the question in South Africa. And four hours of violence and bloodshed confronted the audience with what they did not want to see – a mirror of their own violent society. 'We are so removed', he said. 'You can't kill people "decently" in a corner.'

David Haynes suggested that people took political exception to the African setting and costumes. 'In the end you have all these white people lying dead around a giant anthill', he told me. 'People weren't sure what was implied.' He added:

> It was good that they did it, because the play was really performed in the context of this 'palace of culture'. They built this great piece of fascist architecture. The production made a statement about the state being the major provider of culture.

CAPAB did not invite Dieter Reible to direct another production.

In 1975 François Swart directed Anna Neethling-Pohl's Afrikaans translation of *Othello* for PACT, the Performing Arts Council of the Transvaal, at the Alexander Theatre in Johannesburg and the Breytenbach Theatre in Pretoria. Swart told me that he had considered offering the title role to Ken Gampu, a distinguished black actor who spoke excellent Afrikaans, because he (Swart) saw Othello as a Gatsha Buthulezi figure. He said:

> I wanted to communicate very strongly the contribution Othello was making to the Venetian state. The Venetians were very effete, very ineffectual, very cowed by the threat of the Turkish invasion. (Personal interview, 23 July 1985).

In the context of mid-seventies South Africa, however, he decided against casting Gampu. Said Swart, 'If I cast a black man, the play would vanish in the process of the physical shock and obsession in this country of witnessing the intimacy between a black man and a white woman.'

Instead he chose Louis van Niekerk, a white Afrikaans actor. Said Swart, 'He had the size, the weight, the authority, the passion, the raw intensity, the obsessive qualities needed.' It was decided to play Othello as black, rather than Arabic or 'coloured'. Van Niekerk himself stated, 'The rages Othello displays are partly due to the fact that he is of a particular race – I give indications of the rage a few times in the beginning and then have a real attack. I think there was a definite physiological reason behind them' (*Pretoria News*, 19 May 1975).

The interpretation of Iago was unusual. François Swart told me emphatically:

> Iago is not a villain. He is a fine soldier. His actions are motivated out of sheer frustration. Othello, in getting to Desdemona, needs the assistance of the upper-class Cassio to act as go-between, which indicates a failure in integrity

on his part. He is beholden to Cassio and appoints him as lieutenant. This is the first chink in Othello's armor – a lack of integrity. This triggers the chagrin, the frustration, the malice, the venom in Iago. (Personal interview, 23 July 1985).

Louis van Niekerk in the title role was praised. According to one Afrikaans critic, van Niekerk's Othello remains the disciplined warrior until 'the honour of his wife – and thus also his masculine ego – is injured'. Then 'the layer of varnish peels off and the earthy black man whose spiritual home is still Africa comes to the fore. Then Othello is rough and violent' (Louis Smit, *Vaderland*, 4 June 1975).

An English-speaking reviewer found a contemporary relevance.

> The colour of the hero's skin is what turns the domestic tragedy into a depiction of the contemporary and universal problem of cultural conflict. Othello's innocence of guile, his almost 'primitive' belief in the virtues of honesty and integrity, contrasted with the ambiguity [sic] and artifice of the super-civilized White society surrounding him, are the causes of his downfall. (*Star*, 3 June 1975)

In this production, the 'ambiguity' and artifice of the white society ensured that the only blacks on stage were stagehands. One critic noted: 'Othello is played on the open stage, the scene changes being done in full view of the audience, by Black scene shifters dressed in costume of the period' (A.B., *Star*, 20 June 1975) – a kind of indexing signifier of the society outside the theatre.

The relevance of *Othello* to South African society can hardly be missed. There are, therefore, a number of interesting questions raised by this production. The central one is whether the play should be seen as an indictment of Othello (and by inference, of all blacks) or as an indictment of the white society in which he finds himself. The issue is further complicated by having a white actor in the title role, interpreting the thought processes, motives, and emotions of a black man. Louis van Niekerk's comments that Othello's rages 'are partly due to the fact that he is of a particular race', that they have 'a definite physiological reason behind them' suggests a reinforcement of the belief that blacks are fundamentally different from whites (with the corollary that they should be treated differently). The critic's remark – 'the layer of varnish peels off and the earthy black man whose spiritual home is still Africa comes to the fore. Then Othello is rough and violent' – seems to confirm the well-accepted white prejudice that, with blacks, civilization is only skin deep, so to speak: scratch the surface and you find a primitive savage underneath. Such prejudice was underlined by the director's suggestion that Iago is not a villain, but rather that his venom is triggered by Othello's lack of integrity. Deflecting Iago's culpability could only fuel racist beliefs. Yet the English-speaking reviewer suggested that Othello's innocence of the artifice of super-civilized white society causes his downfall. Perhaps we can conclude that conservative Afrikaner critics saw the production as reflecting evidence of the unreliability of blacks whereas more liberal English critics saw an indictment of white attitudes, with an underlying patronizing implication that blacks are too simple to cope with the cunning sophistication of white society.

Director Swart's perception of Othello as a Gatsha Buthulezi figure suggests another analogy with contemporary South Africa. Buthulezi, the leader of Kwazulu (the Zulu homeland), is seen by many whites as a moderate black leader with whom they could realistically negotiate (as opposed to the 'radicals' and 'Communists' of the African National Congress). The catch, however, is that Buthulezi's willingness to compromise at all with the Afrikaner government disqualifies him in the eyes of most blacks from being a legitimate black leader. The recent government support for his Inkatha movement in their struggle against the pro-ANC United Democratic Front has only reinforced his rejection by most black South Africans.

This production, then, resonated powerfully in the South African context. François Swart showed us a black man (played by a white Afrikaner), noble and highly regarded in the beginning, disgraced and destroyed by the end. His interpretation was sufficiently ambiguous for the audience to bring their own prejudices to bear on the production: for some it validated white racist beliefs that blacks cannot be trusted; for others it attacked white insincerity in their dealings with other cultures.

These three productions offer an intriguing pattern of comparisons and contrasts. Both *Titus Andronicus* and *King Lear* consciously aimed to subvert the dominant ideology by confronting the audience with the violence their system begets. Both productions were controversial cultural events, quite apart from the dramatic interpretations: *Titus* because of the translator's anti-apartheid stand, *Lear* because of the banning of Coloureds from the theatre. Yet *Titus* was hailed as one of the finest Shakespeare productions ever in South Africa, whereas *Lear* was panned as one of the worst. One possible explanation is that audiences could dismiss *Titus* as an example of the primitive savagery of the ancient world, or even blame the violence on the villainous black character. In *Lear*, by contrast, the characters were all white, yet the costumes and set were too South African to be dismissed as exotic and inapplicable. Although none of the critics articulated it, the implication was too clear that white South African society was somehow primitive, violent, and self-destructive. Worse, they suddenly saw themselves depicted as the Other. The production of *Othello*, on the other hand, avoided controversy by casting a white actor in the title role. The directorial choices were ambiguous enough for both liberal and conservative commentators to claim that the play vindicated their respective positions:

either that Othello's fall results from the racial prejudice of society or from his racial background.

As one might expect, then, violence in Afrikaans Shakespeare productions is never interpreted by the Afrikaner establishment as reflecting the apartheid system, the great perpetrator of institutionalized violence in the country. Instead Afrikaners perceive the clear relevance to other societies, especially those in Black Africa, confirming their belief that violence is the inevitable concomitant of primitive blood.

A streetcar named misogyny*

KATHLEEN MARGARET LANT

> Tennessee gave me a lot of clues to Blanche. He was a sly fox ... Tennessee said, 'Just remember, everybody thinks the last line is: "I've always been dependent on the kindness of strangers." That's not the last line. The last line is: "Gentlemen, the name of this game is five-card stud." '
>
> Elizabeth Ashley

> Rape is not a crime of irrational, impulsive, uncontrollable lust, but is a deliberate, hostile, violent act of degradation and possession on the part of a would-be conqueror, designed to intimidate and inspire fear.
>
> Susan Brownmiller

> In the moment of rape a woman becomes anonymous. Like all victims of terrorism, there is something awesomely accidental about her fate. She is like the duck flying in formation which the hunter chose to shoot down – she appeared in his gunsight. Absorbed by his violence, her soul and the history of her soul are lost, are irrelevant.
>
> Susan Griffin[1]

A Streetcar Named Desire is, like an elusive lover, compelling, vexing, confusing, and ultimately heartbreaking because – like the lover one never quite wins – it refuses to conform to our expectations or fulfill our hopes. It leads us on, promises much, but in the end defies our attempt to understand, to approach, to control it, even to find pleasure in it.

In fact, that is just the problem with Williams's most popular play. It doesn't tell a straight story, it won't conform to a narrative or dramatic structure we recognize, it won't – like that reluctant lover again – make up its own mind about what it wants, who it is. Williams's play has proved vexing to audiences, directors, actors, readers, and critics because it seems to hover between two completely antithetical approaches to its own materials. The work shimmers with tension, it glows by the very heat of its own ambivalence.

The widely differing responses the play seems to generate may be the result of what Foster Hirsch calls Williams's 'own ambivalence' toward

---

* A draft of this paper was read at the *Themes in Drama* International Conference held at the University of California, Riverside, in February 1989.

the antagonists of the drama – Stanley and Blanche. According to Hirsch, the two find themselves locked in a 'deadly sex war', in which 'Stanley and Blanche are a solid match.' Williams's commitment to both characters – his attraction to 'Stanley's animal vigor' and his sympathy for Blanche's 'sensibility' – enable him to write 'with a fine balance'. As Hirsch puts it, 'Though he is almost always divided in his feelings about his characters, Williams here makes capital dramatic use of his contrary impulses, and *Streetcar* thrives on its imbalances.'[2]

But the imbalances and tensions Hirsch points to are more extensive, more fundamental, than Williams's merely personal ambivalences. When Hirsch observes that 'Romantic Blanche and naturalistic Stanley are locked in a symbolic conflict: culture fights vulgarity, and is trampled',[3] he restricts his reading of the play to only one of its dramatic conflicts. It is, in fact, as if in *Streetcar* Williams dramatizes two mutually exclusive narratives, reveals two archetypal dramatic situations which dictate completely antithetical roles for Blanche. On the one hand, the play does present Blanche as a tragic figure and Stanley as the cruel agent of her destruction. Stanley brings about Blanche's downfall by unmasking her pretensions and her lies, by physically unclothing and raping her. In this dramatic situation, Blanche is – indeed – flawed, culpable, tragically imperfect, but she is fully and flagrantly human. As a tragic figure she functions as subject, to be judged by her action or inaction, her will to save herself, her sister, her home. She is a being wholly female, driven beyond her ability to cope with the wholly male world. At this level of the play, we may grieve as the environment (Stanley) destroys Blanche, or we may rage as Blanche backs herself into a corner with her lies and evasions. But no matter how we view Blanche – with pity or anger – we see and judge Blanche *as Blanche*, as a fully developed human character.

But the play dramatizes another situation in which Blanche becomes merely a figure, a component of one of our culture's most pernicious, most deeply entrenched narratives – the story of rape. As a figure in this story, as its victim, its object, Blanche ceases to be human. She becomes – instead – a repository for all the mistaken notions our culture harbors about rape. She is acted upon, objectified, and ironically made guilty for her own victimization. No longer fully human, she is simply a metaphor for all that is vile about women. Blanche cannot, then, claim tragic stature or even our sympathy precisely *because* she is a victim of rape. And as she becomes responsible for her own victimization, Stanley is left to glory in his ascendancy. This aspect of *Streetcar* arises from the misogyny which colors the play and our responses to it and which undermines the very moving presentation of Blanche that Williams offers.

Even overtly feminist readers of Williams's work do not fully explore the implications of Blanche's rape by Stanley. Focusing on the imbalances of the work and arguing that Williams's attitude toward the rape are 'ambivalent', Sandra Gilbert and Susan Gubar, for example, assert that in *Streetcar* Williams 'records, rationalizes, and critiques the use of the penis as weapon that he preceives as essential to Stanley Kowalski's relations with women'. Gilbert and Gubar find Blanche a 'sympathetic heroine whose imaginative energy surpasses the creativity of any of the other characters in the play'; for Williams, Blanche is, nonetheless, guilty of abusing and using 'sensitive men' so that her 'punishment' – her rape – fits her crime.'[4]

Gilbert and Gubar conclude, however, that while Stanley does seem to triumph over Blanche, does seem to punish her, what we really observe is Williams's 'scathing critique of the heterosexual imperative which is driving Blanche mad'.[5] Gilbert and Gubar assert that in the final scene of the play, Stanley's guilt 'may be' revealed as 'greater than Blanche's' because Stanley is accused by one of his poker buddies of being responsible for driving Blanche to her breakdown.[6]

But Gilbert and Gubar – like Hirsch – read or view *Streetcar* somewhat myopically. They too seem unaware of resonances in the play to which most audiences and readers would respond. While they focus their attention on a feature of the play that has not been fully considered yet – Stanley's violent assault against Blanche – Gilbert and Gubar ignore the *implications* of Blanche's rape. In effect, Gilbert and Gubar place the play so forcefully in a feminist context that they fail to hear the reverberations the work would inevitably create in a context less than sympathetic to women, the very context in which the play was created and first produced.

There is, in fact, hostility toward women in Williams's work which has been ignored or tacitly applauded by his critics. This misogyny is not peculiar to Williams but exists in his work as a reflection of the society (and its attitudes toward women) to which he belongs. In this light, we can understand why *Streetcar* expresses a great compassion and affection for Blanche (a humane response to the suffering woman, a respectful acknowledgment of her humanity) and at the same time an intense hostility and prejudice toward her (a misogynist response to her very femaleness and to her vulnerability to rape, a reduction of Blanche to the status of metaphor, bearer of meaning rather than creator of meaning).

To understand that this double attitude toward Blanche exists in *Streetcar* is to take a step toward discovering why the play fails to hold together in important ways, why it is difficult to feel pity and terror for Blanche's plight (when we know we should), and why it is difficult not to feel vindicated at Stanley's brutal ascendancy (when we know we should not). Both attitudes, toward women in general and Blanche in particular, exert strong influence on readers and viewers, encouraging at one moment an intense compassion for Blanche and inciting in the next a distaste for and hostility toward her.

Thus, *Streetcar* reveals Williams's desire to render Blanche fully human, though flawed and put upon. Williams displays great compassion for Blanche and insight into the position of women in the twentieth century. He is aware of both their dependence on men and their vulnerability to the passionate excesses of men. In a sociological approach to the play, Robert Emmet Jones shows that the degeneration of Southern aristocratic society left women like Blanche in a peculiarly imperiled position; he characterizes these women as 'the passive pawns of social forces and their own emotions'.[7] Blanche, raised to be decorative, fragile, and delicate, finds herself out of place, alienated from the real world, as Williams's description of her demonstrates:

> Her appearance is incongruous to this setting [Elysian Fields]. She is daintily dressed in a white suit with a fluffy bodice, necklace and earrings of pearls, white gloves and hat, looking as if she were arriving at a summer tea or cocktail party in the garden district . . . Her delicate beauty must avoid strong light. There is something about her uncertain manner, as well as her white clothes, that suggests a moth. (scene 1, p. 15)[8]

Blanche's genteel, feminine world has fallen apart, destroyed by the 'epic fornications' of all her *male* relatives – 'improvident grandfathers and father and uncles and brothers' (scene 2, p. 43). Blanche 'stayed and struggled', she tells Stella, trying to justify to her sister the loss of Belle Reve: 'I . . . tried to hold it together . . . but *all* the burden descended on *my* shoulders.' Jones characterizes Blanche's situation this way: 'The tragedy of these women is the tragedy of the civilization which bore them, nourished them, and cast them out.'[9] What Robert Brustein calls 'the dark masculine forces of society'[10] are pitted against Blanche's typically feminine qualities. And in the struggle, Blanche is pathetically lost and brutally exploited.

Williams is not unsympathetic to the fact that Blanche must exist in a male world on male terms. He shows us that she is trapped economically and socially. When she says to Mitch of Stanley, 'The first time I laid eyes on him I thought to myself, that man is my executioner!' (scene 6, p. 93), she demonstrates her awareness that it is the brutal male ethic, the 'Napoleonic Code', which has reduced her to virtual prostitution. Nor is Blanche unaware of the rules of the games she must play in this men's world or of the power every male has over her. From the beginning of *Streetcar* she is frightened ('Her voice drops and her look is frightened', scene 1, p. 23), and her reaction to Stanley is consistently edged with terror ('looking apprehensively toward the front door', scene 1, p. 27; 'She darts and hides', scene 1, p. 28; 'drawing back involuntarily from his stare', scene 1, p. 29).

Moreover, Williams is aware (as he shows Blanche is) that the games she plays with men – the coyness, the flirting, the submissiveness – are necessary for survival in a masculinist environment. As Andrea Dworkin points out in *Women Hating*, self-denigrating female social behavior is 'learned behavior' that allows woman 'survival in a sexist world'.[11] Blanche must please and placate those in whose hands her destiny rests. When she apologizes to Mitch for not being an interesting companion on their date, he asks why she tries so hard to please: 'I was just obeying the law of nature ... The one that says the lady must entertain the gentleman – or no dice' (scene 6, p. 86). She leads Mitch on in a shameful way, it is true, but she is not unaware of her deception ('She rolls her eyes, knowing he cannot see her face', scene 6, p. 91). Williams has made perfectly clear why the deception is necessary: Blanche is alone, vulnerable, penniless, and – most pathetic of all – desperately lonely.

Williams expresses his sympathy for women in a male-dominated world in one other way: his development of the violent and frequently physically abusive relationships between Stanley and Stella and between Steve and Eunice. Williams's sympathy is qualified, however, for – in the final analysis – in spite of the fact that he perceives the horror for women in these relationships, Williams comes out in favor of them; they are, he tells us at the end of *Streetcar*, life giving, fueled by desire, whereas Blanche's way represents a surrender to death.

The most revealing character in this respect is, of course, Stella. Critics are fond of accusing Blanche of refusing to face facts and of lying, but it is Stella (and Eunice, too) who constantly refuse to *look* at things, to listen to the truth, or even to tell the truth. Stella lies to Blanche throughout and her final, most devastating lie represents her complete betrayal of her sister: she allows Blanche to think she is going on a trip when, in fact, she is being sent to a state mental hospital. Stella, good wife that she is, concerns herself only with maintaining the status quo. She knows, at a deeply unconscious level, that she must keep Stanley happy to preserve the economic and emotional security she has achieved as his woman.

Every time Blanche confronts Stella with the facts of Stella's situation (that Stella deserted Blanche and Belle Reve, leaving Blanche to endure death and degradation; that Stanley is crude and brutal; in short, that Stella is 'married to a madman!' scene 4, p. 64), Stella turns her eyes away from these facts. She willingly blinds and anesthetizes herself to what her life with Stanley has become: 'Blanche! You be still! That's enough!' (scene 1, p. 27); 'I want to go away, I want to go away!' (scene 3, p. 60); 'She crosses in a dazed way from the kitchen' (scene 7, p. 101); 'Her eyes and lips have that almost narcotized tranquility that is in the faces of Eastern idols' (scene 4, p. 62). In fact, Blanche finds Stella's complete abnegation of self in the face of Stanley's brutality so astonishing that she asks Stella, 'Is this a Chinese philosophy you've – cultivated?' (scene 4, p. 65).

Williams demonstrates, moreover, that Stella is abused physically and degraded sexually in her relationship with her husband: she participates in and enjoys sex with Stanley after he has beaten her. There is, too, something unsavory in Stanley's equation of sex and violence (he feels that his brawling with Stella and Steve's with Eunice are perfectly natural expressions of sexual appetite) and in Stella's description of her sexual attachment to Stanley. She tells Blanche, 'I can hardly stand it when he is away for a night . . . When he's away for a week, I nearly go wild! . . . And when he comes back I cry on his lap like a baby' (scene 1, p. 25). Marion Magid remarks quite incisively of this scene:

> It is hard to know what is more unpleasant in this image: the overt sentimentality it expresses or the latent brutality it masks: a fascination with the image of the helpless creature under the physical domination of another, accepting his favors with tears of gratitude.[12]

Magid is, however, mistaken when she implies that Williams glorifies this relationship without qualification, for Williams demonstrates throughout the play that Stella is blinded and drugged and that she has shut herself off from the truth in order to maintain her relationship with Stanley.

Wiliams is not, then, unaware of the self-sacrifice a woman makes to live with a man like Stanley, for, as Stella says finally when she forsakes her sister so that she can stay with her husband, 'I couldn't believe her story and go on living with Stanley' (scene 11, p. 133). The irony of the situation is that Stella *has* believed Blanche's story all along; she – Stella – has called Stanley drunk, pig. She has reviled him but also has shut her eyes to her revulsion for him. This is, Williams shows us, the predicament of the heterosexual woman in the modern world. For Williams, Blanche is clearly the only female – the only fully *human* female – who has the will to set herself against Stanley. Only she refuses to blind herself to Stanley's evils. This pride, her insistence on her right to see and to name, may well be her tragic flaw. She may be quite simply too noble to exist as a female in a world run by a phalanx of Stanley Kowalski's.

In many ways, however, *A Streetcar Named Desire* dehumanizes Blanche, undercuts her tragic situation, and renders her by the end of the play a maddened hysteric with no place in a well-ordered society. In this respect, Williams draws on the most heinous and trivializing myths about women and about rape that inform our culture, and he demonstrates that he bears as many prejudices toward the modern woman as does a brute like

Stanley. These prejudices, Williams's misogynous attitudes, irrevocably flaw this play, for a human being viewed as weak, neurotic, hysterical, dishonest, emotional, affected, and fragile (which, the prejudice tells us, women are and which Blanche certainly is) cannot at the same time aspire to the conditions of the tragic figure. Williams wants Blanche to be tragic (in the final scene he describes her so: 'She has a tragic radiance in her red satin robe following the sculptural lines of her body', scene 11, p. 133), but woman – as conceived in a system of patriarchal myth, especially the myth of rape – cannot be tragic. Blanche is, most clearly after Stanley's assault, too weak and too oppressed to convey tragic grandeur. Williams demonstrates this contradiction beautifully if unconsciously; for as soon as he characterizes Blanche as 'tragic', his stage directions indicate that she must speak 'with faintly hysterical vivacity' (scene 11, p. 133). A neurotic woman may speak in this manner, but never an Oedipus or a Faustus.

If we look at Blanche's flaw, at the action or attitude which brings disaster and ruin upon her, we can understand the nature of Williams's predicament. In the first place, Blanche is, like most women, viewed primarily as a sexual being. As Naomi Weisstein points out, even psychologists, biologists, and anthropologists 'assert that a woman is defined by her ability to attract men',[13] and Dworkin develops her thoughts on misogyny by indicating that woman is perceived as either the wicked (that is, sexually active and knowledgeable) witch or the beautiful, innocent, victimized princess.[14] Thus, woman is categorized by her sexual activity, and sexual activity outside of marriage can be viewed only as degeneration; indeed, in *Streetcar* Blanche's sexual activity is an indication of her moral degeneration. She moves from sixteen-year-old virgin Southern princess (when she married Allan) to aging, sexually promiscuous whore. Sex is – to put it simply – sinful when Blanche engages in it. With respect to Blanche as rape victim, such blatant disclosure of her sexual history is absolutely necessary. It is as though her entire sexual background must be brought before us so that we can see that she, indeed, got what she deserved.

Stanley Kowalski, on the other hand, is applauded for his sexuality, for his crude, sadistic exploitation of Stella, for his love of the 'colored lights'. He is certainly sexually active and, given his attitudes and manner, probably promiscuous as well (this is hinted at in Eunice's accusation of Steve, for the two couples are often compared). Williams's description of Stanley is almost fulsome in its veneration of Stanley's virility:

> Since earliest manhood the center of his life has been pleasure with women, the giving and taking of it, not with weak indulgence, dependently, but with the power and pride of a richly feathered male bird among hens ... everything that is his ... bears his emblem of the gaudy seed-bearer. He sizes

women up at a glance, with sexual classifications, crude images flashing into his mind and determining the way he smiles at them. (scene 1, p. 19)

Gilbert and Gubar point out that the 'submissive Stella seems sexually enthralled by [Stanley's] violence'. But clearly Williams too is enthralled by Stanley, by his violent sexuality, by his masculine threat. While Gilbert and Gubar feel that Williams, as a homosexual, stands 'apart from heterosexual institution' and critiques Stanley's abuses of power,[15] it may be more likely that Williams has created his own Galatea in Stanley. In fact, Williams seems to fall victim to Stanley's sexuality to such a degree that he revels in it – irresponsibly and appallingly – at Blanche's expense. Elia Kazan's production notes to *Streetcar* are even more extravagant than Williams's own words concerning Stanley; Kazan calls Stanley a 'walking penis'.[16]

The play is rent, then, by a thematic inconsistency. Are we to elevate Blanche to a tragic figure or simply consign her to ignominy for the same activity which we applaud in Stanley Kowalski? Some critics of the play would have us suppose that Williams means us to perceive Stanley's attitude toward sex, with its alternations of violence and pleading (in scene 3 Stanley first assaults Stella then sobs, cries, and begs until she returns to him) as somehow superior to Blanche's. Others find Stella's sexual submissiveness healthy; Robert Jones, for example, tells us that Williams's heroines

> believe that through physical desire and its consummation they will belong, that they will achieve life and escape Death. They do not realize that desire fails unless it is accepted wholeheartedly, as by Stella Kowalski.[17]

How anyone could find Stella Kowalski's comatose endurance of Stanley healthy or whole-hearted is, indeed, a subject for wonder.

Tennessee Williams claims to share D. H. Lawrence's view of life, 'a belief in the purity of sensual life, the purity and the beauty of it'.[18] The inconsistencies of *Streetcar*, however, would lead us to believe that sexuality, no matter how debased or desperate (and it is debased and desperate between Stanley and Stella) is pure only for males. Sexuality for females seems to involve a virtuous narcosis (Stella) or a profligate frenzy (Blanche). The attitudes expressed by the characters in *Streetcar* also uphold this sexual double standard, for Stanley is quite willing to protect Steve from Eunice when she suspects him of infidelity. But Stanley feels it his bounden duty to reveal Blanche's sordid past to the impressionable Mitch.

Even more damning than Blanche's promiscuity (a promiscuity we must attribute to her to justify Stanley's raping her), however, is her behavior toward her young, homosexual husband, Allan, years before. Critic after critic berates Blanche for her 'betrayal of the defenseless homosexual ... the supreme sin',[19] for her 'rejection of Allan Grey',[20] for her 'cruelty' which 'consists of unveiling her young husband's true sexual nature, forcing his suicide',[21] for 'her failure to be compassionate':[22]

> Blanche's most fundamental regret is not that she happened to marry a homosexual ... [but that] when made aware of her husband's homosexuality, she brought on his suicide by her unqualified expression of disgust.[23]

Unhappily, the play completely supports these readings. Williams does consider Blanche guilty for not saving her husband from his homosexuality (although it is certainly not clear how she is to do this) and for not showing more womanly support and compassion for the young man when she did discover the truth. She tells the story to Mitch:

> There was something different about the boy, a nervousness, a softness, and tenderness which wasn't like a man's ... He came to me for help ... and all I knew was I'd failed him in some mysterious way and wasn't able to give the help he needed but couldn't speak of! ... on the dance-floor – unable to stop myself – I'd suddenly said – 'I saw! I know! You disgust me ...' (scene 6, pp. 95–6)

By the logic of the play, Blanche is guilty for not saving her husband from himself; she is also to be held responsible for his suicide. Both charges can be made only in a world where a woman's primary duty is self-sacrifice to man, where her appropriate role is that of supportive object not assertive subject. Where is there room in this situation for Blanche's own feelings? What about her rejected love, her jealousy, her anger? What about what Blanche wants?

We see, then, that Williams – investing the tragic significance of his play in Blanche – undercuts this very significance by his own sexist attitude toward her. He defines her in sexual terms (since she is no longer a virgin, she must be a degenerating whore), and he condemns her for failing to provide the self-sacrificing, womanly support her husband, Allan, needed. Williams's unacknowledged, unconscious misogyny weakens his development of Blanche as a strong, exciting character, and Blanche is damned no matter how she behaves.

Furthermore, just as Blanche is denounced for her lack of compassion for Allan and for her failure to conceal her disgust with his homosexuality, she is damned again and again for telling the truth. Women have traditionally been punished for saying what others do not want to hear: Cassandra was laughed at, scorned, and finally raped by Ajax; critical and vociferous women were burned as witches; aggressive, vocal Hedda Gabler was considered unnatural. What is especially interesting about these women is that not only are they intimidated into silence, but also the little they are permitted to say is denounced as falsehood. Cassandra is misled, insane, the Trojans believe; the witch is a 'liar by nature' according to the church;[24] and Hedda is, finally, discredited as evil. In the same way Blanche Dubois is accused of lying by Stanley Kowalski and by critics of the play. Stanley begins to enumerate Blanche's lies to Stella: 'Lie Number One: All this squeamishness she puts on! You should just know the line she's been feeding Mitch' (scene 7, p. 98). Most critics agree with Leonard Quirino that Blanche seeks to deny reality, 'to combat actuality', and that she has a 'preference for soulful illusion'.[25]

But, in fact, if we look closely at the play, we see that Blanche tells the truth consistently and that it is for *this* she is punished. Of course, her first great moment of truth-telling is when she challenges Allan with his homosexuality. This does, on the surface, seem a cruel act, but imagine for a moment Stanley rather than Blanche in this position. Suppose now that Stanley finds Stella in a compromising situation with another woman. We would expect and applaud shock, rage, even violence from Stanley. We would not dream of condemning him for a lack of compassion for the errant Stella. And in a way this is exactly what we admire Stanley for doing in *Streetcar*. His wife, it seems, is forming a threateningly close attachment with another woman (though the relationship is by no means lesbian), and surely we are to approve of Stanley's efforts to protect his marriage. Why then should we revile Blanche for a very natural, jealous, furious reaction to a threat to *her* marriage? The answer is, of course, because she is female. It is not her place to protect what is hers; it is for her to support, love, cherish, accept. And, in fact, with respect to Blanche's ultimate role, her role as the victim of Stanley's rape, we *expect* her to lie. If the rape victim isn't terrified into an appropriate and docile silence, she will be – or has been, traditionally – discredited by police, courts, medical professionals, family and judges.

Through the course of the play, Blanche – in much the same way and with similarly disastrous results – continues to tell the truth, but now about Stanley. She reveals him as she revealed Allan; she shows her disgust for him. In scene 1 she confronts Stella with the degradation in which Stella lives: 'I'm going to be honestly critical about it' (scene 1, pp. 19–20). And a little later she upbraids Stella for letting herself go – which Stella has done: 'you messy child, you, you've spilt something on the pretty white lace collar!' (scene 1, p. 22). After Stanley beats Stella, Blanche describes Stanley as an animal, an ape, a brute, a beast. She admonishes her sister not to 'hang back with the brutes' (p. 72). Of course, Stanley hears this, and Blanche's fate is sealed. She has wounded male pride once too often; she has seen a little too clearly and spoken far too forcefully. She must be punished.

Williams's difficulty in characterizing Blanche as a complex, fully developed figure becomes obvious here. He suggests on one level that Blanche has erred in being cruel and insensitive to her husband, that her failure was simply a lack of compassion; what he conveys, however, is that Blanche has broken the one inviolable rule of relationships between men and women. Women do not tell the truth, they do not challenge, they do not unmask. This notion is so interwoven into the fabric of our society that it makes its way into Williams's play in spite of the fact that it diminishes the effect of the work, and it renders Blanche's sin more a crime against the sanctity of marriage and a threat to the power of men than a brief lapse in sympathy or love.

This brings us to one of the most interesting problems of *Streetcar*: Blanche's punishment. The fact that Blanche has incurred male wrath by seeing too much and criticizing too freely makes it entirely appropriate that she be punished by the one sure means of male domination and power over women: rape. Susan Brownmiller points out that rape is 'not only a male prerogative but a man's basic weapon of force against women, the principal agent of his will and her fear'.[26] And herein lies Williams's inconsistency in having Stanley rape Blanche. The rape is to be a punishment, a retribution brought on by Blanche's great crime (beginning with her cruelty to Allan and culminating in her unmasking of Stanley). But to be a rape victim in a sexist society is to be deserving of the punishment simply because of who one is (a woman) rather than because of what one has done. It is, too, to be somehow sullied by the crime of which one is a victim. It is to be lowly and despicable; it is to be *guilty for* the act rather than *punished by* the act. Thus, Blanche's only crimes are that she is female and therefore subject to masculine will and that she is a bad enough woman (in sexual terms) to be raped. Her real crimes (if they are, indeed, crimes) are forgotten, completely obscured by the fact that we have an entire set of myths to explain rape and that these myths vigorously affirm the rape victim's guilt – which has nothing to do with how Blanche may have treated Allan in the past or with how she treats Stanley now.

These false notions about rape include the idea that all women want to be raped, that a woman – in effect – brings the rape on herself,[27] that it is not logically possible to rape a woman who is not a virgin,[28] and that rape is a crime of sexual desire, brought on by the overwhelming attraction of the victim or by the unbearable sexual deprivation of the rapist.[29] Williams goes to great lengths to obscure the fact that rape is a political crime of 'uncontrolled hostility' toward women, 'a brutal bullying of a smaller, weaker person',[30] by ensuring that the rape in *Streetcar* conforms to all the false stereotypes we hold about the act. Blanche is made to flirt with and entice Stanley; Williams shows that Blanche has an extremely unsavory sexual history, so the act of raping her seems insignificant, indeed; and he indicates that Stanley finds Blanche attractive ('come to think of it – maybe you wouldn't be bad to interfere with', scene 10, p. 129), making this seem a crime of passion and desire rather than one of violence, cruelty, and revenge – which every rape is. We tend, therefore, to forget why Stanley really attacks Blanche – not because she is attractive or because she is promiscuous but because she threatens masculine power with her honesty.

The issue becomes impenetrably muddled. Because Williams harbors false notions about rape, its causes and its intent, Blanche comes off simply as a loud-mouthed, flirtatious whore who really asked for what she got. In other words, she deserves to be raped not for some crime she committed against her husband or against Stanley, but because she has committed a crime against male privilege: she has been as sexually free as Stanley. But Williams attempts also to create a tragic figure in Blanche; she is a human being who has set in motion forces which have brought about her own ruin. To represent her ruin as a sexual assault, however, certainly diminishes the effect of it, for if only whores are raped, where is the tragedy? What can possibly be tragic about the rape of a promiscuous woman to an audience or a playwright in a misogynist society? Anyone watching the play knows enough about the myths of which our world is made to realize that Blanche has brought this rape on by her own sexual promiscuity and nothing else. She is, therefore, certainly not possessed of tragic stature.

On a deeper level, however, the play acknowledges the true intent and character of the act of rape, that it is a crime of domination and power. It is clear, at this level too, that Stanley is punishing Blanche for more than her profligacy; he is punishing her for all the insults she ever hurled at any male, beginning with Allan. This is what Stanley means when he tells Blanche, 'We've had this date with each other from the beginning!' (scene 10, p. 130). But given the false notions the audience harbors about rape – false notions the play itself promotes – the fact that Blanche is raped necessarily diminishes her in our eyes. She becomes no longer a tragic figure but merely a sordid victim of a nasty crime, no longer fully human but merely a metaphor for all the feminine evils the real men of the world must face and deal with.

According to Normand Berlin, *A Streetcar Named Desire* is a tragedy, but one whose effect is determined by the attitudes we hold toward Stanley and Blanche. We must, he says, keep the scales balanced between the two antagonists in order to understand the play fully:

> Desire is the common ground on which Stanley and Blanche meet ... The needs of both are clearly presented by Williams and should be understood by the audience which must neither wholly condemn Blanche for her whorishness nor Stanley for his brutishness.[31]

We cannot keep these scales balanced, however, for Blanche has been violated in such a way that she loses her tragic stature and even her status as an appropriate antagonist for Stanley. Susan Griffin observes that at the moment of rape 'a woman becomes anonymous ... Absorbed by ... violence, her soul and the history of her soul arc lost, are irrelevant.'[32] Indeed, Blanche is anonymous at the end of *Streetcar*; like Stella, she has been rendered comatose, catatonic by the sexuality and brutishness of the masculine world of power. Stanley triumphs, and his rape of Blanche conforms to Brownmiller's characterization of the violation of woman by man:

> rape is not a crime of irrational, impulsive, uncontrollable lust, but is a deliberate, hostile, violent act of degradation and possession on the part of a would-be conqueror, designed to intimidate and inspire fear.[33]

Stanley is more than a would-be conqueror in Williams's play, for he has protected his domain and destroyed the enemy. He has taken all. As Tennessee Williams himself has said, the play doesn't end with Blanche, it ends with Stanley:

> Just remember, everybody thinks the last line is: 'I've always been dependent on the kindness of strangers.' That's not the last line. The last line is: 'Gentlemen, the name of this game is five-card stud.'[34]

And in this masculine world – as in this masculine game – Stanley holds *all* the cards.

NOTES

1 Epigraphs are from 'Liz Ashley: An Outrageous Adventuress', *San Francisco Examiner and Chronicle* (Datebook, 14 August 1983), p. 31; Susan Brownmiller, *Against Our Will: Men, Women, and Rape* (New York: Simon & Schuster, 1975), p. 14; and Susan Griffin, *Rape: The Power of Consciousness* (San Francisco: Harper & Row, 1979), p. 53.
2 Foster Hirsch, *A Portrait of the Artist: The Plays of Tennessee Williams* (Port Washington, NY: Kennikat Press, 1979), p. 30.
3 Ibid., pp. 30–1.
4 Sandra Gilbert and Susan Gubar, *No Man's Land: The Place of the Woman Writer in the Twentieth Century* (New Haven: Yale University Press, 1988), pp. 50–1.
5 Ibid., p. 51.
6 Ibid., p. 52.
7 Robert Emmet Jones, 'Tennessee Williams' Early Heroines', *Modern Drama*, 2 (December 1959), p. 218.
8 Tennessee Williams, *A Streetcar Named Desire* (New York: Signet, 1947). All references to this work appear in the text.
9 Jones, 'Williams' Early Heroines', p. 219.
10 Robert Brustein, 'Williams' Nebulous Nightmare', *Hudson Review*, 12 (Summer 1959), p. 259.
11 Andrea Dworkin, *Woman Hating* (New York: Dutton, 1974), p. 21.

12 Marion Magid, 'The Innocence of Tennesse Williams', *Commentary*, 35 (January 1963), 38.
13 Naomi Weisstein, 'Psychology Constructs the Female', *Radical Feminism*, ed. Anne Koedt, Ellen Levine and Anita Rapone (New York: Quadrangle, 1973), p. 179.
14 Dworkin, *Woman Hating*, pp. 32–3.
15 Gilbert and Gubar, *No Man's Land*, p. 52.
16 Magid, 'The Innocence of Williams', p. 37.
17 Jones, 'Williams' Early Heroines', p. 218.
18 Tennessee Williams, quoted by Jim Gaines, 'A Talk about Life and Style with Tennessee Williams', *Saturday Review*, 55 (29 April 1972), p. 29.
19 Foster Kirsch, 'The World Still Desires "A Streetcar",' *New York Times*, 15 April 1973, sec. 2, p. 1.
20 Bert Cardullo, 'Drama of Intimacy and Tragedy of Incomprehension: *A Streetcar Named Desire* Reconsidered', *Tennessee Williams: A Tribute*, ed. Jac Tharpe (Jackson: University Press of Mississippi, 1977), p. 138.
21 Richard B. Vowles, 'Tennessee Williams and Strindberg', *Modern Drama*, 1 (May 1958), 167.
22 Cardullo, 'Drama of Intimacy', p. 140.
23 Leonard Berkman, 'The Tragic Downfall of Blanche Dubois', *Modern Drama*, 10 (December 1967), 253.
24 Dworkin, *Woman Hating*, p. 133.
25 Leonard Quirino, 'The Cards Indicate a Voyage on *A Streetcar Named Desire*', *Tennessee Williams: A Tribute*, 87.
26 Susan Brownmiller, *Against Our Will: Men, Women, and Rape* (New York: Simon & Schuster, 1975), p. 14.
27 Ibid., p. 311.
28 Susan Griffin, 'Rape: The All-American Crime', *Women; A Feminist Perspective*', ed. Jo Freeman (Palo Alto: Mayfield, 1975), pp. 30–2.
29 Angela Y. Davis, *Violence against Women and the Ongoing Challenge to Racism* (Latham, New York: Kitchen Table: Women of Color Press, 1985), p. 6.
30 Ibid.
31 Normand Berlin, 'Complementarity in *A Streetcar Named Desire*', *Tennessee Williams: A Tribute*, pp. 98–9.
32 Griffin, *Rape: The Power of Consciousness*, p. 53.
33 Brownmiller, *Against Our Will*, p. 391.
34 'Liz Ashley: An Outrageous Adventuress', p. 31.

Languages of violence:
Fugard's *Boesman and Lena*

MARCIA BLUMBERG

Athol Fugard's *Boesman and Lena* evokes the violence of a society built on divisions and privilege. Begun in 1967 and first performed in 1969, it offers neither the hopeful nor the satiric dramatized protest of the post-1976 Soweto watershed years; instead, it portrays the voiceless victims and a vicious cycle of violence in which Arendt maintains: 'impotence breeds violence ... and violence itself results in impotence'.[1] Moreover, the play depicts concentric circles of violence in a hierarchical structure which posits the impersonal violence of the apartheid ideology. The victims within the inner circle, the specific characters, dramatize the modes of personal violence, whether psychological, physical, gestural or verbal, which interact throughout the play in a dialectical relationship to societal violence.

While *Boesman and Lena* speaks to an international audience, Fugard writes of the specific South African milieu. Therefore, an analysis of violence in the play emphasizing the particular nuances of languages and landscape yields more than the mere mud of Swartkops; in the dross is a rich vein of images, speech patterns and dramatic tensions. Besides, the notion of circles of violence in the play reflects a central icon of Afrikaner history and mythology, the *laager* – a circle of oxwagons interlaced with thornbushes protected nineteenth-century hinterland Afrikaner families, their servants, animals and effects, enabling them to fire outwards at the enemy. Although many of the then deracinated Afrikaners now oversee the apartheid system, they retain the *laager* mentality to mask the insecurity of their position as a dominant minority amidst an ever-increasing population victimized by a system of violence. In Lambley's view, apartheid takes its toll on the violators too, since for those Afrikaners 'the prevailing ethic of manipulation ... [highlights] a brutalized society living on its wits and on its nerves'.[2]

The play's circular structure also reflects a claustrophobic containment of the cycle of violence. However, within the circles the eponymous victims manifest antithetical tendencies. Boesman emulates his oppressors in a chain of gender and racial violence that intermittently glints with feeling for the shared experiences of past love, children, laughter, and pain and also bares fear and self-hatred in a progression stressing the impotence of brutality. The doubly-victimized Lena erupts sporadically and, according to Cohen, 'the development of the play depends upon the explosions of Lena's passions and their dangerous subsidences'.[3] While urgency to fathom her plight burgeons into courage, Lena's rebellion is finally subsumed. The play's bleak structure repeats the beginning in the end but adds one variant, her indomitable will to survive.

Boesman and Lena confronts the audience with the starkness of an empty stage, a harsh landscape, which offers a temporary locale for two characters in search of an abode, both physical and metaphysical. The presence of a violating force is evident even in their silent entrance as minutely detailed stage directions set the scene: '*Heavily burdened*'[4] evokes an overarching image of the literal and symbolic weight of exhausted, shabbily attired, old people bearing worn-out possessions, their sum total of worldly goods. They rank more disadvantaged than the lowly snail that carries his burden yet can withdraw for shelter. Boesman and Lena, who are later equated with animals in naming, expletives and action, are unquestionably victims of an ideology that inflicts impersonal violence and accords them sub-human status. Harsh laws such as the Group Areas Act delineated specific localities for each race and empowered agents of violence to remove squatters. Lena's litany of place names, 'Redhouse–Swartkops–Veeplaas–Korsten' (p. 204), systematizes her past to make the present comprehensible and bearable but speaks of areas where her racial group, the Coloureds, could stay yet where she has been unable to find a permanent home.

On the one hand Boesman and Lena are an entity, a Coloured couple, who are victims of an impersonal violence in which Lena conflates the oppressor and his instrument of violence: 'Blame the whiteman. Bulldozer!' (p. 194). On the other hand the play's opening differentiates the two characters and depicts a pattern of personal violence with its hierarchical structure, which forms the depth and richness of the play. Fugard claims: 'my "statement" – the "action" of the piece is in the sub-text',[5] which is emphasized by the silence of their entrances; Boesman leads and Lena later follows until she stops without consultation when he is ahead no more. In the opening tableau Boesman's relief at dropping his goods contrasts with Lena's extra effort to raise the load off her head onto the ground; her action foreshadows the wells of inner vitality and marks a re-emerging attribute of the female characters throughout Fugard's canon. Yet, concomitant with Lena's innate spiritedness is reduction by Boesman's silence and 'hard, cruel objectivity ... to a dumb animal-like submission' (p. 193), which sounds a *caveat* and anticipates the final submergence of her rebellion in the overwhelming violence.

Languages of violence: Fugard's Boesman and Lena

Boesman and Lena comprises two acts yet structurally involves four distinct phases framed by a prologue and an epilogue. Whereas the first phase involves Boesman and Lena, the second and third phases dramatize the altered dynamics of a stranger's intrusion. The final phase supposedly reverts to a dyadic relationship, but the indelible presence of Outa's corpse bears witness and brings menace. The imperative, 'Give!' (p. 246), marks the transition to the epilogue, which repeats motifs of the prologue while portraying Lena's psychic growth, then lapses into repetition of the unending struggle as the play comes full circle. Accordingly, Boesman and Lena laden with their belongings walk off into the literal darkness of night and the gloom of the fact that survival is the acme of their existence.

In Act I Lena's opening monologue forms a microcosm of the entire play. It combines the gestural fury of the opening tableau with verbal and psychological violence as well as notions of the past, the present, and the future forming an ever-repeating cycle of violent repression and submission, unattainable freedom, and the central linked metaphors of mud and garbage. Lena bares her violated psyche, 'Another day gone. Other people lived it. We tramped it into the ground' (p. 196), for she is literally and figuratively enmired: 'This piece of world is rotten. Put down your foot and you're in it up to your knee' (p. 194). As the system imposes violence, so the landscape has dominion over her and she therefore directs expletives and gestural violence at a bird, who has freedom and potential for escape.

As members of the human species, Boesman and Lena will complete the cycle from dust to dust yet their daily existence categorizes them as rubbish. Boesman later uses this image to emphasize the commonality of their plight: 'We're whiteman's rubbish ... he can't get rid of his rubbish ... his rubbish is people' (p. 231). Ontological violence associated with the equation of certain groups with trash infects personal relationships. Thus, Lena is Boesman's property:

> it's **me**, that thing you *sleep* [drag] along the roads. My life ... been used too long ... Time to throw it away. How do you do that when its yourself? (p. 198)

She finally taunts Boesman about his derisive epithet for Outa, 'vuilgoed' [rubbish] (p. 231), as concretized in Outa's death: 'Real piece of rubbish now, hey ... How do you throw away a dead *kaffer*?' [offensive term for a Black] (p. 240). Lena's abusive categorization reflects a view sometimes held by Coloureds of the inferiority of Blacks, yet her tone towards Outa throughout the play is caring and never moves beyond frustration, or verbal anger. In contrast, Boesman denigrates Outa by marginalization and vicious disgust, which fuses with jealousy and explodes in a cataclysmic moment, when he kicks and pummels the body. Although

Boesman regards the corpse as mere rubbish that must be disposed of, they both know that they in turn are the whiteman's detritus that pollutes the atmosphere and landscape of any locale where they sojourn.

In Act 1 Lena's three monologues chart a process of grappling and growth yet provoke vehement reactions from Boesman. Lena's first word, 'Here?' (p. 193) highlights her dominant lexical mode, the questioning that incessantly recurs in Act 1 as she contends with her predicament. Boesman's answer, he 'clears his throat and spits', is not merely a criminal act – bilingual signs in public places declare: 'Spitting is prohibited' – but it signifies his vehement disgust at himself, Lena, and the world and is later verbally concretized in his climactic speech: *Sies*, Boesman! . . . *Sies*, Lena! . . . *Sies, wêreld*! [Ugh, world]' (p. 238). Further gestural violence and a refusal to speak causes brutalizing silence; although her body is a road-map of bruises, she withstands the physical abuse, but the psychic scars are only assuaged by empathetic communication. Boesman utilizes silence as a weapon and her only defence is, thus, self-expression. Unlike the loquacity of some Pinter and Mamet characters, who verbally bombard and dominate their adversaries with bigger and better stories, Lena's survival mechanism stems from a utilization of language to question and confront her existence: 'I verbalize therefore I am.'

Boesman withstands her reminiscences but breaks his silence when she mimics his obsequiousness. His verbal violence ridicules her words, 'rubbish . . . That long *drol* [turd] of nonsense that comes out when you open your mouth' (p. 195). Earthy language mirrors their state and the *potpourri* of English and Afrikaans that Fugard uses throughout the play furnishes their lexical landscape with

> texture . . . the problem of the form and content of one language as opposed to another . . . an important aspect of my writing is an element of 'translation' . . . [in this play] to begin with phrases were all in Afrikaans – some are still, and still defy 'translation'.[6]

While the Samuel French version offers few Afrikaans words and is easier for international audiences to grasp, it lacks the richness of expression of the often more guttural and violent sounds and negates the speech patterns of many Coloureds of Boesman and Lena's ilk, who utilize language and form sentences from words as they construct shacks from the flotsam and jetsam they acquire.

Lena's feisty nature wards off much of Boesman's verbal abuse but proves vulnerable to the ruthlessness of rejection. The white children need no 'girl' [the term often used for a maid, regardless of age] and Boesman ostensibly requires no one either: 'You think *I* want you?' (p. 198). The ironic disclaimer negates his every action, for whether abusive or neutral Lena is involved: 'they are each other's fate'.[7] The very fibre of Lena's being craves empathy; perhaps unfulfilled motherhood and trying times with Boesman compel her to nurture, even a '*brak*' [mongrel] (p. 196) or a dying stranger. Also, her desire to possess and need for self-objectification make the phrase, 'I want him' (pp. 210, 222), central to Lena's *modus vivendi*.

The second monologue and its aftermath characterize the first phase of the play, Lena's subjugation. Boesman's harsh address, 'Make the fire', contrasts with Lena's plea, 'Let's have a *dop* [drink] first ... Please, Boesman!' (p. 201), but automaton-like she complies until the words allow her to unwind. Her soliloquy is a momentary antidote to violence, a formula for survival, that also embraces forms of violence. In a montage of impersonal and personal violence, past and present, Lena strives to order her world through language but violates that too as she mimics her white oppressors in sentences, which conflate English and Afrikaans, '*Loop, Hotnot!* So *Hotnot loops*' (p. 201), and acknowledge her oppressors in both languages. The Samuel French version, 'Walk *Hotnot*! So *Hotnot* walks' (p. 13), dilutes the effect since it does not show the violation whereby the Afrikaans verb is made to take on the English 's'. Besides, '*Loop Hotnot!*' connotes the expletive 'Bugger off', rather than the tamer translation, which chiefly offers abuse in the term '*Hotnot*'. Lena confronts her dilemma by naming places of past crises in forms that utilize metatheatre, physical location, questions, comments, humming and the laughter that make Boesman suspicious of her good spirits. Lena's song and dance offer fleeting release epitomizing Fanon's notion that 'violence is canalised, transformed and conjured away ... the circle of dance is a permissive circle'.[8] A furious Boesman retaliates with threatened assault, but his laughter inflicts psychological violence and exacerbates Lena's confusion, which is verbally and spatially dramatized. He answers her plea for help in a grotesque pantomime that subverts her tentative physical situation and assails her very selfhood.

Boesman's exultant salute to patriarchy ironically displays power over Lena and subservience within the system, as he exhibits gender violence in an imagined dialogue with the police on assault:

> 'She's my woman, *baas* [master]. *Net a bietjie warm gemaak* [Just warmed her a little].' 'Take her' ... finish *en klaar* ... They know the way it is with our sort ...
>
> Lena. You'll go too far one day. Death penalty.
> Boesman. For you? (*Derisive laughter.*) Not guilty and discharge. (p. 207)

Physical beatings project his self-hatred and concomitantly verify her existence and their inseparability, but this dyad manifests loneliness: 'you and the other person, who doesn't want to know you're there. I'm sick of you too, Boesman!' (p. 209). His striking monosyllabic pronouncements, 'I know my way, I know my world' (p. 209) mask self-doubt and foreshadow a speech in which the monosyllable, '*sies*', is pivotal. The first phase ends with Boesman's apparent control as he taunts Lena with the imperative, 'Walk!' (p. 209).

Although the second phase begins with Lena's simple statement, 'There's somebody out there' (p. 209), the Black stranger, who emerges from the darkness as a catalyst, alters the dynamics of interaction and compels confrontation with their inner selves. Besides, her stage positioning is significant; Lena literally and figuratively turns her back on Boesman since Outa's intrusion polarizes them. Antithetical stances surface but Boesman's objections and invective are overruled by Lena's need to converse, 'I'm not thinking of him. It's another person . . . To hell with you! I want him' (p. 210). Momentary qualms at Outa'a approach place them together, but an old, decrepit Black man poses no threat. Though Outa's shapeless, shabby clothing parallels their garb and homelessness unifies them all as victims of impersonal violence, the Coloured couple regard the Black stranger as an inferior in a hierarchy of racial groups.

While Lena's urge to converse negates feelings of superiority, Boesman readily exhibits racial violence and she, thus, rebuts his categorization of Outa, 'He's not brown people, he's black people', with 'They got feelings too' (p. 212). However, the introduction of a third language, Xhosa, confounds clear discussion and results in further abuse – Boesman transforms Lena's invitation 'sit and rest' into 'Hamba' [go] (p. 211) and a frustrated Lena describes Xhosa as 'baboon language' (p. 212). Whereas the Samuel French version gives Outa fixed Xhosa dialogue and English translation, other versions set no specific words and merely offer murmuring and mumbling in Xhosa. Fugard notes: 'I didn't write anything for Outa. Each actor makes up his own piece';[9] Walder's endnote maintains that 'the audience is not meant to understand him, any more than Lena does'.[10] The Samuel French version, therefore, diminishes the effect since the well-made speeches order the chaos evoked in the other texts when non-comprehension increases the verbal and psychological violence.

Boesman conflates gender, racial, and pornographic violence in his fantasy of Lena and Outa as participants in sexual games: 'Some sports. You and him. They like *Hotnot meide* [Hottentot girls]. Black bastards!' (p. 213). Boesman not only relishes his role as imaginary spectator, he revels in what he regards as a degrading image of forced coupling between a Coloured woman and a Black man. Despite his abuse, Lena, irritated at non-communication with Outa, returns dejectedly to the fire but Boesman's stick and his denial of brandy precipitate a literal and metaphoric redrawing of battle lines as Lena runs to Outa as witness. Although Boesman exits, his tyranny is evident in her gestural tic as she checks his absence.

Lena cements the new alliance with physical contact when she pats the old man and teaches him her name. Her third monologue integrates Outa's mumblings into an illusory dialogue, that provides the much-needed empathy of communication. The importance of the dog, who befriended her and disappeared, and his replacement by Outa, hinges on their role as witness, 'Eyes, Outa. Another pair of eyes. Something to see you' (p. 216). In an outburst of anger at the non-completion of her agenda she physically restrains him and ends the monologue with a reminder of his function: 'You've got two eyes. Sit and look' (p. 220). An earlier touching summation of her metaphysical landscape revealing gender violence, 'Boesman's back. That's the scenery in my world' (p. 197), now takes on a new awareness: 'Boesman's back gets in the way these days' (p. 217).

Lena philosophizes in a poignant poetry of pain:

> Once you've put your life on your head and walked you never get light again ... The right time on the wrong road, the right road leading to the wrong place. (pp. 218, 219)

This litany of their plight attesting to impersonal violence is only eclipsed by Lena's elegy for a miscarried foetus:

> Pain? Yes! Don't *kaffers* know what that means? One night it was longer than a small piece of candle and then as big as darkness. Somewhere else a donkey looked at it ... Boesman was too far away to call ... I didn't even have rags! ... Pain is a candle *entjie* and a donkey's face. (p. 219)

A violent juxtaposition of Lena's powerful monologue to Outa as observer contrasts with Boesman's demand for Outa's expulsion and dehumanization in the exchange of pronouns, 'Who's going to give *that* a job?' (p. 221). Lena substantiates the thrice-repeated 'I want him' (p. 222) by buying off an amazed Boesman with wine, 'For that!' She, thus, opts for communication and memory over the forgetfulness and fog of alcohol and makes a momentous decision to withstand the tyranny of his ultimatum, whereby she chooses Outa and the elements rather than Boesman and his shack. Lena's *caveat* metamorphoses Boesman's fear into the ferocity of impotent violence for in Lena's fleeting absence he rips off Outa's blanket and pushes him down, 'If you tell her, I'll kill you' (p. 224). The final tableau of Act I ends this second phase with a definitive spatial statement; Boesman, alone in his shack, watches them enact 'Lena's mass':[11] 'this mug ... Bitter tea, a piece of bread ... The bread should have bruises. It's my life' (p. 225), while his bread and tea are untouched.

Act II provides a mirror image of the two phases of Act I in the interaction of the triadic relationship, which is supposedly curtailed in the final phase. Reversals abound, for the entire act counters his apparent brutal confidence and displays the course of Boesman's self-hatred and vulnerability evident in his first overt gesture of fear in the final tableau, yet

Lena's self-awareness and courage of the second phase deepen. The third phase opening tableau emphasizes spatial positioning as Lena and Outa huddle on a box, while Boesman stays alone with his bread and tea untouched. Their stasis parallels his at the opening of Act I, but contrasts with his *'characteristic violence [which] is now heightened by a wild excitability'* (p. 226) as intoxication releases the dam wall of repressions and torrents of fear, hatred and jealousy gush out.

Unlike Act I, where Lena's monologues are the structural determinants, Act II is heavily weighted with Boesman's long speeches. Verbal anger replaces his silent mode as he utters the first word, an imperative, 'Again' (p. 226). Her forced re-enactment of obeisance to the Whiteman incenses Lena, who retaliates with curses: 'Whiteman's dog – *Voetsek*! [Bugger off]' (p. 226). Her Afrikaans expletive echoes the Xhosa, '*Hamba*' (p. 221), that he aimed at Outa. Boesman's metatheatrical malevolence transforms into vivid story telling as the repeated impersonal violence of man and machine literally and metaphorically gobbles up their goods and themselves. Here, they actively engage in dialogue that dredges memory as well as admitting present chaos, while Outa serves as silent witness.

Boesman's gratitude to the oppressor for purging them of the rubbish that is themselves and their world emphasizes their lack of self-image in a physical and psychological landscape suffused with violence. It stems from Boesman's ironic notion that they thereby gain freedom, but Lena puts the idea in perspective:

> We had to go somewhere. Couldn't walk around Korsten carrying your Freedom for ever ... Bad day for Lena. Three empties and Boesman's Freedom in pieces. (p. 230).

As Boesman reins the dialogue in from Freedom to the rationale for Lena'a acquisition of Outa, his bafflement bounds into vicious jealousy as he questions: 'Why? Why?' (p. 232). In this reversal of modes Lena, unlike Boesman, provides serious answers:

> That's not a *pondok* [shack], Boesman. It's a coffin ... You bury my life in your *pondoks* ... Crawl into darkness and silence before I'm dead. No! I'm on this earth not in it ... The walks led here. Tonight. And he sees it. (p. 232)

Although Outa's only intelligible word is 'Lena', it acknowledges her identity and self-worth and she, therefore, shakes him awake in a continued appeal as witness. Boesman's refusal to share his bread and tea is concretized in violence as he discards both and withdraws, setting the scene for her only monologue in Act II.

Whereas her Act I monologue to Outa is predicated on a minimal response, here Lena performs alone. Analysis of the past and speculation about the future constitute an awareness that the present is all important. Lena fills the void with songs, a medley of place-names, people and her predicament, while Boesman watches and quietly releases a bombshell, 'I dropped the empties' (p. 235). His confession provokes emotions and perceptions that range from non-comprehension and disbelief, to the deep pain of undeserved bruises, the querying of motive, and white-hot rage of curses. Lena channels outrage at Boesman's projection of self-hatred as she implores Outa to observe her plight and begs Boesman to hit her again. Mounting disgust crystallizes in 'Boesman's poem of destruction',[12] which contains a ten-fold repetition of the monosyllable, '*Sies*' (p. 237), and reduces his world to an expression of utter repulsion, detritus on the scrapheap of language.

The realization of Outa's demise initiates the fourth phase – a reinstatement of the initial dyad; yet his corpse remains on stage as a lingering testament to what has transpired. Lena's action of gently moving the body juxtaposed with Boesman's violence to the corpse concretizes their differing modes as voiced by Lena:

> Put your hands on the things in your life. Yours were full. Mug of tea, piece of bread ... Me. Somebody else. Touch them, hold them ... or make a fist at them. (p. 240)

However, Boesman's agitation and explosion of brutality to Outa is concomitant with a subtextual statement of impotence. For Fugard:

> If a society emasculates [a man] – how difficult it is for him to relate decently to any other individual. But equally, how hellish it is for somebody who lives with an emasculated individual.[13]

Lena parallels Boesman's fingerprints on the body as indictment for murder with her beating for 'dropping the empties ... It hurt more than your fists ... Inside. Where your fists can't reach' (p. 244); she thus, exposes the devastating nature of psychological violence.

Boesman's imperative, 'Come!' (p. 244) elicits Lena's 'No', the most vital word in a play punctuated with monosyllables. A Camusian stance, 'I rebel – therefore we exist',[14] marks the zenith of her journey of self-discovery and propels Boesman into a paroxysm of panic emulating the societal oppressors: '*Hotnot* bulldozer' (p. 245). Boesman's silence speaks through action as he carried their goods and bears Lena's barrage of verbal violence: 'Goodbye! Okay, now go. Go! Walk!!' (p. 246). Boesman is transfixed for while she repeats his imperative at the end of the first phase and turns her back to commune with Outa's corpse she repeats the gesture that starts the second phase and, therefore, completes a circle of exchanged modes.

Lena's imperative, 'Give!' (p. 246), initiates the epilogue with an acknowledgement of the overwhelming impact of violence in their lives. As she approaches Boesman and takes her share of their belongings, she manifests the rich complexity of a Fugardian protagonist. On the one hand, her rebellion is subsumed in the reinforcing concentric circles of hierarchic violence. On the other hand, in the endless cycle of life, her journey of self-awareness yields one specific night, where she emerges from a crucible of violence metaphysically recast. In contrast, Boesman's response to victimization is an ever-increasing intensity of violence until confrontation with a stranger and a new Lena lays bare his self-loathing.

A vanquished Boesman offers Lena his only gift, the litany of places that is their story, but she now knows that the answer reveals nothing of their predicament. In a repeated linkage of dog and Outa, 'somebody saw a little bit. Dog and a dead man' (p. 247), Lena stresses the vital role of witness as an antidote to brutality and a confirmation of existence. Her last speech is a confident chain of mostly monosyllabic caveats that connote the staccato rhythm of a *Zeitgeist* of violence. The play comes full circle in the final tableau but variation of the entrance is significant, for Boesman and Lena leave together in the dark night cognizant of their altered personal dynamics and the inexorable force of impersonal violence that must be withstood for mere survival.

NOTES

1 Hannah Arendt, *On Violence* (New York: Harcourt, 1970), p. 54.
2 Peter Lambley, *The Psychology of Apartheid*, (London: Secker & Warburg, 1980), p. 128.
3 Derek Cohen, 'Athol Fugard's *Boesman and Lena*', *The Journal of Commonwealth Literature*, 12.3 (1978), p. 80.
4 Athol Fugard, *Boesman and Lena* in *Athol Fugard Selected Plays* (Oxford: Oxford University Press, 1987), p. 193. All further references are taken from this edition and appear in the text. In his introduction to this volume Dennis Walder declares: 'the texts are the most recent approved by the author, and have been carefully checked' (p. x). Other versions of *Boesman and Lena* are as follows: (Cape Town: Buren, 1969), (New York: Samuel French, 1971), and (Oxford: Oxford University Press, 1973). The chief differences between the Samuel French version and the other texts are the substitution of English for much of the Afrikaans and the provision of a set Xhosa dialogue for Outa with the English translation, both of which I discuss in the paper.
5 Athol Fugard, *Notebooks 1960/1977*, ed. Mary Benson (London: Faber, 1983), p. 184.
6 Ibid., p. 156.
7 Ibid., p. 169.
8 Frantz Fanon, *The Wretched of the Earth*, trans. Constance Farrington (New York: Grove, 1963), p. 45.
9 Mary Benson, 'Keeping an Appointment with the Future: the Theatre of Athol Fugard', an interview with Athol Fugard in *Theatre Quarterly*, 28:7 (1977), p. 81.
10 Dennis Walder, *Athol Fugard Selected Plays* (Oxford: Oxford University Press, 1987), p. 249.

11 *Notebooks*, p. 173.
12 Ibid., p. 173.
13 Melvyn Bragg, 'Athol Fugard, Playwright: a Conversation with Melvyn Bragg', *The Listener*, 5 December 1974, p. 734.
14 Albert Camus, *The Rebel*, trans. Anthony Bower (New York; Vintage, 1956), p. 22.

Stage violence as thaumaturgic technique*

MARY KAREN DAHL

Thauma (meaning 'a wonder' or 'miracle') is the Greek root of thaumatology (the study of miracles) and thaumaturge (the worker of miracles). It is, according to *Webster's New World Dictionary*, linked with the notion of theatre through the Greek word *theasthai*, meaning 'to see, to view', which is the base for *theatron*, the name of the seating space or auditorium in the ancient Greek theatre. When I happened upon the word 'thaumaturgical' in a play by David Rudkin, it provoked the following speculations.

Stage representations of violence are a hallmark of contemporary British playwriting. The 'New Jacobeans', especially the 'two Howards', Brenton and Barker, often construct physically violent images of considerable visceral power. These images are designed to encapsulate and bring home to the spectator a particular politic. Among these contemporary playwrights, however, David Rudkin is unique: he melds political and religious purpose in the theatre, and his use of staged violence could be described as miraculous, or wondrous, in intent.

In a series of early plays, including *Afore Night Come* (1962), *The Sons of Light* (1965–6 ; 1975–6), and *Ashes* (1974), Rudkin uses staged violence to effect change in the spectator – a change analogous to that depicted through the characters and events of his playtexts. The playwright structures a sacrificial undergoing of physical and psychic torture that strips both characters and spectators to bare bone, purifies them, and thus prepares them for what he calls, not 're-surrection', but, tellingly, 'surrection'.

Rudkin himself points to his strategy in representing violence on stage. The indicators appear in *The Sons of Light*, a play of considerable poetic power that Rudkin conceived 'soon' after the 1962 Royal Shakespeare Company production of his first play, *Afore Night Come*, and which he finally saw produced only after he had written *Ashes*. Because writing *Ashes*

---

* A draft of this paper was read at the *Themes in Drama* International Conference held at the University of California, Riverside, in February 1989.

occupied a comparatively brief interlude in Rudkin's long struggle to bring *The Sons of Light* to the stage, it seems particularly appropriate to read the one text through the other. Thus, after identifying the strategy *The Sons of Light* suggests, the discussion will focus on *Ashes* in performance.

The action of *The Sons of Light* is described by Rudkin in a short article in the May 1976 *Plays and Players*: 'the basic idea was of a new nonconformist pastor coming, to redeem a "damned" island: his three sons were to dive down into the island like seeds of resurrection and bring it to life ...'.[1] The play provides two models of the strategic use of violence, each embodied by a major character. The first of these, Dr Nebewohl, has caused a subterranean worker hive to be constructed in the quarry below the surface of the island. He has devised a method of physical and psychic torture that transforms human beings into brainwashed automatons. This rocky chasm is their prison. When they are not working, the captives sleep, sealed up in the rock. Nebewohl is, in fact, the 'technologue of tyranny' (p. 36),[2] and he speaks of his underworld creation with what he calls 'thaumaturgical pride' (p. 35).

Nebewohl's technique is never explicated in the play. Instead, we see it in practice, erupting into the on-stage action. The 'Programme', as it is called, includes a schema labelled 'Deserter Pursued, Recaptured, Purgatively Judged' (p. 25). Whether there are other schemata in the Programme we do not discover; this one appears twice. In each instance, an escapee from the underworld is apprehended, and Nebewohl's creatures search out the flaw that made him defect. The searching is physical and pornographic. The first victim (who remains anonymous) is reamed, that is, raped, with a guard's truncheon (pp. 24–6). Although the act takes place off stage, the actors' gestures and aspects make clear the nature of the violation. The second victim (named Gower) is handled similarly, according to his report. He was 'rent and gouged' with 'white-hot blades: to ease between my hides: along my arms, calves, sides, to slit me, long and parallel and deep'. Then, as with the first victim: 'My legs raised up before me, up, over my face, to bend me like a hoop: there into me ... with a searing implement, opening me and pumping into me such scalding shocks –'. Until at last he is 'hagged', hacked apart. He 'came apart quite easy then', he says (p. 58). According to Nebewohl, by 'over and over through this schema experiencing his dysfunction', the subject will achieve 'the ultimate – salvation for him to which this apparent ordeal is the only path ...' (p. 25).

Nebewohl's interest in salvation recalls his pride in thaumaturgy and introduces the idea that violence may be used strategically to effect miracles. What, then, of the playwright as thaumaturgist? Does Rudkin's use of violence on stage correspond in any way to Nebewohl's schema? The answer would seem to be 'Yes'.

Rudkin explains in *Plays and Players* that Nebewohl is a 'portrait ... in reverse' of his own 'healer' and mentor, Reichian therapist Robert Ollendorff (p. 26). In other words, Nebewohl is a negative exemplar. His are the techniques and implements of destruction. His is the kingdom of death. Opposed to him in the play's action is the eldest of the sons of light, John. It is this character, whom Rudkin describes in the same essay as the 'most morally powerful and ruthless' of the sons, who represents the healer (p. 26). Thus, while Nebewohl's technology of tyranny is suspect, John describes and demonstrates the potentially beneficial thaumaturgic function of staged violence.

The demonstration occurs near the end of the play, when John descends into Nebewohl's underworld kingdom to liberate the entombed. The doctor has methodically used physical torture to control men's minds; now John must find a way 'down in to those heads' to restore them to the kingdom of life (p. 65). The way he chooses is storytelling and poetry.

John addresses the soldiers who control their brother slaves:

> A text you ask of me, older than all speech. A picture must I bring now: image, like a dream, to trouble you: to beat its wings within these heads, within each head, and trouble it and have you wake and have you rise and in your rising haul your brothers with you, up, up, up, up into the light of the Sun. (p. 68)

And he begins to create an image that will beat within their heads: he tells them the story of a soldier who worked in a palace of stone, to whom a milk white sea bird came, singing, pursuing him from room to room, until at last, terrified by 'the beating of her wings above his head; and the song she sang', he killed her. And then, only then, he knew that he had done wrong, and that the beautiful white sea bird would come never again to the 'poor benighted soldier'. He was lost ... turned to stone (pp. 68–9).

John plants the image, and his strategy is successful. When the time comes, he issues a call, and the soldiers and their brother slaves pour out into the light, healed, redeemed. Simultaneously, Nebewohl's kingdom is destroyed, and the earth he polluted, cleansed.

If storytelling, the simple narration of fictive events, can plant an image that bears redemption within it, what of theatre? Staged and spoken images must also create the possibility of new life for those who attend, who listen and watch. John's strategy suggests how the dramatist might conceive himself a thaumaturgist or maker of miracles and how he might deploy techniques to effect wonders.

The character John also describes a specific aspect of Rudkin's dramatic technique that deliberately relies on the spectator's active, imaginative, participation. When Gower is punished for his defection from the cavern kingdom, the spectators are told of the violence, not shown. The figure representing Gower relates the story of his evisceration. He speaks in Gower's persona, but we do not see the torture re-enacted. We see instead a series of signs or indicators: (1) the *'charnel, smoking still'*; (2) Nebewohl's surrogate, the fog king, enfeebled by torturing Gower; and (3) Gower himself, transformed through torture and appearing *'white, golden-headed, pure, the primal essence'* (p. 57). The character John again suggests the playwright Rudkin's technique: 'I cannot tell you the terror that he felt; but you can make it in your heads, the terror that he felt' (p. 69). In other words, at a certain point, if the playwright is to succeed, he or she must stop showing, must stop telling, must let the image take hold, let it beat within our heads so that we the subjects, the spectator/auditors, can take over the creative work and through that process be changed.

Nothing I have said so far will come as a surprise to those familiar with Rudkin's comments about his own psychological crisis and healing. According to the *Plays and Players* article cited above, the therapeutic process he underwent involved 'an address, physical, often brutal, to nervous and psychological and sexual difficulties by means of manipulating muscular and fibrous tensions away'. He writes of his therapist, Ollendorff, as a kind of religious interrogator/healer: Ollendorff had a 'Rabbi-like technique of having the patient somehow dredge up himself from his own insights the necessary responses to his own problems.' Rudkin writes:

> [H]is honesty and simplicity were quite frightening: only now did I begin to understand . . . the impression the Christ of the Gospels made on such people as . . . the Woman at the Well. I also understood how a Christ, or an Ollendorff, could be politically very 'dangerous' in the very best sense: because of his insistence that every man should take upon himself the full moral responsibility for his own salvation and greater destiny. This [assumption of responsibility by individuals for their own salvation and destiny] is something that political systems have to take *from* people in order to survive as systems; and not, for all their mythic pretensions otherwise, bequeath to people. (p. 25)

The passage quoted contains several ideas that are helpful for interpreting Rudkin's playtexts. Note the following: his assumption that individual moral activity presents a political threat; his suspicion of political systems and of mythologies promoted by the state; his respect for a therapeutic technique that stimulates individuals to generate the responses that heal; his recognition of the effectiveness of a kind of brutal, physical address that 'manipulates muscular and fibrous tensions away'; his model of the rabbi who induces the subject to dredge up painful and healing insights; and fundamentally, his respect for the human being and the salvation within.

These comments in Rudkin's own voice and the views filtered through John, the son of light, combine to suggest that *Ashes* is a political play of the most radical sort. Spectators are to be stimulated to begin a process of dredging up insights that will allow them to create their own salvation and destiny. And that process – if allowed to go on with any regularity – would indeed shake the foundations of current political systems.

The play is about a couple, Anne and Colin, and their desire to become parents. First they struggle to conceive a child of their own; then, when that child miscarries, they attempt to adopt. That option refused them, they are left to construct a new image of their life together that does not involve parenting.

The play opens in darkness. Over loudspeakers we hear a man's post-coital rhythmic breathing, and the following exchange:

C. Ow No – do you have to do that now?
A. When else do I get? Never still enough.
C. Gouging.
A. Not gouging.
C. Each twinge runs to the knackers like some Turkish torture.
A. Poor knackers . . .
C. Leave over!

Anne, it seems, is removing a blackhead from some unspecified part of Colin's anatomy. He, not unnaturally, is protesting.

C. I never had blackheads till you started purging them.
A. Not true. None of your other bedmates bothered, you mean. Whatever sex they were.
C. They: weren't cannibals.

The mood changes slightly, as they prepare to move apart.

A. Getting heavy love.
C. Sorry.
A. Mop up now.
C. Ay. Load delivered, back to yard, cold half of bed.

And finally we get an inkling of what the play is about:

A. Perhaps we did it this time. (pp. 9–10)[3]

The stage lights 'snap up' and we see Anne 'supine, head toward us, bare legs raised in a coital posture'. The doctor 'palps her lower belly to feel that everything is in its proper place'. They matter-of-factly discuss the fact that Anne and Colin have 'been trying for conception' for two years, and the doctor requests a post-coital sample (pp. 10–11). Blackout . . . alarm clock . . . Anne and Colin set about the necessary business. Anne, whom we see in silhouette, raises her legs again; there is a quick switch back to the doctor's office; he seems to take a sample, prepares a slide, and discovers all Colin's sperm dead. Now it is Colin's turn. Specialists, tests, treatments – again we see and hear all the details: science applied to intercourse; intercourse reduced to propagation mechanics. At last Anne conceives; a new phase begins.

What does this play have to do with the subject of thaumaturgic stage violence? To begin with, as is evident from the dialogue quoted, this is not a sentimental look at a romantic young couple. In addition, it is not enjoyable to sit in the audience watching Anne and Colin go through a series of ludicrously dehumanizing actions. Rudkin describes the effect he desires:

> As to the indignities to which COLIN and ANNE submit themselves, they must not make light of them, nor ever clown them; but rather bring us into a wry factual sharing of them. We might here or there be tempted into a tasteless or ignorant laugh: if so, the character must by stillness deliver any necessary rebuke. (p. 7)

The couple's efforts to conceive are painful, humiliating, human. We come indeed to share in their indignities and their dilemma. We are balanced on the edge of revulsion and recognition, and the discomfort generated is considerable. Friends of mine have barely been able to sit through performances, and my students report not being able to eat while reading the play. One and all, they are profoundly affected by it. Rudkin has structured an experience that involves undergoing an agony roughly analogous to the 'brutal, physical address that "manipulates muscular and fibrous tensions away" '. We have to decide whether to stay or go; whether to 'attend to' the characters, or not. We are active and engaged as spectators, hence ready to wrestle with meanings.

I hasten to add that Rudkin's theatre is neither destructive nor coercive. But he does not romanticize. He returns always to the material facts of copulation and conception – our mortal, corporeal, condition. The experience is painful. Sometimes.

As the play goes on, Rudkin presents specific images, verbal and visual, that force viewers to penetrate his meaning and dredge up from their own insights an appropriate response. Those images that are most telling have violence as their primary content, a fact that ceases to surprise once we realize that this play is not about birth and parenting as thought, but about their obverse: death, destruction, and violation. And it may be, haltingly, about a world to come.

I interrupted the story at the point where Anne finally had achieved pregnancy. In the second section of the play, she struggles to carry the child full term. It miscarries; she undergoes a hysterectomy; Anne and Colin will have no children of their own bodies.

The overriding image for this section is of Anne bedridden, haemorrhaging, monitoring the blood for signs she can interpret, as she wills the embryo to stay within her body. She is martyred by this pregnancy, and the stigma is revealed in a moment of jarring intensity. Colin has brought Anne a three-minute egg, which she

> Beheads . . . with [a] knife. Suddenly a most convulsive recoil – she hurls herself from bed, reels down – with a shock we see her nightdress stained where she bleeds. Crouches shuddering, utterly upturned. C O L I N re-enters; sees her gone; looks into egg. Utters almost inaudible choke of abomination; covers egg with first thing to hand; stands, bottling nausea, shock.

Anne speaks aloud, 'What am I trying to save? Some monster to be born, they'll take one look at – . . . Or a Mozart, Darwin?' (p. 39). This is the moment that caused my students to stop eating. No actual physical violence occurs: Anne moves convulsively, but no one touches her. She is alone. Colin certainly has not meant to hurt her; he has been waiting on her hand and foot. Yet all the violence that the play is about is implicit in this moment. It is an important example of the kind of image that beats within the spectators' minds, until, when Rudkin issues the call, they finally see what the playwright has been leading toward: the connections he means them to draw between private anguish and radical politic.

The call comes in the last section of the play, when the image of the egg recurs twice. Each time it is embedded in a long monologue, which, like Gower's in *The Sons of Light*, describes a scene of terrifying destruction. In the first, Colin is telling Anne about the trip he has just taken to Belfast for his Uncle Tommy's funeral. He paints a vivid picture of the terrorist bombing in which his uncle died and of the family gathered to bury him. Among the family members is Lily Martin; Colin describes their encounter as follows:

> I clapped eyes on – that trunk of her, no legs, no arms; the head as bald as an egg, half the features blown away. The breath was dashed out of me, I had no breath left to – hide my horror. (p. 59)

Lily is the survivor of another terrorist bomb. We see not her, but her terrible deformity, transmitted by means of Colin's recollected response. The scene Colin now conjures triggers in the spectator an imaginative response that overlays and is modified by the remembered image of Anne's convulsive recoil at the abomination in the egg.

It is at this moment that the various elements Rudkin has prepared begin to coalesce into a recognizable pattern. Anne connected the chick embryo with her own child unborn, the feared monster. Colin now transposes the image from the nursery into the adult world of sectarian violence. In the process, the most important link of the play is forged: that between inherited values and beliefs, and the atrocities humans perpetrate on nature and on one another.

Lily's deformity is the consequence of a terrorist bomb. That bomb was laid by what Colin terms 'an undertribe', the Catholic Irish, against the dominant tribe, the Protestants, who have occupied Northern Ireland for generations. The violence, Colin says, has revealed to him the suffering caused by the occupation. He is himself one of the Protestants and he and all his tribe must relinquish their hold on Ireland. They must recognize also that their commitment to remain oppresses them as well. The twofold 'tyranny of our ... *inheritance*' (p. 60) must be overthrown.

For this opinion, his Cousin Sammy excluded Colin from the company of menfolk that carries Tommy's coffin to the grave. Sammy insists: 'We here [in Ireland] have to fight. To save the land we love' (p. 59). To affirm this belief, Sammy will marry Lily Martin. He was pledged to her before her wounding; he now will not fail in his obligation. Their union represents the continuation of that tyranny Colin has identified. Lily embodies the atrocity created by tribal warfare; Sammy, the willed enforcement of beliefs in rights, privileges, and national heritage. The outcome of their alliance is inevitable, if we draw the parallel Rudkin indicates between private and public spheres. As Colin knows, his insistence on fathering a child, despite the evidence that his and Anne's chemistries were incompatible, cost his wife her womb: 'If I had been content', he says, 'my wife would have her womb this day' (p. 54). Just so, enforcing Britain's heritage will lay waste, de-fructify, Ireland. Anne's body haemorrhaging, blood staining her night dress, now can be seen to emblematize the warring tribes' struggle to inhabit one mother, their common homeland.

The second of the monologues that end the play requires of the spectator still more attention and imaginative work. The idea of Ireland made barren through tribal warfare shifts to a generalized vision of an earth blasted by man squandering his inheritance. In a densely imagistic passage, Anne tells of a dream she has had:

> A child came. No child that I would call a child. A child of ice, moving without seeming to move, crossing the black flat of the marsh beneath the red sky. He-she-it, featureless, white, its head in a dome like a child from space. I was so frightened, so weak I could not lift myself at all; I felt I was going out, like water down a drain: into extinction. (*Thinks, does not say: 'But no.' New tone of coming resurrection:*) I woke. A voice overlapped from the dream: the child's and mine: the same. 'Take *off* your dead.' (p. 63)

Here again is the likeness of an egg: 'He-she-it, featureless, white, its head in a dome, like a child from space.' But now that egg, symbol of life and fertility, no longer stinks of abomination. It adorns the long-awaited child, the child miraculously born of the imagination of this woman without a womb, the child who joins its creator mother in proclaiming the way of life to come: Take off your dead, the inherited beliefs that enslave and destroy, and freedom will be yours.

The process of casting off our dead, of stripping away the 'selves' that dictate expectations and behaviors, attacks the mortar that binds political alliances, institutions, and policies. It involves psychic violence and violation. The stage picture that completes the play *Ashes* figures the result. Anne is seated on the 'rostrum' that has served as marriage bed, doctor's couch, and ambulance interior; Colin leans beside her, pretending to read a newspaper. He has just given her the County's letter rejecting their petition to adopt a child.

> *It is pitiful, but they are released. Their hopes for parenthood lie in ashes, but on some other road must lie whatever is for them. After a moment she turns herself, without standing, toward Colin; with right hand she quite strongly seizes his hair, forcefully raises his face to her own. On his face suddenly the beginning of a strange light.* (p. 64)

In terms drawn from *The Sons of Light*, Anne and Colin have been 'stretched on the torturer's last' (p. 31). From the ashes, they are reborn, severed from their heritage, with no blueprint for the future, but radiantly face-to-face.

And what of the spectator – the object of the playwright's 'thaumaturgical pride'? Through a complex process of revulsion, recognition, and ultimately identification, we have undergone an experience analogous to that depicted by the actors. Moreover, we have wrestled with meanings, and created our own from the series of images the playtext presents. Rudkin gives us pieces; we make up the whole. In so doing, we effectively escape from Nebewohl's kingdom. For Nebewohl, like other technologues of tyranny, employs actual physical violence to eradicate his victims' power to imagine: 'Our monitoring', he says, 'reveals no trace of dream-activity. It would seem the old image-factory is quite empty: even of schema' (p. 37). Rudkin counters the forces of darkness by structuring an ordeal through which we will at least glimpse salvation. 'Powerful and ruthless', he brings 'A picture', a playtext, an 'image, like a dream, to trouble' us: 'to beat its wings within [our] heads, within each head, to trouble [us] so [we] will wake and draw our [sisters and brothers] with us, up . . . into the light of the Sun.' So that we leave the theatre taking with us healing images of life and freedom.

NOTES

1 David Rudkin, 'Seeing the Light', *Plays and Players*, May 1976, pp. 24–6, p. 24.
2 David Rudkin, *The Sons of Light* (London: Eyre Methuen, 1981).
3 David Rudkin, *Ashes* (New York: Samuel French, 1974).

Violation and implication: *One for the Road* and *Ficky Stingers**

DAVID IAN RABEY

The observations in this article arise from the experiences of playing Nicolas in a rehearsed reading of Harold Pinter's *One for the Road* and Tel (The Man) in a production of Eve Lewis's *Ficky Stingers* within a space of four months. Both characters act out their power fantasies through the rape – or perhaps in Nicolas's case, the licensing of a rape – of a female character. Both plays aim to shock and disturb their audiences through depicting an almost casual and apparently irresistible perpetration of criminal injustice, to which the audience are ostensibly the sole, mute witnesses. But their management of theatrical dynamics, and audience sympathy, in terms of energy and effect, make for a mutually enlightening contrast.

Pinter states in the Introductory Interview, in the 1985 Methuen illustrated edition of the play, that 'The facts that *One for the Road* refers to are facts I wish the audience to know about, to recognize.' His exploration and investigation centre on the premise 'Given a certain state of affairs, what would the attitude of the interrogator to his victims be? ... I wasn't thinking then of my audience. Having started on the play, letting the images and the action develop, I did go the whole way, to the hilt, as far as I could. The end result being that the play is pretty remorseless' (pp. 14–15). He adds, 'It is also, however, true that many of the natural sadistic qualities which we all possess, are given free rein in the play. The audience felt fear – but what was it fear of? Fear not only of being in the position of the given victim, but a fear also born of recognition of themselves as interrogator. Because think of the joy of having absolute power' (p. 17). He also records audience reaction: 'When the play was done in New York, as the second part of a triple-bill, a goodly percentage of people left the theatre when it was over. They were asked why they were going and invariably they said, "We know all about this. We don't need to be told." Now, I believe they were lying. They did not know about it and did not want to know' (p. 18).

* A draft of this paper was read at the *Themes in Drama* International Conference held at the University of London, Queen Mary and Westfield College, in March 1989.

One for the Road dramatizes the ethical certainty and relish of tactical play enjoyed by government representative and interrogator, Nicolas, over the three family members he holds in captivity. Pinter: 'He has all the power within those walls. He knows this is the case, he believes that it is right, for him, to possess this power, because, as far as he's concerned, he's acting for his country legitimately and properly' (p. 16). Within the framework of the play, Nicolas's energetic initiative is incontrovertible – he is the controlling figure, analogous to stage manager or dramatist, even more completely than the Duke in *Measure for Measure* or Prospero in *The Tempest*, who remain vulnerable to surprise. Nicolas's first interview with Victor establishes the interrogator's idiosyncratic blend of ostensible courtesy thinly veiling coarse taunts and threats, alongside his complete control of the situation. Like Victor, the audience pieces together the enormity and implications of this situation by way of exposition; their viewpoint is the shared perspective of hypnotized victims held in the gaze of an unpredictable predator who talks the reality of circumstances into existence as if, as he claims for himself, 'God speaks through me.'

The second scene is, in certain ways, dramatically analogous to *Macbeth* IV.2, in which the defiant son of Macduff is murdered by Macbeth's hirelings. Preceding events have given the audience an awareness – albeit tantalizingly, horrifyingly imperfect – of the oppressor's capabilities; the child is doubly pitiful, in his youthful innocence (allied with the sense that the father's 'treacheries' are to be visited upon him) and in his specific innocence as to the dangers of the situation, to which he is giving additional provocation by his laudably spirited but excruciatingly impractical non-co-operation. Whilst the audience fears for the child, its awareness of the world of the play corresponds with the superior vantage point of the oppressors, to the extent that they may even fearfully imagine the fatal treatment that the child may receive. The on-stage occurrence of Young Macduff's murder confirms our sense of his murderers' baseness but resolves the tension of the scene, as they prove only capable of realizing our worst imaginings (though imaginative stagings of the action have featured its performance under a shockingly playful guise, for example bouncing the child on a murderer's knee, with a dagger only visible when he falls). Nicolas prises open the terms of Nicky's vulnerability with the question why 'do you like your mummy and daddy?' – implicitly highlighting Nicky's dependence on Victor and Gila as the audience struggle to formulate the poignantly basic reasons why any child 'likes' its parents. Nicky claims not to like 'those soldiers' he spat at and kicked on his parents' arrest. Nicolas firmly identifies them to Nicky as 'your country's soldiers' and counters 'They don't like you either, my darling', his arch show of benevolence suggesting that the forced courtesy of his office is the sole fragile bastion between the child and the wrath of the amassed national military force. But the circuit of threat is unclosed, unlike the scene in *Macbeth*: Nicolas and the forces he represents decline to reveal their planned impositions of events.

Nicolas's interrogation of Gila contains the most harrowingly overt displays of callousness, and the brutality of the scene paradoxically relies upon Nicolas being less superior than hitherto: rather, in identifying himself as a virtual 'son' of Gila's father and losing control of his temper in abusing her, he builds up a sense of personal equivalence and, hence, personal offence. He is also a more direct personal threat to Gila on the level of gender: he is a potential sexual attacker who appears to find her answers and her existence increasingly provocative. His deliberately blunt reminder of her vulnerability, 'How many times have you been raped?', licenses scorn when she in unsure, 'And you consider yourself a reliable witness?' This is the climactic moment of his destructive onslaught on Gila's sense of self; his characteristic note of prurient sexual nausea (previously evident in his withering reflection on her probable menstruation, 'Women do that') returns to dismiss her as a damaged object: 'You're a lovely woman. Well, you were.' This statement compounds senses of both desirability and desecration, Nicolas's former sexual interest and his current mocking rejection: compare Chiron and Demetrius' rape and mutilation of Lavinia in *Titus Andronicus*, after which the victim, former emblematic beauty, is mocked and shunned as a sub-human 'thing' or 'object'. This might constitute a relief from possible misery, at first impression; then, Nicolas's comments about the matter of Gila's son now being 'academic' (i.e. irrelevant), and his line 'But I should think you might entertain us all a little more before you go' opens up a yawning pit of horrific possibility once more. The threat is rendered immediate in Nicolas's gloating use of the words 'us all' – he no longer dissociates himself from the soldiers as he did with Nicky.

Nicolas returns to his former airy *bonhomie* for his final interview with Victor, and the dramatic tension is located between this superficial cheer and the dawning sense of Victor's mutilation – probably the loss of his tongue – and Nicky's murder. Again, Nicolas can beg horrific questions through his studied casualness: when Victor affirms to the banter-question, has he been surviving, Nicolas jabs in 'Really? How?'. Again, he purports to find his victims' plights somehow unimaginable: he displays the oppressor's terrifying, wilful lack of imagination, the liberation into cruelty by deliberate self-blinding and robotic self-brutalization.

As Pinter claims, *One for the Road* fulfils a documentary purpose in that it forces an audience to recognize facts of challenging brutality and moral enormity which, despite pronouncements to the contrary, they are unlikely to have confronted so insistently or pursued imaginatively and politically, in terms of international analogue practices and alliances.

Nicolas acts as the audience's guide through a world of his making. The actor playing Nicolas is likely to find the first scene, the initial interview with Victor, the hardest work, in that he is required to set the pace, establish character and information, with a necessary lack of practical support. The pointed status-inequality of Nicolas's interview with Nicky outrages the audience and involves them emotionally, almost tangibly, and the actor playing Nicolas will feel he can 'play off' something not solely of his own making – namely, the audience's reactions to Nicky's conduct given the power context established by the first scene. After this unequal dialogue, the Nicolas–Gila scene is frighteningly compulsive in Nicolas's alternation between playing high-status and performing personally invested vengefulness, as he plays injured brother/lover/voyeur out of an exaggerated sense of personal hurt and disgust which only intermittently conceals sexual excitement. The last scene forms a gruellingly slow tempo coda to leave Victor and the audience pondering the implications of Nicolas's words, but without providing frameworks of response: for example, the sense of injury to Victor and Gila is not explored as tragedy, as is Lear's loss of Cordelia, nor do we see them released into hate as are the interrogatees of Martin Lynch's *The Interrogation of Ambrose Fogarty* (1982) and Ron Hutchinson's *Rat in the Skull* (1984). The cast members of *One for the Road* have to play, with as much vulnerability as they dare, in support of the actor playing Nicolas, meeting and feeding his energies: he in turn has to develop a sense of play with on- and off-stage audiences, zeroing in to plant seeds of impressions, building a sense of cumulative suggestiveness where, by the end of the play, the exercise of imagination is tantamount to anticipating horror, and yet always challenged, from a different direction, by a new partial disclosure. Pinter acknowledges that the audience may confront in themselves a shocking capacity for manipulative power, as the actor playing Nicolas is obliged to do; but more likely, their dominant viewpoint will be that of Victor and Gila, their dominant impression one of outrage, vulnerability and impotence before the irresistible power of the human vivisectionist Nicolas, who is the principal imaginative and dramatic agent/force of the play. I take this to be the sense of Pinter's comment 'I wasn't thinking then of my audience', in writing the play: the investment of imaginative and dramatic energy observes the structural and situational patterns decreed by Nicolas from beginning to end, with no check to, nor conflict with, his control. The interaction of the drama is, rather, between Nicolas's actions and the audience's capacities for disbelief or dissociation. But Pinter 'stacks the deck', with all his power, in Nicolas's favour, and the interrogator plays out his tricks right up to the flourish of the final trump line. The play *One for the Road* is, I contend, inevitably something of a celebration of his power as its most skilful player, even its inventor – as are the first half of Shakespeare's *Richard III* and the eventual through-line of Brenton and Hare's *Pravda*, despite their musterings of nominal opposition. There is no suggestion in *One for the Road* that anyone can defeat, significantly resist, or know more than Nicolas: the play demonstrates, in its appalling simplicity, the extent of his power. It is a chastening experience, implicitly challenging any sense we may have of being able to withstand the imposed pressure of any authoritarian political regime we might offend, however strong or liberal we might consider ourselves.

Eve Lewis's play *Ficky Stingers* (staged 1986, published in *Plays by Women Volume 6*, ed. Mary Remnant, Methuen 1987) is another study in victimization, involving rape. Its protagonist, called simply Woman, narrates and enacts, with the choric support of Woman 1 and Woman 2, the events preceding and succeeding her rape by the Man, named Terry/Tel. Woman 1 and Woman 2 act as the Woman's playful peers, her incomprehending family, unreliable bitchy friends and general female social context as well as speaking her thoughts in her voice during the rape and traumatized aftermath, creating the dramatic sense of a fractured consciousness and splintered self. Lewis stipulates in her play notes that this is 'not a play about Terry': the play in performance is, rather, an exploration of the woman's injured consciousness via internal monologue and of the lack of any support or sympathy around her. The play concludes with Tel's joke, involving a drunken dragon vomiting over a hapless little dog: its ostensible humour centres on the dragon's misunderstanding of, even obliviousness to, the dog's suffering, mistaking it for an object of his thoughtless devouring. Woman 1 and Woman 2 join in with Tel's own laughter at his joke, excluding the Woman, who '*sits, lights a cigarette and smokes it*' whilst the other characters' laughter and movements become larger and more distorted.

Like *One for the Road*, *Ficky Stingers* is a bleak play which offers no images of the victim gaining relief or revenge over her victimizer. But even as *Ficky Stingers* essentially depicts the isolation and trauma of the rape victim, it contains fragile seams of sensing alternative possibilities. The Woman is shown assimilating the shock and implications of her violation, however falteringly and painfully, in her 'confessional' narrative to the audience, and the audience provide an appreciation of her viewpoint when she is both together with and apart from Tel; there is a muted but poignant image of female supportiveness when Woman 1 and Woman 2 embrace the Woman, wash and comfort her and try to send her to sleep, after she has broken down in tears at her own question after the rape, 'What do you do?'; and, even as the Woman fails to repel Tel's approach in the final pub scene, there is a knowledge gleaned, if not acted upon, and shared in her address to her fellow women in the audience: 'I sit back down. Like I always do. Like we always do. Sit. Sit and take it. Sit back down.' This startling bonding of character and female audience members implies the character's breakthrough to a sense of *communal* injury, not at all lessened by habituation; and calls on women witnesses to show solidarity with the character in her misery by accommodating significantly less of the pointed harassment of which the rape is posited as the logical extension. This builds towards the sense that character and audience have learned, and will be better prepared next time against Tel-like behaviour of whatever shade or degree.

In playing Tel, I discovered two principal things: firstly, not to make him visibly demonic from the outset, as rapists rarely are – rather, he was shown initially as recognizably laddish, larky, even amiable; secondly, that, in contrast to my experience of playing Nicolas, the performance was in no way a theatrical celebration of Tel's energies and could not be played or construed as such – the audience are bonded firmly in sympathies with the Woman and against Tel. This by no means involved playing Tel in a spirit of irony or criticism, rather the performance involved depicting Tel as vehemently as possible (based on the character's possible senses of sexual revenge and loss of masculine identity after redundancy). Also, whilst Tel is an impulsive, boorish small-time thief compared to the systematic sadist and murderer Nicolas, Tel's criminality felt morally worse to performers and audiences in post-production comparative discussion. This is in line with Pinter's professed interest in exploring 'the attitude of the interrogator to his victims' involving what he views as 'the natural sadistic qualities, which we all possess', whereas Lewis says in her Afterword that her play is not about Terry, 'The events all take place within the narrative of the Woman and Terry is given no real justification for his behaviour. To make him the focus would distort the whole purpose of the piece.'

Whilst both *One for the Road* and *Ficky Stingers* are written, I believe successfully, as rebuffs to our tendencies to distance ourselves from the suffering of others, they leave audience sympathies in different configurations after their principal shocks. *One for the Road* steadily steps up pressure on interrogated characters and audience witnesses alike, challenging them to cope with each revelation of cruelty, and presents no image of a world beyond the room presided over by Nicolas, no imaginative space or narrative time for the assimilation of his actions or any non-passive reaction to them. *Ficky Stingers* follows its protagonist, the Woman, through a variety of settings, attempting to resolve her emotional reaction to violation, and depicts her final conscious impatience with herself and her sex for their passive reactions. But impatience can involve the anticipation of identity. *Ficky Stingers* thus invites its audience to discover what Augusto Boal in *Theatre of the Oppressed* (1979) terms a 'precondition for action' – action in this case involving the resisting of the Man. *One for the Road* invites its audience to admire the artistry of Nicolas or to share the sense of pathetic, vulnerable littleness experienced by his victims: it is a formally coercive play, though Pinter regards its message as anti-coercive, and the dramatic experience it offers is either that of authorized sadism or of fearful impotence in the face of violation. *Ficky Stingers* paves the way for its women witnesses to free themselves from the condition of spectator and to take on the status of actor, to cease to be an object and to become a subject, to change from witness to protagonist, Boal's objectives of dramatic analysis. Victor and Gila in *One for the Road* face a dilemma which in fact now confronts the eponymous hero of David Edgar's play *The Jail Diary of Albie Sachs* (1978) who was recently maimed by a car bomb: accorded sympathy whilst his outrageous injury is still newsworthy, he is faced with the problem of rebuilding his life beyond this brief highlighting of his plight. *Ficky Stingers* goes further than *One for the Road*'s brief, chill illumination of injury and presents its audiences – victims and potential victims alike – with a rehearsal for revolution.

Acknowledgement: Thanks to my fellow cast and team members in our performances of the plays cited: Stella Blackburn, Emma Ferguson, Ashley Wallington, Nikole G. Bamford, Gill Entwistle, Catherine McQuade, and Maryjane Stevens.

The mask as sign of violence in contemporary Latin American theatre*

SEVERINO JOÃO ALBUQUERQUE

In a well-known article on theatre semiotics, Tadeusz Kowzan examines the mask along with the make-up because, from the material viewpoint the two signs seem to be deprived of mobility.[1] Kowzan submits that if a gradation from sign mobility to immobility is to be attempted, facial expression is placed at one end as the most mobile, and mask at the other end as the most immobile of signs, with make-up somewhere in the middle. This paper examines the diverse ways Latin American playwrights have used masks for the purpose of conveying violence and seeks to show that in the plays of the period the mask sign is endowed with more mobility than Kowzan would allow.

In the Latin American theatre of the sixties and seventies, the vast majority of uses of masks for the expression of violence appear in works which include sessions of physical torture with hooded men at work. In violation of Article Five of the Universal Declaration of Human Rights ('No one shall be subjected to torture or to cruel, inhuman or degrading treatment or punishment'), the use of torture figures among the forms of harassment repressive governments have inflicted on the people of Latin America. As Amnesty International and other organizations have abundantly documented, there have been cases of torture in every Latin American country in the period under consideration.

With the severe curtailment of the freedom of the press, the theatre had a unique contribution to make, and not just because many of its own people were at the forefront of the resistance. In spite of the arrests and torture experienced by Augusto Boal and others, Latin American playwrights seized the political moment and countered the victimization with an art form that was often as urgent as the confrontations on the streets. Drawing from Brecht, Artaud, the Theatre of the Absurd, and freely adapting to their needs other imported trends such as documentary theatre, Grotowsky's poor theatre, theatre as game, as ritual, and as role-playing, a number of playwrights in search of a language found in violence

* A draft of this paper was read at the *Themes in Drama* International Conference held at the University of California, Riverside, in February 1989.

both a pertinent theme and a mode of expression remarkably suited to the artistic manifestation of their often intense commitment to socio-political change.

Aware that 'el teatro no necesita confirmar la existencia de la tortura sino entenderla ('theatre does not need to confirm the existence of torture but rather to understand it'),[2] playwrights of the period have resorted to the eloquence of the theatre in order to express their repugnance of such practices. The appropriateness of the theatrical medium is ascertained as one considers the similarities between the stage and a torture chamber. In her brilliant book on torture and war, Elaine Scarry states that because it is 'built on ... repeated acts of display and [has] as its purpose the production of a fantastic illusion of power, torture is a grotesque piece of compensatory drama'; thus, it is perfectly understandable that in different parts of the world victimizers refer to the torture chamber as the 'production room' (the Philippines) or the 'blue-lit stage' (Chile).[3]

In the plays which call for the use of hoods in torture sessions, the degradation such scenes evoke is intensified by the fact that the audience does not see the faces of the participants. I submit that the conveyance of this feeling of degradation endows the mask with a degree of mobility which Kowzan fails to acknowledge. Indeed, there are other issues than those treated by Kowzan that must be taken into account when one considers the use of the mask as a sign of violence. In addition to the more practical function of hiding the torturer's identity, two important factors should be mentioned in connection with the use of hoods on stage. First, given the deeply-rooted association of the theatre with masks, it is evident that hoods on stage may enhance (and not impede or 'immobilize') the effectiveness of a dramatization of torture. Second, as variations of the foremost elements of ceremony and ritual – masks endowed here with the malignancy of contemporary events – hoods contribute to the ritualistic atmosphere of a ceremony of violence such as a torture session. In such an interpretation, the participants in a torture ritual would be involved in exorcism of an undesired sentiment – dissension – within the community, and the sacrificial act offered by the united, hooded congregation would then propitiate the repressive entity which demanded the ritual. Nevertheless, since the victim stands for all of his kind, torture assumes an additional ritualistic dimension which sanctions the symbolic destruction not only of a group, faction or race but of all of humankind.

The mere appearance of a hooded person in front of a prisoner can elicit intense fear and suggest unbearable pain, especially to those who, like Latin American political activists, are well aware of the atrocities committed in torture chambers in several countries of the region. A theatrically effective presentation of torture will convey such feelings of fear and pain to the spectator, who may then reflect on, and take action against the evils perpetrated by an illegitimate power structure without his or her consent.

It should be noted that in those plays which depict torture sessions, hoods can be worn by either torturers or victims. Hoods worn by torturers have holes for the eyes, and are found in Enrique Buenaventura's *La audiencia* (*The Hearing*),[4] Oduvaldo Vianna Filho's *Papa Highirte*,[5] and Eduardo Pavlovsky's *El Señor Galíndez*,[6] while hoods worn by victims (naturally without holes, to prevent later identification of the torturer) are seen in João Ribeiro Chaves Neto's *Patética* (*The Pathétique*),[7] Alfredo Dias Gomes's *Campeões do mundo* (*World Champions*),[8] and Mario Benedetti's *Pedro y el capitán* (*Pedro and the Captain*).[9] It is noteworthy that one play of the period, César Vieira's *Morte aos brancos* (*Death to Whites*),[10] requires the audience as well as the victims of torture to wear masks. The lengthy directions in the beginning of the text specify that a hood is to be attached to the back of each chair in the area where the spectators are going to be seated (p. 20). In scene 12, the actors who play the roles of torturers leave the stage and move among the spectators putting the hoods on them (p. 116). Audience empathy with the victims is thus facilitated. Moreover, since there isn't time for the cast to interact with everyone in the audience, most spectators have to put on the hoods themselves, thus highlighting the collaborative aspect of some forms of victimization.

With the sole exception of *Papa Highirte*, which calls for Mariz's tormentors to wear '*caixa de papelão na cabeça, com dois furos para os olhos*' (p. 20) ('a carton on the head, with two holes for the eyes'), stage directions in these plays make no definite specifications concerning shape, material or color of masks: the playwrights kept their indications about masks deliberately succinct to allow the stage director more latitude in staging the play.

Drawing on examples from important Latin American plays of the period under consideration, I will next address several issues pertinent to the use of the mask as a sign of violence. Although only two of the seven men in Buenaventura's *La audiencia* are directly involved in torture, the other five individuals also wear hoods to show that they condone the practice. However, while those five men eventually remove their hoods, the two torturers keep theirs on for the entirety of the play. In fact, they constitute a rare example of torturers who wear masks for the duration of a stage performance. Playwrights understandably avoid such presentation of the torturer since the spectator may be unable to relate fully to characters who have been thus deprived of an identity. Still, it is noteworthy that in *Milagre na cela* (*Miracle in a Prison Cell*)[11] and *Un despido corriente* (*A Regular Lay-Off*)[12] – plays whose impact depends to a large degree on the theatrical effectiveness of the torture sessions represented – Jorge Andrade and Julio Mauricio have absolutely refrained from including masks in their works: this emphasizes the audacity and impunity of its practitioners, and the casual attitude to torture adopted by repressive establishments.

In contemporary Latin American theatre, the mask as a sign of violence also occurs in plays which, while political in nature, are not primarily concerned with the practice of torture. A masterful use of the mask as a sign of violence is made in the collective work *El asesinato de X* (*The Assassination of X*) in a scene meant to illustrate each individual's responsibility for the violence in Latin American society. In scene 9, titled 'El Sistema', when five actors present the 'official version' of the 1968 uprising in Córdoba, Argentina, '*al tiempo que dicen los textos se colocan unas monstruosas máscaras*'[13] ('they put on some monstrous masks as they say their lines'). Following the reading of the 'comunicado oficial', the actors enact the consequences that an individual's political awakening have on the entire system or 'máquina'. Deftly removing and then putting their masks back on, the actors perform the liberation of one member of society and his or her influence on others, and then represent the violent reaction coming from the 'máquina':

> *Uno intenta quitarse la máscara y escapar de la máquina. Lo logra. En ese momento es reintroducido brutalmente. Otro sale y logra quitarse la máscara. La máquina se desparrama por todo el espacio circular, transformándose en seres que caminan como autómatas, menos el que se quitó la máscara, que camina normalmente. Se acerca a una mujer e intenta quitarle a su vez le máscara. Los demás separan a la pareja. El hombre es arrojado y cae. La mujer es obligada a retomar el ritmo mecánico. La máquina vuelve a armarse.* (pp. 47–8)

(One of them attempts to remove his mask and thus escape the machine. He succeeds. At that moment he is brutally forced back inside. Another one goes out and manages to remove his mask. The machine scatters all over the circular area, as it transforms itself into beings that walk as automata. The only one who walks normally is the group member who managed to remove his mask. He approaches a woman and tries to remove her mask. The other members of the group separate the couple. The man is pushed away and falls, while the woman is forced to return to the mechanized movement. The machine is put together anew.)

Although not as blatantly political a play as *El asesinato de X*, Egon Wolff's *Flores de papel* (*Paper Flowers*)[14] also resorts to the use of masks to indicate violent change. Wolff's play documents the upheaval experienced by an individual, Eva, who seems to represent an entire social class, as it succumbs to the demands of the lower classes, which are represented by a mysterious man called simply 'El Merluza' (*The Hake*) who one day follows Eva home, and proceeds to question the woman's certainties and ultimately destroys her comfortable existence. When at the play's end Eva, '*ausente, perdida*' (p. 245) ('absent, lost'), follows 'El Merluza' outside, thus leaving her once orderly, middle-class apartment for the disorder of the victimizer's world, her face is literally hidden behind a grotesque mask, an enormous paper flower, and her identity completely destroyed.

The plays mentioned so far were written (and some of them had brief runs) during military dictatorships. Since the mid-eighties return to civilian rule in most countries of South America's Southern Cone, a number of playwrights have returned to the theme of torture in an attempt to come to terms with the reign of terror that dominated those countries for the better part of two decades. A representative play from this period is Luiz Maria Lima's *A nossa voz* (*Our Voice*), which was written in 1986 and first performed in 1987; the work has yet to appear in print. *A nossa voz* is a representative play of the post-military regime because it denounces the impunity of well-known murderers and torturers who have not been prosecuted and probably will never be brought to justice, thanks to the very generous amnesty legislation which Congress (in Brazil as well as in Argentina and Uruguay) was prevailed on to pass, by a military that remains in the wings, ever watchful of the fledgling democracies.

A nossa voz depicts the efforts of a group of community leaders to honour the memory of an outspoken critic of the dictatorship, the radio personality, Isaura do Amaral, who was killed under torture in a military facility, and whose body has never been found. To commemorate the tenth anniversary of Isaura's death, the activists have erected her statue in the main square of their working-class neighborhood. In a parallel plot, Isaura's well-heeled husband, Raul, and his friend Hipólito, continue their search for the master torturer, known to them only as 'Anjo' (the Angel), who was responsible for Isaura's death. The two plots converge when Raul accidentally discovers that 'Anjo' is no less than the husband of one of the activists, Marta, who one day comes to invite him for the dedication of Isaura's statue. Marta is attracted to the gentle and good-looking Raul as an obvious escape from her brutal and impotent husband, Benjamin. When Marta returns home from a second encounter with Raul, an unusually soft-spoken Benjamin persuades her to confess not only to the affair but also to the fact that Raul knows that Benjamin is Isaura's torturer and murderer.

At this point there is a complete transformation in Benjamin as well as in the settings. 'Anjo' returns to his former, brutal self and goes into an uncontrollable rage while the living-room becomes a veritable torture chamber. He suspends Marta from a parrot's perch and slowly tortures her to death. In addition to the fact that a husband is torturing his wife, what makes this torture scene unique among the plays under consideration is that Benjamin puts on a hood before he begins to victimize Marta. While in other situations the torturer wears a mask to hide his identity from the victim, this is obviously not the case in *A nossa voz*. Benjamin puts on the hood to torture his wife because he cannot function outside the role he learned to play in the barracks. Although he has been retired from the Armed Forces because of 'excessive zeal in carrying out his duties', Benjamin repeatedly vows allegiance to the repressive apparatus that resorted to torture in order to perpetuate its control of the country. His donning of a mask stresses not only his belief in and loyalty to a way of thinking that will stop at nothing to achieve its goals, but also the perpetuation of such state of affairs beyond spatial and temporal confines – spreading terror beyond the walls of the military facilities and the chronological limits of a regime that was officially over when Benjamin tortures and kills Marta.

A nossa voz won the First Prize Award in the 1986 Concurso Nacional de Dramaturgia (National Playwriting Contest) sponsored by Rio de Janeiro's prestigious Casa de Cultura Laura Alvim. In spite of the award and its long run, the play did not enjoy critical acclaim, with virtually every theatre critic pointing out its didacticism and 'panfletarismo' (pamphleteerism). Perhaps as attenuating factors, some theatregoers did recall that the play was authored by a very politically committed individual, and that it reflects the concerns of former as well as potential new victims of terror as the country lives through a difficult transition period marked by uncertainty and instability.

The mask has been an effective sign in the theatrical treatment of social conditions which follow the loss of a community's ability to fight for legitimate power. When torture is involved, regardless of the different approaches selected by contemporary Latin American playwrights to give theatrical configuration to a phenomenon which notoriously resists representation, the mask sign must be a crucial (and mobile) element if the staging of torture sessions is to succeed in denouncing a practice which 'explicitly announces its own nature as an undoing of civilization, [and] acts out the uncertainty of the created contents of consciousness'.[15] The mask has been an important element in the portrayal of torturers and victims in contemporary Latin American theatre. As an element endowed with a certain degree of mobility, the mask sign has facilitated the interplay of verbal and nonverbal expressions of violence. Whether the victims survive their plight or perish as a consequence of the torment, the use of masks during a stage representation constitutes a powerful evocation of the horrors of torture. Physically hurt and psychologically destroyed, each victim succumbs to fury and brutality; driven by the kind of unbridled aggression only illegitimate power can sanction, torturers inflict often unbearable suffering. However, neither victims nor torturers are consistently identified by unequivocal mask signs. Both groups present different degrees of sign mobility which contribute to the impact of the plays in which they occur. From their interaction there evolves a vision of widespread pain, oppression and inhumanity whose powerfulness is attributable to the playwrights' mastery of the theatre's multisignation.[16]

NOTES

1 Tadeusz Kowzan, 'The Sign in the Theatre', trans. Simon Pleasance, *Diogenes*, 61 (1968), 52–80; p. 66.
2 Erminio Neglia, 'El tema de la tortura en el teatro hispánico', *N/S*, 8:16 (1983), pp. 91–102.
3 Elaine Scarry, *The Body in Pain: the making and unmaking of the world* (New York and Oxford: Oxford University Press, 1985), p. 28.
4 Enrique Buenaventura, 'La audiencia', *Teatro* (Havana: Casa de las Américas, 1980), pp. 113–39.
5 Oduvaldo Vianna Filho, *Papa Highirte* (Rio de Janeiro: Serviço Nacional de Teatro, 1968).
6 Eduardo Pavlovsky, *El Señor Galíndez* (Buenos Aires: Editorial Proteo, 1976).
7 João Ribeiro Chaves Neto, *Patética* (Rio de Janeiro: Editora Civilização Brasileira, 1978).
8 Alfredo Dias Gomes, *Campeões do mundo* (Rio de Janeiro: Editora Civilização Brasileira, 1980).
9 Mario Benedetti, *Pedro y el capitán* (Mexico City: Editorial Nueva Imagen, 1979).
10 César Vieira, *Morte aos brancos: a lenda de Sepé Tiaraju* (Porto Alegre: Tchê, 1987).
11 Jorge Andrade, *Milagre na cela* (Rio de Janeiro: Editora Paz e Terra, 1977).
12 Julio Mauricio, 'Un despido corriente', *Teatro latinoamericano de agitación* (Havana: Casa de Las Américas, 1972), pp. 177–310.
13 Grupo Teatro Libre, 'El asesinato de X', *Teatro latinoamericano de agitación* (Havana: Casa de las Américas, 1972), pp. 13–62; p. 45.
14 Egon Wolff, 'Flores de papel', *Tres obras de teatro* (Havana: Casa de las Américas, 1970), pp. 125–245.
15 Scarry, *The Body in Pain*, p. 38.
16 Passages in this essay appear in Severino João Albuquerque, *Violent Acts: a study of contemporary Latin American theatre* (Detroit: Wayne State University Press, 1990).

'night Mother and True West: mirror images of violence and gender*

RAYNETTE HALVORSEN SMITH

Playwrights Sam Shepard and Marsha Norman have both raised the ire of feminist critics. For example, Jill Dolan, responded in a review of Norman's *'night Mother*, a play which ends with the suicide of its female protagonist, with this criticism:

> If feminist plays are defined as those that show women in the painful, difficult process of becoming full human beings, how can a play in which the suicide is assumed from the first moments be a thorough consideration of women? ... To add to the crimes this play perpetrates in the name of women's theatre, the daughter is killing herself for self-indulgent, easy-way-out reasons that are placed only in a personal, instead of societal, context ... Norman sets up a hopeless, insular situation that doesn't allow other women to generalize from their own lives to the play's situation.[1]

The play was largely dismissed by feminists as reflecting only stereotypical feminine masochism. The suicide of the main character Jessie is viewed as neurotic, personal, and therefore void of any depth in social meaning. The play's characters are criticized as uncompelling, serving as another example of women only 'animated by the absent male'.[2]

Sam Shepard has also been criticized for the stereotyped, macho-violent cowboy characters that dominate his work. He certainly sounds like a firm defender of the patriarchal order when he makes comments such as this one to Robert Coe:

> I [Coe] asked him why he doesn't write more women characters. He [Shepard] said he thinks men are more interesting: the real mystery in American life lies between men, not between men and women.[3]

The purpose of this essay is to demonstrate that while neither playwright lays claim to any feminist orientation (especially not Shepard), use of the exaggerated gender stereotypes and violence for which they have been criticized actually functions to deconstruct these gender myths. In *True West* and *'night Mother* both playwrights approach their characterizations with a wit and sense of irony that critiques their stereotypes,

* A draft of this paper was read at the *Themes in Drama* International Conference held at the University of California, Riverside, in February 1989.

even as they create them. In their frightening and sometimes violent characterizations, they share a fearless pursuit of subconscious imagery. This imagery moves the characters beyond stereotype into archetype. The work of both authors explores the paradoxical nature of gender definition and violence. They portray a 'divided self' that is a result of gender identification and source of violence in the two plays.

Both take place at 'Mom's' or 'Mama's' house. In *True West* Austin is house sitting while 'Mom' is in Alaska. He is caretaker of her plants while working on a script idea for a Hollywood producer. Jessie, from her very first actions in *'night Mother*, also is clearly caretaker of 'Mama's' house. Although she is there ostensibly because she had no place else to go after her divorce, she is clearly the one who brings order to the household. A striking detail in both author's set descriptions is the lack of doors. In the *True West* set description Shepard dictates that there are to be no doors at all. In *'night Mother* there is only one door, center. As Norman describes the door:

> It should be, in fact, the focal point of the entire set, and the lighting should make it disappear completely at times and draw the entire set into it at others ... It is an ordinary door that opens into absolute nothingness.[4]

Both plays open with the image of mother's house that is positively claustrophobic: in one the characters are given no defined exits, in the other only a door to 'nothingness'. This is only the first in a sequence of images where mother is superimposed with smothering. In both plays the authors trap the characters in a way that makes violent attempts at escape inevitable. But one set implies there will be no escape, the other only escape into nothingness.

The setting for *True West* is uncharacteristically realistic for Shepard. Indeed, Shepard comments on this in his notes in the beginning of the script:

> The set should be constructed realistically with no attempt to distort its dimensions, shapes, objects, or colors. No objects should be introduced which might draw special attention to themselves other than the props demanded by the script. If a stylistic 'concept' is grafted onto the set design it will only serve to confuse the evolution of the characters' situation, which is the most important focus of the play.[5]

As in previous Shepard plays, however, the visual imagery is laden with symbols. The realism serves to underscore the banality of these images. With the mental pictures evoked by the play's title, *True West*, juxtaposed against the setting of 'Mom's kitchen', it becomes clear that Shepard perceives the reality of modern Southern California as surreal. But in the subtle visual symbols Shepard describes, the open rugged lands of the old west have not been so much civilized as 'sissified'; tumbleweeds have been replaced by orange trees, cacti by ruffly Boston ferns, grasslands by astroturf.

In *True West* Shepard creates a collage of contrasting images which polarize around gender difference. The artificiality of Mom's kitchen is associated with domestication, domestication with feminization, and feminization with emasculation. In the dialogue he consistently chooses docile images of the encroaching civilization, such as Safeways and color TV sets, over other more virile representations such as towering office buildings or stadiums. Although Mom's house is supposedly in a typical overdeveloped suburban neighborhood, the only sounds from the outside are the crickets and a coyote howling. The 'true west' is outside somewhere, asociated with the wild, the natural, the isolated, the violent, the masculine. Shepard acknowledges this importance he places on the role of violence defining the American male:

> I think there's something about American violence that to me is very touching. In full force, it's very ugly, but there's also something very moving about it because it has to do with humiliation. There's some hidden, deeply rooted thing in the Anglo male American that has to do with inferiority, that has to do with not being a man, and always, continually having to act out some idea of manhood that invariably is violent.[6]

In contrast to Shepard, Marsha Norman sets up a different visual image of opposition in the setting of *'night Mother*; there is only the confining reality of the mother's house, and nothingness. This becomes a metaphor for the dilemma of the main character, Jessie. She can choose only between the world of her mother (femininity and all that represents), or death. In both of these plays, violence is seen as the agent for the transformation out of this domesticity to freedom, autonomy, and individualism.

The plot of *True West* involves the meeting of two brothers, Austin and Lee, in the kitchen of 'Mom's house', in a suburb 40 miles east of Los Angeles. As the play opens, we observe two brothers who are as surreal in their contrasting difference as this suburban house grafted onto the desert. Shepard describes Austin as in 'his early thirties, light blue sports shirt, tan cardigan sweater, clean blue jeans, white tennis shoes'. Lee is described as the antithesis of this yuppie image:

> ... his older brother, early forties, filthy white t-shirt, tattered brown overcoat covered with dust, dark blue baggy suit pants from the salvation army, pink suede belt, pointed black forties dress shoes scuffed up, holes in the soles, no socks, no hat, long pronounced sideburns, 'Gene Vincent' hairdo, two days growth of beard, bad teeth. (p. 2)

Lee has arrived to 'make a little tour' of the neighborhood houses. He collects 'Electric devices. Stuff like that' (p. 7). By the beginning of scene 2 it looks as though he might even rob his own mother's house when he states: 'Made a little tour this morning. She's got locks on everything. Locks and double-locks and chain locks and – What's she got that's so valuable?' (p. 10). The audience is left to ponder that very question; what is Lee looking for in returning to this house?

To contrast with the wild cowboy Lee, Shepard consistently superimposes on Austin images of Mom and femininity. The play opens with Austin displaying a romantic bent in writing by candlelight. Austin speaks to Lee with feminine diffidence and fear, unsuccessfully trying to placate him with offers of coffee, a trip 'up north' to stay with his family, etc. Later in the play he drives Lee to violence by pestering him with maternal offers of toast from the toasters he stole to impress him.

Shepard's stage directions for Austin also contain some subtle feminine images. In the opening of scene 2 Austin is watering the plants with a vaporizer as Lee sits and drinks beer. In his next stage direction he makes coffee. Austin begins scene 5 'at sink washing a few dishes' (p. 28). Even when he decides to break out of his domesticated role and break into people's homes like his brother Lee, he steals toasters (the subliminal image of the housewife ever lurking).

A developng rivalry between the 'ivy-league' Austin and the wild cowboy Lee becomes apparent as Lee 'bullshits' his way into a round of golf with Hollywood producer Saul Kimmer to whom Austin is attempting to sell a script idea. This eventually leads not only to Lee receiving an offer to develop his idea for one of his 'True-life stories' (a 'Western that'd knock your lights out' (p. 18)) but also, to add insult to injury, Kimmer's decision to drop Austin's project, a romance story. Shepard takes another stab at domestication by making 'ivy-league' educated Austin artistically impotent.

Shepard's point, however, is not to valorize Lee. Even as Austin is starting to come apart at the seams over this turn of events, Shepard starts to tip the scales in the other direction. Lee, is 'not a man of the pen'. He needs Austin and his literary skills to write his script so he blackmails him, first by taking the keys to his car, and later by promising to take the completely disillusioned Austin to the desert with him.

By this point in the script Shepard's imagery is clear: the loss of the 'true west' is brought about by the feminization of the frontier; feminine = domesticated = emasculated. In stark opposition to domestication (Mom's kitchen), is the frontier (the desert) which, in this critique by Florence Falk,

> symbolizes those open spaces where law, order, and social restrictions have never invaded and primitive longings for individual power gain prompt release. The 'frontier' also represents conquest, the settling of territories by means of violence, and an alien environment where outlaw cowboys stake out the land and claim their victim before he gets them first . . . It is the domain of

Male Homo Erectus, whose bulging muscles and veins streaked with violence bespeak daring and conceal any trace of vulnerability.[7]

In some ways Lee certainly fits the description, he's just returned from the Mojave where he has spent 'Three months of just passin' through' (p. 12), and where he had a pit bull he used in dog fights. Even though he is a thief stealing television sets, Shepard takes the opportunity for another little jab at domestication when Lee says 'They don't need their televisions! I'm doin' them a service' (p. 22). Nevertheless, as Bonnie Marranca points out,

> The heroism and strength of the cowboy is revered by Shepard but in actuality the men he creates are ineffectual, fearful, and emotionally immature. They show no strength of character or will, yet they are allowed to dominate because it is their due as men.[8]

Although Lee personifies in many ways the violence and wildness of the cowboy, he betrays this romantic image with these comments:

> *Lee.* Hey, do you actually think I chose to live out in the middle a' nowhere? Do ya'? Ya' think it's some kinda' philosophical decision I took or somethin'? I'm livin' out there 'cause I can't make it here! (p. 49).

Shepard carefully balances these two characters, who can be viewed as two halves of a self,[9] because he is not standing as an advocate of either position. He is more interested in the dilemma posed by these character polarities:

> Commenting on *True West* Shepard has said: 'I think we're split in a much more devastating way than psychology can ever reveal. It's not so cute. Not some little thing we can get over. It's something we've got to live with.'[10]

The characterizations of Lee and Austin are examples of Shepard's 'stereotypes' actually functioning as archetypes. This idea of the painfuly split human and its relationship to gender identity can be traced as far back as a story told by Aristophanes in Plato's *Symposium* about the birth of desire:

> in the beginning we were nothing like we are now. For one thing, this race was divided into three . . . besides the two sexes, male and female, which we have at present, there was a third which partook of the nature of both . . .
> . . . each of these beings was globular in shape, with rounded back and sides, four arms and four legs, and two faces . . . And such . . . were their strength and energy, and such their arrogance, that they actually tried to scale the heights of heaven and set upon the gods.
> At this Zeus took counsel with the other gods as to what was to be done . . . At last . . . after racking his brains, Zeus offered a solution.
> I think I can see my way, he said, to put an end to this disturbance . . . What I propose to do is to cut them all in half, thus killing two birds with one stone, for each will only be half as strong, and there'll be twice as many of them . . .

> Now when the work of the bisection was complete it left each half with a desperate yearning for the other, and they ran together and flung their arms around each other's necks, and asked for nothing better than to be rolled into one. So much so that they began to die ... Zeus felt so sorry for them that he devised another scheme. He moved their privates round to the front ... and made them propagate among themselves ... So you see ... how far back we can trace our innate love for one another, and how this love is always trying to reintegrate our former nature, to make two into one, and to bridge the gulf between one human being and another.[11]

By scene 8 of *True West* Mom's house appears thoroughly trashed. The plants are dead and drooping. Bottles and cans litter the floor around the drunken men. The typewriter is wrecked. During the scene, crushed toast is added to the debris. In the violence and passion of Lee and Austin's attempt to collaborate (or integrate), Mom's house has been reduced to the likeness of a desert junk yard.

When Mom finally appears upon the scene, she is an absurd apparition from the sterile, shallow, and meaningless culture from which Austin now feels compelled to flee. The motivating factor in her return is to see Picasso (who she mistakenly believes is alive and in town), and because she missed her plants. This is perhaps Shepard's most brutal blow to the feminine and maternal which he portrays as trivial, empty, and emasculating. Her presence is a reminder to Lee why he dare not allow Austin to return to the desert with him. Yet when he takes Mom's antique china and silverware, it becomes clear that he has not come to Mom's house merely as a thief; perhaps behind his stealing is a genuine hunger for the domesticating influence of the feminine.

Jessie and Austin share a common struggle. In order to be free, to be fully individual, they must shed their suffocating domestication. The task is to exorcise the Mother. Violence becomes the only means to this transformation. For Austin this involves leaving 'civilization' as he knows it: the 'wife and kiddies', his writing, and education. All must be sacrificed if he goes to live the life of a free man in the desert. When he finally has Lee down on the floor with a telephone cord around his neck, in this act of violence we know he has transformed – he is no longer domesticated – he is wild, maybe even more so than Lee.

Lee is frightened. He is the rugged individual. His identity hinges on his opposition to the feminine domestication that Austin represents. Austin represents several threats; that he will domesticate his last frontier, the desert, or that Austin might actually succeed in the desert, beat him at his own game. Lee indeed fears he might actually wind up 'turned inside out'.

In the final moments of the play, we realize they have reached an inevitable impasse:

> They square off to each other, keeping a distance between them. Pause, a single coyote heard in the distance, lights fade slowly to moonlight, the figures

of the brothers now appear to be caught in a vast desert-like landscape, they are very still but watchful for the next move, lights go slowly to black as the after-image of the brothers pulses in the dark, coyote fades. (p. 59)

Paradoxically, the threat of violence that pervades most of this play builds to a climax and then is frozen unresolved.

Both Norman and Shepard portray gender as fixed, immutable, and defined by opposition. Therefore, the attempts to integrate these two opposing facets of personality, as symbolized by the characters Lee and Austin, into a complete human being are thwarted because, being opposites, they neutralize and destroy each other. Paradoxically in *True West*, each character is also portrayed as ineffectual and incomplete without his complementary half. Austin's 'art' is too tame, soulless. Lee does not have the control, the discipline, to capture his 'true stories'.

True West and *'night Mother* are about the cost of autonomy. Both plays are placed in Mother's house which represents the psychic locus of the first struggle for autonomy and the first split in the human psyche. As Shepard demonstrates in *True West*, this split from the Mother (the feminine), leaving her home to become an individual (and masculine) is costly. The brothers are left in an eternal struggle of violently expelling the feminine parts of their personality and leaving Mom's home, only to return and desperately attempt to reclaim these missing parts of themselves.

There are many parallels between Jessie's and Austin's struggle for autonomy, but their gender difference poses very different dilemmas. A female cannot eject the 'Mother', and thus the feminine aspects she represents, without risking loss of her basic gender identity. Therefore, the project of becoming a self is more complicated.

Adding to this complication is the fact that in western culture these two halves, masculine and feminine, are not equal in value. As opposites, the masculine is defined as the positive pole and the feminine as the negative. The feminine gender defined by 'lack' or 'other' is reflected in the basic postulates of psychoanalysis. In 'Some Psychical Consequences of the Anatomical Distinction Between the Sexes', Freud conceptualized female and male gender as both opposite and complementary. Freud's theories polarize around the penis which he refers to as 'large' and 'superior' and what he assumes to be its female opposite, the clitoris, which he labels as 'stunted' and 'inferior'. The argument for this assessment is contained in the same essay:

> There is an interesting contrast between the behavior of the two sexes ... when a little boy first catches sight of a girl's genital region, he begins by showing irresolution and lack of interest; he sees nothing or disavows what he has seen ... It is not until later, when some threat of castration has obtained a hold upon him, that the observation becomes important to him ...

> A little girl behaves differently. She makes her judgement and her decision in a flash. She has seen it and knows that she is without it and wants to have it. (XIX. 252)

Kaja Silverman in *The Subject of Semiotics* elaborates on how, in this same essay, Freud extends this idea of opposition to more general definitions of gender difference:

> Not only does the male subject possess the privileged appendage, but the female subject acknowledges the importance which that possession confers. Thus the value of the penis depends entirely upon the twin assumptions of female lack and envy.
> ... He associates the male subject with aggressivity, voyeurism, and sadism, and the female subject with the antithetical but complementary qualities of passivity, exhibitionism, and masochism.[12]

In this definition masculinity is totally dependent on the subjugation of the feminine. In Freud's model for gender there can be no such thing as feminine violence. The two concepts neutralize each other. Violence is associated with aggression and sadism which are by his definition masculine. According to Freud's Oedipal theory, the male's violent disassociation from the mother to carve out an identity as individual does not occur for the female. Therefore, individuality and independence are the domain of the male.

Both Norman and Shepard use violence to manipulate their characterizations, underlining the unresolvable contradictions inherent in gender defined as opposition. The plot of *'night Mother* is very direct in this use of violence. Jessie announces to her mother that she is going to commit suicide and then effectively blocks her mother's attempts to prevent it. In the dialogue that follows both mother and daughter struggle for some mutual understanding before the inevitable act of suicide occurs. At the end of the play Jessie finally goes through the door to 'nothingness' and shoots herself.

In Marsha Norman's script any melodramatic reasons for Jessie to commit suicide have been carefully neutralized. Everything is wrong with her life, but no one thing is all that unusual or dramatic. Norman gives us no overwhelming reasons why her life should be such a failure, choosing instead to point to a more universal and general malaise. She is very careful to give us nothing for which we can really overtly blame the character. Fault is not the issue. For example, one reason given is epilepsy, something outside of Jessie's control. Norman leaves the reason for the husband's departure opaque. Jessie's son is apparently a disaster, but she refuses to place any blame, 'He's hurt me, I've hurt him. We're about even' (p. 25). Norman is arguing that Jessie's choice is a rational one, and not idiosyncratic. The point is that Jessie, in fulfilling the feminine role, perceives that she has never become an autonomous person.

Jessie. I found an old baby picture of me. And it was somebody else, not me ... That's who I started out and this is who is left. That's what this is about. It's somebody I lost alright, it's my own self. Who I never was. Or who I tried to be and never got there. Somebody I waited for who never came. So see, it doesn't much matter what else happens in the world or in this house, even. I'm what was worth waiting for and I didn't make it ... (p. 76)

So finally Jessie says 'no' to this untenable position in life.

It's interesting how unacceptable critics have found Norman's simple premise of a rational suicide. Rather than confronting the larger issues posed by the script, they invented more 'solvable' reasons for Jessie's suicide. For example, Jill Dolan points out how the physical appearance of the actress in the original ART and later New York production, Kathy Bates, was collapsed onto the character of Jessie; she points to critic John Simon's descriptions of Jessie as 'fat, unattractive, and epileptic'.[13] At least two of these accusations would then be perceived as the character Jessie's own fault, and as an acceptable explanation for why her husband left. But this issue of fat or unattractiveness is not in the script. Norman is very neutral in her description of Jessie saying only that she is 'pale and vaguely unsteady, physically'. She is even more insistent on that neutrality in the description of the setting, 'Under no circumstances should the set and its dressing make a judgement about the intelligence or taste of Jessie and Thelma.' Norman is pointing emphatically to larger, more universal reasons than personal quirkiness for Jessie's suicide. It is ironic that even as Norman expresses the problem of women achieving the status of full personhood, critics were unable to extrapolate these dilemmas of a female as relating to the larger human condition. Even though her tragedy is that as a woman she could not become a person, this was not considered a true tragedy because she is not part of what this society can relate to as a universal person, *man*kind.

Even though Jessie's predicament has been criticized as 'a hopeless, insular situation that doesn't allow women to generalize from their own lives to the play's situation' (Dolan), her suicide could also be viewed as a metaphor for a pervasive modern malaise that manifests itself in real women. This malaise adopts guises such as anorexia and agoraphobia. Contemporary women are beginning to exhibit these 'neurotic' behaviors in alarming numbers. This play makes conscious the unconscious decisions of many women to 'shut down' or go on strike. This behavior can be viewed as having a definite political meaning.

Central to Jessie's struggle for autonomy are issues about control, and more specifically loss of self-control. In *Women Who Marry Houses* Seidenberg and DeCrow point out that this is a major factor in agoraphobia:

> The agoraphobe often states that she will not venture from the security of the home because of her fear of losing control. It is difficult for her to be more specific. Pressed, she may say she fears going berserk, going out of her mind, or running amok.[14]

The authors then move on to explain why this is a greater problem for women than for men:

> Women fear loss of control more frequently than men. Losing control has a different meaning for the female than for the male, as a result of societal conditioning. Generally, while growing up the girl is made to feel that her prime task is self-control, being quiet, passive, obedient, and silent. Loss of control for her then may mean not being able or no longer wanting to follow this programming. Boys, on the other hand, are taught less about self-control than about the need to control others, the environment, the world.[15]

Here is the basic tender archetype that determines the different focus of the violence in *True West* versus *'night Mother*. Lee and Austin attempt to control each other and their surroundings with violence. Jessie uses violence (suicide) as the ultimate way to gain control over herself.

Seidenberg and DeCrow note the irony of women fearing the loss of control in an arena (outside the home) where historically they have never exercised control. They go on to state:

> Agoraphobics may well be the most completely uncompromising feminists of our times. They will not be placated or bribed by small favors or grants of limited access. Sensing that they are not welcome in the outside world, they have come to terms with their own sense of pride by not setting foot on the land that is deemed alien and hostile.[16]

Those same ideas resonate in the character of Jessie. When Jessie explains that she can't hold down a job or anything else because of her epilepsy, Mama screams 'But I can't do anything about that!' And Jessie replies:

> No. You can't. And I can't do anything either, about my life, to change it, make it better, make me feel better about it. Like it better, make it work. But I can stop it. Shut it down, turn it off like the radio when there's nothing on that I want to listen to. It's all I really have that belongs to me and I'm going to say what happens to it. And it's going to stop. And I'm going to stop it . . . (p. 36)

A serious question that is raised by both plays is why the return home, and metaphorically to Mother, doesn't nurture or nourish these characters but rather threatens to smother them. In *The Mermaid and the Minotaur* Dorothy Dinnerstein provides at least a partial explanation:

> So long as the first parent is a woman, then, woman [sic] will inevitably be pressed into the dual role of indispensable quasi-human supporter and deadly quasi-human enemy of the human self. She will be seen as naturally fit to nurture other people's individuality; as the born audience in whose awareness

other people's subjective existence can be mirrored; as the being so peculiarly needed to confirm other people's worth power and significance ... At the same time she will also be seen as the one who will not let other people be, the one who beckons her loved ones back from selfhood, who wants to engulf, dissolve, drown, suffocate them as autonomous persons....[17]

That Jessie decides to spend her final evening with her mother, attempting to make her understand, underlines how difficult she finds this separation from Mother to be an individual. In one exchange it is particularly clear how troublesome this is for both mother and daughter:

> *Mama.* Everything you do has. to do with me, Jessie. You can't do *anything*, wash your face or cut your finger, without doing it to me. That's right! You may as well kill me as you, Jessie, it's the same thing. This has to do with me, Jessie.
> *Jessie.* Then what if it does! What if it has everything to do with you! What if you are all I have and you are not enough? What if I could take all of the rest of it if only I didn't have you here? What if the only way I can get away from you for good is to kill myself? ... (p. 72)

Jessie cannot clearly define her personal boundaries with the other members of her family either. Her identity is blended with that of her son ('Ricky is as much like me as it's possible for any human being to be' (p. 59)) and with her ex-husband when she confesses she actually wrote his farewell note: 'I said I'd always love me, not Cecil. But that's how he felt' (p. 61). Her body is the only aspect of herself she can truly identify as her own. Sometimes she even seems to relate to this body in the third person, as though it were a foreign object. When she tries to explain to Mama why her husband left her behind she can only state 'you don't pack your garbage when you move' (p. 61). Much like the anorexic, she is determined to exert total control over this self she whose only clear boundaries are her body.

The violence in *'night Mother* must be suicide. It transforms the character Jessie into an individual and into nothing. The audience is placed in a painful position of ambivalence; they are both horrified at the impending suicide and yet rooting for this bold act of emancipation. But, in contrast, in *True West* the violence of the two irreconcilable halves of a man, as represented by the characters of Lee and Austin, ends at a standoff. The problem for Lee and Austin is not that they are incapable of exorcizing the Mother, but that ultimately the cost of this amputation is too high. They can be independent, but they cannot be complete without the qualities she represents.

In viewing the plays as mirror images, it is interesting to note that the characters in *True West* spend most of the play destroying Mom's house, while in *'night Mother* Jessie's action consists mostly of putting her mother's house in order. Lee and Austin have trashed their mother's house until it has been reduced to the likeness of a sterile desert junkyard. Their violence was turned outward focusing on their mother's house. At the end of the play Mother has gone. She leaves stating that 'this is worse than being homeless' (p. 58). The feminine has been banished. In the final scene of *'night Mother* only Mama remains, washing the hot-chocolate pan. Jessie is gone. All is finally in order. Through the violence of suicide Jessie finally makes the transformation to individual, but to be that individual she had to murder her own female body. The feminine remains (her mother), but the individual was expelled (Jessie). The violence of separation from mother leaves the split male, Lee and Austin, and the absent female.

Even though no claim to feminist intent is made by either author, their two plays foreground the feminist concern with definitions of gender. Both plays lay open the psychic pain of characters caught in a struggle to define a self within these gender archetypes. Through the devices of violence these playwrights employ, the meanings, traps, and tragic ironies of gender roles in American culture are explored. The two plays stand as mirror images: violence as a means to define gender, and gender definition as a cause for violence.

NOTES

1 Jill Dolan, Review of *'night Mother*, *Women and Performance: A Journal of Feminist Theory*, 1: 1 (1983), pp. 78–9.
2 Sue-Ellen Case, 'The Personal Is Not the Political', *Art & Cinema*, 1: 3 (Fall 1987), p. 4.
3 Ellen Oumano, *Sam Shepard: The Life and Work of an American Dreamer* (New York: St Martin's Press, 1986), p. 137.
4 Marsha Norman, *'night Mother* (New York: Hill & Wang, 1983), p. 3. Hereafter cited parenthetically in the text.
5 Sam Shepard, *True West*, in *Sam Shepard; Seven Plays* (New York: Bantam, 1986), p. 3. Hereafter cited parenthetically in the text.
6 Michiko Kakutani, 'Myths, Dreams, Realities – Sam Shepard's America', *New York Times*, 29 January 1982, sec. 2, p. 26. Also cited by Lynda Hart in *Sam Shepard's Metaphorical Stages*, Contributions in Drama and Theatre Studies, no. 22 (New York: Greenwood Press, 1987), p. 138.
7 Florence Falk, 'Men Without Women; The Shepard Landscape' in *American Dreams: The Imagination of Sam Shepard*, ed. Bonnie Marranca (New York: The Performing Arts Journal Press, 1981), p. 105.
8 Bonnie Marranca, 'Alphabetical Shepard; the Play of Words' in *American Dreams*, p. 30.
9 William Klep, 'Worse Than Being Homeless: *True West* and the Divided Self' in *American Dreams*, p. 117.
10 Hart, *Sam Shepard's Metaphorical Stages*, p. 105.

11 'The Symposium', trans. Michael Joyce, in *Collected Dialogues of Plato*, ed. Edith Hamilton and Huntington Cairns (New York: Pantheon, 1961), pp. 542–4.
12 Kaja Silverman, *The Subject of Semiotics* (New York: Oxford University Press, 1983), p. 138.
13 Jill Dolan, *The Feminist Spectator as Critic* (Ann Arbor: UMI Research Press, 1988), p. 30.
14 Robert Seidenberg and Karen DeCrow, *Women Who Marry Houses; Panic and Protest in Agoraphobia* (New York: McGraw-Hill, 1983), p. 112.
15 Ibid., p. 113.
16 Ibid., p. 7.
17 Dorothy Dinnerstein, *The Mermaid and the Minotaur: Sexual Arrangements and Human Malaise* (New York, 1976), pp. 111–12.

The role of the theatre in Czechoslovakia's 'velvet revolution'[1]

JEREMY ADLER

I

The launching of a new political system from a Prague stage has resurrected the Baroque image of politics as theatre in a wholly unexpected way, putting it on television screens across the world. Suddenly, the theatre became an acknowledged arbiter of reality, as the playwright Václav Havel stripped away the illusion and deceit which had bedevilled Czech political life for over forty years. Spontaneously, commentators revived the image of Fortune's Wheel, and nowhere was this more appropriate than in Baroque Prague, where in less than a year, Havel had risen up from prison to become king-maker, and – by popular acclaim – King of Bohemia. In 1968, the writers had played a leading role in reforming the system; but in 1989, a small band of dissidents having tirelessly preserved the nation's conscience, and the students having taken the decisive public step by demonstrating in enormous numbers, it was the turn of dramaturgs, directors, actors and musicians to provide a channel for the general will, and so help to transform the protest into political action. The cohesion between these different groups, with the unusual role of the theatre soon supported by television, won the day by dislodging the Party from its pre-eminent place in the constitution. Until the contingency which brought the groups together gives way to firm structures, the situation remains precarious. However, the scenario was not pure chance.

II

Havel's personality is inseparable from the events. As playwright, philosopher and dissident, he provided a focal-point for the population in general, and for the actors in particular. Crossing the divide between dramatist and politician, he became the director of real events which, as a political philosopher and the author of essays like *The Power of the Powerless* (1978), he had effectively been preparing for twenty years. He thus combined those opposites, seemingly mutually exclusive, which Plato des-

13 17 November 1989: drama in the streets (photo: Jan Šibik)

cribes in the *Republic*: the artist, whom Plato excluded from his State, and the philosopher, who has seen the truth that lies beyond the confines of the cave and is thus fitted to lead the State as a philosopher-king. Havel's unusual linking of these roles is, perhaps, a measure of his wider significance, and his success is a call to re-interpret the relationship between the citizen and the State elsewhere, too. The relevance of Havel's political writing to such changes needs no elaboration here. However, it is worth recalling that his ideas on theatre also contributed to the political scene. He sees theatre as an institution in which society can renew itself, constituting as a living body, and re-forming around a shared awareness of Truth. Writing from prison on 21 November 1981 in his *Letters to Olga*, he puts the matter like this:

> The first embryonic appearance of genuine socialness happens the moment those participating in the theater cease to be a mere group of people and become a community. It is that special moment when their mutual presence becomes mutual participation; when their encounter in a single space and time becomes an existential encounter; when their common existence in this world is suddenly enveloped by a very specific and unrepeatable atmosphere; when a shared experience, mutually understood, evokes the wonderful elation that makes all the sacrifices worthwhile. It is a moment when a common participation in a particular adventure of the mind, the imagination and the sense of humor, and a common experience of truth or a flash of insight into the 'life in truth' suddenly establishes new relationships between the participants. Halfhearted coexistence suddenly blossoms into a feeling of mutual solidarity or brotherhood, even of brotherly love, despite the fact that many of the participants may not have known or seen each other before. This electrifying atmosphere of 'alliance' and 'fellowship' is a central aspect of the 'socialness' of the theater I am talking about.[2]

Havel's vision of good theatre reads like a blueprint for the 'velvet revolution', and, taken in connection with subsequent events, implies a new relation between art and politics. Considering his views historically, the contrast to Brecht is the most marked. Whereas in the neo-Aristotelian theatre of catharsis, as renewed in the German Classical theories of Lessing and Schiller, who are the real butt of Brecht's criticism, the stage provided a school and forum where the emotions could be exercised and purified thereby (so the optimistically enlightened view ran) inculcating a sense of humanity in the audience which, once at large again, would become a more humane society, Brecht, of course, re-interpreted the relation of stage and society dialectically, so that the distorting mirror of his anti-Aristotelian theatre should lead audiences to recognize the true political (i.e. economic) situation, and then act politically (i.e. in Marxist–Leninist fashion) outside the theatre. Havel's situation when he emerged as a young writer in the 1960s could be defined in terms of the failure of both these theories. Neo-Classicism had not forestalled the rise of barbar-

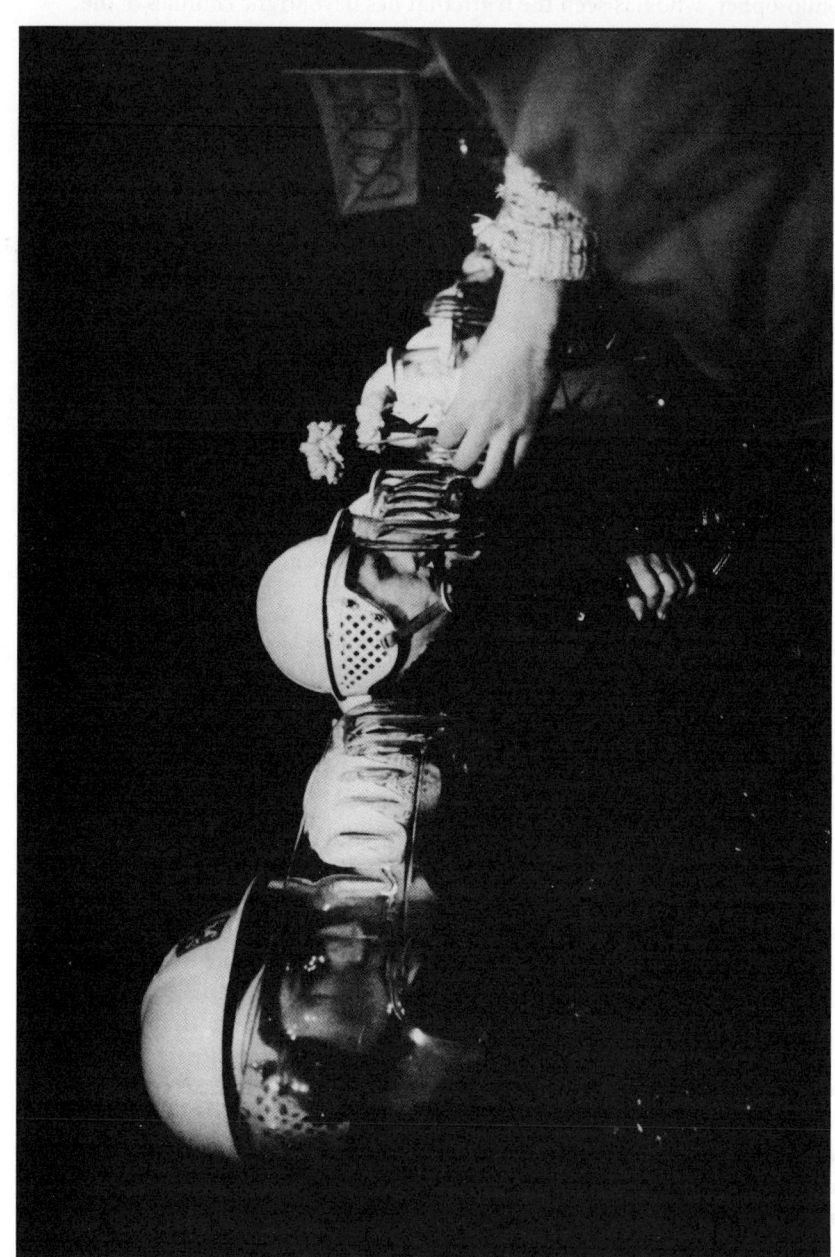

14 17 November 1989: riot police and theatre students (photo: Pavel Štecha)

ism in Germany; and Brecht's politics, especially when viewed from a Stalinist society, were demonstrably bankrupt. In opposition to these essentially contrastive views, Havel makes a less rigid distinction between theatre and society, treating the two as reciprocally permeable: mentally speaking, this implies a theatre without walls, which enables a continuous, and continuously altering, interaction between art and politics. He shares both a Brechtian sense of active engagement, and an explicitly Schillerian vision of universal brotherhood, combining the historical opposites in his own new synthesis. There is a very specific Czech tradition for Havel's views, too, but within the wider European context of the 1960s, they take their place not just beside Absurdism (which is only one element of Havel's theatre), but beside the anti-institutional experiments of the Happening, and the 'language games' of anarchic bodies like the Vienna Group. From such ingredients, he derives a vision of theatre and of historical change which is not only post-tragic, but essentially post-absurd, and non-violent: because, in his political writings, he sees change as inevitable (there is no epoch which has not been succeeded by another),[3] the true political actor must wait for, and peacefully help to bring about, a non-violent transition from one epoch to the next. The inevitability of change means that all effort can be directed towards ensuring that it will be peaceful when it eventually occurs. The pivotal role of theatre resides in its ability to strip away illusions, and reveal an authentic, vital 'truth' which, without further mediation, holds equally within and outside the theatre; correlatively, 'theatre' – it could be argued – does not depend on any specific institution, but can take place anywhere, and in society at large. It was this view which won the day in 1989.

III

Havel had more than once referred to conditions as resembling those in a 'pressure-cooker', people in the provinces reported 'simmerings', and the whole situation had been steadily building up for fifteen months, with the escalating student attendance at demonstrations after 21 August 1988, the twentieth anniversary of the Warsaw Pact invasion. New groups of young people had begun to mushroom, many with striking names like the Independent Peace Organization, the Children of Bohemia, and the John Lennon Peace Club. Even when they demonstrated in relatively small numbers, they took heart from the fact that onlookers began to smile and wave at them. As one youngster put it, 'demonstrating' was now 'elating'. By Mayday 1989, the students and young people were exploiting official parades to make their own protests, and by the triple anniversary of 28 October 1989, up to 20,000 students and others had taken to the streets. Officially, the main anniversary was the Communist one, Nationalization

15 17 November 1989: riot police and theatre students (photo: Jan Šibik)

Day (1948); but it was also the date of Czech and Slovak Federalization (1968), and the Foundation Day of the Republic itself (1918). This last was the ideal that the demonstrators were celebrating in 1989, as even the regime was now forced to recognize. Such activity disorientated the opposition as well as the authorities, who were confronted by an unexpected generation gap. Here were students dissatisfied with their parents, who wanted more radical activity than the beleagured dissidents could offer. Crucially, they were desperate for public meeting places of any kind, since halls, studios, and rooms were all in the hands of the Party.

By early in 1989, the actors had taken over from the writers and they began to rally around Václav Havel. His arrest in January prompted a letter from Josef Kemr to *Rudé Právo*. When Havel was sentenced, the actors petitioned for his release. The decisive point was that a group of public figures now spoke out in favour of a dissident branded as a 'lunatic criminal' by the Party. Such was the background for the seven-point manifesto *Several Sentences* issued on 29 June 1989, which gained 40,000 signatories in four months. The title recalls Ludvík Vaculík's *2,000 Words*, the key statement of the Prague Spring. But whereas Vaculík's title refers to the typical length of a *feuilleton*, suggesting the central role of the writers at that time, the new one indicated the spoken word, and hence the leading part now played by actors. Nearly the whole theatre community signed the document, and Václav Neumann and the Czech Philharmonic refused to appear on television until its demands were met. The players were calling the tune.

Theatre people were already in close touch with the students, and the link was strengthened by drama students, who act in professional theatres during their studies. A whole series of joint ventures prepared the way for the revolution, and also established the tone of subsequent events. Actors belonged to the organizing committee of the Society for a More Cheerful Present, which put on hybrid political 'happenings', like appearing in the streets on 15 August 1989, armed with cucumbers and salami truncheons; another memorable event was the launching of an artificial whale on the Vltava on 21 August. Local fishermen lent a helping hand at the launching, but the police did not see the joke; they destroyed the objectionable creature, and prosecuted the 'criminals' for polluting the river. The absurdity of such actions signified a new pluralism, and broke through the barrier of fear. How potent the recipe turned out to be was proved by the revolution. Other changes occurred within the theatre itself, most importantly, perhaps, at the Realist Theatre. On the eve of 27 October 1988, the seventieth anniversary of the founding of the Czech Republic, the Realist Theatre mounted its collage, *Res Publica*, and a year later came *Res Publica II*. This performance dismantled the barrier between 'persons' (nomenclatura) and 'non-persons' (dissidents), by combining banned texts from

16 The National Theatre, Prague: political meeting of theatre practitioners and theatre students (photo: Pavel Wellner)

the sixties by figures like Havel and Kryl together with others by Holan and Seifert. Thus, the Realist Theatre was a focus for oppositional activity, and this explains why it became a rallying-point after Friday 17 November.

Clearly, even before that day change was possible, though scarcely anyone seriously envisaged it, and the party line remained rigid. But in the morning of what was to become Bloody Friday, the man who unwittingly triggered off the revolution by authorizing independent groups to participate in the official demonstration gave an unprecedented interview which offered a new insight into the split forming in the highest echelons. Vasil Mohorita, as Political Employee of the City Committee of the Socialist Youth Organization in Prague in 1978, had no qualms about bearing false witness against Havel and other dissidents; but in 1989, as the Head of the Union of Socialist Youth, he was learning to change his tune, and this agility has since earned him the job of Party Secretary. In the interview on 17 November 1989, he declared: 'My heart feels with Gorbachev'. He explained that he was in touch with youth organizations in all countries – Poland, Hungary, the Soviet Union – and 'had been taking lessons from them', to the extent that 'free discussion' was now occurring among Czechoslovak youth, and that he had explicitly permitted 'opposition groups' to join in 'the legal procession'. When challenged whether this meant a split between the Youth Organization and the Party, he asserted that 'he was not, and never had been, the "cogwheel" of the Party'. This reversed one of the Party's most well-worn slogans.

The new division was reflected in the day's events that provided the spark for the revolution. By chance, the climax that evening was witnessed by some important theatre people during an interval in the performance of Büchner's *Danton's Death*. This barely credible historical irony is typical of the new symbiosis of politics and theatre which continued during the days to come. That Friday, the enormous peaceful demonstration of some 40,000 students and young people to commemorate the fiftieth anniversary of anti-Nazi protest in Prague, and the death then of the student Jan Opletal, became – as the demonstrators were quick to cry out – a macabre re-enactment of Gestapo brutality. The police 'white helmets' and the feared anti-terrorist 'red berets' turned their clubs and dogs on men, women and children. This was the scene observed by several actors from a balcony of the National Theatre. The police drove the youngsters into side-streets, and tried to winkle them out from nearby apartments where they sought refuge. The news spread like wildfire. Propitiously, the drama students had immediate access to their teachers, who (as actors) were just finishing the evening performances at the Theatre on the Balustrade and other small theatres. Next morning, students from the Theatre Faculty at the Academy of Performing Arts issued a proclamation which called for a

17 25 November 1989: soldiers and a priest (photo: Karel Cudlin)

government commission of enquiry, and a week-long strike of students and teachers. Simultaneously, the actors were mobilizing, and with a unanimity which they themselves sometimes found hard to understand, agreed to meet. In the afternoon, students, actors, directors and dramaturgs gathered at the Realist Theatre. Several students described their experiences at the demonstration, and a drama student read out their proclamation. A discussion ensued. Participants included Professor Milan Lukeš, dramaturg of the National Theatre, and Jiří Frehár, Director of the Realist Theatre and Chairman of the Czech Union of Dramatic Artists. It was this group of establishment figures (nomenclatura) and others outside the system which took up the students' initiative. The debate turned on three propositions: to read a statement, and to perform daily (as had happened in some East German theatres); to read it and close; or to read it and debate instead of performing. The turning-point came when one actor argued: 'We've acted for forty years like fools. If we play tonight, we'll act the fool for another forty years.' The meeting endorsed and extended the students' demands. For once, a wide variety of views, from Party-members to opposition, had galvanized into unity on a single issue. Crucially for the emerging political process, the theatres joined the student strike, and 'instead of planned performances' agreed to 'read to the audience our standpoint on the events [of 17 and 18 November] and ... offer the theatre premises for a broad public debate.' Suddenly, here were public meeting places, put at the disposal of the opposition. For the first time, independent dialogue was to have a public home, open to all-comers. Further, the same meeting called for what was to prove the vital General Strike on 27 November; and for an end to *all* 'bloodshed and political despotism'. The demands were becoming bolder, the means clearer. The public was further incensed by the news that a student, Martin Šmíd, had been killed on Friday, his face beaten to pulp by the police. This was probably disinformation, intended to provoke a violent reaction, but it back-fired. General dissent increasingly turned into moral outrage.

That night, all Prague theatres struck. They turned into debating clubs. Then, on Sunday, Václav Havel called opposition groups to a debate at the Drama Club Theatre, and at 10.00 p.m. Civic Forum was established, and soon set up its Headquarters (its 'crisis committee') in the bunker-like basement of the Magic Lantern Theatre. The new organization endorsed the central demands of the students and actors, but added its own, notably that everyone implicated in the Soviet invasion resign from office; and (echoing *Several Sentences*) that all prisoners of conscience be released. This Forum spread its basis of support more widely than any other grouping hitherto, bringing some twelve existing bodies under its umbrella (including Charter 77) and members of several others, including the Socialist Party and the Churches. It further extended its base by associating itself with the signatories of *Several Sentences*. Simultaneously in private houses and theatres throughout the country, new groups were forming independently which were shortly to join the Forum. The week of 20–27 November was declared a National Theatre Strike, and by Monday it had spread to Brno and every major town, except where communist directors closed the buildings. There, people gathered with the actors outside. In Bratislava, the authorities alternately opened and closed the theatres, but the crowds and actors gathered, too. What was probably the first National Strike in the history of the Republic since 1945 had begun, and at a stroke, the new political movement had won a highly efficient national network. The student/theatre axis remained strong, as evidenced by the setting-up of the students' strike co-ordinating committee at the Academy of Performing Arts.

Over the week beginning 20 November, actors and other theatre people joined with the students and dissidents, mobilizing opinion; by day, they went out into the factories and other enterprises with the students, putting their case, inviting condemnation of the injustice, encouraging and helping the workers to form strike committees. Only the agricultural collectives appear to have remained relatively Stalinist in all this. In the evenings, the actors debated with the public. Videos of the police brutality on Bloody Friday were shown (as they were in Prague shop-windows), and with humour and histrionics, the actors would help people grasp and believe what had happened. Typically, a student might speak (say, a local girl, come home from Prague), then a dramaturg, then some respected local figure such as a painter or doctor. Open discussion would ensue. Since every aspect of life had been corrupted, everything invited discussion. Concepts needed clarifying. Elementary practical problems cried out for solution.

IV

As the theatres became major centres of political reality, video took over as the main means of representation, creating instant history from the speeches, debates, and press-conferences. No less, however, throughout the country, the old tradition of the strolling player seemed to revive, as actors travelled out to collectives and factories, or organized fresh happenings in the provinces. This combination of a resurgent, practically forgotten tradition, and the most modern medium available, typifies the revolution in general, but it was a link which the actors, by the nature of their profession, were particularly well-suited to exploit. To give an idea of what such 'theatrical' activity was like, I shall sum up two recordings made by Civic forum in the small provincial town of Děčín, which were smuggled out over the border and sent to England via Vienna. The tapes cover two evenings at the local theatre. On 30 November, some six speakers shared the stage, including two Communists, and a Civic Forum chairman. The event fell into no existing category, resembling by turn a public enquiry, a party-political meeting, a psycho-therapy session, a trial, a philosophy seminar, and a nascent parliament. Issues debated included local pollution, the Party's role in the work-place, the opening-up of the local Party building, and the role of the militia. Here is a sample of the dialogue:

> *Interlocutor.* When one party has all the power, it cannot follow the new constitution.
> *Communist.* Comrade Urbanek gives us our line.
> *Interlocutor.* But the situation changes daily.
> *Communist.* Comrade Urbanke says it is a complicated issue and we shall have to prepare a special Congress. Then, the issue will be discussed.
> *Interlocutor.* Does that mean that the local Party has no opinion? (*Laughter*)

The Communists were given a fair hearing, and hecklers were silenced, but eventually, the highest local figure, the chairman of the District National Committee, just gave up and left. Three days later, the actor Jan Přeučil (who had joined the Party after 'Normalization' in the 1970s) came from the Theatre on the Balustrade in Prague, and after the night's agenda had been read out, gave a tremendously affecting speech. As he exploited his every skill as actor, raconteur and orator, the audience was spell-bound. He summarized events, described how the students had come to him on Bloody Friday, took in his own family history, his father's friendship with Jan Masaryk and subsequent imprisonment for fifteen years, blending anecdotes, jokes, and analysis. Throughout, most striking was the apparent nobility of his appeal to ethical values: to truth, to charity, and wisdom; to political caution and civic calm. The population had been warped, twisted without exception, and now required 'moral, inner reconstruction' to create a peaceful homeland. Havel's idealism, his will to 'live in truth', had inspired the entire acting profession to become his disciples, it seemed, and now they had set out to proselytize the nation.

Outside the theatre buildings in the provinces, the theatre people inspired the same jolly mood that prevailed in Prague. For example, in Hradec Králové, they organized a human chain to link the town with its traditional rival, Pardubice. Another time, they built a wall out of cardboard boxes in a public square surrounded by the offices of the secret police, the local National Committee, and the Russian military representatives. The wall was about three metres high, and everyone was encouraged to cover it with slogans: the protest was visible, but peaceful, and immune to military intervention.

Thus, although the students had started the revolution on 17 and 18

November, it was instantly mediated by the actors, and quickly spread everywhere. Crucially, it also united young and old. In a provincial town, an octogenarian organized shifts to look after her great-grandchildren, so that she, her daughter, and her grand-daughter could take part in demonstrations and debates in the theatre. For a five-year-old girl in Brno, life became a fairy-tale when she and her class-mates joined the human chain for the release of a political prisoner, Petr Cibulka, and he was really released. A research scientist put it like this in a letter:

> I am extremely happy, and many of us are, that we can witness the putting down of the fortress of communist power-holders, and I am extremely grateful that I could be part of it. I am sure that we have won, and it will be up to us to decide our life from now on ... I visited my mother twice today; for the moment, it is always necessary to be in the right place at the right time ... I can't switch off the radio and television, they're both permanently on, since Friday evening; in two hours the meeting in the City Square is starting, it's snowing outside, and I'll have to go out and dig a tunnel to get to the street ... Forgive us our emotions, you over there, but they were suppressed for too long, and now they must be ventilated, particularly at the start, they're one of our main motors, they carry along those who are still hesitant and filled with fear. The discipline of all participants is amazing, particularly the young, who are unnaturally well behaved; it's a shocking experience for my generation to discover that the children from the secondary schools showed greater political maturity and organizational skills than the whole governing apparatus. I am only writing on politics, but all of a sudden it's everywhere ...

What Schiller and Brecht had perceived as *opposite* purposes of the theatre, to inspire the moral bond of humanity and to provoke political action, both now occurred without any script at all. To grasp what happened requires, amongst much else, an understanding of Czechoslovak theatre history, for in Czechoslovakia, the actor occupies an unusual social position, and combines the popularity of a folk-hero with the moral authority of a *philosophe*.

v

Symbolic of the place occupied by the stage is the fact that the Czech National anthem started life as a song in a play. Echoing Lessing's call for a German National Theatre in Hamburg and Herder's prompting of national self-awareness, during the later eighteenth century, there was a revival of the Czech language, which had been ousted by German, both among the strolling players and at the Tyl Theatre (where *Don Giovanni* was first performed). Actor-dramatists like Václav Tham wrote and adapted new plays, and a style based on the Viennese popular theatre developed in Czech. It had a strong social meaning in the nineteenth century, and was politicized after 1848. Improvizations between the acts developed (replacing the jugglers and acrobats of the old strolling players), and provided socio-political comment. Voskovec and Werich continued the satire in the Republic. Their formula of mixing politics with the absurd won them the affection of intellectuals, bourgeois, and simple people alike, and the style has survived as a living legend until the present day. Here, then, was a tradition, which had helped to re-awaken the Czech national consciousness, which itself had led to the birth of Czechoslovakia in 1918.

State ownership of the theatres from 1948 effectively ended the tradition in all but memory. The wider power-base of the contemporary theatre originated in the 1950s, when the little theatres emerged, breaking the state monopoly of the big enterprises, which were moribund with 'ideological purity'. New dramatists came up like Vyskočil and Suchý. In the sixties, Kundera and Havel were put on. The enormously popular production of *Ubu Roi* at that time was interpreted by the director Jan Grossman and audience alike as a satire on Communism. Even so, the main changes were to begin with the Writers' Congress in 1967. Only after the subsequent crackdown, and when a new law was passed banning demonstrations and gatherings in public places in August 1969, the theatres and cinemas came into their own as the only public places where people could meet openly and express common feelings more or less freely.

The rigid system of censorship imposed compromise and self-censorship on every stage. Active opposition gave way to passive resistance, until this lapsed into passivity; similarly, audience sensibilities blunted. Up until 1975, people responded to nuances and shifts in dramatic meaning; by 1980, only the word elicited a response. One solution was to revert to unscripted utterance. This avoided textual censorship, but might be challenged at the obligatory pre-dress-rehearsal for the local National Committee. Choices were tied to quotas (so and so many new and old Soviet and Czech plays), and to anniversaries (1917, 1945, 1948). This generally led to listless, apathetic performances, but it could also be exploited. The opportunity to stage *Macbeth* at the Ypsilon Theatre was the anniversary of some South American revolution. This led to a typical absurdity. Four years on, the theatre was due to perform a comedy when Brehznev died; but as this was a day of mourning, after some negotiation, the National Committee agreed that the theatre could open if a tragedy were put on. *Macbeth* was duly done, with inordinate pauses at the relevant points, and a minute of dead silence after 'Yet who would have thought the old man to have had so much blood in him?' It was a black mass. Acting had become a tacit conspiracy with the public, and thus particular theatres earned the national credit on which they capitalized in 1989.

VI

However, television provided the crucial bridge. By the seventies, immensely popular soap operas developed. In the wake of Socialist Realism, they purveyed what can be termed a 'new (dis)honesty'. Enormous quantities of these series covered every aspect of life – the police, the factory, the hospital, the agricultural collective, and so forth. The formula permitted an element of localized criticism that stopped short of the real malaise: indignation was to be indulged, and to be aroused against individuals like the corrupt official, the chairman of the milk co-operative, or whoever, and away from the Party' itself. A telling Slovak example I saw in December 1989 revolved around some mischief at the local brothel. Party officials were somehow implicated, but the culprits were the Jewish brothel-owners, dressed to resemble the traditional anti-semitic stereotypes. It was all good, clean, racist fun. Ideologically, it was intended to reveal a socialist society able to recognize and criticize its own failings. (This same formula of 'limited' or 'focused' criticism could be seen in some Soviet and East German films, too. It also succeeded in duping some Western audiences.) This well-written rubbish by the likes of Jaroslav Dietl could be funny at more than one level, and was forgiven as well as loved because it touched a raw nerve. But it boomeranged. Many excellent actors like Ladislav Mrkvička, Jiři Labus or Vladimir Kratina gained instant access to every home. No politician ever won affection and adulation like this. When the soap operas could call on the camera-work of the Gorbachev era, political broadcasts still offered only the turgid full-frontal mumblings of inarticulate despots. By about 1975, the politicians having retreated to anonymous limbo, these actors were becoming major public figures. When they struck on 18 November 1989, and went out into the factories, they effectively smashed through the lie of the silver screen. Their 'coming out' denounced that same reciprocal conformism which had previously tied them to their equally self-disgusted audience. Less sophisticated viewers who, apparently, could not properly distinguish between the actors and their roles, were equally open to their influence. Suddenly, the television heroes were real heroes, who risked their careers if things went wrong; and that provided a signal example to their safer, anonymous followers. Exploiting their own professional sense of the public, they functioned as social barometers, and stepped into the political void, playing the parts of the democratic politicians that had not yet been created.

Unlike 1968, this was a 'media revolution' from the very start, beginning with the televising of the protest in Tiananman Square. This helps to explain very different aspects of the events of 1989, such as the internationalizing of spontaneous revolution, and the extraordinary speed of events. In East Germany, the almost incidental announcement on television on 9 November that travel restrictions would be eased initiated the sudden, wholly irresistible storming of the Berlin wall that led to the unplanned abandoning of *all* visa controls: the immediate communication produced instantaneous action. Where previously the 'medium' had operated to control the so-called 'masses', the people now acted on the news to snatch control of their own destiny. In Romania, coming after Berlin and Prague, things actually focused on the television building. This indicates both the closer connection between the 'medium' and the revolt, but also the more problematic aspect of events in Romania, the continuingly centrist monopoly of power, which passed from one clique to another. In Czechoslovakia, events were more individualistic, and the use of new technology more republican. Orwell's spectre of state-controlled television dissolved as if by magic under the impact of individual, hand-held video cameras: nothing more potently expressed the student cause than their videos of the beatings; their debate with the authorities revolved in part around the release of the secret police's own videos; and by the end of the first week of the theatre strike, television, too, had joined the reformers, for the first time in the history of Czechoslovakia giving live, impartial coverage. Meanwhile, the police sabotaged the delivery of newsprint to the provinces, and it took *Rudé Právo* over a week more to offer Václav Havel a space. The printed word lagged behind at every stage.

VII

Various aspects of theatre were an essential part of the public mood on the streets. The old mass-psychosis of what Canetti calls a 'double crowd'[4] based on the mutual hatred and fear of ruler and ruled came under attack from a jubilantly unifying mass, which appropriately focused on an entertaining and civilizing place (the theatres), whereas in Poland it had centred on labour and the spiritual world (the factories and the church). The spectrum of crowd behaviour was remarkable. No window was broken. No car burnt. From the start, there was an element of ritual, when the students knelt on Bloody Friday, and demonstrators lit candles for the victims on the Saturday. Celebrating the canonization of St Agnes, Cardinal Tomášek's support simply reinforced and articulated the mood. But when the police drew blood, they broke a taboo. Their barbarism smashed the veneer of the citizens' reluctant quiescence upon which the terror of the regime depended. The blood on the street and on the national flag provided the focal point where the long-standing struggle of the dissidents and the long-suppressed sensibility of the public could meet. The police calculated on their own instincts: a violent counter-attack, which would justify any further measures. But the crowd fought back by destroying *all* the rules. That meant removing the morbid atmosphere of hatred, fear and repression, which had prevailed in public for years, with the spirit of carnival. One student friend spoke of 'our merry revolution'. Suddenly, everything was possible. It was the citizens' turn to break the taboo. Their choice, for the first time in years, was unequivocal, liberal, and democratic, and hence they could dispense with revenge and violence by embracing sheer fun. It was a technique which, for once, left the Party helpless and frustrated. Its role was just written out of the script. During the strike, taxis hooted as on New Year's Eve. Everywhere, the crowd responded to speakers and events with the verbal wit of stand-up comedy: suddenly, they learnt to use the countless jokes they had been inventing for years *about* their rulers against their rulers. On a video, one saw how the Prague Party Secretary Štěpán helplessly tried to explain the strike to a crowd of workers, arguing that it was put on by children. 'We're not children! We're not children!' the crowd taunted in reply. Elsewhere rhyme proved a potent weapon: 'Jakeše do koše' (stick Jakeš in the basket) they called; and when news came that he had gone, they quipped 'Už je ve koši' (now he's in the basket). The absurd and the folk traditions which the small independent groups had tried to bring to the streets in the months before now reigned supreme. When people rang out the old order with keys and little bells, this echoed the end of many a good Czech fairy-tale ('zazvonil zvonec a pohádky je konec'). But it also recalled those magic bells of the popular theatre that Papageno found so useful. Perhaps the irony of ironies was to turn the fairy-tale bell into a Liberty Bell, which the students wittily placed on the site formerly occupied by the monster Stalin monument, now decked out like a carnival float. Stalin's image had been dismantled. Now his followers would go. And indeed, only two weeks after the General Strike, bells throughout the land tolled the knell of Czech Communism. Thus the carnival focused on iconoclastic symbols, transforming instant history into legend.

Everything combined in such symbols and moments: religious sentiment, protest, joy, and national fervour. A poignant moment came with the return of the singer, Marta Kubišová, who had epitomized the spirit of the Prague Spring. She had remained loyal to those ideals, become a Chartist, and suffered odious indignities. On her return, she was like a living legend, resembling St Martha herself, one of whose emblems is a bunch of keys; few playwrights could have risked the concentrated symbolism which sprang from reality itself when she once again sang 'A Prayer for Martha', one of the most popular hits of 1968. The sentiments are those of Commenius, the Czech Humanist; the song itself comes from a Dietl soap opera, but it had been forbidden during 'normalization'.

18 Marat Kubišová (photo: ČTK)

> Let peace dwell in the countryside,
> Let anger, envy, spite,
> Fear and feud
> Pass away, pass away.
>
> Now, when the lost
> Government of your things
> Will return to you
> Oh people, back to you ...

This being 'magical Prague', literature and poetry blended with reality. But the new iconoclasts also smashed through the most potent modern sterotypes, Kafkaesque bureaucracy coupled to the mocking obedience of the Good Soldier Švejk. Instead, people re-activated an older layer of history and myth. 'The Knights of Blaník are here!' a woman cried out in Wenceslas Square: she referred to the Czech legend that a hord of warriors lay asleep in the Blaník rock, and would one day break out, resplendent in full regalia, to save the nation in its direst hour.

Tiananman Square had inspired East Germany and Czechoslovakia, and it remained a constantly lurking threat. No-one doubted that the so-called 'People's Militia' (the Party's private army) was armed with real guns. It took just over two weeks for its disarmament and, then, its disbandment to begin. Behind the display, the bitter power-struggle remained the one pivotal fact.

Observers and participants alike may well have recalled the euphoria in the early phase of the French Revolution, before the terror began, which seems to have had a similarly theatrical irreality. Writing from Paris on 4 August 1789, the German commentator Joachim Heinrich Campe asked:

> Is it really true . . . that the great and marvellous dramas that are being acted out here now, and are still being played, are not the creations of my imagination, not dreams, but facts?[5]

Five days later, he remarked on the extraordinary suddenness of the changes, which seemed to come as quickly in 1789 as in 1989:

> The entire ancient building of feudalism, with all its brilliant rights for the rulers and all its oppressive burdens for the subjects, was toppled and destroyed in a few minutes.[6]

In the midst of the reversal, the crowd appeared as self-possessed to Campe as the people in Prague were two hundred years later:

> Public law and order are not maintained by bayonets, but by request and friendly encouragement . . .[7]

However, Campe turned a blind eye to the actual violence that had already taken place, grotesquely exaggerating the citizens' peaceableness, in order to hail the Revolution as a 'Sentimental-Comic Drama'. Appropriately, Campe exploited the analogy with the then popular anti-Aristotelian genre, bourgeois drama. Good humour and human sentiment, so the analogy implies, were forging the bonds of humanity in society, as they had previously done in the theatre. To recall views like Campe's during the events of 1989 intensified the lurking fear that terror and tragedy might ensue in Prague, too. Yet apart from the political differences, there were important differences in attitude, and in the artistic situation. The theatre itself had been gagged, and when the revolution broke out in November, 'theatre' was not so much a metaphor as a reality: the previously censored desire for carnival suffused the events themselves. Consequently, the participants shared a theatrical self-awareness, which created a sense of ironic distance from the political events and from politics as such. This probably helped to ensure that the ideals of truth and non-violence were actually maintained.

This suffusing of actions with a new consciousness helps to explain why the November Revolution of 1989 is only partially to be understood as a reversal. Of course, outwardly, things may look like a theatrical change and the East German writer Christa Wolf captured this feature, equally true in Prague, with her epigram on the totalitarian tools of power, the endless march-pasts, displays, and tattoos: 'Today, the people are the tribunes before which the leaders parade back and forth.'[8] But besides a *reversal*, the events entail *substitution*, as everywhere demonstrators take the State's 'republicanism' at its word and substitute the truth for the lie. Practically, things can run so quickly, because the opposition re-establishes the moral value of existing institutions. This can be observed at every level, whether linguistically, or oganizationally. For example the students simply adopted relevant Communist slogans, like the actually Talmudic 'If not now, when? If not us, who?'. The Party insistence on the role of the workers was also a point well taken.

VIII

To trace the progress of the Revolution and its success involves following the way in which the demands of the dissidents, students, and actors translated into political action before the new government was finally sworn in on 10 December and Havel became President at the end of the year. The commission demanded by the students was formed on 29 November, and on 4 December presented its findings that the police had acted brutally, and should be punished. That same day, going far beyond a point from *Several Sentences*, and as reformulated by Civic Forum, the Soviet Union condemned the 1968 invasion. As if to symbolize the role of the actors, Milan Lukeš, who took part in the original meeting with students at the Realist Theatre, became Minister of Culture in the new Czech Regional Parliament. And to cap it all, the actors' brilliant proposal for a two-hour National Strike – too long to be dismissed as a lunch-break, short enough to unite divers views without causing total chaos – was taken up by Andrei Sakharov in his campaign to abolish the Party's leading role in the Soviet Union.

But it is proving difficult for some people to end the role-playing, and on both sides they bungle their lines. Dubček blundered by repeating inappropriate slogans from 1968; Jakeš voted for a resolution whilst actually speaking against it. Some shop-assistants and workers managed to continue to work while striking. And young soldiers meant for use against the crowd, locked away for days without any access to the media, tripped delightedly into freedom after the general strike, but reflected sadly that they would have to remove their tricolours when they returned to barracks. If the success is to last, it will require more substitution, more than acting, and the theatres will have to find a new role. As one Civic Forum spokesperson put it on 1 December: 'The time of civic responsibility has now begun.'

19 President Havel (photo: Pavel Štecha)

NOTES

1 This article first appeared in a shorter version in *The Times Literary Supplement*, 22 December 1989. I am indebted to many friends in England and Czechoslovakia for information, but above all to Julek Neumann, formerly of the Ypsilon Theatre; without his help, the article could not have been written. The present version incorporates some revisions and additions, but is essentially a record of the events, an attempt to understand things as they occurred. For background on the contemporary Czech theatre, see Paul I. Trensky, *Czech Drama since World War II*, Columbia Slavic Studies (White Plains, NY: Columbia University Press, 1978); also Marketa Goetz-Stankiewicz, *The Silenced Theatre: Czech Playwrights without a Stage* (Buffalo and London; University of Toronto Press, 1979). A full study of the theatre's part in the revolution is being prepared by Barbara Day for the published revision of her thesis, 'The Theatre on The Balustrade and the Small Stage Tradition in the Czech Theatre' (Diss., University of Bristol, 1986). See also her 'Czech Theatre from 1918 to the Present Day', *New Theatre Quarterly*, 2, August 1986, pp. 250–74; and 'When Actors Really Act', *The Independent*, 21 December 1989, p. 12.
2 Václav Havel, *Letters to Olga. June 1979–September 1982*, translated by Paul Wilson (London and Boston: Faber and Faber, 1990), p. 250.
3 See Václav Havel, Letter to Dr Gustáv Husák', in *Living in Truth*, ed. Jan Vladislav (London and Boston: Faber and Faber, 1989), pp. 25–33.
4 Canetti's concept of the 'double crowd' assumes greater parity between the two groups than prevails between governors and governed (two armies provide a better paradigm), but the term excellently captures the reciprocal dependency of Party and People in a totalitarian regime. See Elias Canetti, *Crowds and Power*, trans. Carol Stewart (London: Gollancz, 1962), pp. 63–73.
5 Joachim Heinrich Campe, 'Briefe aus Paris, zur Zeit der Revolution', in *Die Französische Revolution. Berichte und Deutungen deutscher Schriftsteller und Historiker*, ed. Horst Günther, 4 vols. (Frankfurt am Main: Deutscher Klassiker Verlag, 1985), vol. 1, p. 9.
6 Campe, 'Briefe aus Paris', p. 43.
7 Campe, 'Briefe aus Paris', p. 12.
8 This was the version of Christa Wolf's words publicized in several newspapers; what she actually wrote in her speech for a mass demonstration in East Berlin on 4 November 1989 was: 'A suggestion for 1 May: the leadership should march past the people.' See *'Wir sind das Volk'. Die DDR im Aufbruch. Eine Chronik in Dokumenten und Bildern*, ed. Micha Wimmer, Christine Proske, Sabine Braun and Bernhard Michalowski (Munich: Heyne Verlag, 1990), pp. 103–8; see p. 108.

Index

Achard, Marcel, 151
Adam, Villiers de L'Isle-, 156
Aeschylus, 27
   Agamemnon, 22, 24, 26
   Choephori, 25
   Eumenides, 25, 26
   Niobe, 38
   Oresteia, 24, 26, 35
   Prometheus Bound, 19–20
   Suppliant Maidens, 15, 18–19, 20–1, 22–4
Afrikaans theatre, 215–24
Albery, James, *Pink Dominoes*, 153
Andrade, Jorge, *Milagre na cela*, 271
Antoine, André, 153, 154, 155, 167
Antona-Traversi, Camillo, 159
Aristotle, 9, 47
Arrabal, Fernando, 151
Artaud, Antonin, 177, 197, 212, 269
Ashley, Elizabeth, 225
Axelos, Kosmos, 198

Bakhtin, Mikhail, 70, 177
Baqué, Françoise, 198
Barker, Howard, 251
Barthes, Roland, 196
Battle of Angiers, the, 1
Beaujour, Michel, 198
Benedetti, Mario, *Pedro y el capitán*, 271
Bergson, Eva, 169, 170
Berlin, Normand, 236
Blood Beast Terror, The, 162
Boal, Augusto, 266, 269
Bowers, Fredson, 101
Brecht, Bertolt, 11, 269, 293, 295, 304
   Threepenny Opera, 9
Brenton, Howard, 251; and David Hare, *Pravda*, 265

Breytenbach, Breyten, 216–17, 218
Brownmiller, Susan, 225, 235, 237
Brustein, Robert, 228
Büchner, Georg, *Danton's Death*, 299
Buenaventura, Enrique, *La audiencia*, 271
Buthulezi, Gatsha, 221, 223

Caillous, Roger, 198
Campe, Joachim Heinrich, 310
Camus, Albert, 191–201
   Caligula, 191–201
Canetti, Elias, 307, 313
Chester play, 97–9
Choisy, Camille, 168
Chaves Neto, João Ribeiero, *Patetica*, 271
Clark, Kenneth, 10
Cocteau, Jean, *The Human Voice*, 156
Colette, 151
Corneille, Pierre, 88
   Polyeucte, 88
Corpus Christi plays, 93–100
Courteline, Georges, *Les Boulingrin*, 151, 154–5
Cronenberg, David, 152
   Fly, The, 152
   Scanners, 152
Croxton *Play of the Sacrament*, 69–78, 82, 83
Cruickshank, John, 192

DeCrow, Karen, 285–6
Deerhunter, The (film), 5
Dekker, Thomas and Philip Massinger, *The Virgin Martyr*, 88
Dickens, Charles, 3, 7
Dietl, Jaroslav, 306, 308
Digby play, 99

Dinnerstein, Dorothy, 286–7
Dolan, Jill, 285
Douglas, Alfred, 181, 182
Duvernois, Henri, *The Bronze Lady and the Crystal Gentleman*, 155
Dworkin, Andrea, 229

Edgar, David, *The Jail Diary of Albie Sachs*, 267
Ehrman, Jacques, 198
Equalizer, The (film), 5
Euripides, 26
   Bacchae, 2, 27, 35
   Erechtheus, 39
   Hecuba, 35–44
   Heraclidae, 39
   Iphigenia at Aulis, 39
   Orestes, 9
   Medea, 27, 39
   Suppliants, 39
   Troades, 27
   Trojan Woman, 39

Fink, Eugen, 198
Forster, E. M., *A Passage to India*, 7, 10
Foucault, Michel, 196, 197
Fourie, Peter, 217
Freeman, Edward, 192, 196
Free Theatre Movement, 153–4, 155, 167; *see also* Théâtre Libre
Frehár, Jiří, 301
Freud, Sigmund, 15, 283, 284
Frijda, Nico, 10
Fugard, Athol, *Boesman and Lena*, 239–49

Gaillard, Pol, 197
Gampu, Ken, 221
Ganz, Arthur, 180
Gay-Crosier, Raymond, 192, 196
Genet, Jean, *The Maids*, 180
Gilbert, Sandra, 227, 232
Girard, René, 11, 70, 107
Gomes, Alfredo Dias, *Campeões do mundo*, 271
Grand Guignol, 151–63; *see also* Théâtre du Grand-Guignol
Gréban, Simon and Arnoul, *Mystery of the Acts of the Apostles*, 84, 86–8
Griffin, Susan, 227, 237
Grotowsky, Jerzy, 269

Grossmann, Jan, 305
Grupo Theatre Libre, *El asesinato de X*, 272
Guber, Susan, 227, 232

Hall, Radclyffe, 181
Hammer Films, 162
Harrow, Kenneth, 192
Haynes, David, 220, 221
Havel, Václav, 291–7, 299, 301, 305, 307, 311, 312
Heidegger, Martin, 197
Hernandez, Mario, 206
Hirsch, Foster, 225–6, 227
Hizinga, Jacques, 198
Homer, 6, 15
   Iliad, 4, 16–18
   Odyssey, 4, 9, 38
Horace, 132
   Ars poetica, 7, 79
Hutchinson, Ron, *Rat in the Skull*, 264

Ibsen, Henrik, *Ghosts*, 153
Ionesco, Eugène
   Bald Soprano, The, 198
   Chairs, The, 197

Jarry, Alfred, *King Ubu*, 197
Jefferson, Mark, 7, 10
Jones, Robert, 232
Jonvin, Jacques, 168–9

Kahn, Coppelia, 133
Kazan, Elia, 232
King, Stephen, *Pet Semetary*, 162
Kowzan, Tadeusz, 269, 270
Kratina, Vladimir, 306
Krige, Uys, 218
Kubišová, Marta, 308, 309
Kundera Milan, 10, 305
Kyd, Thomas, 123

Labus, Jiři, 306
Laillon-Savona, Jeanette, 192
Lawrence, D. H., 232
Lenormand, Henri-René, 151
Lessing, G. E., 35, 293, 304
Level, Maurice
   Le Baiser dans la nuit (*The Last Kiss*), 157

Un Drame à la salpetrière, 168
Lewis, Eve, *Ficky Stingers*, 261, 265–7
Lewis, R. B. 192
Lima, Luiz Maria, *A nossa voz*, 273–4
Lord, André de, 153, 155, 162
  Au téléphone, 156
  Horrible Experience, 162, 168
  Last Torture, The, 156, 168
  Masters of Fear, 155
  (with Henri Bauche) *Laboratory of Hallucinations, The*, 157, 168
Lorca, Federico García
  Blood Wedding, 203
  La casa de Bernarda Alba, 203
  Public, The, 203–4, 207–12
  Shoemaker's Prodigious Wife, The, 203–7, 212
Love story, 3
Lugné-Poë, A.-F., 151
Ludus Coventriae, 80, 83, 95
Lukeš, Milan, 301, 311
Luppe, Robert de, 192
Lynch, Martin, *The Interrogation of Ambrose Fogarty*, 263

Machard, Raymonde, 170
Magid, Marion, 230
Magnier, Maurice, 167
Mallarmé, Stéphane, 156
Mandela, Nelson, 215
Marcadé, Eustache, *La Vengeance Jhesucrist*, 82
Marlowe, Christopher
  Edward II, 102
  Jew of Malta, The, 102
  Spanish Tragedy, The, 102, 110
  Tamburlaine, 102
Maupassant, Guy de, 153
Maurey, Max, 155, 159, 163, 167, 168
  Weekend Cottage, 159–62
Mauricio, Julio, *Un despido corriente*, 271
Méténier, Oscar, 151, 154, 167
  In the Family, 154
  Him, 156
  Little Bugger, The, 154
  Mademoiselle Fifi, 167
  Meal Ticket, The, 154
miracle plays, 79–91; *see also individual titles*
Mirbeau, Octave, 151

Mohorita, Vasil, 299
Molière, J. B. P., 141
Mrkvička, Ladislav, 306
My Life as a Dog (film), 3
Mystère du Vieil Testament, 79
mystères, 79–91; *see also individual titles*

Nadal, Martínez, 207
Neumann, Václav, 297
Neethling–Pohl, Anna, 221
Niekerk, Louis van, 221
Nietzsche, Friedrich, 196, 197
Night of the Shooting Stars, The (film), 5
Nonon, Charles, 162, 170
Norman Marsha, '*night Mother*, 277–8, 279, 283, 284–9

On Golden Pond (film), 3
Ovid, 123–35 *passim*

Pascal, Blaise, 193, 199
Pascal, Fred, 170
Patton (film), 8
Pavlovsky, Eduardo, *El Señor Galíndez*, 271
Pielmeier, John, *Agnes of God*, 88–9
Pinter, Harold, *One for the Road*, 261–5, 266, 267
Plato, 4, 6, 11, 291–2
Platoon (film), 5
Plautus, 47–68
  Asinaria, 51
  Casina, 47, 51, 53–65
Poe, Edgar Alan, 153
Přeučil, Jan, 303
Puccini, 7

Quirino, Leonard, 234

Rabe, David, *Streamers*, 93
Racine, Jean, *Bajazet*, 141–50
Realist Theatre (Prague), 297–8, 301
Reible, Dieter, 216–21 *passim*
Robbe-Grillet, Alain, 197, 198, 199
Royal Shakespeare Company, 251
Rubinstein, Richard, 162
Rudkin, David, 251
  Afore Night Come, 251
  Ashes 251–2, 255–9
  Son of Light, The, 251, 252, 257, 259

Sainte Apoline, 84
Sainte-Hostie, La, 82–3
Sartre, Jean Paul, 193, 197
Scarry, Elaine, 270
Schiller, J. C. F. von, 293, 304
Scott, Clement, 153
Seidenberg, Robert, 285–6
Sewell, Vernon, 162
Shakespeare, William, 15, 101–21, 215–24
  Comedy of Errors, The, 113–15
  Coriolanus, 107, 112
  Cymbeline, 120
  Hamlet, 103–4, 111, 215
  2 Henry IV, 119
  Henry V, 103, 120
  1 Henry VI, 103, 112
  2 Henry VI, 103, 107, 111
  3 Henry VI, 104–5
  Julius Caesar, 105–6, 112
  King John, 108–9
  King Lear, 1, 11, 12, 102–3, 114, 194, 216, 218, 223
  Macbeth, 1–2, 101–2, 106, 107, 109, 111, 114, 262, 305
  Measure for Measure, 262
  Merry Wives of Windsor, The, 117–18, 120
  Othello, 114, 216, 218, 221–3, 224
  Richard II, 108
  Richard III, 107–8, 265
  Romeo and Juliet, 103, 104, 216, 217, 220, 223
  Taming of the Shrew, The, 115–17
  Tempest, The, 262
  Timon of Athens, 112–13
  Titus Andronicus, 104, 110–12, 113, 124–40, 152, 263
  Troilus and Cressida, 106
Shaw, G. B., 178–89
  Candida, 178, 179
  Heartbreak House, 183–4
  Major Barbara, 178, 179
  Man of Destiny, 178
  Man and Superman, 177–8, 188
  Music Cure, The, 178–9
  Pygmalion, 184–7
  Widowers' Houses, 179–81, 182–3, 184
Shepherd, Sam, *True West*, 277–83, 286, 287–8
Silverman, Kaja, 284

Sollers, Philippe, 198
Sophocles, 2, 27, 153
  Ajax, 15, 35
  Electra, 35
Steinem, Gloria, 8
Steiner, George, 1
Storey, David, 15
Strauss, Richard, 3, 7
Swart, Francois, 221–2, 223

Tate, Nahum, 2
Taxi Driver (film), 5
Terence, 49
Tertullian, 79
Tham, Václav, 304
Theatre of the Absurd, 269
Theatre of Cruelty, 177, 211, 212
Théàtre du Grand-Guignol, 151, 162, 165–75
Towneley/Wakefield cycle, 80, 95–8
Tolstoy, Leo, *Power of Darkness*, 154
Tourneur, Cyril, *The Revenger's Tragedy*, 151

Uys, Stanley, 218

Vaculik, Ludvík, *2,000 words*, 297
Vergil, 123–35 *passim*
Vengeance de Notre-Seigneur, La, 82
Vernant, Jean–Pierre, 18
Vianna Filho, Oduvaldo, *Papa Highirte*, 271
Vieira, Cesar, *Morte aos brancos*, 271
Vorster, B. J., 219

Wakefield cycle, 80, 95–8
Warriors, The (film), 5
Weiss, Peter, *Marat/Sade*, 152
Weisstein, Naomi, 231
Whitney, Frederick
  Last Kiss, The (trans.), 157
  Say it with Flowers, 156
Wilde, Oscar, 182
Williams, Tennessee, *A Streetcar Named Desire*, 225–38
Wolf, Christa, 3, 10–11
Wolff, Egon, *Flores de papel*, 272–3

York cycle, 93–6, 97

Zola, Emile, 153